Florian Resatsch

Ubiquitous Computing

GABLER RESEARCH

Informationsmanagement
und Computer Aided Team

Herausgegeben von Professor Dr. Helmut Krcmar

Die Schriftenreihe präsentiert Ergebnisse der betriebswirtschaftlichen Forschung im Themenfeld der Wirtschaftsinformatik. Das Zusammenwirken von Informations- und Kommunikationstechnologien mit Wettbewerb, Organisation und Menschen wird von umfassenden Änderungen gekennzeichnet. Die Schriftenreihe greift diese Fragen auf und stellt neue Erkenntnisse aus Theorie und Praxis sowie anwendungsorientierte Konzepte und Modelle zur Diskussion.

Florian Resatsch

Ubiquitous Computing

Developing and Evaluating Near Field
Communication Applications

With a foreword by Prof. Dr. Helmut Krcmar

GABLER

RESEARCH

Bibliographic information published by the Deutsche Nationalbibliothek
The Deutsche Nationalbibliothek lists this publication in the Deutsche Nationalbibliografie;
detailed bibliographic data are available in the Internet at http://dnb.d-nb.de.

Dissertation Technische Universität München, 2009

1st Edition 2010

Editorial Office: Ute Wrasmann | Anita Wilke

Gabler Verlag is a brand of Springer Fachmedien.
Springer Fachmedien is part of Springer Science+Business Media.
www.gabler.de

Coverdesign: KünkelLopka Medienentwicklung, Heidelberg
Printed on acid-free paper

ISBN 978-3-8349-2167-3

Foreword

Ubiquitous Computing has been the subject of discussion in various research areas for some time now. Over the past several years RFID and Near Field Communication (NFC) technologies have become the driving force behind the vision of Ubiquitous Computing. In particular, NFC could become a real Ubiquitous Computing technology in consumer hands if it succeeds in capturing distribution channels, for example due to integration into the mobile devices market. Even if that will be the case in the future, application developers and entrepreneurs interested in using RFID or NFC technologies will be faced with the challenges of negotiating the process of moving early prototypes into a final product. In particular, given the physical nature of the technology, it is imperative that the user be involved in the very early stages of development in order to bring successful, consumer-accepted applications to market.

In 2009, NFC technology still finds itself in the starting blocks—accordingly, these research results come at the right time. Previous approaches to the challenge of developing NFC applications have neither applied research methods specific to Ubiquitous Computing, nor have they integrated the appropriate design guidelines. Florian Resatsch's work focuses specifically on these issues and makes use of a unified developmental and evaluation process model.

The work draws on knowledge from a range of disciplines and combines these into a process for developing and evaluating Ubiquitous Computing applications using Near Field Communication (NFC) as an enabling technology. Various design guidelines for NFC applications are developed based on three engaging case studies. With these results Florian Resatsch shows the importance of combining various disciplines into a single multi-methodological approach in order to better understand the subject of "Ubiquitous Computing" from the user's perspective. His work makes clear the necessity of a process-oriented approach in enabling the development of information technology applications based on NFC.

Researchers in information systems will gain new insight into which research methods are applicable to which phases of product and prototype development. Important insights into the use and application of generic technology acceptance models and the piloting/prototyping of NFC-based applications are succinctly presented. Three case-studies, each in a different phase of the development cycle, add to the insights.

For practitioners a number of recommendations for orchestrating the development of user-friendly applications are provided. In particular, the compiled design guidelines can help entrepreneurs to focus early on important issues in the application development process. The specific guidelines on how to user-test the infrastructure and the detailed design parameters will prove helpful.

Given these contributions to the field I hope that this book by Florian Resatsch will find the attention it deserves.

Prof. Dr. Helmut Krcmar

Acknowledgements

From first recognizing the idea of a world in which ubiquitous computing would be a reality to the final version of this book more than five years have passed. A very long list of people contributed to this work and I would like to express my gratitude to everyone involved—I enjoyed and appreciated every single minute of their time they made available.

First, I would like to thank my advisor Prof. Dr. Helmut Krcmar for his continuous support during the Ph.D. process. Prof. Krcmar accepted the subject of this dissertation—he was open to and interested in the very new topic of Near Field Communication. I highly appreciate this open attitude and interest. Second, I thank Prof. Dr. Serge Miranda from the Université de Nice Sophia Antipolis in France who was so kind to be on my committee. Third, I am very thankful for the support of Prof. Dr. Jan Marco Leimeister who provided constructive feedback, thorough help, contacts to fellows, and advice during the entire development of this thesis. He initiated the ubiquitous computing working group at the department and got me involved in it.

Particular thanks go to Prof. Dr. Dr. Thomas Schildhauer for his generous support during the time I worked at the Institute of Electronic Business e.V. (IEB) in Berlin, where I was able to work while completing my Ph.D. studies, and for the many contacts he shared over the last several years. A thank you also goes to Heiner Andexer who supported the idea of ubiquitous computing and who helped me maintain a realistic vision of things. There is also Jörg (Dr. Jörg Aßmann) whom I thank for his unconditional support, his wicked humor, his insightful remarks on the thesis, and encouragement to pursue my empirical studies.

This thesis would not have been possible without the help of the project partners of the case studies Easymeeting, Mobile Prosumer, and Public Transport Company. I thank the management of the DVZ and all the employees of the DVZ who were willing to answer my questions in two interview sessions. In the case of the Mobile Prosumer, I would also like to thank Guido Leuchtenberg for his highly appreciated help in conducting the focus groups for the project, and Peter Sonneck and Franz Kilzer for arranging for the support of the project. For the Public Transport Company project I would like to thank Peter Preuss for making this whole study possible. Peter continuously supported the research efforts with very constructive business-minded feedback. Thanks also to Petra Krallmann who advised me in how to approach the statistical analysis of the study. I would also like to thank Eva Münkhoff from the University of Paderborn and Prof. Dr. Robert Wilken from the ESCP-EAP—both provided feedback on the research setup and calculations.

Furthermore I would like to thank my friends and colleagues Daniel Michelis and Thomas Nicolai, with whom I got into the topic of ubiquitous computing in the first place. Over the years they have given me support—mentally and also in terms of content. We began our research together in 2005 and discovered our topics over the course of time.

Thank you to Dr. Christian Kaspar who read the work several times, gave feedback at various stages, and helped me with his Ph.D. related experience. His input considerably improved the thesis. There is also Uwe Sandner for helping me to quickly become a Java developer and to understand theoretical computer science which I needed in order to start the Ph.D. program at the University. Tony Modica without whom my theoretical computer science would not have been as good as it was in the exams. Tony helped me to understand many facts and theories.

Thanks to Stephan Karpischek for initiating the Mobile Prosumer project and getting me involved in it. I enjoyed our fruitful discussions and continuous quest for making the Mobile Prosumer a good research project despite the many stumbling blocks. Martin Pischke who read my thesis at a very early stage, long before it was finished, and his useful feedback.

Erik Smith for the fantastic short notice general editing and proof-reading of the thesis, and also Marilyn Tremaine who edited parts of the thesis in the context of the paper publications.

But there is more: First, the colleagues in the department of Information Systems at the Technische Universität München, who helped me as an external Ph.D. student to keep up with all the organizational demands of the university. In particular, thanks to Stefanie Leimeister, Uta Knebel, and Dr. Peggy Sekatzek who were all available to give me feedback on my work and tips in the process. Second, all my colleagues at the Institute of Electronic Business e.V. who were aware of my intention to finish the Ph.D. and supported my decisions.

Finally the most important people need to be thanked: my parents, who have given me the freedom to pursue my studies and for their great understanding during the long phase of my life when I was constantly under some sort of time pressure…and always running out of time for regular visits. And my girlfriend Corina Weber! There is more to thank her for than what fits on these pages: for listening to my complaints and the (from time to time arising) frustrations, and for believing in me during this long period. For her continuous support and love, and her endless patience. She knows how much I owe her.

                                                                                                Florian Resatsch

Abstract

The term ubiquitous computing (Ubicomp) describes a reality in which numerous computers are woven into the fabric of daily life. Radio Frequency Technology (RFID) is considered the primary micro-processing technology driving the Ubicomp vision. Similar technologically to RFID, Near Field Communication (NFC) was first introduced to markets in 2005. NFC is a standardized interface technology for the exchange of data between electronic devices such as PCs, mobile telephones, and RFID tags. The use of NFC in mobile phones is the focus of this thesis. A subset of RFID technology, NFC has the potential to directly impact vast numbers of mobile phone users worldwide. But not much is known about how users will react to NFC technology when introduced to markets on a large scale. The challenges for companies interested in developing and marketing NFC applications lie in: being able to justify the high initial investments in NFC infrastructure, not knowing whether users will accept the technology, not knowing which technology future users will employ in their daily lives, and recognizing that consumers need to experiment with NFC to get a better idea of what it has to offer. So that companies may respond to these challenges, this thesis presents a directed process for developing and evaluating NFC applications from initial idea to final product, and introduces a set of guidelines for designing future applications.

The focus of the research lies in developing and evaluating NFC-based Ubicomp applications. It combines existing theories of Ubicomp, human-computer interaction, and technology acceptance in proposing an iterative process model: the ubiquitous computing application development and evaluation process model (UCAN) as a utility theory for developing and evaluating NFC applications. To test the process model the thesis uses three NFC-based artifacts from specific case studies, all of which solve a general domain-specific problem and target the end-user.

To answer the research problem the thesis makes use of the paradigm of design science. In employing this problem-solving paradigm, artifacts are developed within the framework of a utility theory. The utility theory, or process model, is in this case UCAN. The three artifacts are embedded within case studies that are subjected to the UCAN process. The case studies are: "Easymeeting" (office), "Mobile Prosumer" (retail), and "Public Transport Company" (ticketing). To analyze the artifacts, multiple methods were used and compared during the evaluation process. UCAN is used to determine which evaluation methods are applicable to each phase of the process—it is theorized and refined throughout the thesis.

In addition to the UCAN process model, a set of guidelines for designing NFC-based Ubicomp applications are the two primary results of this thesis. UCAN covers four phases: from initial idea, to low-fidelity prototype, to working prototype, up to the final product, and specifies evaluation methods for each prototype phase. These methods are: expert interviews, focus groups, talking-out-loud, and a survey that employs the UTAUT technology acceptance model. Companies can use the process model to determine various requirements for building successful NFC-based applications. The guidelines for designing NFC applications apply to four categories: NFC technology, tag infrastructure, devices, and human factors. The guidelines provide recommendations for how to approach designing NFC systems in terms of: process, promotion, privacy and security concerns, implementation of services, relevance, tag appearance, tag distribution, target groups, simplicity, haptic feedback, and existing infrastructures. The guidelines make possible initiating the development process of NFC according to user desires.

This work adds to the growing scientific body of Ubicomp knowledge by contributing the empirical results from three case studies and providing new theoretical insights. The thesis expands upon existing research in the ubiquitous computing field. It presents a view of Ubicomp through the lens of the relatively new technology NFC, and makes use of several evaluation methods, including a technology acceptance model (UTAUT), in developing the research. In particular, the artifact studied in relation to public transportation was measured at three points during the evaluation process. The case study featured a significant sample size and was conducted in the field. It was the largest NFC-based pilot test conducted in Germany. This thesis is the first to research NFC on a large-scale.

The thesis addresses practitioners by offering them a directed process model for developing NFC-based Ubicomp applications. The process model provides specific evaluation methods for each phase of development. Companies can use these methods to design successful applications. Because of the structure of the UCAN process, it is possible to determine unnecessary and even unwanted functions at a very early phase of application development. Furthermore, it allows changes to be made to the product at later developmental stages before significant investment in infrastructure has taken place. The applied UTAUT model helps companies to determine how to better market their products to consumers and how to improve the final NFC-based Ubicomp product. With UCAN and the set of design guidelines, a company has two solid resources that it can use to justify initial investments in NFC infrastructure, forecast whether users will accept the technology, and allow consumers to experiment with NFC to determine what it has to offer from the very beginning.

The research setup of this thesis has three limitations: the selection of the case studies, the extent of the research process, and the addition of added methodologies for analyzing the artifact. Future research needs to examine in more detail (also quantitatively) user-centered design approaches and acceptance models for Ubicomp applications. The following questions represent potential areas of future research: Is the UCAN process model developed here meeting the needs of Ubicomp application developers and does it enhance the development process? And: Do the developed NFC guidelines have a direct influence on technology acceptance, product success, and system usage?

Contents

List of Figures

List of Tables

Abbreviations

AI	Application Identifier
API	Application Programming Interface
CCC	Chaos Computer Club
CDMA	Code Division Multiple Access
CDT	Cognitive Dissonance Theory
CET	Cognitive Evaluation Theory
CHI	Computer-Human Interaction
CMS	Content Management System
CRM	Customer Relationship Management
DNS	Domain Naming Service
DOI	Digital Object Identifier
EAN	European Article Number
ECC	Error Checking and Correction Algorithm
ECMA	European Computer Manufacturers Association
EDGE	Enhanced Data Rates for GSM Evolution
EMID	Electromagnetic Identification
EPC	Electronic Product Code
EPCIS	Electronic Product Code Information Service
ERP	Enterprise Resource Planning
ETSI	European Telecommunications Standards Institute
FCC	Federal Communications Commission
FIFA	Fédération Internationale de Football Association
GHz	Gigahertz
GLN	Global Location Number
GOMS	Goals, operators, methods, and selection rules
GPRS	General Packet Radio Service
GSM	Global System for Mobile Communications
GTIN	Global Trade Identification Number
GUI	Graphical User Interface
GUID	Global Unique ID
HCI	Human Computer Interaction
HF	High Frequency
HTML	Hypertext Markup Language
ID	Identification
IDE	Integrated Development Environment
IEEE	Institute of Electrical and Electronics Engineers
IS	Information Systems

ISBN	International Standard Book Number
ISO	International Organisation of Standardisation
ISSN	International Standard Serials Number
IT	Information Technology
J2ME	Java Platform, Micro Edition
JAVA ME	Java Platform, Micro Edition
JDK	Java Development Kit
JSR	Java Specification Request
KB	Kilobyte
KBIT	Kilobit
KHz	Kilohertz
KLM	Keystroke-level Model
LAN	Local Area Network
LBS	Location-based Services
LED	Light Emitting Diode
LF	Low Frequency
LLCP	Logical Link Control Protocol
MIDP	Mobile Information Device Profile
MHz	Megahertz
MIDP	Mobile Information Device Profile
MM	Motivation Model
MNO	Mobile Network Operator
MP	Mobile Prosumer
MSA	Mobile Service Architecture Specification
NDEF	NFC Data Exchange Format
NDEF	NFC Data Exchange Format
NFC	Near Field Communication
ONS	Object Naming Service
OR	Operations Research
OS	Operating System
OTA	Over the Air
PC	Personal Computer
PDA	Personal Digital Assistent
PET	Privacy Enhancing Technologies
PLM	Product Lifecycle Management
PML	Physical Markup Language
POS	Point-of-Sale
PTC	Public Transport Company
RF	Radio Frequency

RFID	Radio Frequency Identification
RQ	Research Question
RSS	Reduced Space Symbology
RTD	Record Type Definition
SCT	Social Cognitive Theory
SDK	Software Development Kit
SDT	Self-determination Theory
SE	Software Engineering
SIM	Subscriber Identity Module
SME	Small and Medium Enterprises
SMS	Short Message Service
SOA	Service-oriented Architecture
SoC	System on Chip
SPT	Self-perception theory
SSCC	Serial Shipping Container Code
TAM	Technology Acceptance Model
TPB	Theorie of Planned Behaviour
TRA	Theorie of Reasoned Action
TTF	Task Technology Fit
TV	Television
UCAN	Ubiquitous Computing Application Development and Evaluation Process Model
UCC	Uniform Code Council
UHF	Ultra-High Frequency
UMTS	Universal Mobile Telecommunications System
UMTS	Universal Mobile Telecommunications System
UPC	Universal Product Code
URI	Uniform Resource Identifier
URL	Uniform Resource Locator
URN	Uniform Resource Name
UTAUT	Unified Theory of Acceptance and Use of Technology
WIMAX	Worldwide Interoperability for Microwave Access
WLAN	Wireless Local Area Network
WORM	Write-Once, Read Many
WSN	Wireless Sensor Networks

1   Introduction

The Ubiquitous Computing paradigm was introduced in the early 1990s by Weiser (Weiser 1991, 1993). The term *ubiquitous computing* (Ubicomp) is used to describe a reality in which numerous computers are invisibly woven into the fabric of daily life. At the time Weiser wrote his papers the use of personal computers was on the rise, the Internet was still in its infancy, and mobile communication was a long way off—let alone the actual reality of being surrounded by ubiquitous invisible computers (Bell/Dourish 2007, 134). The technological advancements in recent years have made realizing the early Ubicomp vision possible (Gershenfeld/Krikorian/Cohen 2004; Leimeister/Krcmar 2005; Mattern 2003a, 2003c, 2005b).

However, still the *computing* aspect was centered primarily on the personal computer until *Radio Frequency Identification* (RFID) was introduced in various industry segments (Knebel/Leimeister/Krcmar 2006). RFID is an automatic identification method that relies on the storage and remote retrieval of wireless data with what are known as RFID *tags* or transponders. The transponders contain unique identification numbers and other pertinent data. They make it possible to track and trace all kinds of physical objects (Fine et al. 2006) and enable the integration of virtual data in the physical world (Fleisch/Christ/Dierkes 2005a, 8). RFID technology is becoming more and more relevant to businesses and organizations around the globe. According to a recent study, the market for RFID systems grew from 1.5 Billion EUR in 2004 to 22 Billion EUR in 2010 worldwide (Heng 2006).

Convergence effects of RFID and end-user devices—especially in the combination of mobile phones and RFID—open up further fields of possible Ubicomp applications (Resatsch et al. 2007b; Riekki/Salminen/Alakärppä 2006). For example *Near Field Communication* (NFC) (NFCForum 2007a, 2007b, 2007c) allows mobile phone users to simply touch things equipped with RFID tags for initiating interactions and for taking advantage of offered mobile services (Jalkanen 2005). NFC represents a new technology with extreme functionality. But what kind of applications potential users will accept, and whether consumers want this type of Ubicomp in real life, remains unclear.

Companies considering providing this kind of enabling technology are facing many challenges. Chief among these are the high upfront costs of hardware infrastructure, unknown user technology acceptance, as well as a lack of specific design guidelines for the applications. These problems expose the need for a directed approach to development and evaluation in order to gain insight into relevant application elements and usage patterns from a very early stage in the application development process (Abowd/Mynatt 2000; Reilly et al. 2005).

This analysis will present three case studies of NFC-based artifacts in creating a process model for developing and evaluating Ubicomp applications. The book should help companies understand user acceptance of NFC to create successful applications, and help researchers make use of appropriate evaluation methods in various phases of application development.

1.1 Field of Investigation

The book focuses on the oft-cited realm of Ubicomp (Weiser/Gold/Brown 1999; Weiser 1993; Abowd/Mynatt 2000). This section briefly outlines the concept as the primary field of investigation. Technological Ubicomp developments are described first (1), followed by (2) an explanation of the focus technology in this analysis: RFID in the forming of NFC. The section finishes with (3) a description of possible use scenarios of NFC in mass consumer markets.

(1) Ubiquitous Computing: Recent technological developments influence the ongoing integration of Ubicomp in our life today (adapted from (Fleisch/Mattern/Billinger 2004)):

* *Miniaturized micro chips:* In 1965 Moore's Law stated that the complexity of an integrated circuit doubles approximately every 18 months. With respect to minimum component costs, the industry experiences an increase in available micro-processors with many potential application scenarios due to the small size and the wireless capabilities. RFID is seen as a major micro-processor technology driving the Ubicomp vision (Fine et al. 2006). NFC relies on RFID as a standardized interface technology for exchanging data between devices (NFCForum 2007c).

* *Ubiquitous consumer devices:* The mobile phone is a truly ubiquitous device of our times (MLR 2006 ; o.V. 2006). New shapes and forms, and even completely new devices are created to help users use the underlying infrastructure of Ubicomp (Ballagas et al. 2006).

* *Network capabilities and infrastructure:* Internet download bandwidth has increased significantly in recent years. More wireless-frequency wave bands are now allocated for business and private use and are globally available. This increases network reach for Ubicomp applications as also wireless mobile transfer rates reach new heights (Hagenhoff/Kaspar/Resatsch 2008; Mattern 2002).

* *Interaction technologies:* Smart phones with high resolutions displays are common. New devices integrate miniaturized screens with touch or point technologies (Poupyrev/Okabe/Maruyama 2004; Luk et al. 2006; Rukzio 2007). NFC phones have been recently introduced to the marketplace (NFCForum 2007c).

* *Software:* Web services enable fast and easy access to distributed content on the Internet, with the potential to link physical objects and data (McIlraith/Zeng 2001; Paolucci et al. 2002).

* *Production technology:* New self-assembly techniques have arisen in recent years that make cost-efficient productions possible (Kommandur 2004). RFID chips can be produced in self-assembly processes[1].

* *Standards:* With the Internet providing an already standardized backbone, further identification schemes for various industries and purposes are being standardized (Auto-ID-Center 2003; NFCForum 2007c).

---

[1]   Examples can be found at http://www.pb.izm.fhg.de/izm - Self-assembly and interconnection of silicon chips

These technological developments enable new kinds of applications for bridging virtual and physical worlds (Mattern 2005a; Fleisch/Mattern 2005). From human-computer interaction with natural interfaces to context-aware computing, the diversity of applications in these scenarios is immense (Abowd/Mynatt 2000). Depending on one's point of view, the Ubicomp vision is either still just a vision (Mattern 2005b) or is already here but in a different, "messier" form than originally envisioned (Bell/Dourish 2007).

(2) RFID in the forming of NFC: One type of Ubicomp technology is the focus of this analysis: Radio Frequency Identification (RFID). RFID as a Ubicomp technology has been broadly discussed in literature (Abowd/Mynatt 2000; Fleisch/Christ/Dierkes 2005a; Fleisch/Mattern 2005; Knebel/Leimeister/Krcmar 2006; Mattern 2004, 2003a, 2005b; Want 2006; Want et al. 1995; Krcmar 2005). Many of today's RFID approaches concentrate on process optimization or supply chain processes; RFID was first introduced to the retail sector in order to optimize logistics, solve out-of-stock problems and improve the supply chain (Fleisch/Christ/Dierkes 2005a; Fleisch/Mattern 2005; Fleisch/Mattern/Billinger 2004; Fleisch/Thiesse 2007; Mattern 2005b; Resatsch et al. 2007a; Murphy-Hoye/Lee/Rice 2005; Leimeister/Krcmar 2005) —but not as a *consumer* technology (Resatsch et al. 2007a).

Although not much different technologically than RFID, Near Field Communication (NFC) was introduced to markets in 2005 (NFCForum 2007c). NFC is a standardized interface technology for the exchange of data between electronic devices such as personal computers (PCs), mobile telephones, and RFID tags. NFC has an operating range of a few centimetres, and works in combination with RFID technology and contactless smart card infrastructure. Using NFC, a mobile phone for example can read amounts of data from RFID tags by touching or waving the phone to a tag. With this functionality, NFC phones directly enable the user to bridge physical and virtual worlds (Rukzio et al. 2006a). NFC is usually applied in three major areas: service initiation, peer-to-peer and applications (NFCForum 2007c). NFC is used to initiate a service, for example by opening another communication link for data transfer, it is used to enable communication between two devices, or is build on top off existing services, such as ticketing, and electronic payment infrastructures (NFCForum 2007c). NFC makes mass market services of RFID possible.

(3) NFC in mass consumer markets: Thus far NFC has not suffered from the negative reputation relative to privacy issues as RFID (Resatsch et al. 2007a). From a technological standpoint however it is very similar since both use radio frequency to transmit data. What is special about NFC is that it can also be implemented in a mobile phone (GSM-Association 2007; NFCForum 2007a). By implementing RFID in mobile phones the technology previously used for tracing and tracking could be used by consumers in once unimagined ways (Jalkanen 2005). Considering the ubiquity of mobile phones and their growth potential (GSM-Association 2006), an NFC-equipped phone would be a true Ubicomp device and even a potentially disruptive technology (Christensen 1997) if there is a physical infrastructure (NFC tag or devices) that can be used.

This study investigates NFC in combination with RFID and mobile phones. Both terms, NFC and RFID, are used in parallel in the first chapters, especially when analyzing the impact of showcases and prototypes on consumer perception. The latter stages of the analysis focus on NFC as the used technology.

The main questions are whether ubiquitous computing technologies such as RFID represents a significant value to consumers in forming NFC, whether these technologies are accepted on a technological level, and how applications should be developed and evaluated in designing them according to the needs and demands of future users.

1.2 Research Problem

Technologies that are new—or perceived to be new—to a certain domain, industry, or field take a long time to impact the lives of ordinary people (Norman 1999b; Kaasinen 2005). The adoption of so called "disruptive technologies" is an even longer and more complicated process (Christensen 1997). *Disruptive technologies* are technologies that may cause revolutionary changes in people's lives, a fact that is being spread by many Ubicomp visionaries (Mattern 2003a, 2002).

Christensen uses the term disruptive *innovation* in his later work to emphasize that the *strategy* creates the disruptive impact, not the technology in itself—only a few technologies have the intrinsic potential to be disruptive (Christensen 2003). True "disruptive technologies" provide new use case categories for technologies that were previously unavailable. Although the technology at the root of RFID has been around since the late '40s (Stockman 1948), the dawn of a new era of mass usage has occurred only recently (Knebel/Leimeister/Krcmar 2006). Supporters of the technology, such as huge retail companies, regard RFID only as an incremental improvement for optimizing their processes (Loebbecke/Palmer 2006). In North America, the efforts of EPCglobal[2] in particular have dominated the development of RFID applications with a focus on industry use cases, and have in the process generated a fundamental interest in supply chain management (Fine et al. 2006). Although interest in RFID has focused primarily on supply chain applications, Fine and others also see the potential of RFID and tagging technologies to impact the lives of end-users (Fine et al. 2006)—a not yet realized reality for RFID (Wilding/Delgado 2004) and especially not for NFC in this early market stage. A shift in this status would significantly increase the potential for disruptive rather than incremental improvements. Advancements related to NFC with mobile phones may also prove disruptive. This holds especially true given that more and more ideas have cropped up on bridging the gap between real and virtual worlds since the introduction of NFC phones by large mobile phone producers (Rukzio/Schmidt/Hussmann 2004; Smith/Davenport/Hwa 2003; Välkkynen/Niemelä/Tuomisto 2006). These recent mobile phone introductions point to NFC's mass-market potential.

Given the physical dimension of the technology both NFC and RFID first require investments in a tag infrastructure to make it viable. Such investments in large-scale Ubicomp information technology infrastructure are high. Serious market and user-acceptance-based research may help to mitigate high investment risks in such technologies (Degenhardt 1986).

---

[2]   Source: http:// www.epcglobalinc.org/ - accessed 24.02.2008

Fig. 1 shows a possible benefits cycle that would evolve around RFID-based applications—
here consumer RFID applications include NFC applications.

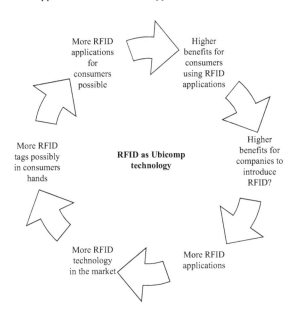

Fig. 1: Benefits cycle for the market introduction of RFID

While many current RFID-based Ubicomp applications are used for managing supply chains
and logistics (Fleisch/Thiesse 2007), end-user benefits also likely exist. If RFID works well
for supply chain management (a fact that retail businesses seem to confirm (Thiesse 2007)),
then companies can profit from the introduction of an RFID infrastructure with a greater
range of RFID applications and an increase in RFID technology. From this the conclusion can
also be drawn that more consumers will have touch points with RFID technology (e.g. the
tags on product labels left on products), also making more consumer-useful applications
potentially possible (e.g. an RFID-reader in a NFC mobile phone used to determine product
ingredients from the product tag). If applications providing tangible benefits to consumers
were adopted in significant numbers the advantages for companies would increase further
since their infrastructure would be used multiple times—thus leading to even more RFID
implementations. The challenge is first getting the benefits cycle started.

In terms of supply chain and logistics, RFID is more likely to be seen as an incremental
improvement, but in the area of consumer application, RFID could still be a disruptive
innovation. The adoption of important industry use-cases such as item-level tagging initiates
the benefits cycle that is indicative of broad consumer acceptance. According to Sheffi
(2004), RFID "is still not out of the fog of innovation: the benefits of the technology are not
entirely clear, especially its advantages over bar code technology" (Sheffi 2004). Furthermore
Sheffi states that the discussions about standards and privacy issues (Spiekermann 2005; Juels

2006) are indicative of a technology still in its infancy. One critical aspect of technology is that the move from invention to innovation is only possible if consumers adopt and accept the particular technology in large numbers (Sheffi 2004).

As described above, a broader availability of RFID technology in supply-chain applications may lead to more RFID availability at a consumer level in the future. This means new product and service potential for companies in mass markets. But the high initial investments in infrastructure that are currently needed, as well as the uncertainty surrounding both user acceptance of the technology and the potential of NFC as a technology itself, prevent the RFID benefits cycle from getting started. Because of the limited availability of NFC phones and therefore consumer applications in the German market, people have little opportunity to experiment with applications, let alone to get to know the technology itself. This prevents the consumer from being able to properly assess potential NFC applications benefits (Abowd et al. 2005). Furthermore, companies are aware of the challenges related to establishing the technology as previously outlined, which limits the number of applications being developed and tested. Compared to other new technologies, both RFID and NFC are still mostly unknown (NFC) or perceived negatively (RFID) (Resatsch et al. 2007a). This is why some consider technology-push as a strategy for creating a market entry for RFID in consumer applications. However, the technology-push effect is also considered a reason for innovation failures (Utterback 1971, 124-131):

Technology-push is used when potentially successful market applications are unknown. This contrasts with market-pull, in which details of the market are well known and define consumer needs and wants. The relation of technology-push to market uncertainty implies the use of anticipatory and exploratory methods for entering the market (Herstatt/Lettl 2000; Lender 1991). These methods include early integration of future users to help develop applications to suit their needs. This has the potential to lead to better product acceptance in the latter stages of market entry.

NFC as a subset of RFID technology could potentially target all mobile phone users worldwide. The number of mobile phone users is immense—to date, more than 3.3 billion people use mobile phones worldwide[3]. But less is known about how users will react to the introduction of the NFC technology to larger segments of the market. Nevertheless, considering the overall market potential, decisions about investments in NFC infrastructure have become important for mobile operators, mobile service providers, and handset manufacturers.

The challenge lies in: (1) justifying the high initial investments in infrastructure, (2) not knowing whether users will accept the technology, (3) not knowing which technology future users will employ (NFC) and (4) understanding the need of consumers to experiment with NFC to determine what is has to offer (see Fig. 2).

---

[3]   Source: http://www.itu.int/ITU-D/ict/newslog/Global+Mobile+Phone+Users+Top+33+Billion+By+End2007.aspx – accessed 31.08.2008

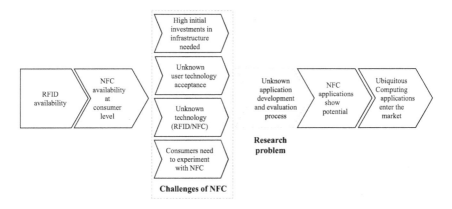

Fig. 2: Challenges of NFC and the research focus in overview

To overcome these barriers and challenges, the research problem of this thesis is to help companies develop successful NFC-based Ubicomp applications and researchers evaluate these applications in their early stages.

1.3 Research Questions and Objectives

The study is based on three research questions. The first research question is (RQ1):

• **RQ1: What are the defining elements of RFID- and NFC-applications (information systems) and what specific challenges are implied by the development of these applications?**

Once the defining elements of the technology and other factors influencing RFID- and NFC as Ubicomp technologies are explained, existing technology acceptance models and evaluation methods will be examined to determine which one fits the development process and the specifics of Ubicomp applications (RQ2):

• **RQ2: Which technology acceptance models and which evaluation methods support the development of Ubicomp applications?**

The results of RQ1 and RQ2 help to answer the final research question (RQ3) regarding how companies might use the models and methods to successfully develop and evaluate Ubicomp (NFC-based) in a way that keeps infrastructure investments low, determines technology acceptance, helps people understand the technology, and lets future users experiment with the technology to create a set of design guidelines:

• **RQ3: How can companies develop successful Ubicomp applications in a directed process and what are the design guidelines for these applications?**

The three research questions follow from one another, from RQ1 to RQ2 to RQ3.

Beyond examining the research problem and related questions, the following objectives belong to the stated goals of this research:

- To propose a *process model* for the development and evaluation of ubiquitous computing applications using the example of Near Field Communication

- To establish *design guidelines* for outlining the positive and negative factors related to user acceptance of NFC-based ubiquitous computing artifacts in three exemplary domains.

To answer these questions, the study needs to describe the theoretical background that is necessary for an understanding of the characteristics of Ubiquitous Computing technology using the example of NFC and RFID. It aims to state initial requirements based on human-computer interaction theory for NFC-based applications due to the notion of *ubiquity* and *daily life* in Ubicomp. It further consolidates and integrates technology acceptance models to be used in Ubicomp settings. Based on existing theory it needs to develop a process model as a utility theory for the development and evaluation of Ubicomp applications and finally to theorize about and test the process model with different evaluation methods and use the findings of the cases to prepare design guidelines for NFC-based Ubicomp applications.

This work is addressed to practitioners and the information systems (IS) research community. It seeks to introduce a potential process for mapping evaluation methods into the course of Ubicomp application development using the example of Near Field Communication. It will also supplement the scientific body of knowledge related to these questions with empirical results from three case studies as well as new theoretical insights on ubiquitous computing.

The target practitioner groups of this study are managers who are responsible for the development and implementation of innovative user-centered services in the area of NFC and RFID. The relevant target group within the specific area of research is the ubiquitous computing, information systems, and human-computer-interaction community.

This study supplements existing research in the field of ubiquitous computing.

1.4 Methodology

Currently Ubicomp does not allow a broad ex-post quantitative analysis of existing solutions since only a few real life applications for consumers exist. To find answers to the aforementioned research questions, existing Ubicomp application artifacts will be evaluated according design science principles. This chapter profiles (1) design science, and explains (2) the design science process, (3) utility theories in design science, and (4) the research process.

(1) **Design science:** This study makes use of the problem-solving paradigm of *design science* (Hevner et al. 2004). Design science is based on the work of Simon (Simon 1980; Simon 1996). Design means to create something that does not occur in nature. "Design science attempts to create things that serve human purposes" (March/Smith 1995). Simon called it "science of the artificial" (Simon 1996). The *science of the artificial* aims to explain the difference between the natural and the artificial world, the creation of the artificial, and the design of evolving artifacts in socio-organizational environments. The production of relevant

knowledge differentiates design research from design itself (Vaishnavi/Kuechler 2004). "Design Science" is "Technology Invention" (Venable 2006).

(2) Design science process: Design consists of a set of activities (processes) and a product (artifact). According March and Smith, design science consists of two processes: develop/build and justify/evaluate. These processes produce four types of artifacts: constructs, models, methods, and instantiations (March/Smith 1995). Fig. 3 illustrates how the develop/build and justify/evaluate processes are connected according to Hevner et. al.; Development and building refer to theories and artifacts, whereas justification and evaluation refer to analytical research, case studies and further methods. The creation of design science relies on existing "kernel theories" that are applied, tested, and possibly modified by the researcher (Walls/Widmeyer/El Sawy 1992). In between the develop/build and justify/ evaluate processes an assessment and refinement cycle is maintained (see Fig. 3).

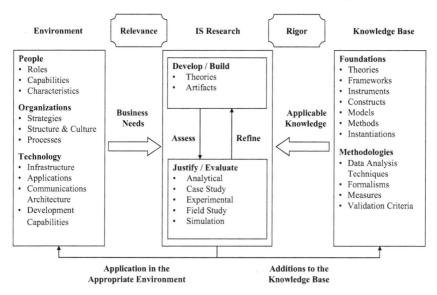

Fig. 3: IS research core activities
Source: (Hevner et al. 2004)

The design science process addresses the building and evaluation of artifacts to meet business needs. IS research derives from foundational theories, frameworks, and instruments of various disciplines used in the develop/build phase of the research study. Methods provide relevant guidelines for the justify/evaluate phase. The application of existing foundations and methodologies conforms to the rigorous nature of the research (Hevner et al. 2004). There is a close research cycle between design-science and behavioral-sciences, insofar as technology and behavior are inseparable in information systems (Hevner et al. 2004) and potential methods can be derived from social science.

(3) Design artifacts: Artifacts are the primary output of design approaches in the build/develop phase. Instantiation refers to the realization of an artifact in its environment. To evaluate an instantiation one must take into account the efficiency and effectiveness of the artifact within the environment as well as its impact on users. For assessing impacts on users, related behavioral science approaches are employed. In the case of built artifacts, the application of data and underlying research methods are critical for understanding and justifying the theoretical dimensions of the artifact. In this analysis built artifacts are evaluated according to their intended functions in the environment.

Artifact design contributes invaluably to the body of IS knowledge, making it an important part of research (March/Smith 1995; Simon 1996) with implications for the scientific community. Design science has already been used successfully in several IS research approaches (Walls/Widmeyer/El Sawy 1992; Markus/Majchrzak 2002; Aiken/Sheng/Vogel 1991).

Hevner et al. asserts that a combination of technology-based artifacts and people-based artifacts are necessary to address the acceptance issue of information technology systems. Design science approaches this goal through the construction of innovative artifacts "aiming at changing the phenomena that occur" (Hevner et al. 2004).

This work aims to solve the research problem by developing and evaluating such artifacts using a utility theory as a frame. Gregor points out the importance of theory to IS research, stating at the same time however that March and Smith (1995) as well as Hevner et al. (2004) only use the word theory to describe natural-science based research (Gregor 2006). In response to this Gregor (2006) then quotes Weick (1995): "Writers should feel free to use theory whenever they are theorizing" (Weick 1995).

(4) Utility theories: In view of this, the utility theory described by (Venable 2006) can be seen as a potential means of overcoming deficiencies in existing approaches. Utility theory asserts that an IS system or IS process can help to improve a problematic situation. The utility of the IS system or process should be announced by its efficacy and efficiency in addressing the problem. A theory is a utility theory if a new or newly applied technology, when applied properly, is more effective than another technology or will provide otherwise identified improvements. The problem space (see Fig. 4) is similar to the business needs of Hevner et. al. (2004) as mentioned above. Furthermore the notion of the problem space extends to causal links of multiple problems in a context.

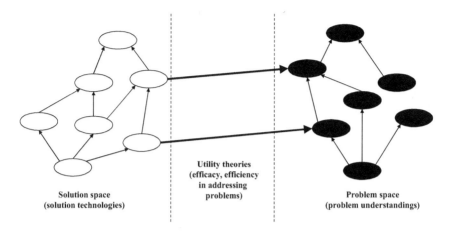

Fig. 4: Utility theories in between solution and problem space
Source: (Venable 2006)

The utility theory needs to clearly identify the general problems that the technological solution addresses. Although problems are perceived differently among individuals and especially researchers, the problem scope is determined by the person conducting the research. The theoretical aspects of this analysis are related to realizing a process model for solutions and realizing new applications for existing technology (Venable 2006). A utility theory links a concept or group of technology concepts (NFC prototypes) to the aspects of the problem (end-user acceptance) that it addresses.

A utility theory should be stated clearly at the beginning and be revised further during the research process. The ongoing development of hypotheses and re-conceptualizations is called the emergent theory (Vaishnavi/Kuechler 2004). When artifacts are evaluated on how well they solved a problem or improved a process, the emergent utility theories are further examined.

Theoretical speculation is central to design research. Utility theory can help as a starting point for a design-based research process. In order to evaluate the technology in terms of the problem, this thesis intends to make use of a utility theory in the form of a process model based on established IS theories. The developed design or utility theory is well substantiated (Goldkuhl 2004):

(5) Research process: In addition to its theoretical grounding, a research process is set up. Pfeffers et. al. (2006) propose a design science research process model based on process elements from other IS approaches (Archer 1965; Eekels/Roozenburg 1991; Hevner et al. 2004; Nunamaker/Chen/Purdin 1991; Pfeffers et al. 2006; Takeda 1990; Walls/Widmeyer/El Sawy 1992).

Based on the design science research process a problem is identified for each artifact (instantiation). The objectives of the solution are stated, and artifacts are designed and developed. In addition, the ability of the artifact to solve the problem is demonstrated before using a utility theory to examine the artifact with various behavioural science methods. This integrated multi-dimensional and multi-methodological approach helps to generate "fruitful research results in IS research" (Nunamaker/Chen/Purdin 1991). Although there are many barriers to using multi-methodological approaches in terms of philosophy, cultures, psychology, and practice, the results are still encouraging (Westfall 1999). Multiphase research designs generate very rich data of different types, and evaluate phenomena from multiple perspectives (Zmud 1998).

Fig. 5 illustrates the research process. After a description of the theoretical background in chapters 2 and 3, the utility theory is developed in chapter 4. The theoretical background also provides the necessary knowledge for developing and building artifacts and to evaluate them according the process mentioned by Hevner (Hevner et al. 2004). Three artifacts are featured in this analysis, all of which solve a general domain specific problem, are based on NFC (as a Ubicomp technology) and are focused on the end-user. The utility theory is a process model for connecting the artifacts under evaluation. Every artifact contributes to the Ubicomp body of knowledge, it also helps to test the process model and refine it in the course of the analysis.

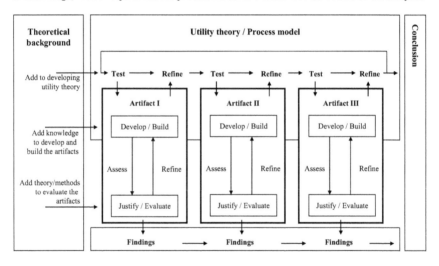

Fig. 5: Research process and incorporation of design science in the analysis

Bearing this research process in mind, the following section explains the structure of this analysis in which the three artifacts are lined up in a chapter structure.

1.5 Thesis Structure

The thesis analysis combines methodology, theory, and empirical studies. Design science provides the framework for the research process, the employed methods and the case studies.

Based on the aforementioned design science process the remainder of this analysis is structured as follows (see Fig. 6)[4]:

• Chapter 1 outlines the field of investigation, the research problem and objectives, relevant work in the field, and the methodology of design science.

• Chapter 2 covers aspects relevant to the research problem in the ubiquitous computing field, RFID and NFC in general.

• Chapter 3 expounds on the theoretical framework developed in chapter 2 and explains in more detail human computer interaction theory, as well as innovation adoption and technology acceptance models.

• Chapter 4 provides a utility theory relating to the design science research process. This utility theory is a process model for developing and evaluating Ubicomp applications. It is the basis for the evaluation of the artifacts in chapters 5 and 6.

• Chapter 5 presents two artifacts for analysis. Both artifacts are part of a case study and are evaluated according to utility theory explained in chapter 4. The artifacts are in earlier prototype stages.

• Chapter 6 expounds on the view of a later-stage working prototype evaluation in the field.

• Chapter 7 summarizes the findings and draws conclusions. In addition future research directions in the area are presented.

---

4   A note on the writing style: To increase readability, neutral persons will be referred to using the male pronoun only (he instead of, e.g., she or he) throughout this thesis. The parts of the thesis are named as follows: a single number Y denotes a chapter; Y.Y is also referred to as a chapter and all other parts are called sections. Further: every figure that has no source mentioned is an illustration by the author.

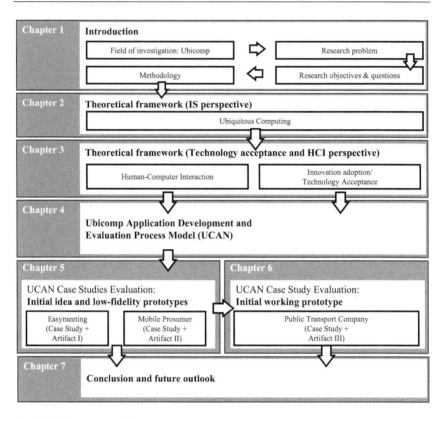

Fig. 6: Thesis structure overview

2   Theoretical Framework

Goal of this chapter is to describe the theoretical background that is necessary for an understanding of the characteristics of ubiquitous computing (Ubicomp) technology. The sub-goals of this chapter are to

- define Ubicomp and Ubicomp applications in a working definition (in Chapter 2.1),

- describe available Ubicomp technologies and attributes of the underlying technology (in Chapter 2.1),

- define building blocks of an Ubicomp infrastructure and narrow these blocks down for an initial model (in Chapter 2.1),

- and to research what the user knows about the Ubicomp technologies to look at the current state of everyday use of technologies such as RFID (in Chapter 2.2).

- Finally a conclusion is drawn (in Chapter 2.3)

2.1 Ubiquitous Computing

Ubiquitous computing (Ubicomp) is about the ubiquitous availability of miniaturized computers surrounding human beings. To understand the implications of this concept, a working definition of Ubicomp is given in section 2.1.1. Ubicomp building blocks are enumerated in section 2.1.2, followed by an overview on Ubicomp technologies (Section 2.1.3). Section 2.1.4 details the technology Radio Frequency Identification (RFID), while Near Field Communication (NFC) as a subset of RFID is described in section 2.1.5. The differences between NFC and RFID are summed up in section 2.1.6.

2.1.1 Definition

Depending on the context, several definitions of *Ubiquitous Computing* can be found in literature. Sometimes it is also referred to as "Pervasive Computing" (Burkhardt et al. 2001; Hansmann et al. 2003) or "Calm Computing" (Rogers 2006).

According the Merriam-Webster Online dictionary, *ubiquitous* means "existing or being everywhere at the same time: constantly encountered" (Merriam-Webster 2006d). The word pervasive comes from pervading or tending to pervade which means "to go through" or "to become diffused throughout every part of" (Merriam-Webster 2006c). In a definition given for the word *calm* that means quiet and free from disturbance, Merriam-Webster states: "Calm often implies a contrast with a foregoing or nearby state of agitation or violence" (Merriam-Webster 2006a). The words alone could symbolize that Ubicomp should have an implicit (calm) and everywhere (ubiquitous) simplicity supporting humans in their lives (pervasive).

In Mark Weiser's text (Weiser 1991, 1993), Ubicomp is described as invisible computers in different sizes, situated to specific tasks. "People will simply use them unconsciously to accomplish everyday tasks" (Weiser 1991, 2). Bearing this definition in mind, it becomes clear that Ubicomp's original intention was human-focused. The basic idea meant computing that occurs independent of the desktop where the machines suit human needs and do not force people to adapt the needs of the machine. An early definition of this was given by Abowd for whom ubiquitous computing is "any computing technology that permits human interaction away from a single workstation" (Abowd 1996).

This definition also led to the often-cited "internet of things" (Fleisch/Mattern 2005; Gershenfeld/Krikorian/Cohen 2004; Leimeister/Krcmar 2005; Mattern 2003a), a concept in which the focus is on objects that are able to interconnect and interact with each other. Thus the *Internet of things* is one possible characterization of the overall vision.

An attempt to standardize the topic is given by the National Institute for Standards and Technology (NIST 2001): Ubiquitous computing is (1) numerous, casually accessible, often invisible computing devices, (2) frequently mobile or imbedded in the environment (2), and (3) connected to an increasingly ubiquitous network structure.

(1) refers to the ubiquity and invisibility of computers, while (2) also draws attention to mobility and mobile devices. Mobile phones are ubiquitously available devices although not invisible in themselves, but invisible in terms of how they transfer data actions. According to Pfaff and Skiera, mobile computing is a subset of ubiquitous computing (Pfaff/Skiera 2005). Mobile computing relies on a mobile device that the user interacts with directly, whereas in some forms of Ubicomp no interaction with a single device is necessary. (3) is important, because of the necessity of adequate infrastructure—without which the idea of connected devices would not be possible. A network and communication infrastructure is needed to bring the desired services into everyday life.

As for the notion of invisibility sometimes associated with Ubicomp, it actually refers more to simplicity of use than the actuality of an invisible computer. Weiser used the term in his work to describe an integral part of life, computers as an "invisible part of the way people live their lives" (Weiser 1991, 2). Furthermore he states that computers "will be invisible in fact as well as in metaphor" and "will come to be invisible to common awareness. People will simply use them unconsciously to accomplish everyday tasks" (Weiser 1991, 2). Ease-of-use and the unconscious usage is the main proposition of Ubicomp.

As for today, further wireless technologies can also be part of Ubicomp. To sum up, the working definition of *Ubiquitous Computing* for this study is:

Ubiquitous network and communication infrastructures are defined by the presence of various, miniaturized, networked, and often invisible technology situated within the range of everyday human actions encompassing applications, supporting interaction, and processes with ease of use.

The focus is on applications in the Ubicomp domain. To detail the term application and what is understood in the context of this work, the definition of application is important.

Here a Ubicomp application is defined as an application that:

- functions as an information technology system for end users

- features relevant hardware (infrastructure plus networked technology)

- features software (interaction, communication, services and process)

- features a human-computer interface

- is in the *everyday range* of human beings.

According to IBM[5], an application is "the use to which an information processing system is put". The use is relative to the user. In our case, *application* refers to the combination of soft- and hardware parts of the NFC-based Ubicomp system, including the infrastructure, which is the focus of computing systems development (see also the concept of the "machine" in (Bjorner 2006)). The *application program* is the written software that controls the system (software application). With the possibility of various combinations, this distinction is important for the later evaluation of the applications developed throughout the analysis.

2.1.2 Building Blocks

Fleisch and Thiesse state a list of smart object functionalities, that can also be extended to a list of building blocks in the Ubicomp context (Fleisch/Thiesse 2007):

- *Identification.* Objects need to be uniquely identified. This identification alone allows the object to be linked with services and information which are stored in the network.

- *Memory.* The device needs storage capacity so that it can carry information about its past or future.

- *Processing logic.* Smart objects may be able to make decisions automatically without a central planning instance, e.g. in the sense of an industrial container which determines its own route through the supply chain.

- *Networking.* In contrast with the simple pocket calculator, smart objects have the capability of being connected with resources in a network or even amongst themselves (referred to as *ad-hoc networking*) for the reciprocal use of data and services.

- *Sensor technology.* The object collects information about its environment (temperature, light conditions, other objects, etc.), records it and/or reacts to it (referred to as *context awareness*).

---

[5]   http://publib.boulder.ibm.com/infocenter/printer/v1r1/index.jsp?topic= /com.ibm.printers.ip4100 opguide/ic3o0mst218.htm - Accessed 25.02.08

- *User interface.* With the merging of computer and physical objects new requirements arise that the user interface needs to address. This calls for new approaches similar to the mouse & desktop metaphor of graphical user interfaces, e.g. in the form of haptic interfaces.

- *Location & tracking.* Smart objects know their position (location) or can be located by others (tracking), for example at the global level by GPS or inside buildings by ultrasound.

A Ubicomp application does not necessarily include all these building blocks, but the list shows the relevance (and complexity) of Ubicomp systems.

2.1.3 Technologies

The working definition states the presence of *various, miniaturized, networked, and often invisible technology* as the driving force of Ubicomp. Furthermore the notion of being unobtrusive in everyday life demands some sort of wireless technology. Table 1 gives an overview of current wireless technologies and the integration of NFC in this context (Fine et al. 2006).

Technology	Frequency	Typical Range	Data Range
Dedicated RFID	125-134 kHz (LF) 13.56 MHz (HF) 400-930 MHz (UF) 2.5 GHz & 5 GHz (microwave)	20 cm passive 400 cm (active)	1-200 kbps
Near Field Communication (NFC)	13.56	**0-20 Centimetres**	**106,212,424 kbps**
Zigbee 802.15.4	2.4 GHz	70 meters	250 kbps
Bluetooth 1.1 802.15.1	2.4 GHz	10 meters	780 kbps
Bluetooth 2.0	2.4 GHz	10 meters	3 Mbps
Ultra-Wideband 802.15.3a	3.1 GHz	10 meters, 2 meters	110, 480 Mbps
802.11a	5 GHz	100 meters	54 Mbps
802.11b/g	2.4 GHz	100 meters	54 Mbps
802.16 WiMAX	10-66 GHz	1-3 miles	134 Mbps
802.16a WiMAX	2-11 GHz	30 miles	75 Mbps
802.16e WiMAX	6 GHz	1-3 miles	15 Mbps
GPRS	900, 1800, 1900 MHz	National Network	160 kbps
EDGE	900, 1800, 1900 MHz	National Network	160 kbps
UMTS	900, 1800, 1900 MHz	In selected cities	2 Mbps
CDMA2000/1XRTT	1900 MHz, others	National Network	156-307.2 kbps
CDMA2000/1xEV. DO	1900 MHz, others	In selected cities	2.4 Mbps

Table 1: Overview on wireless technologies
Source: (Fine et al. 2006)

RFID and Near Field Communication (NFC) have the shortest communication range. Then come the Wireless Personal Area Network (WPAN) technologies, such as Zigbee, Bluethooth 1.1, Bluetooth 2.0, and Ultra-Wideband, followed by Wireless Local Area Network (WLAN) with different frequencies and reach. The Wireless Wide Area Networks (WWAN) typically represent mobile phone network technologies, such as GPRS, EDGE, UMTS, and CDMA.

The Radio Frequency Identification (RFID) technology is widely recognized as the main force behind Ubicomp (Fleisch 2004; Gillert/Hansen 2007; Landt 2005; Mattern 2003a), given how it matches the Ubicomp notion of small, miniaturized microchips embedded in daily life. NFC runs at the same frequency as RFID, but has different use cases and standards. This analysis focuses on RFID in the forming of NFC, and takes as its use case mobile phones with RFID reader capabilities.

However, there are more technologies that fall under the domain of ubiquitous computing. Mainly driven by the idea of linking virtual data to real world objects (Nicolai/ Resatsch/Michelis 2005), authors also used barcodes in the area of Ubicomp (Adelmann/Langheinrich/Flörkemeier 2006). This commonly coined "tagging" (Thiesse 2007), is shown in Fig. 7 as the bigger tagging picture.

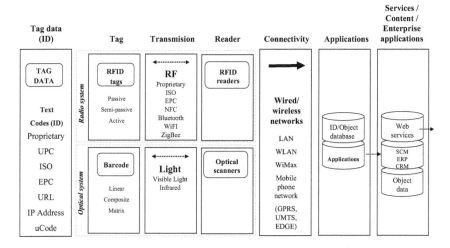

Fig. 7: Tagging
Source: (Fine et al. 2006)

The tag data is stored on the physical tag with either text or codes (ID)—these can be data standards, such as UPC, ISO, EPC, URL, the IP address, or the ucode. These codes can be stored on the RFID chip, but also be encoded in optical systems, such as Barcodes (Toye et al. 2005). RFID tags can be passive, semi-passive (or semi-active), and active. The radio frequency transmission may use various frequencies and is read by RFID readers. On the other hand, optical systems may use barcodes (linear, composite, matrix) that are transferred by visible light or infrared and read by optical scanners, such as cashier systems or optical scanners. In both cases, the data has been transferred from the tag to the RFID reader or optical scanner. To make use of the data, it is being transmitted from the reader to the computer system by wired or wireless networks (using common technologies, such as LAN, WLAN, WiMAX, GPRS, UMTS, EDGE). The applications match the code or ID with certain applications, which in turn may start web services, use other object data, or also enterprise applications.

Barcodes—compared to RFID—have major technical drawbacks: They need a line of sight to be read, thus making barcodes more obtrusive, less integrated in a daily life, and not as *invincible* as the contactless NFC. Therefore the case studies in this work concentrate on the use of RFID for Ubicomp applications.

2.1.4 Radio Frequency Identification (RFID)

An RFID system consists of the following components (see Fig. 8) (Fine et al. 2006):

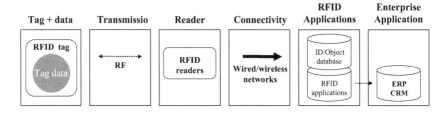

Fig. 8: Components of an RFID system
Source: (Fine et al. 2006)

Every system uses RFID tags on which data is stored. The data transmission results from electro-magnetic waves, which can have different reaches depending on the frequency and the magnetic field. The RFID readers can read and write data from and to the tag. The connection between the readers and the application uses Wireless LAN, Bluetooth, or wires. In a database (the content), the data on the tag is assigned specific information.

The following paragraphs describe the technology from an IS perspective in terms of (1) standards, (2) RFID tag and data, (3) capacity, (4) shapes and form, (5) frequency, (6) RFID transmission, (7) RFID readers and connectivity, and (8) cost of RFID.

2.1.4.1 Standards

Several organizations are involved in the development and definition of RFID standards. Hardware standards establish the air interface protocol and tag data format. Tag ID standards define the coding system or namespace. Application standards then describe the data handling in RFID services (Fine et al. 2006). The following organizations take part in standardization: International Organization of Standardization (ISO), EPCglobal Inc, European Tele-communications Standards Institute (ETSI), and the Federal Communications Commission (FCC). The following standards are applicable in Germany (see Table 2):

Standard	Content	Frequency
Auto-ID Class 0 / Class 1	Air Interface Communication	860 – 930 MHz
EPCglobal Gen 2	New standard for Air Interface Communication	860 – 930 MHz
ISO 14443	Air Interface and Identification for Customer cards	13.56 MHz
ISO 15693	Unique Identifier	13,56 MHz
ISO 15993-2	Air Interface and Identification	13.56 MHz
ISO 15993-3	Air Interface, Anti-collision and transmitter protocol	13.56 MHz
ISO 18000	RFID Air Interface Standard; New standard – ranges from 18000-1 (Generic parameters for the Air Interface for globally accepted frequencies) to 18000-7 (433 MHz).	All
ISO 18092	Also ECMA 340; Near Field Communication standard	13.56 MHz

Table 2: ISO and EPCglobal standards
Source: (BITKOM 2005)

2.1.4.2 RFID Tag and Data

RFID tags contain a microchip and a transponder. They can be either active or passive. Active tags require a power source, such as an integrated battery or a powered infrastructure. The lifetime of a battery in an active tag is limited by the number of read operations and the amount of energy stored. Having its own power source enables active tags to constantly transmit their signal up to several hundred meters. Active tags are larger in size compared to passive tags. Because of size, cost, and the need for its own power supply, active tags are used for high value items that need to be tracked from considerable distance (Fine et al. 2006; Want 2006).

Active tags are impractical for low value products and retail trade. Passive tags are of interest because they do not require batteries or maintenance. Passive tags have an indefinite operational life and can be printed into adhesive labels. The tags consist of an antenna, a conductor chip attached to the antenna, and an optional form of encapsulation (Want 2006, 26). The conductor chip stores data related to the object it is attached to or the tag itself. The data can be written either at the stage of production (factory programming) or at the end user (field programming).

The tags can be read-only, write-once, read many (WORM), or read/write:

- *Read-only:* At the point of manufacture, an *n bit* serial identification number is assigned to the chip. Information related to the identification number is stored in a central database.

•   *WORM:* WORM tags allow one writing procedure and an infinite number of reading processes.

•   *Read/Write:* Data can be written and read.

In between active and passive tags, the semi-passive tag systems require the tag to use battery power for the chip logic, but use harvested power for communication. They have a greater reading range than passive tags, but have shorter lives due to battery life (Ward/ Kranenburg/Backhouse 2006).

2.1.4.3 Capacity

Passive tags can store from 64 bits up to 64KB of non-volatile memory. Active tags have a larger memory.

2.1.4.4 Shapes and Form

RFID tags come in many shapes and sizes (see Fig. 9).

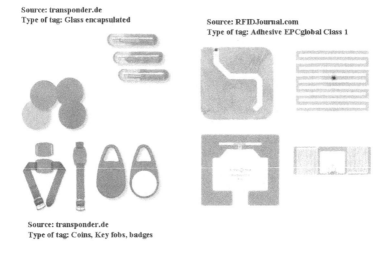

Source: transponder.de
Type of tag: Glass encapsulated

Source: RFIDJournal.com
Type of tag: Adhesive EPCglobal Class 1

Source: transponder.de
Type of tag: Coins, Key fobs, badges

Fig. 9: Different shapes of RFID tags
Source: transponder.de; RFIDJournal.com, 2006

The different tags are used in a variety of ways. Fine et. al described a creative experiment in which pigeons ate a tag, and were tracked as they flew by (Fine et al. 2006). Common use cases are animal tagging (Informationsforum-RFID 2006b), and at ski lifts (Informations forum-RFID 2006a).

Conventional RFID tags are silicon-based. The tag itself is connected to an antenna with attachment technologies or fluidic self-assembly. These approaches do not scale adequately to decrease the cost of the tags. An approach for realizing cheap RFID tags is to use printed electronic technologies, particularly organic electronics (Baude et al. 2003; Subramanian et al. 2006). The projected costs for high-throughput printed RFID tags are expected to be much lower than today's RFID technology, because of the elimination of current lithography and vacuum processing requirements. The possible frequency for printed RFID tags is 13.56MHz. Currently the performance of printed tags is inadequate for operation, further improvements should enable the realization of all-printed RFID tags (Subramanian et al. 2006). Printed RFID chips are not yet available on a larger scale, and are therefore not used for the case studies.

2.1.4.5 Frequencies

RFID makes use of frequencies ranging from 300kHz to 3 GHz, the exact range depends on country regulations. Generally, radio frequency (RF) frequencies are divided into low frequency (LF), high frequency (HF), ultra-high frequency (UHF), and microwave. *Active tags* transmit at higher frequencies only, while *passive tags* transmit at all frequencies. Table 3 shows the communication range of different frequency bands and system types.

Frequency band	System type	Communication Range						
		3cm	10cm	30cm	1m	3m	10m	>10m
LF	Passive							
HF	ISO14443							
	ISO15693							
UHF	Passive							
	Active							
Microwave	Passive							
	Active							

Legend: |||||| =Widely available   ///// = Available   = Not available

Table 3: Communication range of RFID systems
Source: (Dressen 2004)

Table 4 lists typical applications relevant to the available frequencies (see Table 3):

Frequency range	LF (126 – 134 KHz)	HF (13.56 MHz)	UHF (400, 868 – 915 MHz)	Microwave (2.45 GHz)
Typical Applications	Point-of-sale theft prevention; access control; SpeedPass, animal tracking	Item-level tracking; library & book tagging; luggage, *Identification* Standard tag.	400 MHz: Car key remote control; 868 MHz: Logistics (Europe) 915 MHz: toll collection; pallet tracking;	Supply chain management, container, toll collection, ISM (industrial, scientific, medical) Higher GHz (5,4) are developed.
Data rate	less than 1 kilobit per second (kbit/s)	approx. 25 kbit/s	30 kbit/s	100 kbit /s

Ability to read near metal or wet surfaces	Better	>	>	Worse
Coupling	Inductive	Inductive	Backscatter	Backscatter
Cost	Very low (<5c)	Low (5c for 1 Mio)	High	Very high
Maturity	Very mature	Established	New	In development

Table 4: Typical applications and characteristics
Source: adapted from (Fine et al. 2006, 8; BITKOM 2005; Ward/Kranenburg/Backhouse 2006; Dressen 2004)

As with every technology, the quality of RFID tags increases over time. Physical constraints cannot be overcome, but tag readability and data rates are improved and costs are dropping.

2.1.4.6 Transmission

Two different RFID design approaches exist from transferring energy from the reader to the tag: magnetic induction and electromagnetic wave capture. The two designs are either *near field* or *far field*. Through modulation techniques, RFID signals can transmit and receive data. The electromagnetic wave capture is also called back scatter transmission (Want 2006).

A distinction is made between the (1) far-field RFID and the (2) near-field RFID:

(1) Far-field RFID: Tags using far-field principles operate above 100 MHz, typically in the 865 MHz / 915 MHz range up to 2.45 GHz. Back scatter technology reflects back the reader's signal, modulating the signal to an alternating potential difference in order to transmit data. The system's range is limited by the energy transmission sent by the reader. Due to the advances in semiconductor manufacturing, the energy required to power a tag continues to decrease. In recent years the distances have increased up to 3 meters. EPCglobal's Class-1 generation 96-bit tag (see list above) receives the most attention and was used in show cases from Wal-Mart and Tesco (Want 2006, 29). The Metro Future Store in Germany used UHF technology (BITKOM 2005).

(2) Near-field RFID: Near-field RFID uses magnetic induction between a reader and a tag. Fig. 10 shows the principle of near-field induction. The RFID reader passes an alternating current through a reading coil, generating a magnetic field in its location. If a RFID tag with a smaller coil is placed within range of the reader, the alternating voltage appears across it and the magnetic field is affected by tag data. The voltage is rectified and powers the tag chip. Once powered, the data is sent back to the reader, using load modulation.

Using induction for power coupling from reader to tag and load modulation to transfer data from tag to reader

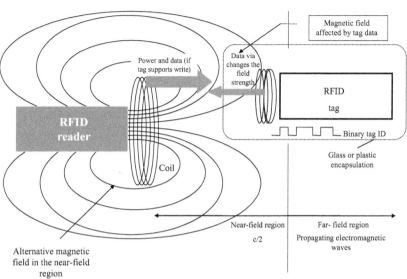

Fig. 10: Using induction in the near field region
Source: (Want 2006)

Any current drawn from the tag coil will have its own magnetic field—opposing the reader's field—detected by the reader coil. A variety of modulations are possible depending on the number of bits required and the data transfer rate. Near-field coupling was the first approach to implementing a passive RFID system. The physical limits of the near-field coupling prevented some use cases. The range of magnetic induction approximates to $|r| = c/2\pi f$ with constant c (speed of light) and f the frequency. If f increases, the distance over which near-field coupling works decreases. A further limitation is the energy. If applications need more ID bits or to be able to discriminate between multiple tags in the same locality for a fixed read time, each tag requires a higher data rate and a higher operating frequency. This limits the amount of tags and range (Want 2006). NFC (see section 2.1.5) uses the limitations of near field RFID as a competitive advantage.

2.1.4.7 Readers and Connectivity

RFID readers can be implemented into large gates or small handheld devices. The reader captures the data transmitted by the tag and delivers it to the infrastructure for further processing, e.g. retrieving content connected to the identification number on the tag. Readers are either capable of reading single frequencies, whereas multi-protocol readers can read the spectrum of most available bands.

While *gate* readers are used at large entry points in which large distances need to be monitored, so-called *compact* readers are used by a small combination of read/write devices.

Vehicle readers are attached to trucks or forklifts. Mobile readers are carried by their users and are used in combination with wireless transmission.

Specific to RFID readers is the interference between readers—known as reader collision. The reader collision is similar to the tag collision, where too many tags are in the same field. Several anti-collision schemes have been invented, one called *time division multiple access* (Auto-ID-Center 2003). This instructs readers to read at different times. For tag anti-collision, the first digits on the tag are interpreted and compared with the reader's scheme. If more than one tag responds, the digits are counted upwards until only one tag matches (Auto-ID-Center 2003). The connection between readers and the underlying infrastructure uses Bluetooth, Wireless LAN or GSM, GPRS. An Ethernet connection is also possible.

The RFID infrastructure must be capable of handling all incoming events in real-time. RFID systems require a server architecture capable of handling many events. Databases commonly used in such systems are Oracle™, Microsoft™, and others. In between incoming events and the back-end system, a middleware is used to integrate data in enterprise systems. In consumer scenarios this can also be a connector to the Internet itself, if information needs to be retrieved from independent data sources and is not stored anywhere (Maass/Filler 2006).

2.1.4.8 Cost

Several costs are directly or indirectly related to RFID (Smith/Konsynski 2003):

- Cost of the tag itself

- Cost of applying the tag to objects

- Cost of purchasing and installing tag readers

- System integration costs

- Cost of training and possibly reorganization

- Cost of implementing application solutions

- Tuning of the RFID system (Chappell et al. 2002)

- Maintenance (Chappell et al. 2002)

In many studies regarding the financial side of RFID implementations, improvements in the supply chain seem to have cost cutting potential over time (Loebbecke/Palmer 2006; Heinrich 2005). Loebbecke et al. observed two cost-based benefits when introducing RFID into the fashion industry: time savings in moving merchandise through the supply chain and lowering the labor costs in existing processes. Chappell at. al. (Chappell et al. 2002) also sees the largest benefit in a reduction of safety stock inventory and labor. Labor costs decline by automating processes and removing process-specific verification or auditing steps. Shrink can also be reduced, while other benefits come from indirect cost savings.

When introducing RFID, Wal-Mart experienced several similar benefits: reduced labor costs, out-of-stock supply chain cost reduction, theft reduction, improved tracking, and reduced inventory holding (Asif/Mandviwalla 2005). However, one of the main challenges to implementing RFID over time is the middleware, which has not yet been advanced to a *plug-and-play* stage. This means that initial adopters still have to make an effort to integrate RFID in the existing business processes (Asif/Mandviwalla 2005). First movers still have a disadvantage in total costs because there are no ready-to-go software packages.

Loebbecke et al. state that RFID transponder costs need to decrease in order to make a large-scale adoption economically viable (Loebbecke/Palmer 2006). The Auto-ID labs mention 5 cents per tag as a target cost (Chappell et al. 2002). This can be best reached by the introduction of printed RFID tags (Subramanian et al. 2006), although Subramanian et. al. declare a per tag cost of less than 2 cents as necessary for item-level tagging.

2.1.5 Near Field Communication (NFC)

Near Field Communication (NFC), is a standardized interface technology for the exchange of data between electronic devices such as PCs, mobile telephones and RFID tags. If NFC compatible devices are held together closely, they register one other and determine how to exchange data. The technology can be integrated into various kinds of user devices such as personal digital assistants (PDA), mobile phones or even television (TV) sets, etc. (NFCForum 2007a, 2007b, 2007c). In this analysis, the term *Near Field Communication* is used to describe the NFC ecosystem as the basis of mobile phones, terminals, devices, tags and readers. NFC is a technology related to RFID, but due to the physical limitations of near-field RFID (see also the previous section) the maximum connection distance is approx. 10 cm. However based on personal experience (Resatsch et al. 2007c), the maximum working distance is 1 to 2 cm. NFC is standardized in ISO 18092 (ECMA 340) (ECMA-340 2004).

2.1.5.1   NFC Forum Technology Architecture

The NFC Forum has specified a general architecture for various end user devices, such as smart cards as well as mobile phones.

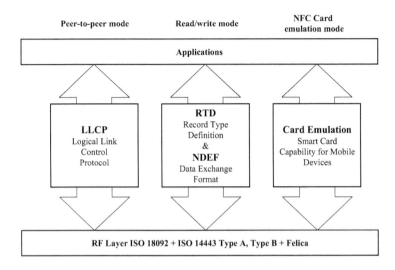

Peer-to-peer mode   **Read/write mode**   NFC Card
                                                           emulation mode

Fig. 11: NFC Forum technology architecture
Source: © 2006 by NFC Forum (nfc-forum.org)

The NFC Forum standardizes the peer-to-peer mode, the read/write mode, and the card emulation mode from the application to the radio frequency layer. The radio frequency (RF) layer is specified accordingly with the NFC forum tag specification (see below). Applications that use NFC can be in peer-to-peer mode, read/write mode, or in an NFC card emulation mode. Within peer-to-peer, the Logical Link Control Protocol (LLCP) is used to connect to the RF layer. For the read/write mode, Record Type Definitions (RTD) and NFC Data Exchange Format (NDEF) are being used, while the card emulation mode is a special smart card capability protocol for mobile devices. This card emulation can enable payment or public ticket services.

On the radio frequency level, various application selection processes are considered. Decisions on which application to choose can be based on information previously extracted from the RF signal or assuming a certain technology is used. These uninformed decisions could be solved by a trial and error selection method, which results in slower transaction times and less user experience. In the case of a reader who supports different contactless technologies, a divergence in the selection algorithm could result in a deadlock (GSMAssociation 2007). An anti-collision and initialization procedure is implemented to avoid this case.

The technology architecture includes the NDEF and three RTDs for specific applications all of which are described in (NFCForum 2006a, 2006b, 2006c, 2006d, 2006e). The NDEF is the standard exchange format and consists of messages, records, and the payload. The NDEF message contains one or more NDEF records. The NDEF record consists of type, type format, identifier for the payload and the actual payload in a byte array[6]. The payload is the application data carried within the NDEF record. The RTD is an NFC-specific record type and type name carried in an NDEF record[7]. Based on the architecture several communication and interaction styles are possible.

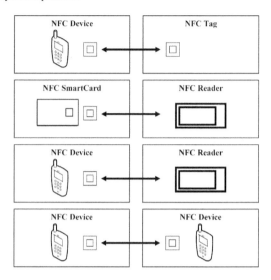

Fig. 12: NFC interaction styles
Source: (adapted from (Rukzio 2007)

The NFC devices include an NFC reader. An NFC reader is capable of a bi-directional information transfer with another NFC reader and therefore device. If the reader is implemented in a mobile phone (device), NFC can operate on different interaction levels between phone and tag, smart card and reader, NFC device and reader or device with device (see Fig. 12). The focus lies on the first case of an NFC-enabled mobile phone as NFC device and a NFC tag. It is important to look at the mobile NFC architecture to understand the complexity.

2.1.5.2 Mobile NFC Architecture

Figure 13 (Fig. 13) shows the reference mobile NFC architecture as defined by the GSM Association.

---

[6]   Source: http://mobilezoo.biz/jsr/257/javax/microedition/contactless/ndef/NDEFRecord.html - accessed 11.02.2009

[7]   Source: http://java.sun.com/developer/technicalArticles/javame/nfc/ - accessed 11.02.2009

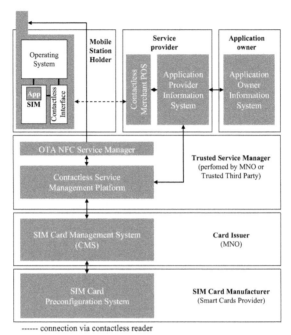

------ connection via contactless reader

Fig. 13: Mobile NFC technical architecture
Source: (GSMAssociation 2007)

Various components play a role in the mobile NFC technical architecture description: the mobile phone itself needs the operating system, the application (potentially on the SIM card), and the contactless interface. A service provider (here a merchant Point-of-Sale (PoS) system) with his information system is contacted to the application owner (if different). A trusted service manager supplies a contactless service management platform with the Over-the-air NFC service manager. A card issuer (usually the Mobile Network Operator (MNO)) operates the Subscriber Identity Module (SIM) card management system, which is related to the SIM card pre-configuration system of the SIM card manufacturer. To build an NFC ecosystem and develop NFC applications, more attention has to be paid to the surrounding ecosystem than in a standard mobile service architecture.

2.1.5.3 Available NFC Phones

Several NFC phones are currently available in the market: In the first case studies the Nokia 3220 was used as the test phone with NFC shell, in later case studies, the Nokia 6131 NFC was used. In the case of the Nokia 3220, the NFC shell is extending the common Nokia phone cover with a NFC reader/writer antenna. The shell has a pre-installed Java Service Discovery application for creating shortcuts such as call dialing, SMS sending, and web browsing. The shortcuts are written on the tag, automatically starting the relevant application if the NFC device is close enough to read the tag. In case of the Nokia 6131 NFC, the NFC antenna was seamlessly integrated in the phone. NFC tag recognition was turned on automatically. Recent developments include the Nokia 6131 NFC, which was introduced in 2007 and the Nokia 6212 NFC introduced to the market in late 2008 (see Fig. 14).

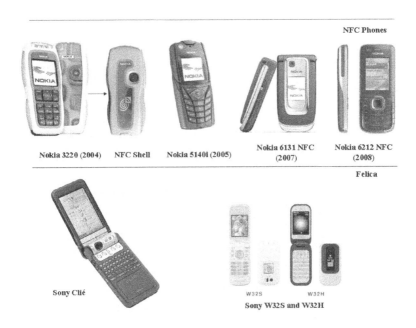

Fig. 14: NFC and Felica™ phones
Source: Nokia™, Sony™

Early Nokia NFC phones were shipped with a Nokia NFC shell, a *pad extender* to connect the phone with the NFC shell, a pre-installed Java application (for the Service Discovery) for creating shortcuts such as call dialing, SMS sending, and web browsing and NXP MIFARE® 1K Standard RFID sticker tags to identify objects and tasks. Newer phones have a seamlessly integrated NFC antenna and tag.

NFC integrates a different paradigm than RFID based infrastructures. While the typical RFID use case is a tag that is carried by the user, e.g. in a contactless card, the NFC idea is based mainly on a combination of mobile phone at the user and stationary tag. There are two NFC modes: active and passive. In the active mode, both devices generate a radio field to transfer data. In passive mode, only one device generates a radio field with load modulation by the other device (usually a tag). The NFC protocol specifies that the initiating device is responsible for generating the radio field (NFCForum 2007a). This solution keeps infrastructure costs down. The RFID infrastructure would need many readers in many locations, assuming the user would like to use his RFID card for a certain service. While with NFC, the user could interact and use services based on NFC tags that are distributed.

Chipset manufacturers are currently working on an integration of NFC as an add-on to existing Bluetooth chip sets to further decrease costs per unit. To add NFC functionality to a Bluetooth system, NFC is built as *System-on-Chip* (SoC). From a technical perspective, many of the requirements for NFC are already integrated in other RF-based technologies: Antenna, power, clock, data bus. NFC is then implemented as a peripheral on a host system. In high volume products, SoC implementations offer significant unit-cost savings and very efficient integration. A lower overall need exists for space, processing, and power value (NFCForum 2007b).

2.1.5.4 Developing with NFC

Mobile handset manufacturers support NFC development with several Software Development Kits (SDK): The Nokia 6131 NFC SDK emulates Java applications (so-called MIDlets from the Mobile Information Device (MID)) for the Nokia 6131 NFC mobile phone. The Nokia 6212 NFC SDK may be used for the new 6212.

For the development of mobile phone Java applications for Symbian mobile phones, Java Platform Micro Edition (Java ME) can be used. Java ME is a subset of the standard Java available with additional mobile phone-related Application Programming Interfaces (API). Another option is Flash Lite. For Java ME development, a Java SE Development Kit (JDK) is needed. Furthermore a wireless toolkit, a mobile-phone SDK, such as the Nokia Symbian OS SDK for Java or in this case a Nokia NFC SDK, as well as an IDE plus an add-on for Java ME development (EclipseME or NetBeans can be used).

Developing applications with NFC for Java handsets is based on the contactless API (in this case the JSR-257)[8] and the Mobile Information Device Profile (MIDP)[9]. The MIDP allows a developer to write applications and services for network-connectable mobile devices. For security related applications, the security and trust API for J2ME is used (JSR 177)[10]. Various Java Specification Request (JSR) will be bundled in the near future in the Mobile Service Architecture specification (MSA)[11].

The contactless JSR-257 has two features: the contactless communication itself and a visual component for the bar codes. NFC phones implement the contactless side (see Fig. 15). The phone application uses Over-The-Air (OTA) implementations and provides the user interface.

---

[8] JSR 257: Contactless Communication API – Source: http://jcp.org/en/jsr/detail?id=257 – accessed 01.02.2009

[9] Mobile Information Device Profile (MIDP); JSR 37, JSR 118 – Source: http://java.sun.com/products/midp/ - accessed 01.02.2009

[10] JSR 177: Security and Trust Services API for J2ME – Source: http://jcp.org/en/jsr/detail?id=177 – accessed 01.02.2009

[11] JSR 248: Mobile Service Architecture – Source: http://jcp.org/en/jsr/detail?id=248 – accessed 01.02.2009

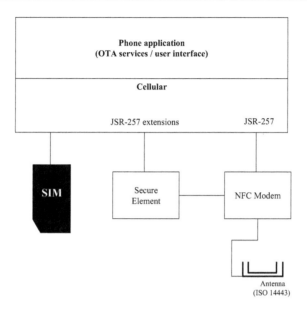

Fig. 15: Overview JSR-257
Source: (GSM-Association 2007)

The NFC contactless features include read/write NDEF data, the extension to access the secure element (requires a signed MIDlet), and the extension to utilize native communication with various NFC tags. The JSR-257 is attached to the NFC modem, which makes use of the RFID antennta (standardized according to the NFC standards ISO 14443).

2.1.5.5 NFC Tags

NFC works on a 13.56 MHz frequency. Each NFC tag has a unique identification (ID) code, ranging from 4 to 10 bytes, depending on the manufacturer of the tag. The ID codes are sufficient within the numerical range of one manufacturer (Jalkanen 2005). The following tags (see Table 5) have been initially defined by the NFC Forum as a standardization forum:

NFC Forum Type	Based on ISO	Chip Name	Memory Capacity	Data rate	Unit Price	Unique ID	Security	Available from
Type 1	ISO 14443 A	TOPAZ	96-byte	106kbit/s	Lowest	Yes	16- or 32-bit digital signature	Innovision Research & Technology
Type 2	ISO 14443 A	MIFARE	48-byte	106kbit/s	Low	Yes	Unsecure	Philips / NXP
Type 3	FeliCa	FeliCa	2kbyte	212kbit/s	Higher		16- or 32-bit digital signature	Sony

Type 4	ISO 14443A/B	Several names: Example is MIFARE DESFire	>3kbyte	106kbit/s up to 424 kbit/s	Higher	Yes	Variable	Several

Table 5: NFC Forum tag types
Source: (NFCForum 2007a)

Larger NFC tags can store approx 10 kilobytes (KB), whereas small tags store 40 bytes in addition to the ID code. NFC tags are usually shipped with a NFC device in a small amount. (Fine et al. 2006). Tag types 1 and 2 can be read/write or read-only. In this dual state, the tag can be read and then set to be read-only after. Type 3 and 4 are single-state, which means, they can only be read-only.

Each NFC tag can initiate several services in the mobile phone by default: open an Uniform Resource Locator (URL) in the mobile browser, initiate a phone call to a number written on the NFC tag, send a SMS text message (Short Message Service – SMS), start a client application on the mobile phone, and further services defined with the handset providers. NFC allows users to use their mobile phone to program the read/write tags with desired services depending on the capacity of the tag. This allows for a great flexibility in end-user service provision. For professional applications, the tags are read-only.

2.1.6 RFID and NFC Information Systems

The building blocks in section 2.12 demanded the following functions: identification, memory, processing logic, networking, sensor technology, user interface, and location & tracking. To develop such a system based on RFID and mobile phones (NFC), the user is the starting point. An RFID chip with a certain identification number (ID—identification), is read by a reader in the phone with memory capabilities (Memory). A Graphical User Interface (GUI) enables the user to interact with the system. On the phone an application uses the ID or it is routed through the phone (http/app—processing logic). A sensor technology can be implemented in the RFID chip if desired. The networking is based on various connecting frequencies such as GSM, UMTS or Bluetooth (Hagenhoff/Kaspar/Resatsch 2008). A backend framework may connect the ID with specific services (also third (3rd) party services) via its service management component, matching tag data with user data.

This analysis focuses on the ubiquitous computing technology application and the interface between user and Near Field Communication (see Fig. 16). The domains are *human-computer interaction* (interface), *technology acceptance* (application development and evaluation) and *Ubicomp technology in the forming of an NFC system* (NFC phone, chip, and environment).

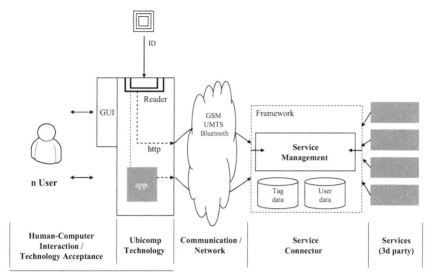

Fig. 16: NFC information systems structure

In practice such systems have been researched on an academic level (Rukzio/Schmidt/Hussmann 2004; Abowd et al. 2005; Öquist 2006; Lumsden/Brewster 2003; Jalkanen 2005; Rukzio 2007). In order to make planning of these systems possible, companies must better understand the end-user. The following section describes how consumers understand RFID today and what conclusions can be drawn for NFC as a successor.

2.2 Ubiquitous Computing Technologies and the Consumer

Incorporating NFC in the design of mobile phones is very new to markets. RFID however has been around as a technology for a while and is in many cases already in consumer hands— although people are not aware of it. In many contactless smart cards an RFID chip is at work. To determine if and how RFID acts as a consumer technology, and why NFC is different, it is important to first categorize RFID applications (Section 2.2.1) and to take a look at how people are aware of the technology (Section 2.2.2).

2.2.1 Categorization of Applications Using the Example of RFID

RFID applications can be categorized in (1) open loop vs. closed loop applications and (2) machine-centered vs. people-centered approaches (see Fig. 17).

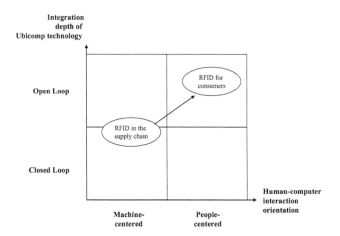

Fig. 17: Classification of RFID applications
Source: Integration dimensions adapted from (Fleisch/Christ/Dierkes 2005a))

(1) **Open loop vs. closed loop:** A definition of open and closed loop is necessary as the terms are used in several different sciences with various meanings. A closed loop Ubicomp application is defined as an application in which an Ubicomp technology, such as RFID, is only used within one single system (Wray et al. 2006) and the technology component (the RFID tag) does not leave the process of the system in which it was initially used. By contrast an open loop application is an application in which, for example, an RFID tag and its information can be used outside of the initial system in one or more systems. According Fleisch et al. (2005) most applications today begin with closed loop systems because of the clear cost advantages and benefit calculations (Fleisch/Christ/Dierkes 2005b). The option of participating in open loop systems also depends on choosing the right standards (Fleisch/Christ/Dierkes 2005b). The depth of technology integration varies of course between open and closed loop systems.

(2) **Machine-centered or people-centered applications:** Machine-centered applications are applications that do not include interactions with people on a user level. This counts for most of business-to-business applications where the purpose of the application is to use the information on the tag for controlling other machines or use it as information source for applications. People-centered applications are primarily designed for direct people interaction and built for end-users and consumers. Examples are the FIFA World Cup 2006 tickets (FIFA 2004) or the address book desk by Timo Arnall (Arnall 2005a). The reason for this distinction has much to do with media reactions due to privacy and data security questions. As soon as people-centered applications are considered, discussions arise. In the case of 2006 World Cup tickets, usage of RFID led to a number of reactions ranging from critical articles (FoeBUD 2006) to the public call of the Chaos Computer Club (CCC) to send in the tickets to let the CCC read and research the information on the ticket (CCC 2006).

This analysis focuses on NFC. NFC is a people-centered open-loop technology—it targets end users with open-loop infrastructure. This focus on NFC implies a certain user awareness of the technologies employed. Since NFC was not widely introduced into markets by 2004, the next chapter uses RFID as a technology to further understand user perception on Ubicomp technologies. RFID may serve as a basis here, because NFC has the same components as RFID (tag, device, information system) and a similar infrastructure system.

2.2.2 User Awareness and Perception of RFID

The free Internet tool *Google Trends*[12] was used to cull information regarding RFID discussions, and presents the interests of Internet users for specific topics. Search queries produce late majority indicators since people start searching for a specific term once they have already heard about it via a different channel. For example, if someone had heard about RFID in the media they might be conducting a search about it. Fig. 18 shows that search queries for RFID and supply chain show a similar course over time.

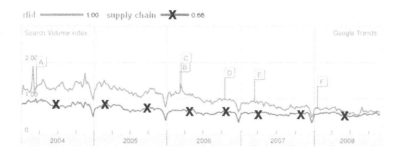

Fig. 18: Search queries for RFID and supply chain
Source: google.com/trends

The queries maintain a stable level; therefore people might search for supply chain and RFID in the same manner. Fig. 19 compares a real consumer product like the Apple™ iPod® with RFID. It can be clearly seen that for a significant period the news reference volume remained almost steady while the iPod® related search queries quickly exceeded the RFID search queries. The news reference volume maintained the same relation for a while until new iPods® were released. However, iPod® search queries rose sharply, consistently maintaining a higher amount than RFID-related queries. This indicates significant media-based coverage and shows the interests of the majority of Internet users following the adoption of previous groups (Fig. 19).

---

[12]   Source: http://www.google.com/trends - Accessed 2008-05-26 - Google Trends lists the amount of search queries on a specific topic or keyword. It also allows comparing search queries in different countries.

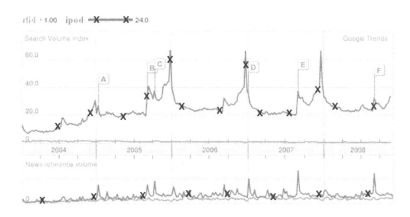

Fig. 19: Comparison iPod vs. RFID
Source: google.com/trends

Comparing the amount of search results for the term *spychips* (German: Schnüffelchips) with *RFID* in Google shows 302.000 search results for spychips vs. 55.400.000 for RFID. However, more consumers might remember discussions pertaining to *spychips* than any industry RFID proposal. The usage possibilities of RFID have led to many discussions within the media in terms of data security and privacy issues. The absolute number of Google search queries of the term *RFID* in Google trends worldwide is almost constant. Also, it can be stated that the type of news varied from highly positive to more negative in the last several years. It was initially euphoric (A) while in more recent times we see a focus on negative issues such as RFID viruses (E). Letters B to F reflect other news sources. The influence of negative news is shown in the chart below. Here Scott Silverman announced the idea of implanting RFID chips in immigrants and guest workers. This has led to a very high number of web-logs mentioning the quote (Fig. 20).

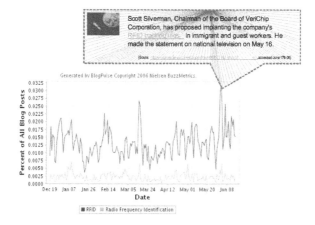

Fig. 20: The reaction in web-logs to bad news
Source: Blogpulse 2007 [13]

Clearly, privacy seems to be an issue for RFID applications, but overall negative media coverage leads to a significant increase of reporting in many communication channels on the Internet, such as weblogs, communities, etc.; since it is not possible to distinguish between the difference of opinion of opinion leaders and other consumers with the tools used above, it appears that the search queries represent an interest in the technology that is not at the same intensity than it could be for being consumer good (A test with myspace.com instead of iPod® shows an even higher difference). Although researchers and experts are highly aware of the potential opportunities and threats represented by RFID, consumers might not be able to judge them appropriately. The Digital Methods Initiative (DMI) presents another recent example of RFID perceptions in a Folksonomy analysis (Fig. 21):

---

[13]   (Source: BlogPulse - Search conducted for both the acronym RFID and the term Radio Frequency Identification, because some web-logs use the acronym while others the whole set)

Substantive Composition of RFID according to Folksonomy

Research Question_Which issue (tag) language is associated with RFID?
Findings_The folksonomic space shows a commitment to a DIY hacking culture with
privacy concerns.

privacy (8) security (7)

sv (5)   technology (4)   hardware (4)   hacks (4)

diy (3)   radio (3)   wireless (3)   resistance (2)   electronics (2)   internet (2)

research (2)   nfc (2)   interactiondesign (2)   make (2)

politics (2)   reference (2)   id (2)   fashion (2)   tags (2)

barcode (2)   mobile (2)   news (2)

software (2)   wallet (2)

Source_del.icio.us
Method_Harvest tags related to RFID in del.icio.us. Visualize language, sized by frequency of mentions.
Query_RFID
Tools_Harvester, Issue Discovery Tool and Tag Cloud Generator
Date_20 October 2007

Product_of the Digital Methods Initiative,
dmi.mediastudies.nl. **Analysis**_by Marijn de
Vries Hoogerwerff and Uschi Reiter. **Recalling
RFID Icon**_by Léon&Loes. **Design**_by Anne
Helmond.

Fig. 21: Which issue (tag) language is associated with RFID?
Source: DMI ©Digital Methods Initiative 2007 - digitalmethods.net

To sum up: people tend to appreciate what they know. For a more detailed understanding of this, a survey was conducted at a large technology trade fair in Germany to determine the current status of RFID perception among people. A sample of 336 (N=336) visitors was randomly chosen, out of which 70% were male and 30% were female. This ratio is representative for the average number and demographics of visitors to the trade fair. The quantitative survey was conducted with mobile personal digital assistants and a standardized questionnaire. Table 6 shows the research framework.

Research framework	Quantitative analysis
Method of data collection	Personal interview with questionnaire
Period	Thursday, March 9th 2006 and Saturday, March 11th 2006
Measuring method	Interval 5/7-item-scale
Universe	World's largest trade fair for digital IT and telecommunications solutions for home and work environments; halls 5-7; Visitors of the fair.
Sample type	Random
Sample number	n=336

Table 6: Research Framework

To get an overview of the participant's basic knowledge, the first question asked what the abbreviation R.F.I.D. stands for. Around 90% correctly identified the acronym RFID as Radio

Frequency IDentification. Following that, the participants were asked to rate what they knew about RFID, defined as subjective knowledge (Fig. 22).

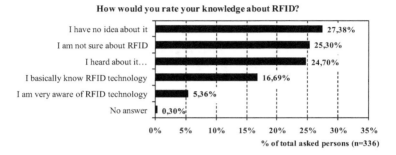

Fig. 22: Question on subjective knowledge
Source: (Resatsch et al. 2007a)

More than 75% of all participants rated their knowledge from *non-existent* to *I heard about it*. Only a few people considered themselves significantly informed. Although people did not think they knew much about RFID, a clear connection emerged between answers to the question *In which areas do you see the most value of RFID?* and the industries that have been exposed to the most RFID media coverage: logistics and retail (Fig. 23).

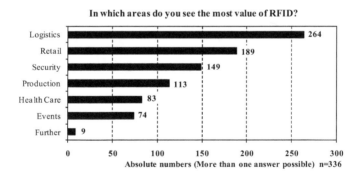

Fig. 23: Industries in which the participant sees the highest value for RFID
Source: (Resatsch et al. 2007a)

Evaluating something requires proper background information or people will rely on other resources to determine personal opinions. The first question concentrated on the importance that people place on RFID in their daily lives. Only a few—19%—rated RFID as being important for their lives today. The rest (almost 75%) responded either neutrally or did not see any relevance for RFID (Fig. 24).

Is RFID currently important for your life?

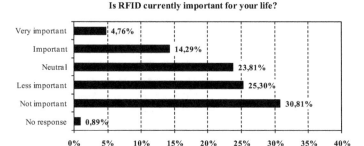

Fig. 24: Importance of RFID in daily life
Source: (Resatsch et al. 2007a)

A possible explanation is that people do not see any benefits in RFID or they have not had any real contact with RFID, or finally there is currently no application that would add substance to people's lives. RFID functions within the context of ubiquitous computing that is often times associated with control or perceived control. Research on perceived control (Günther/Spiekermann 2005) exists in this area in order to increase the acceptance of RFID applications. In the study, 47% strongly agreed that RFID would give others control over their lives, however, this also assumes that the people responding have enough information or experience with the technology to make an accurate assessment—which is not the case according to their own evaluations of how well they are informed (Fig. 25).

RFID helps others to control your life

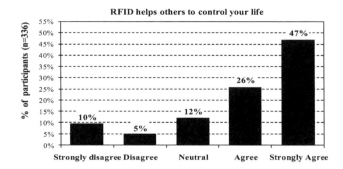

Fig. 25: RFID and control
Source: (Resatsch et al. 2007a)

For a more detailed view of people's opinion of the technology, the question was asked if RFID has already a benefit in the life of the participant personally. While 52% claimed they maybe see a potential benefit, 15% were negative. Overall, 26% saw a personal benefit or could at least imagine a use for RFID, 7% strongly agreed that RFID has benefits (Fig. 26).

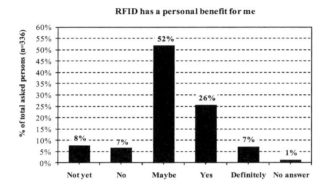

Fig. 26: Personal benefit of RFID
Source: (Resatsch et al. 2007a)

Another question concerned RFID and its influence on people over time. About 15% of the participants assumed negative to very negative changes, and 20% rated the change rather positively. Based on these descriptive data, the picture of RFID that people had at the trade fair was rather negative. People are not necessarily informed about RFID, but in most cases rate RFID in exactly the same way that it is discussed in the media.

Discussions concerning RFID revolve around tracking & tracing issues, supply chain support, and privacy and security issues. Privacy is definitely a very important topic, but should be discussed when people have had the chance to experience and learn about the technology with showcases and hands-on prototypes. If the model that Beckwith (Beckwith 2003) proposes according to Adams is used, information on the following topics should be given to the user: *information receiver* (who will use or have access to the data?), *information usage* (how will the information be used?) and *information sensitivity* (how sensitive is the data?). People will then have the opportunity to use the application and decide freely if they like it, thereby giving technologies such as RFID the chance to enter the consumer market place and cycle back on a major scale into industry and the world of small-and-medium enterprise. The acceptance of the technology and the potential benefits that come with it depend on information and perception.

The study makes clear that people do not know enough about RFID to rate it properly. Other studies showed similar results with different underlying sample groups (Knebel/ Leimeister/Krcmar 2006). Using more prototypes to show the real value of RFID in end-consumer areas could ultimately lead to a greater overall acceptance of the technology. This would also lead to more understanding and less fear of RFID-use within operational businesses. Especially in the case of RFID as an Ubicomp technology, the value of prototypes and early user integration is important to successful developing applications.

In his 1993 paper on Ubicomp, Mark Weiser states that the establishment of "working prototypes of the necessary infrastructure in sufficient quantity to debug the viability of the systems in everyday use" is crucial to the research of Ubicomp (Weiser 1993). The study therefore hypothesizes that the benefits of RFID can be demonstrated to consumers with valid and fun prototypes. Doing so will ultimately increase a positive perception. NFC already has a different approach in terms of consumer marketing and prototypes. With many available prototypes and handsets people can experiment with it. With NFC the hurdles of consumer acceptance might be lower, especially as the usage becomes more clear in the combination of RFID and mobile phone.

2.3 The Importance of Prototyping

The goal of chapters 2.1 and 2.2 was to describe the theoretical background that is necessary for understanding the characterizing elements of RFID- and NFC-applications and information systems and what specific challenges the characteristics imply.

The chapter developed a working definition of Ubicomp and Ubicomp applications (Section 2.1.1), defined building blocks of the infrastructure (Section 2.1.2), determined available technologies and attributes of the underlying technology of this *necessary infrastructure* (Section 2.1.3) and deepened knowledge about RFID (Section 2.1.4) and NFC (Section 2.1.5). In the summary (Section 2.1.6) this information is narrowed down to an initial information systems overview.

Chapter 2.2 showed what a user currently knows about RFID, by categorizing applications on the example of RFID (Section 2.2.1) and a study of awareness of RFID as a technology (Section 2.2.2).

This section draws conclusions about the characteristics of RFID- and NFC-applications, and lists the requirements of and challenges related to the importance of prototyping. As a stand alone technology RFID is at a disadvantage due to the lack of a GUI to interact with the user, as well as other awareness issues. NFC could be a more valuable technology for consumers. The study in section 2.2.2 showed clearly that people tend to appreciate and prefer what they already know, but Ubicomp, NFC, and RFID are rather unknown concepts and technologies among regular people. This presents a challenge for raising IT budgets to develop NFC applications, achieving market penetration of the technology, and create a high technology acceptance with the user.

NFC in the combination of mobile phones with RFID reader and writer will be highly relevant for markets if there exists:

•   a high NFC mobile phone distribution and market penetration,

•   a cheap infrastructure component availability (NFC tags), and

•   a significant number of NFC-aware customers.

From an IS perspective, NFC-based applications are yet not widespread because:

- people are not aware of the technology potential (*awareness*),

- there are high initial investments in infrastructure necessary (*mobile phone & tag infrastructure*),

- application developers and companies are not sure which services will be accepted by the end-user (*provider insecurity*), and

- there are not enough usable applications for end users (*application availability*).

These challenges support the idea of a process model for helping companies introduce NFC applications into markets and for integrating a process for determining the successful attributes of a designated application. As stated in chapter 2.2.2 a prototype approach may help in order to allow people to try and test out Ubicomp technologies and to understand their value. Using such a "grassroots" or prototype-based approach implies two questions:

- What are the influencing factors and requirements based on *human-computer interaction* theory for NFC technology?

- What *technology acceptance theories* could assist the development and evaluation of likeable NFC applications?

The following two chapters focus on these questions in order to develop an appropriate utility theory (process model) for Ubicomp applications that makes use of prototypes in following the specified approach.

3 Human Computer Interaction and Technology Acceptance

The focus of this chapter is to state the basic requirements of NFC-based applications relative to human-computer interaction theory (Chapter 3.1). It also seeks to further integrate the technology acceptance models to be applied into the Ubicomp setting (Chapter 3.2).

3.1 Human Computer Interaction

The connection between human computer interaction (HCI) and Ubicomp was discussed from Ubicomp's early stages up to today (Abowd 1996; Abowd/Atkeson/Essa 1998; Abowd et al. 1998; Abowd/Mynatt/Rodden 2002). Abowd also discussed the effects of prototypes in the area of Ubicomp to facilitate technology diffusion (Abowd et al. 2005).

Interfaces of various kinds were discussed intensely in Ubicomp literature—especially because the use of haptic elements, such as RFID chips, changes the established forms of interaction familiar from desktop computers (Henseler 2001; Michelis et al. 2005; Poupyrev/Okabe/Maruyama 2004; Ishii/Ullmer 1997; Blackler/Popovic/Mahar 2003; Öquist 2006; Thevenin/Coutaz 1999; Ballagas et al. 2003; Tan 2000; Shneiderman 1992; Raskin 2000; Mantyjarvi et al. 2006; Välkkynen et al. 2003).

Only few of the known literature approaches discuss the effects of everyday activities and principles associated with routine tasks, although these effects were part of the Ubicomp vision and are relevant for building systems that will be accepted by users (Mattern 2003b, 2003c, 2005b; McCullough 2004; Weiser 1993).

Human beings have one thing in common: an everyday life and the range of actions that life encompasses. The Ubicomp definition presented included applications *within the everyday action range of human beings* (see section 2.1.1). This everyday life is determined by several factors that loop back to the development of—and the interaction with—Ubicomp applications.

Ubicomp use is quite different from desktop computer use. Daily life centers around activity spaces (Golledge/Stimson 1997) within specific contexts. With a link from the virtual into the physical world, an interaction design off the desktop becomes essential (McCullough 2004; Norman 1988). Ubicomp applications should function only when we want them to and in a way in which we do not need to know how they function. These "information appliances" (Norman 1999b, 53) allow people to carry out tasks without needing to be aware of the computers that are involved (McCullough 2004).

Simplicity, as already stated, is the primary motivation driving the design of information appliances. Design the tool to fit so well that it becomes a part of the task (Norman 1999b, 53). This design credo describes a way of creating computers so that they are *invisible* to us perceptually, i.e. so that we are not conscious of them.

Human Computer Interaction (HCI) is defined as "a discipline concerned with the design, evaluation and implementation of interactive computing systems for human use and with the study of major phenomena surrounding them." The focus is "specifically on interaction between one or more humans and one or more computational machines", which together form an adequate context for Ubicomp (Hewett et al. 1992).

HCI has two sides, both the machine and the human side, connected via an interface. An interface can exist in different ways. Raskin gives a broad definition: "The way that you accomplish tasks with a product—what you do and how it responds" (Raskin 2000).

The goal of this chapter is to determine a preliminary set of human related non-functional system requirements. In order to determine a basis set of requirements for developing an initial hypothesis for Ubicomp applications with high user acceptance, this chapter will

* describe the human aspects of Ubicomp in order to identify the specific characteristics of user actions in everyday life (Section 3.1.1),

* describe human computer interface necessities (Section 3.1.2), and

* compare interaction possibilities (Section 3.1.3).

In listing preliminary non-functional requirements, the first section will introduce basic information about the human aspect in Ubiquitous Computing.

3.1.1 Human Aspects

First the *end-user* is defined in terms of his behavioral constraints to using information systems. Then the notion of an *everyday task* is described as well as the *cognitive limitations of humans*. Furthermore a way to overcome these limitations is developed with *context-sensitive* applications.

3.1.1.1 The End-User

In supply chain management *users* are clearly described (Porter 1998). But in the real world the Ubicomp user can be anyone. We might not even be aware of using an application, since it was designed to be seamlessly integrated into daily life (Weiser 1993). In supply-chain management or logistics the focus is on organizations and companies. For this analysis, the focus is on the *end-user*, meaning a consumer, client, or user of a system, or an application. End-user computing has been defined as "the adoption and use of information technology outside the information systems department" (Brancheau/Brown 1993, 439).

In his "Articles of association between design, technology and the people formerly known as users", John Thackara stated in his CHI2000 keynote speech: "We will deliver value to people —not deliver people to systems. We will give priority to human agency and will not treat humans as factor in some bigger picture" (Thackara 2000). The main actors in Ubicomp are human beings, called *users*—people that use things.

Businesses employ user-models to describe pre-existing marketing segments. In contrast, newer approaches to user modeling focus on desires, identity, and intent (McCullough 2004, 160). It is important to know more about the user—his intents, identities, and desires—in order to create and define appropriate scenarios in which users act.

An end-user is defined as the ultimate consumer of a finished product (Merriam-Webster 2006b). This analysis focuses on the end-user—also known as the consumer or customer.

Marc Prensky (2001) advances an explanation for why and how things changed in terms of the user in his essay "Digital Natives, Digital Immigrants" (Prensky 2001a). Kids and students today have spent less than 5000 hours of their entire life reading, but 10000 hours playing video games. Email, cell phones, the Internet, and computer games are an integral part of their lives. Students born in the '90s know mobile phones from growing up around them. As a result of this ubiquitous environment and the increasing amount of human-technology touch points, students think and process information differently. A recent study showed that 57% of all adolescents in Australia received their first mobile phone at age 13, while 16% received theirs at an even younger age (Littlefield 2004). Prensky (2001) calls those *Digital Natives*—native speakers of the digital language. *Digital immigrants* are people who were not born into the digital world, but became fascinated with its possibilities and adopted many of its aspects. If this is true, system designers of Ubicomp worlds need to create environments in which the language of the respective generation of Digital Natives is spoken. Natives are used to receiving information very quickly, they multi-task, and parallel-process. They prefer graphics over text, random access, and games. Therefore the quest for applications is to provide Digital Natives with appropriate content and to create a platform for them where they can share and exchange their own content

A process model with evaluation aspects needs to take into account whether Digital Natives perceive Ubicomp applications differently than Digital Immigrants. In addition to the actual age-based differences in perceptions, the end-user is defined by several behavioral constraints.

3.1.1.2 Behavioral Constraints of the End-User

Norman explained the behavioral constraints that apply to human action: physical, semantic, logical and cultural (Norman 1999a, 1988):

*   *Physical constraints*: Physical limitations constrain possible operations. They are effective and useful if they are easy to see and interpret, and they cannot be ignored.

*   *Semantic constraints*: The meaning of a situation limits the set of possible actions. Semantic constraints rely on the knowledge of the world.

*   *Logical constraints*: Logical constraints use reasoning to determine the alternatives. If logical constraints are applied correctly, users can logically deduce what actions are required.

*   *Cultural constraints*: Even if the logical or physical constraints to not apply, some constraints are based on culture. Cultural constraints are shared by a cultural group. The cultural aspect is not only about different civilizations and their behaviors, but also about learned behavior that has become culturally accepted. The scroll bar on the right is now a cultural constraint, because it is a learned constraint to many users.

These constraints are important in designing how users interaction with the application. The arrangement of controls can be constrained this way. A Ubicomp application designer should take these constraints into account in determining the basic factors of the application. They affect the way a user performs daily actions. The idea of Ubicomp is to bring ubiquitous technology to the people in the context of everyday life. The next section looks at the way users perform daily actions in order to develop an overall set of HCI Ubicomp preliminary requirements.

3.1.1.3 Everyday Tasks

Abowd describes informal daily actions as followed (Abowd/Mynatt/Rodden 2002, 53):

• They rarely have a clear beginning or end. An interaction has no common starting point or closure, thus requires greater flexibility and simplicity.

• Interruption is expected as users switch attention between competing concerns.

• Multiple activities operate concurrently and might need to be loosely coordinated.

• Time is an important discriminator in characterizing the ongoing relationship between people and computers.

• Associative models of information are needed, because information is reused from multiple perspectives.

These daily actions can be seen as everyday tasks. Most of everyday tasks are routine operations performed on a daily basis—eating, meeting with friends. The *not everyday* activities have wide and deep structures and require conscious planning and thought. Psychologists tend not to study everyday or unavoidable tasks, instead they study the complex ones (Csikszentmihalyi 1991). There are also tasks with deliberately set deep structures: games and leisure activities. They need to be entertaining and diverting, thus posing an interesting challenge. Everyday activities must be done quickly and often simultaneously with other activities. The structure of everyday activities minimizes planning and mental computation (Norman 1988; Norman 1999b, 154-155).

Everyday activities are conceptually simple. Simplicity lies in the nature of the tasks (Norman 1988) and follows certain structures (Maeda 2006). Everyday task structures are either shallow or narrow. An everyday task is rather boring, hence people usually want to get it over with as quickly as possible. An everyday task must therefore have either few choices at any point, which requires little planning, or be shallow in order to avoid long-term planning. One way to do so is to improve the process that is involved in fulfilling an everyday task. An example can be the check-out process in a supermarket. It is a rather boring and routine task. Streamlining and speeding-up the task would help a person to concentrate on more important things. To achieve a rapid task performance, Shneiderman suggests the following criteria (Shneiderman 1992):

• Users have *adequate knowledge* of the objects and *actions* necessary for the problem-solving task.

• The solution plan can be carried out *without delays*.

- *Distractions* are eliminated.

- User *anxiety* is low.

- There is *feedback* about progress toward solution.

- *Errors* can be avoided or, if they occur, handled easy.

An optimum in response time and feedback limits the possibility of anxiety concerning a task. Next to the optimal task performance for every day tasks, people suffer from cognitive limitations in everyday tasks.

3.1.1.4 Cognitive Limitations

Cognition occurs as people process external information in executing one part of a larger task. Any task that a human can do without conscious thought will become automatic. This *automaticity* enables people to do more than one activity at a time. If two tasks are performed simultaneously without one being an automatic task, the task performance of each task decreases. Simultaneity can be achieved by altering the attention between tasks (Raskin 2000).

The scope of human mental abilities is set by cognitive limitations. We can be (1) conscious or (2) unconscious of our actions while performing them—many human actions are performed in this way.

(1) A conscious process can be defined as the set of events that "are claimed by people to be conscious, which can be reported and acted upon with verifiable accuracy under optimal reporting conditions" (Baars/McGovern 1996). Optimal reporting conditions imply a minimum delay between event and report.

(2) Unconscious events are defined if "their presence can be verified (by influencing other observable tasks), although they are not claimed to be conscious and they cannot be voluntarily reported, acted on, or avoided even under optimal reporting conditions" (Baars/McGovern 1996).

Subconscious thoughts fit into patterns and proceed rapidly without effort. Subconscious thoughts are biased toward regularity and structure and are limited in formal power. Conscious thoughts are slow and labored. We ponder decisions, think about alternatives, compare different choices, and try to find explanations (Norman 1988). Conscious processing involves short-term memory, which is limited in the amount of available actions. A conscious process is rather inefficient, and the greater the number of conscious steps to a process, the more difficult it is. Whatever we do without effort, we tend to do unconsciously. By using perceptual abilities one can take advantage of memorizing patterns and appropriate responses. Based on previous experiences, patterns assist in performing a task (such as tic-tac-toe game). A conscious event can combine knowledge from different sources in novel ways, and trigger unconscious rule systems that pick up errors in the meaning, syntax world level, sound, intonation, or printing of a "snetnecne" (Baars/McGovern 1996, 8).

Any sequence of actions that are performed repeatedly will become automatic. Repetitive and predictable stimuli tend to fade from consciousness regardless of their physical intensity. Therefore news satisfies our consciousness because of its novel character. Consciousness has the ability to direct mental resources toward novel and significant events. Everyday tasks are routine but biologically or personally important, for example, the need to eat can be conscious without becoming habitual or boring. A set of actions we perform will be clumped into a single action. If single actions consist of a set, we perform the set of actions sequentially until completed. The automatic process of habituation is governed by a similar sequential unfolding. We cannot be conscious of more than one task at a time and we cannot avoid developing automatic responses (Raskin 2000).

In everyday usage, a plan or intention is similar to the notion of *goal contexts*. They describe a conscious or unconscious need or value that shapes selection and action. A goal context is a "future-directed, non-qualitative representation about one's own actions" (Baars/McGovern 1996). People become aware of the goal contexts only if they are missing. We are made aware of everyday tasks that have become unconsciously habituated and part of our routine when something prevents us from performing it. For routine tasks everything should work smoothly in order to not to be distracted from the goal contexts.

The number of decisions needed to perform a task should be limited for everyday tasks. As mentioned in the previous section, a task can include a shallow or narrow decision. These task-related structures are important for the design of applications in terms of cognitive load (see Fig. 27).

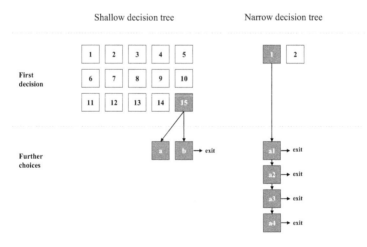

Fig. 27: Decision tree structure
Source: adapted from (Norman 1988)

If in shallow structures there are many alternatives that need to be displayed to the user, there should be few decisions to make after the single top-level choice (Decision 15 leads to (a,b) as further decisions). Shallow structures provide no problem in terms of planning or depth of analysis. Narrow structures incorporate only one or a very small number of alternatives. If the initial possibilities lead to only one or two choices, the structure after the alternative can be narrow and deep (Decision 1 leads to (a1,a2,a3,a4) as linear next steps with exit possibilities in each step) (Norman 1988). To keep the cognitive load on a level that conforms to the ability of our short-term memory, the number decisions the user has to make should be limited. The shallow structure is better in terms of the cognitive load, because it has a clear end with fewer decisions to be made after the first level choice.

If a user needs to perform different tasks he can only concentrate on one at a time. In the Internet, links can be re-organized or limited selection options can be given to a user. This fact hardly applies to real world contexts, where physical objects are the primary interface. In cognitive theory the effort required for making multiple decision might overwhelm us (Norman 1999b). Designing technology that avoids cognitive overload is made possible for example with *collaborative filtering*, which presents only relevant information to the user. The cognitive load of an Ubicomp application should be as low as possible. One possible solution is to determine the contextuality of an application to limit the cognitive load.

3.1.1.5   Context-Sensitive Applications to Limit the Cognitive Load

As described above, performing specific tasks requires specific levels of cognition. The detailed process of relating contextual information to the choice of meaning is rarely conscious. Our experiences are based on unconscious processes. The "context-sensitivity of conscious events extents far beyond language to perception, action control, memory, problem-solving, etc; [...] The less conscious some event is, the less it is sensitive to context" (Baars/McGovern 1996, 8). Baars and McGovern (1996) use the example of driving home from work with the intention to go shopping. If a navigational error occurs it will likely be because the driver was thinking of something else instead of turning right into the shopping center when he or she should have. Contexts can be set up by conscious events.

Ubicomp targets less conscious events, which are less sensitive to context. So long as tasks must be performed consciously, e.g. with the mobile phone, a certain degree of context-sensitivity inside the application will help to lower the cognitive load.

Context is defined as "any information that can be used to characterise the situation of an entity." (Dey 2001). The entities in the case of Ubicomp can be objects, such as the RFID tag attached to some location. On the basis of the available information, received from sensors or alternative sources, an application can react in different ways. This behavior is called context-aware. Context-awareness allows applications to provide only relevant information for a specific location, time or other coordinates and sensor data.

Context-awareness was originally in reference to objects. However, a user is also situated within a context. According to Scheer et. al. (Scheer et al. 2002) this context can be categorized as:

•   *Local context.* Context related to the actual location of the user.

•   *Action-related context.* Action currently conducted by the user.

- *Time-specific context.* Time period or point in time of the user.

- *Personal context.* The personal context describes individual preferences of the user.

Dey states three features of a context-aware application (Dey 2001):

- *Presentation of information and services*, automatic execution of a service, and tagging of context to information to support later retrieval.

- The *automatic execution* is critical to the perception of control. If common context information, time, date, and temperature are used, control is given. If the automatic execution is unforeseeable and undetectable, the user might be afraid of the outcome.

- *Tagging of context to information.*

Marc Langheinrich (2002) stated four principles in the context of privacy and security for use in Ubicomp environments (Langheinrich 2002). These can be added to the contextual factors stated above.

- *Notice*: Install mechanisms to declare collection practices, but also efficient ways to communicate these to the user.

- *Choice and consent*: Provide a selection mechanism so that users can indicate which services they prefer.

- *Proximity and locality*: Encode and use locality information for collected data that can enforce access restrictions. Proximity is a very relevant contextual factor. The closer a person is to the interaction device, the easier it is to experience the feedback channel. Proximity supports restrictions based on the location of the person who wants to use the data (Langheinrich 2002). Furthermore proximity can be a key to secure Ubicomp applications since the user must be willing to use the device. Proximity is a key factor for NFC as the near-field only works within a close proximity.

- *Access and recourse*: Provide a way for users to access personal information in a simple way through standardized interfaces.

These sets of requirements might be used as common criteria to build Ubicomp applications. Besides these general aspects, the interface between human and computer plays an important role.

3.1.2 Human Computer Interface

Interface design has been improved over the familiar Graphical User Interface (GUI) of personal computers in order to make computational processes more convenient for people. Nevertheless up to now no GUI has ever been as convenient as an electronic door opener through which people walk into office or retail buildings without thinking about the process of *opening a door*. Decades after the invention of the revolving door, building better interfaces still remains the goal of much of human-computer interaction research (McCullough 2004).

From a virtual interface in the foreground the aim is to move towards inhabitable interfaces that can be physically accessible but that act discretely in the background (see Fig. 28).

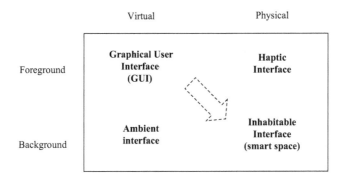

Fig. 28: From GUI to smart space
Source: (McCullough 2004, 71)

To gain control, the massive amount of available technology can be managed by context only. In a natural interaction, context would include information that does not require our attention except when wanted or when necessary. Ambient interfaces show potentially relevant information; haptic interfaces use latent intuitive physics. McCullough (2004, 71) points out the *perceptual intelligence* approach of Alex Pentland (2000) that states that most of the tasks people want performed do not seem to require complex reasoning (McCullough 2004; Pentland 2000). Things and smart devices that have a perceptual intelligence may remain silent and supportive at the same time. To establish control, some kind of interface for physical interaction is needed. The next section describes multimodal interaction to differentiate between various interaction styles.

3.1.2.1 Multimodal Interaction

The scope of multimodal interaction not only includes internal body chemicals (blood oxygen, glucose, pH), but also external chemicals (taste, smell), the various somatic senses (touch, pressure, temperature, pain), and muscle senses (stretch, tension, join position), as well as a sense of balance, hearing and vision (Schomaker 1995). Öquist provided a framework for multimodal interaction with a device (see Fig. 29).

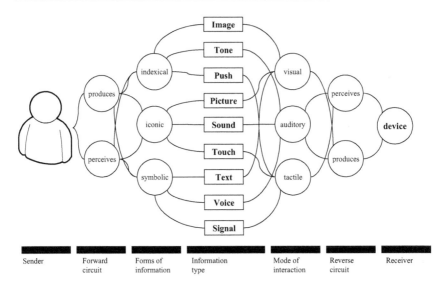

| Sender | Forward circuit | Forms of information | Information type | Mode of interaction | Reverse circuit | Receiver |

Fig. 29: Framework for multimodal interaction
Source: (Öquist 2006)

The information types correspond to the mapping between indexical, iconic, and symbolic forms over the visual, auditory, and tactile modes (Öquist 2006). Between a human being and a device—the sender and the receiver—many forms of interaction may occur, as well as certain modes of interaction. In the indexical form, the sign is directly connected to the object, the iconic form means that a signal is analogously connected, and in the symbolic form, the sign is only arbitrarily connected to the object.

The framework focuses on mobile devices but can also be a reference for general sender-receiver interface classification. Smaller interfaces will allow a different way of interaction than what is common with today's large mobile phone displays. The availability of different interaction possibilities led much research to either employ new forms of interaction or new interaction devices (Luk et al. 2006; Belt et al. 2006; Lumsden/Brewster 2003; Zhao et al. 2004; Foley/Wallace/Chan 1984; Välkkynen/Niemelä/Tuomisto 2006; Mantyjarvi et al. 2006). Feedback is crucial to the user. Haptic interfaces provide an opportunity to develop multi-modal feedback (Kahol et al. 2005).

3.1.2.2 Haptic Interfaces

A haptic user interface refers to devices that enable touch-based interactions with digital environments. Haptic interfaces produce an increase in the usability of a system, because of the cognitive effort the user needs to perceive and manipulate information with usual computing environments. The term *haptic* includes sensing and manipulation through the sense of touch. A haptic sensory system has two components: a tactile (or coetaneous) sensing and kinaesthetic (or proprioception) sensing. Tactile sensing refers to the stimulation of the outer surface of the body. Kinaesthetic sensing refers to the limb position and movement awareness (Boff/Kaufman/Thomas 1986). Tan (2000) gives the example of feeling the softness of a blanket (tactile sensing) and the ability to touch one's nose with closed eyes (kinaesthetic) (see Fig. 30) (Tan 2000).

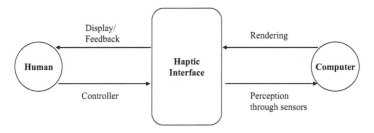

Fig. 30: Haptic interface information flow
Source: (Tan 2000)

An advantage of haptic systems is bi-directionality. Force-feedback controls, mainly used in the gaming industry, are a way to enhance the user's sense of movements in the virtual world. A main aspect is pointing, an interaction from the early times of human-computer interaction. Pointing devices are applicable in different interaction tasks (Foley/Wallace/Chan 1984) mostly framed for screen-based interaction, such as touch screens or tabletops. They can be either direct-controlled or indirect-controlled, whereas the direct-controlled refers to a pen and the best example of indirect-controlled is the common computer mouse.

Abowd (2002) stated that a keyboard is less likely to be our interface of choice for interacting with the physical world. System input has moved from the textual input of keyboards to a greater variety of data types. This has resulted in a shift from an explicit human input to the possibility of more implicit forms. The human body's natural interactions with the environment provide sufficient input to services without further intervention. Natural forms can be the aforementioned handwriting or speech. Although not yet in a state where fluent interaction is possible, technology will some day be capable of interpreting meaning from sensed signals of human activity. The union of explicit and implicit input defines the context of interaction. According to Abowd, an important feature of Ubicomp is the attempt to merge computational artifacts smoothly with the world of physical artifacts. An example is given by augmented reality (Abowd/Mynatt/Rodden 2002).

The possibility to touch things with an NFC-enabled mobile phone is a promising approach towards changing system input from being keyboard-based to touch-based in the real world. On the consumer front-end, several interaction devices can be used. They range from barcode recognition (Adelmann/Langheinrich/Flörkemeier 2006), to mobile phone with RFID interaction (Riekki/Salminen/Alakärppä 2006; Ballagas et al. 2006). The combination of mobile phone with real world interaction is easy to use and adheres to the Ubicomp notion (Rukzio 2007; Rukzio/Schmidt/Hussmann 2004).

3.1.2.3 Affordances

Norman (1988) was the first to use the term "affordance" in the way it was later used by many interaction designers (Norman 1999a). Affordance describes context as "a situation where an object's sensory characteristics intuitively imply its functionality and use" (UsabilityFirst.com 2006). Norman (1999) stated that the term needs to be understood as *perceived affordance*, separated from *affordance* and *feedback* (Norman 1999b, 123). All three concepts can be manipulated differently. Perceived affordances are used by designers to make the user perceive that a certain action is possible. In graphical interfaces, the designer can control only perceived affordances.

The visible icons provide visual feedback that advertises the affordance. In contrast a real affordance does not necessarily have to have a visible presence. The presence of feedback helps to understand and increase the usability of a system, but it is independent from the visibility. Affordances reflect possible relationships among actors and objects (Norman 1999a, 123).

This is important for Ubicomp design in later stages since the feedback channel does not need to be visual, but requires feedback and captions are a way to imply functions and use. The affordance specifies the range of possibilities and therefore must be understandable.

3.1.2.4 The Interaction Design of an Everyday Task

Ubicomp is placed in daily life. Daily life consists of physical interactions taking place in everyday tasks. Everyday tasks should be kept simple. There are seven principles to transform a difficult task into a simple one (Norman 1988):

- "Use knowledge in the world and knowledge kept in the head.

- Simplify the structure of tasks.

- Make things visible.

- Get the mappings right.

- Exploit the power of constraints—both natural and artificial.

- Design for error.

- When all else fails, standardize."

This list from Norman shows that it is possible to simplify the tasks we need to conduct. Norman lists technological approaches to make mappings more natural and to simplify the structure of tasks (Norman 1988, 191-192):

- *Keep the task much the same, but provide mental aids*: Reliance on simple mental aids is inevitable given the limits of one's own memory. Information is presented physically rather than requiring the user to keep the information in his head. One can think of everyday notes or the spell-checker in office documents, things that help people to focus on the relevant aspects of a task.

- *Use technology to make visible what would otherwise be invisible to improve feedback and the ability to keep control:* To make something visible simplifies understanding and performance of a task. Examples are instruments in cars that show relevant information to the driver without overextending his concentration on driving. They are mental aids and reminders, for example to fuel up the car.

- *Automate, but keep the task much the same:* Some impacts on automation can be dangerous as well. Norman (1988) uses the example of an autopilot in a plane. The best is the combination of full control (start and landing) and complete automation (during the flight) in order to assure the necessary safety.

- *Change the nature of the task:* Technologies can help to transform complex tasks into narrower, shallower structures thus simplifying tasks.

Natural mappings help the user to determine which object is related to what action or vice versa. The appropriate use of natural mappings should even reduce the dependence upon labels (Norman 1988). The user cannot see into the computer or mobile phone to gain reassurance that given commands are executed. If users come to expect a certain response time, but the volatility of the time is very high, they may become apprehensive. Extreme variation is unsettling and should be prevented or acknowledged by the system, for example through the usage of a progress bar. Users prefer short response times under 15 seconds. The response time can vary depending on the task: For simplex frequent tasks, 1 second is appropriate. Common tasks may take two to four seconds, while complex tasks may require up to eight to twelve seconds in response time. Because unexpected delays are disruptive, a feedback system should be implemented. To sum up the previous paragraphs, the following design principles make design understandable (Norman 1988):

- *Visibility:* The user can immediately tell the state of the device and the alternatives for action.

- *Conceptual model*: A user demands consistency in the presentation of operations and a coherent system image (see also (Norman 1999b, 177)

- *Mappings*: The relationship between system state and what is visible, between controls and their effects, and between actions and actual results must be clear and easy to determine.

- *Feedback*: A user receives full and continuous feedback about every action.

These principles are highly relevant if designing applications for everyday activities and serve as basic requirements. Besides the object character of Ubicomp, the object itself is not as important as the underlying activity.

3.1.2.5   Interaction between Physical Objects and Mobile Devices

Commands usually apply actions to an object. The interface allows sequencing in both ways, either object-action or action-object. One chooses either the *verb* (action) and then selects the *noun* (object) or vice versa. Both versions have different implications as long as the usability differs. Once a command is chosen in the verb-noun style a delay between issuing the action and selecting an object can lead to surprising results. With a noun-verb system, a command is executed when issued. The user does not need to shift his attention away from the content that triggered his action. A noun-verb paradigm does not need to a cancel feature, because of the instant decision of the selection after an object is active (Raskin 2000). It is important to design for activities, experiences, or processes, but not for objects (McCullough 2004, 51-52).

From picking up an RFID chip to scanning it with an NFC-enabled mobile phone, the user may receive different forms of interaction feedback. Transitions in the form of interaction possibilities pose challenges to discover and select the right services. A possibility is to request a standard framework for requesting pervasive services. An interface is needed to bridge the physical and the virtual world—not necessarily a screen-based one, but a relational interface as Ullmer and Ishii would say (2000).

In a relational interface, the system maps the logical relationships between physical objects and computational representations (Ullmer/Ishii 2000). Riekki et. al. use a framework of visual symbols that communicates to users which objects can be touched and what services are activated. Touching a symbol with a mobile phone triggers a service that is supplemented with context-specific information (Riekki/Salminen/Alakärppä 2006). According to Belt et. al. the interaction between a mobile device and RFID is considered positive (Belt et al. 2006). But also the field study they conducted revealed problems due to erroneous understanding of the interaction technique. Rukzio (2007, 30) gives an overview on the different ways that a mobile device may interact with its environment and the objects within (see Table 7).

Name	Touching	Pointing	Scanning	User-mediated object selection	Indirect remote controls
Description	The user touches an object with a device to establish a connection.	The user points with a device at an object to establish a link.	Object and device interact because of the proximity.	The user actually types in information provided by the object.	The user controls a remote display with a mobile device.
Device-Object Interaction	RFID, NFC, proximity sensors	Visual, light beam, infrared	Bluetooth, WLAN, GPS	No direct link, except body	Bluetooth, GPRS, GSM, cable
Advantages	Natural way of interaction. Unambiguous selection of an object.	Natural way of interaction. Distance to smart object limited.	Possible to discover all nearby located objects. Objects do not need to be visually augmented.	No special device needed.	Control of a remote device that may not have an interface.
Disadvantages	Proximity of user and object needed. User must be aware of the augmentation.	Dexterity is needed.	No direct link between smart object and localization.	Complex input is difficult to type in.	Interaction is intrinsically indirect.

Table 7: Overview on mobile device interaction
Source: (Rukzio 2007, 30)

The various ways of interacting between objects and devices led from a proposed graphical language of touch (Arnall 2005b) to manifestos for networked objects (Bleecker 2005). Ballagas et al. (2006) differentiate even more in detail between various forms of interaction (Ballagas et al. 2006). Touching is a key factor for mobile interactions and theoretically considered to be a valid basis for Ubicomp applications.

The next section sums up the previous sections in determining a preliminary set of requirements for NFC-based Ubicomp applications.

3.1.3 Summary: Preliminary Set of Requirements

To sum up, the following basic requirements for Ubicomp applications provide the framework for the case studies:

The decisions needed to perform a task should be limited to those pertaining to informal daily activities. This led to the first requirement:

•   R1. Few choices after the single top level choice.

A general notion on labels, a graphic language applied to new interaction paradigms (see (Arnall 2005b)) aids the further development of useful applications (see *Affordances*).

- R2. Add general captions on labels.

Adding to Norman's design principles (Norman 1988):

- R3. The user needs to immediately tell the state of the device and alternatives for actions (*Visibility*).

- R4. Consistency in the presentation of operations (*Conceptual model*).

- R5. Relationship between actions and results must be clear and easy to determine (*Mappings*).

- R6. Full and continuous feedback about every user action (*Feedback*).

Dey describes three features of a context-aware application (see chapter 3.1.1.5): Presentation of information and services, automatic execution of a service, and tagging of context to information to support later retrieval (Dey 2001).

- R7. Presentation of information and services.

- R8. Automatic execution of a service.

- R9. Tagging of context to information.

Marc Langheinrich stated four principles for use in Ubicomp environments that help to overcome problems with privacy and security and (Langheinrich 2002) that are adapted to the preliminary requirements.

- R10. Notice: Install mechanisms to declare collection practices, but also efficient ways to communicate these to the user.

- R11. Choice and consent: Provide a selection mechanism so that users can indicate which services they prefer.

- R12. Proximity and locality: Encode and use locality information for collected data that can enforce access restrictions.

- R13. Access and recourse: Provide a way for users to access their personal information in a simple way through standardized interfaces.

The human aspect in Ubicomp is determined by digital natives who perceive applications differently than digital immigrants. It has been made clear that a human being has several constraints (physical, semantic, logical, cultural) that affect the individual in his everyday life and in the everyday tasks that make up this life. These everyday tasks must have either few choices at any single point or be shallow, because human beings are hindered by cognitive limitations—the decisions needed to perform a task should be limited. This means that the cognitive load should be as low as possible—context-sensitive applications can help in this regard by reducing the cognitive load. Finally, proximity is a relevant contextual factor. Looking at HCI, the following aspects are considered relevant for Ubicomp applications:

- *Haptic interfaces* are beneficial.

- Use *affordances* (relationships between actors and objects).

- Follow the *interaction design principles* (Visibility, conceptual model, mappings, and feedback, notice, choice and consent, proximity, access and recourse).

In chapter 2.1, NFC as a technology in ubiquitous computing was described. Matching NFC to the results of HCI shows that NFC follows the HCI design principles already to a large extent:

- It is an everyday technology because it is built into a mobile phone, which is a ubiquitous device nowadays.

- NFC can be used in a context-sensitive manner since the mobile phone device can use system data, system time, and other contextual factors to enrich the tag-based software application.

- Proximity is a key element in NFC, since the NFC technology is based on the RFID 13.56 ISO standards with a maximum reach of 2 to 3 centimeters.

- It incorporates a haptic interface using a *touch* to start an application.

- It uses affordances if the NFC tags are properly labelled.

- It follows the interaction design principles (Visibility, conceptual model, mappings, and feedback):

  - NFC tags are visible in the environment.

  - A conceptual model can be used, when the tags are physically applied in the area of usage (e.g. attaching a tag to a printer will likely start a printer-related task).

  - Mappings are visible because of the mobile phone display in which NFC technology is incorporated.

  - Feedback: the phone provides a) a haptic response (vibration) when the phone successfully reads a tag and b) a visible feedback on the display.

An application using NFC that is built on these factors may positively impact technology acceptance. In order to determine user acceptance and technology adoption for these applications, the next chapter focuses on the question of technology acceptance and innovation adoption.

3.2 Technology Acceptance

This chapter aims to describe and potentially integrate existing technology acceptance models into Ubicomp application development. The chapter identifies relevant aspects of innovation adoption and technology acceptance models with the following questions: What could *innovation adoption theories* add to the development of likeable Ubicomp applications? Which of the known *technology acceptance models* is useful for Ubicomp evaluation?

The idea is to use existing technology acceptance models, eventually consolidate them and integrate the model into a guided process. With a forecast based on technology acceptance at the right time in an application development process, it is possible to avoid making the wrong investments in expensive Ubicomp infrastructure.

First, an overview of end-user related ubiquitous computing is presented in section 3.2.1. Then innovation adoption and its influence on Ubicomp is described in section 3.2.2. Section 3.2.3 lists known technology acceptance models that have been evaluated from a Ubicomp perspective. Section 3.2.4 sums up the innovation adoption and technology acceptance issues and their implications on the development of Ubicomp applications.

3.2.1 Technology Acceptance Evaluation in Ubiquitous Computing

It is not clear what effects the adoption of Ubicomp applications have and whether common technology acceptance models can be applied here (Ajzen 1991; Ajzen/Fishbein 2005; Bandura 1986; Davis 1986; Davis 1989; Fishbein/Ajzen 1975; Gefen/Straub 2000b; Goodhue 1995; Venkatesh/Davis 1996; Venkatesh/Davis 2000; Venkatesh et al. 2003). The following table (Table 8) shows selected end-user related Ubicomp research, based on literature research:

Methodology	Focus of research	Subject	Source
Case study (Method not described)	Gaming	"Smart Playing Cards - Enhancing the Gaming Experience with RFID"	(Floerkemeier/Matter n 2006)
Case study, Field test, Focus group	Consumer	"A case study in pervasive retail"	(Roussos et al. 2002; Roussos/Moussouri 2004)
Case study, Survey research, Descriptive overview.	Consumer (HCI)	"The human experience [of ubiquitous computing]"	(Abowd/Mynatt/Rod den 2002)
Case studies, descriptive overviews	Home	"User-initiated context switching using NFC"	(Jalkanen 2005)
Case study	Consumer	"Case study on retail customer communication applying ubiquitous computing"	(Strüker/Sackmann/ Müller 2004)

Methodology	Focus of research	Subject	Source
Literature review (Analytical)	Consumer	"Consumer Power: A Comparison of the Old Economy and the Internet Economy"	(Rezabakhsh et al. 2006)
Scenario (Descriptive)	User Mobility	"Aura: an Architectural Framework for User Mobility in Ubiquitous Computing Environments"	(Sousa/Garlan 2002)
Show case (Descriptive)	Consumer	"AURA: A mobile platform for object and location annotation"	(Smith/Davenport/H wa 2003)
Field study, survey research	Public space	"Novel methods: emotions, gestures, events: Prototyping and sampling experience to evaluate ubiquitous computing privacy in the real world"	(Iachello et al. 2006)
Field study, survey research	Public space	"User Perceptions on Mobile Interaction with Visual and RFID Tags"	(Belt et al. 2006)
Experiments	Miscellaneous	"RFID toys"	(Graafstra 2006)

Table 8: End-user related Ubicomp research with acceptance measurements

Further Ubicomp related end-user oriented research includes (Want et al. 2002; Iachello et al. 2006; Saponas et al. 2006; Hallnäs/Redström 2002; Pfaff/Skiera 2005; Ballagas et al. 2003; Strüker/Sackmann/Müller 2004; Langheinrich 2002; Pinhanez 2001; Pinto/Jos 2006; Aßmann/Resatsch/Schildhauer 2006). Most of these evaluated application approaches in the area of Ubicomp and consumers were either not evaluated at all or conducted in laboratories and with student participants in evaluations. Since most real life people might not be familiar with—nor mind—RFID and NFC and all these acronyms (see Section 2.2.2) it is very important to also discuss valid development and acceptance evaluation methods with real users.

3.2.2 Innovation Adoption

Rogers described the adoption of innovations as a process "through which an individual [...] passes from first knowledge" (Rogers 1995, 20) of an innovation to finalizing the adoption decision. The adopter categories from Rogers were inserted into the technology adoption life cycle (also referred to as bell curve) with the innovators as enthusiasts who drive a market and demand technology (Rogers 1995). Innovators pursue new technology products aggressively, because technology is a central interest in their life. Next on are the early adopters who buy into new product concepts very early in their life cycle. Unlike the innovators they do not adopt technology just for the sake of the technology. They find it easy to imagine how a new technology may fit into their other concerns, making the early adopters the key to opening a high-tech market segment. The early majority shares some of the early adopters ability to relate to technology driven by practicality. They wait until other people start using the technology. The early majority accounts for roughly a third of the whole adoption life cycle, making it the key to substantial profits. People from the late majority wait until technology has become somewhat of an established standard with support from large companies. The last group, the laggards simply do not want to use new technology for personal or economic reasons (Moore 2002, 13; Rogers 1995, 282).

Moore (2002) figured out a crack in this bell curve, showing the problem of crossing the phase from innovators and early adopters to the early majority. The pragmatists and conservatives reward solutions and convenience. Norman (1999b) adapted from Christensen (1997) the needs-satisfaction curve of a technology (see Fig. 31 - (Christensen 1997; Norman 1999b, 32 - 33)). New technology first delivers less performance than the average customer requires. Customers then demand better technology with better features, until the technology becomes good enough and rather irrelevant.

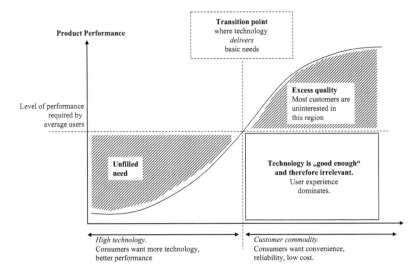

Fig. 31: The transition point of technology
Source: (Norman 1999b, 32)

When that happens consumers want convenience, reliability, and low cost. This transition point marks the change from technology-driven products to customer-driven, human-centered ones. Early adopters need the technology and pay a price for it. Similar to the concept of market-pull vs. market-push, a market-pull is created by designing and engineering a product that meets the needs of a core group of users (Fig. 32). The core group of users needs to feel, trust and accept the product. This is the case if the product meets or exceeds their needs (Smith/Gerth 2006).

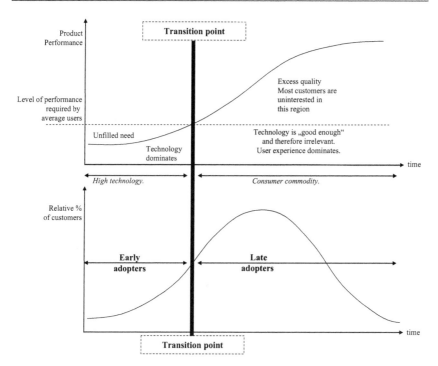

Fig. 32: The transition point
Source: adapted from (Norman 1999b, 33)

The complex world of Ubicomp demands products that are understood and accepted by people, not experts. Therefore there is a need to ask the *common* or *normal* user for evaluations. The dissemination of an innovation is regarded as the process by which an innovation is communicated through various channels among members of a social system (Rogers 1995). The innovation-decision process has five main steps: knowledge, persuasion, decision, implementation and confirmation (see Fig. 33). Rogers defines five adopter categories in his work: innovators, early adopters, early majority, late majority, and laggards. While the innovators are risk-takers, the early adopters are opinion leaders who make the initial evaluation of an innovation and communicate the result to the other members of their group. If the early adopters are convinced by innovators that a technology is worth it, the technology can spread into the mass market after crossing the *chasm*—the different needs of early adopters and early majority (Moore 2002).

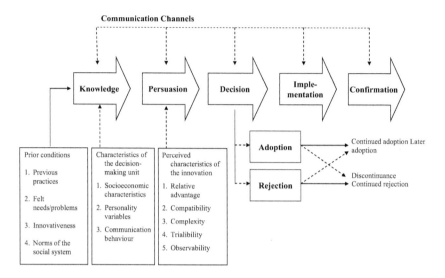

Fig. 33: Innovation-decision process
Source: (Rogers 1995, 170)

The decision to accept an innovation depends on the innovation-decision of other members, and here networking exerts a major influence. This also means that communication channels such as mass media have a powerful effect on spreading the message. But the most trustworthy channel for leaders of opinion is word-of-mouth—even more so than mass media. The adoption of innovation is therefore largely an information processing activity to which potential adopters have gathered enough information on the particular innovation (Hainbuchner 2005).

Rogers also states that the available information about an innovation may positively influence its adoption probability (Rogers 1995, 16). In the case of NFC, this would mean that—if the invention NFC and RFID is an innovation and if we are still *in the fog of innovation*—more information (equals experience and visible benefits) about RFID is crucial for large-scale adoption. In particular knowledge about the technology is critical (see 2.2.2)

The value of an innovation is judged by five aspects (Rogers 1995, 14-16) (see Table 9):

Core Constructs	Definition
Relative Advantage (RA)	The degree to which the innovation is perceived as better than the idea it supersedes
Compatibility (C)	The degree to which an innovation is perceived as being consistent with the existing values, experiences, and needs of potential adopters
Complexity (CX)	The degree to which an innovation is perceived as difficult to understand and use
Trialibility (T)	The degree to which an innovation may be experimented with on a limited basis
Observability (O)	The degree to which the results of an innovation are visible to others

Table 9: Constructs of innovation
Source: (Rogers 1995)

Studies that investigated these constructs from the Innovation Diffusion Theory (IDT) (alternative name: Diffusion of Innovation Theory), concluded that only Relative Advantage (RA), Complexity (CX), and Compatibility (C) play an important role in determining the degree of individual technology adoption (Karahanna/Straub/Chervany 1999; Sultan/ Farley/Lehmann 1990; Karaiskos/Kourouthanassis/Giaglis 2007). Individual technology adoption would be the focus in case of NFC. But, technology adoption is oftentimes used in the context of organizational adoption and for complex technology introductions (Adams/Nelson/Todd 1992; Taylor/Todd 1995; Boudreau/Robey 2005). Innovation adoption processes may take place on an individual, group or on organizational level (Venkatesh 2006). The process in organizations has various perspectives: the technological, the organizational, and the interorganizational. Chwelos et. al. showed that in these perspectives, the readiness, perceived benefits, and external pressure were significant predictors of intent to adopt a software system (Chwelos/Benbasat/Dexter 2001). The external pressure related to managerial decisions influences adoption in organizations, although other processes, such as different mechanisms of innovation diffusion also play an important role (Leonard-Barton/Deschamps 1988; Greenhalgh/Robert/Bate 2004). On an individual level, however, there is no pressure to use a technology unless there are certain needs. Several models of acceptance theory exist to predict human behavior in the domain of information systems— most with organizational foci. Ubiquitous computing on the contrary relates to consumer- and end-users more than to organizations. Because of this, the next chapter reviews various models in technology acceptance theory and if there is a potential model for researching the individual adoption of NFC-based Ubicomp applications. To start with, an overview of technology acceptance models and the idea behind them, is presented in the next section.

3.2.3 Technology Acceptance Models

Various acceptance models have been widely researched in information systems science. In principal the models seek to assess the likelihood of success for new technology introductions. Based on the results, and an understanding of the acceptance drivers, invention can be planned and conducted. Individual reactions to using information technology lead to actual use, which has an influence on the reaction. Intentions to use information technology have an impact on the actual use. Therefore questioning intentions helps to understand actual use (see Fig. 34).

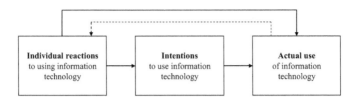

Fig. 34: Basic concept of user acceptance models
Source: (Venkatesh et al. 2003)

Technology adoption occurs on an organizational level and an individual level. Numerous models have been used to explain adoption on an individual level, including the social cognitive theory (SCT), theory of reasoned action (TRA), the theory of planned behavior (TPB), and the technology acceptance model (TAM). Further models are an extension to the TAM (TAM II), task-technology fit (TTF) and the motivational model (MM). The following sections describe key components of the models and theories and result in a combined model.

3.2.3.1   Social Cognitive Theory (SCT)

Social Cognitive Theory (SCT) provides a framework for understanding, predicting, and changing human behavior. The theory identifies human behavior as an interaction of personal factors, behavior, and the environment (Bandura 1977; Bandura 1986). Human behavior is seen as an interaction between personal factors and the environment. This interaction influences the thoughts and actions of a person, involving human beliefs and cognitive competencies. Beliefs and competencies are modifiable by social influences and structures. The interaction between the environment and a person's behavior determines the aspects of their behavior and therefore the environment modifies the behavior. A person might construe a situation differently whereby the same set of stimuli provoke different responses from different people or from the same person at different times (Jones 1989).

The SCT (Bandura 1989, 1977a; Bandura 1986; Bandura 1977b) is the basis of the computer self-efficacy. Compeau and Higgins applied the SCT to information technology in the context of computer utilization (Compeau/Higgins 1995a, 1995b). Core constructs of the SCT are Outcome Expectations—Performance (OE) and Outcome Expectations Personal (OEP), Self-Efficacy (SE), Affect (A), and Anxiety (ANX). OE relates to performance-based consequences of the behavior, OEP are the personal consequences of behavior. Self-efficacy (SE) means the judgement of one's ability to use a technology to accomplish a task. An individual's liking for a particular behavior is called affect (A), while anxiety refers to the feelings of insecurity or unease that are evoked when performing a behaviour (ANX) (Venkatesh et al. 2003). Anxiety is an important interface to the privacy discussions around Ubicomp applications.

3.2.3.2   Theory of Reasoned Action / Theory of Planned Behaviour (TRA/TPB)

Drawn from fundamental theories of human behavior, the theory of reasoned action (TRA) is the antecedent of the theory of planned behavior (TPB) and was described in 1975 by (Fishbein/Ajzen 1975). Specific behavior of people is determined by a person's intention to perform that behavior. To behave in a certain way is a function of an individual's attitude toward the behavior and subjective norms. The attitude of a person is viewed as the major determinant related to his beliefs that performing the specific behavior will lead to certain consequences and his evaluations of those consequences. As core constructs to determine human behavior, attitude towards behavior and subjective norms are used. Main limitation of TRA is the assumption that someone voluntarily forms an intention to act, but in practice time, money or organizational constraints limit the freedom to act. The TPB is supposed to overcome these limitations. The theory of planned behavior (TPB) extends the TRA by adding the core construct of Perceived Behavioral Control (PBC) (Ajzen 1985; Ajzen 1991) (see Fig. 35). Behavioral control is defined as one's perception of the ease or difficulty of performing a behavior. Both constructs have the same objective: to understand human behavior through identifying determinants of behavioral intentions.

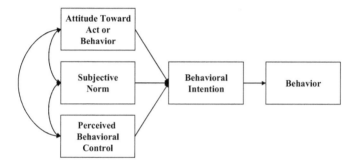

Fig. 35: Theory of Planned Behavior
Source: (Ajzen 1985)

The constructs were not invented especially for information technology research, however they provide a basis for later research in that area and were adopted widely. A reason is the ability to capture social and control factors through Subjective Norm and Perceived Behavioral Control (Taylor/Todd 1995; Yayla/Hu 2007).

3.2.3.3 Technology Acceptance Model (TAM)

The technology acceptance model (TAM) (Davis 1986; Davis 1989) is best known in information systems research and has been applied to different technologies (Davis 1989), such as the Internet (Agarwal/Prasad 1998), personal computer (Taylor/Todd 1995), or in certain domains such as banking (Chan/Lu 2004). It has also been researched in different cultures (Straub/Keil/Brenner 1997). It provided good results for a variety of technologies and domains (Venkatesh 2006). While the TRA is a general theory on human behavior, the TAM intends to specifically predict information technology acceptance. Fig. 36 shows the TAM.

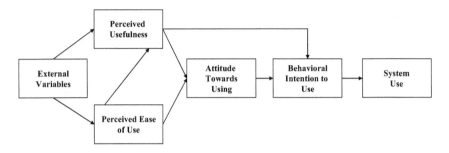

Fig. 36: Technology Acceptance Model (TAM)
Source: (Davis 1989)

The TAM has been extended with various constructs and validated according to the relative importance of singular constructs (Mathieson/Peacock/Chin 2001; Gefen/Straub 2000a). Another research stream investigated in moderating variables, such as gender (Venkatesh/Morris 2000), experience (Taylor/Todd 1995), and age (Venkatesh et al. 2003). These moderators proved to be significant in a meta analysis (King/He 2006). Ease of use (EOU) is the degree to which the user expects the target system to be free of effort. (Davis 1989, 985). Perceived usefulness (PU) is influenced by EOU. Both EOU and PU predict attitude (A), defined as the user's evaluation of the desirability to use the system. A and PU influence the Behavioral Intention (BI) to actually use the system, with I predicting the system use.

Critics suggest that the TAM does not have any socials aspects as influencing factors (Davis/Bagozzi/Warshaw 1989; Melone 1990). The effect of EOU has a lower effect on the technology acceptance (Gefen/Straub 2000b). PU and EOU are also conceptually similar to the aforementioned constructs Relative Advantage (RA) and Complexity (CX) used in the IDT, which are important for the individual adoption of innovations.

3.2.3.4 Task-Technology Fit (TTF)

A weakness of the TAM out from an organizational perspective is the lack of task focus. Although the "usefulness" concept implicitly includes tasks, IT utilization may be better measured with a more explicit inclusion of task characteristics. The task-technology fit (TTF) addresses the assessment of information systems from an ex-post view. The core of the model is the "assertion that for an information technology to have a positive impact on individual performance, the technology: (1) must be utilized and (2) must be a good fit with the tasks it supports." (Goodhue 1995).

The measure of this task-technology fit consists of 8 factors: quality, locatability, authorization, compatibility, ease of use, production timeliness, systems reliability, and relationship with users (Goodhue/Thompson 1995). They measure the fit between certain task characteristics, tasks that need to be done by the user and the technology supporting theses tasks (see Fig. 37).

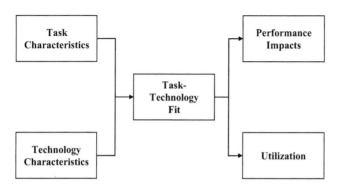

Fig. 37: Task-Technology Fit (TTF) model
Source: (Goodhue 1995; Goodhue/Thompson 1995)

The TTF measure is a predictor of user reports of improved job performance and effectiveness that is attributable to the use of the system. The fit influences the perceived performance impacts and the utilization. The original TTF looks on the individual level in organizations. Other versions of the TTF model exist and include additions, such as utilization or individual abilities (Dishawa/Strong 1999; Goodhue 1995; Goodhue/Thompson 1995). TTF excludes attitudes towards IT, a fact that also led to combinations of TAM and TTF (Dishawa/Strong 1999). As previously described, tasks play an important role in Ubicomp contexts. Another aspect is the motivation to perform a task.

3.2.3.5 Motivational Model (MM)

Psychology supports the general motivation theory as an explanation for many aspects of human behavior in specific contexts (Vallerand 1997). In information systems research motivational theory has been discussed to add to insights on technology adoption (Venkatesh et al. 2003; Venkatesh/Speier 1999). Davis applied both motivational aspects, extrinsic and intrinsic motivation to the domain of IS. It is *extrinsically motivated* if users want to perform an activity that is influenced by achieving valued outcomes that are distinct from the activity itself. Users are *intrinsically motivated* if they perform activities for no other reason than the activity itself. Motivational models do not have specific core constructs.

3.2.3.6 Unified Theory of Acceptance and Use of Technology (UTAUT)

Several of the previously described theories or models have similar constructs of direct determinants of intention or usage. This led Venkatesh et al. to the conclusion that a unified theory of acceptance is possible (Venkatesh et al. 2003). Therefore the authors identified, discussed, and reviewed eight models to determine similarities. The eight models reviewed are: the theory of reasoned action, the technology acceptance model, the motivational model, the theory of planned behavior, a model combining the technology acceptance model and the theory of planned behavior, the model of PC utilization, the innovation diffusion theory, and the social cognitive theory. These models were empirically compared using within-subjects andlongitudinal data from four organizations (Venkatesh et al. 2003).

Seven constructs out of all the other models are direct determinants of intention or usage in one or more of the individual models. Fig. 38 shows the complete UTAUT constructs as tested by Venkatesh et al. (2003)

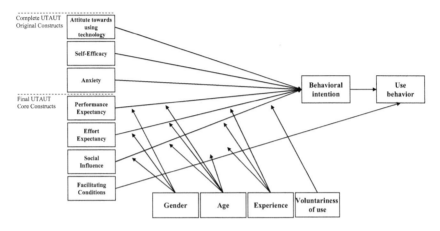

Fig. 38: Original UTAUT constructs
Source: (Venkatesh et al. 2003)

Table 10 shows an overview of all used UTAUT core constructs and their definitions.

Core construct	Original Sources	Definition in source
Performance Expectancy (PE)	(Venkatesh et al. 2003)	Degree to which an individual believes that using the system will help him or her to attain gains in job performance.
Effort Expectancy (EE)	(Venkatesh et al. 2003)	Degree of ease associated with the use of the system.
Social Influence (SI)	(Venkatesh et al. 2003)	Degree to which an individual perceives that important others believe he or she should use the new system.
Facilitating Conditions (FC)	(Venkatesh et al. 2003)	Degree to which an individual believes that an organizational and technical infrastructure exists to support use of the system.
Self-Efficacy (SE)	(Bandura 1986; Venkatesh et al. 2003)	Judgment of one's ability to use a technology (e.g. computer) to accomplish a particular job or task
Anxiety (ANX)	(Bandura 1986; Compeau/Higgins 1995b; Venkatesh et al. 2003)	Evoking anxious or emotional behavior when it comes to performing a behavior (e.g. using a computer)
Attitude Towards Using Technology (ATUT)	(Bandura 1986; Compeau/Higgins 1995b; Davis/Bagozzi/ Warshaw 1992; Venkatesh et al. 2003)	Individual's overall affective reaction to using a system.

| Behavioral Intention (BI) | (Venkatesh et al. 2003) | Intention to use the system in the future. |
| Use behavior | (Venkatesh et al. 2003) | Actual system usage |

Table 10: Core constructs and definitions of UTAUT

The UTAUT synthesizes these known constructs and models to combine exploratory power. Fig. 39 shows the key moderating influences of the proposed and supported model:

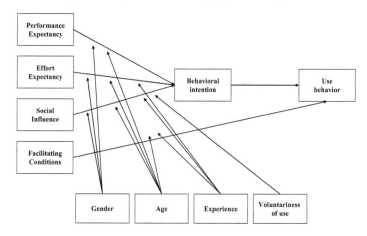

Fig. 39: Unified Theory of Acceptance and Use of Technology (UTAUT)
Source: (Venkatesh et al. 2003)

UTAUT posits four determinants in its final form: Performance Expectancy (PE), Effort Expectancy (EE), Social Influence (SI) and Facilitating Condition (FC). Moderation variables are gender, age, experience and voluntariness of use. The model was empirically tested and cross-validated. While TAM and other established models hardly explain 40% of the variance in use, UTAUT explained 70% or more of the variance in use (Venkatesh et al. 2003).

Items used in estimating the model included seven constructs, the aforementioned four plus Attitude Towards Using Technology (ATUT), Self-Efficacy (SE), and Anxiety (A). Venkatesh et al. (2003) empirically tested the original seven-construct model and found strong empirical support for the UTAUT with three direct determinants of intention to use (PE, EE, SI) and two direct determinants of usage behavior (BI, FC). The tests with all constructs were run in different industries, where individuals were introduced to a new technology in the workplace. The industries included entertainment and telecomm services where use was voluntary, but also organizational settings such as banking and public administration where use was mandatory. Final confirmation of UTAUT was empirically tested in other organizations, in financial services industry, and in retail electronics. The UTAUT model might also lay a solid foundation for researching the individual adoption of Ubicomp technology because of the combination of constructs and the voluntary setting.

Since the UTAUT constructs incorporate eight different acceptance models, of which only a few target individual behavior, it is important to look at experiences in UTAUT research to determine constructs for Ubicomp research. The UTAUT model has already been adapted to a variety of researched topics. The following table lists research approaches and results. The UTAUT suitability for the underlying topic is described in order to determine the possibility for adapting it to NFC-based Ubicomp research. Conceptionally closest to Ubicomp and its ubiquity in the forming of NFC is the domain of mobile business and mobile services where the majority of technology acceptance studies have been conducted.

The following table (see Table 11) lists studies conducted with UTAUT constructs or additional constructs. Studies with a strict focus on industry settings, such as (Lee 2006) "An Empirical Study of Organizational Ubiquitous Computing Technology Adoption: The Case of Radio Frequency Identification in the Healthcare Industry" are not inserted in the table because of the consumer focus of this analysis. Lee focuses on core constructs driven by organizational technology adoption, such as market uncertainty, need pull, vendor pressure, perceived benefits, technology push, and presence of champions, etc.;

Domain (Application)	Title	Short description and research objective	Core constructs used in the study and moderators researched	UTAUT suitability for the proposed research and important factors	Source
Ubiquitous Computing (Wireless Sensor Devices – Motes)	Exploring the Benefits of Using Motes to Monitor Health: An Acceptance Survey N = 103 (anonymous second study)	This paper presents the findings of an anonymous web survey of over 100 participants aimed at investigating the possible acceptance of *Motes* as a reliable and efficient health monitoring tool. The UTAUT was applied to determine how viable this technology will be in medical institutions and patients' homes.	Core Constructs: - Performance Expectancy - Effort Expectancy - Social Influence - Facilitating Conditions - Behavioral Intention - Use behavior Moderators - Gender - Age - Experience - Voluntariness of Use	Use behavior could not have been measured since the underlying technology is not yet commercially available and was only known to a few participants. Participants stated that they would need more information. The results could not be tied closely to UTAUT as the qualitative analysis reveals that people do not know enough about motes. The authors also measured whether people have heard of motes before the study. The authors also suggest a new construct based on the uniqueness of the domain including a richer overall model.	(Lubrin et al. 2006)

Domain (Application)	Title	Short description and research objective	Core constructs used in the study and moderators researched	UTAUT suitability for the proposed research and important factors	Source
Ubiquitous Computing (Tablet PCs)	Acceptance of Ubiquitous Computing	The study investigates user acceptance of table PCs through interviews with employees in four industries during a three-month-trial.	Core Constructs: - Performance Expectancy - Effort Expectancy - Social Influence - Facilitating Conditions - Behavioral Intention - Use behavior Moderators: Not mentioned	The paper uses a rather exploratory approach in describing the factors related to tablet PC acceptance. Nothing is said about the reliability or validity.	(Garfield 2005)
Mobile Business (Mobile Services)	Adoption of Mobile Devices/Servi ces - Searching for Answers with the UTAUT N = 157	The paper looks at answers to the adoption rates of mobile services by testing the applicability of the UTAUT to explain the acceptance of mobile devices/services. The study described in the paper used all hypotheses as given by the UTAUT.	Core Constructs: - Performance Expectancy - Effort Expectancy - Social Influence - Facilitating Conditions - Anxiety - Attitude toward using mobile device/service - Behavioral Intention - Use behavior Moderators: Not tested	The authors results point to the possibility of modifying the original UTAUT, a need to get into a more detailed study of the relationships with some larger random sample and illustrate that there is a difference in the acceptance of mobile technology and the acceptance of mobile services. They also claim that the organizational focus of the original UTAUT is problematic, because of the more personalized nature of mobile services. The authors have some reservations toward the hypotheses in the original model.	(Carlsson et al. 2006)

Domain (Application)	Title	Short description and research objective	Core constructs used in the study and moderators researched	UTAUT suitability for the proposed research and important factors	Source
Organizational (E-Learning)	Students` Acceptance of E-Learning Environments : A Comparative Study in Sweden and Lithuania. N = 67	The 2007 paper of Keller et. al. presents a cross-cultural study exploring the implementation of e-learning environments in two universities. The study used a questionnaire based on the UTAUT and innovation diffusion theory.	Core Constructs (2006): - Performance Expectancy - Effort Expectancy - Social Influence - Facilitating Conditions Additional Core Constructs (2007) - Results demonstrability - Visibility - Rate of use - Duration of time spent on use. Moderators (2007): - Age - Gender - Previous knowledge of computer use - Confidence in computer use	The 2007 paper includes a ranking of the core constructs, namely, 1. FC, 2. EE, 3. PE, 4. SI, 5. RD and 6. V.; Significant correlations were found between several constructs. - The level of acceptance varied substantially between both universities. - A significant relationship was measured between EE and a high rate of usage. Other factors, such as course content are considered to have a higher impact on the rate of use than the level of acceptance. - Cultural factors seem to have a high potential of influence in E-Learning environments. The authors point to (Hofstede 2001) for further constructs to implement in the evaluation of technology acceptance.	(Keller 2006; Keller/Hrastinski/Carlsson 2007)

Domain (Application)	Title	Short description and research objective	Core constructs used in the study and moderators researched	UTAUT suitability for the proposed research and important factors	Source
Mobile Business (Code Reading Applications)	Factors Affecting the Use of Hybrid Media Applications N = 20	The objective of the study was to find out the factors affecting the user acceptance of hybrid media applications. The focus was on code reading applications for camera phones. The research questions of the study were the following: - Which factors affect the intention to use code reading applications in consumer user segment? - Which factors affect the use of code reading applications in consumer user segment? - What kind of expectations do users have towards code reading applications?	Core Constructs: - Performance Expectancy - Effort Expectancy - Social Influence - Facilitating Conditions - Attitude toward technology - Self-Efficacy - Anxiety - Intention to use - Use Moderators - Gender - Age - Experience - Voluntariness of Use	Only two of all UTAUT hypotheses were accepted, the rest was rejected. Due to the very small sample size of only 20 people, no comparison between different user groups was possible. Within the small sample size, attitude towards technology has had the strongest affect on use intention. The results showed a positive intention towards the use of code reading technology.	(Louho/Ka llioja/Oitti nen 2006)

Domain (Application)	Title	Short description and research objective	Core constructs used in the study and moderators researched	UTAUT suitability for the proposed research and important factors	Source
Ubiquitous Computing (Framework)	Activity-centered ubiquitous computing support to localized activities N = 24	The paper presents *ActivitySpot*, a framework (conceptual model plus software implementation) for supporting localized activities, activities that are strongly tied to specific physical environments. Evaluation was done with a combination of UTAUT constructs and SCT.	Core Constructs: - Activity and Action Perception - Performance/ Usefulness - Facilitating Conditions - Personalization - Behavioral Intention - Use behavior Moderators: Not stated	The system was tested in two different scenarios. Only one of the experiments provided enough data for a valid research approach (n=24).	(Pinto/Jos 2006)
Internet (Online stocking)	The Role of Personality Traits in UTAUT Model under Online Stocking N= 196	The paper aims to combine the theory of personality traits with the UTAUT in the context of online stocking.	Core Constructs - Performance Expectancy - Effort Expectancy - Social Influence - Facilitating Conditions - Intention of Adopting Online Stocking Moderators: - Internet Experience (UTAUT) - Extraversion - Conscientiousness - Agreeableness - Neuroticism - Openness	Data analysis in the paper showed that personality traits play more important roles as moderators than external variables. Other moderators than experience were left aside in the study to simplify the research model.	(Wang/Ya ng 2005)

Domain (Application)	Title	Short description and research objective	Core constructs used in the study and moderators researched	UTAUT suitability for the proposed research and important factors	Source
Wireless technology	SME Adoption of Wireless Lan Technology: Applying the UTAUT Model	The authors seek to further validate the UTAUT model and enhance the understanding of the adoption of wireless technologies as well as SME adoption of WLAN technology. Research questions were: - Does UTAUT hold up in the context of SME? - What factors determine the adoption of WLAN in SMEs?	Core Constructs: - Performance Expectancy - Effort Expectancy - Social Influence - Facilitating Conditions - Attitude toward technology - Self-Efficacy - Anxiety - SME Behavioral Intention - SME Use Behavior Moderators: - Gender - Age - Experience - Voluntariness of Use	Not mentioned in the paper. Only the study setup is presented.	(Anderson /Schwager 2004)
Mobile Business (Mobile Technologies)	Adoption of Mobile Technologies for Chinese Consumers N = 221	The authors conducted a service with 221 Chinese nationals and tested a conceptual framework based on UTAUT with moderating variables. The constructs are similar to UAUT with different moderators.	Core Constructs: - Performance Expectancy - Effort Expectancy - Social Influence - Facilitating Conditions - Attitude on using mobile - Using Intention Moderators: - Usage experience - Gender - Education	The results indicate that gender and education are significant moderating factors while internet usage did not register as significant. The authors suggest taking cultural background and disposition into consideration for an extended UTAUT. The UTAUT was able to explain well the low education group's attitude forming process, while the UTAUT failed to explain successfully the high education group.	(Park/Yan g/Lehto 2007)

Domain (Application)	Title	Short description and research objective	Core constructs used in the study and moderators researched	UTAUT suitability for the proposed research and important factors	Source
Mobile Business (Mobile Advertising)	Consumers Perceptions and Acceptances Towards Mobile Advertising: An Empirical Study in China N = 261	The paper presents an integrated model about consumer's perceptions and acceptances towards mobile advertising. The authors created a research framework with constructs from UTAUT, IDT, and TTF. Research questions are centered around mobile advertising.	Core Constructs: - Permission - Performance Expectancy - Effort Expectancy - Social Influence - Facilitating Conditions - Individual Innovativeness - Task- Technology Fit - Behavioral Intention - Use Behavior Moderators: - Age - Gender - Experience - Voluntariness of Use	All major constructs had similar influences than in the original UTAUT model. However, in this case, Facilitating Conditions had a significant influence on use behavior. Effort Expectancy had no influence on Behavioral Intention, because of the easy availability of mobile advertising. The revised UTAUT proved to be valuable for the acceptance research validity.	(He/Lu 2007)

Table 11: Previous research on technology adoption mentioning UTAUT

UTAUT proved to be a valuable model in the literature mentioned above. While He and Lu (He/Lu 2007) researched a mobile service, Park et. al. (Park/Yang/Lehto 2007) took a look at mobile technology in total. Carlsson et al. (Carlsson et al. 2006) selected a combination of device (technology) and service (application). The table below lists used UTAUT constructs in the literature (see Table 12):

Core Constructs ->	PE	EE	SI	FC	BI	UB	ANX	ATUT	SE
(He/Lu 2007)	x	x	x	x	x	x			
(Park/Yang/Lehto 2007)	x	x	x	x	x			x	
(Anderson/Schwager 2004)	x	x	x	x	x	x	x	x	x
(Wang/Yang 2005)	x	x	x	x	x				
(Pinto/Jos 2006)						x	x	x	
(Louho/Kallioja/Oittinen 2006)	x	x	x	x	x	x	x	x	x
(Keller/Hrastinski/Carlsson 2007)	x	x	x	x		x			
(Lubrin et al. 2006)	x	x	x	x	x	x			
(Carlsson et al. 2006)	x	x	x	x	x	x	x	x	
(Garfield 2005)	x	x	x	x	x	x			
(Lee 2006)									
Summary	9	9	9	9	9	8	4	4	2

Table 12: UTAUT constructs and their use in literature

Although the construct ATUT was not used in many of the studies, it proved to be of value in determining BI in the case of Louho et. al. (Louho/Kallioja/Oittinen 2006). Near Field Communication is a mobile phone based service. To research previous use of UTAUT in the context of mobile services or NFC, Table 13 looks at the differences between the original UTAUT validation (Venkatesh et al. 2003) and two recent studies focusing on mobile services (Carlsson et al. 2006; Park/Yang/Lehto 2007).

Core Construct	Impact on (dependent construct)	Original UTAUT validation (Venkatesh et. al. 2003): Organizational setting	Park et. al results (Park et. al. 2007): Mobile services	Carlsson et al. results (Carlsson et. al. 2006): Mobile services
Performance Expectancy	Behavioral Intention	Yes	Yes	Yes
Effort Expectancy	Behavioral Intention	Yes	Yes	Yes
Social Influence	Behavioral Intention	Yes	Yes	No
Facilitating Conditions	Use behavior	Yes	No	No
Facilitating Conditions	Behavioral Intention (Park et. al.)	--	No	--
Behavioral Intention	Use behavior	Yes	--	Yes
Attitude toward technology	Behavioral Intention	No	Yes	Yes
Self-Efficacy	Behavioral Intention	No	--	Not mentioned
Anxiety	Behavioral Intention	No	--	Not clear

Table 13: Organizational technology acceptance vs. individual acceptance

The table shows the different levels of prediction specific to different domains. Most of the UTAUT studies that included the original model originated from the *organizational* use of technology context. In the definition used, Ubicomp is a technology or concept for the individual, thus the original constructs might need to be adapted more toward individual technology acceptance.

3.2.3.7 Critical Assessment of Acceptance Models

Both Mathieson (Mathieson 1991), and Taylor and Todd (Taylor/Todd 1995) compared the TAM with the TPB. The TPB is less parsimonious than TAM, TBP is not specific to information system usage, but seeks to predict a wide range of behaviors and requires instituting unique operations in every situation it is used (Mathieson/Peacock/Chin 2001). In many of the aforementioned studies, UTAUT guided the development of the researched constructs and items. But in some cases the number of participants was too small to add significantly to the validity of the constructs used (Pinto/Jos 2006; Louho/Kallioja/Oittinen 2006). Both TAM and UTAUT address organizational adoption of technology acceptance by individuals. Carlsson et al. nevertheless used all UTAUT constructs for their acceptance study of mobile devices (Carlsson et al. 2006). Their results are based on researching an consumer product outside organizational domains. Performance Expectancy and Effort Expectancy had an impact on Behavioral Intention—supporting the UTAUT hypotheses—but Social Influence did not. In case of this consumer research, Attitude Toward the Technology influenced Behavioral Intention, but Anxiety did not. Behavioral Intention had a positive influence on usage. Facilitating Conditions did not have that effect. Because of these findings it is not clear whether the individual technology acceptance makes such a difference to constructs. They point out that the adoption of Mobile Services (application level) and Mobile Devices (technology level) are asynchronous. In case of the code reading technology researched by Louho et. al., all original UTAUT constructs were used (Louho/ Kallioja/Oittinen 2006). The sample size of the study was possibly too small in order to determine the interlinking effects of the constructs.

UTAUT includes many of the technology acceptance models available and will be used as a basis for Ubicomp research. It will be included in the process model that the thesis plans to develop since it combines the most relevant aspects from the previously researched acceptance models. UTAUT needs larger sample sizes to validly evaluate the constructs. It's not possible to obtain a large sample size at an early stage of application development. The effort would be significantly higher than at later stages, where the product is closer to market launch. This effort is taken into account in developing the application process model.

3.2.4 Summary: Technology Acceptance and Implications

Ubicomp is by all means a techno-social development (Satyanarayanan 2002). By definition this requires knowledge of technological systems, social processes, and their interactions (Orlikowski/Barley 2001, 14). Ubicomp demands applications and products that are understood and accepted by normal people, not experts. In evaluating applications the need to consult the common user is critical. This is especially true considering the fact that up to now only very few people know about the existence of Ubicomp as a concept or are familiar with the underlying technologies (such as NFC) driving consumer applications. In order to get the word out about the existence of the technology and its benefits, Rogers (see section 3.2.2) believes a grassroots approach to spreading the knowledge is needed. Companies need market forecasts and support in making decisions regarding investing in the development of a new product. To generate forecasts of innovation adoption and technology acceptance, a guided process for the evaluation of NFC artifacts and their development is needed. This can be achieved by evaluating Ubicomp with case studies featuring NFC artifacts. The process model should:

• Be capable of a guided evaluation of prototypes and followed by applications before reaching the transition point with future users.

• Measure technology acceptance before a final product enters the market.

- Be capable of giving a company or corporation the possibility to change the application during the development process without risking the loss of significant investments in Ubicomp infrastructure.

- Take into account the specifics of ubiquitous computing discussed here—such as close user integration and the importance of human computer interaction.

The focus of the next section is to propose that this process model be used for developing and evaluating Ubicomp applications.

4 Designing an Ubiquitous Computing Application Development and Evaluation Process Model (UCAN)

In this chapter existing theories are used to develop a process model for developing and evaluating Ubicomp applications.

Very early on Weiser laid out a potential research method for ubiquitous computing: "the construction of working prototypes of the necessary infrastructure in sufficient quantity to debug the viability of the systems in everyday use" (Weiser 1993). Weiser might have known this without needing to experience the potential of Ubicomp technology as we see it today. Unless Ubicomp technology is readily available on the market, a thorough user evaluation is almost impossible without working prototypes (see also 3.2.4). Given this fact, the development of the process model will begin with prototypes (see Chapter 2.3) since they also provide a basis for evaluating technology acceptance (see Chapter 3.2). For the purpose of this analysis the process model is based on combining information from the HCI chapter (see Chapter 3.1) and the section on innovation adoption and technology acceptance (see Chapter 3.2). Following these sources, the process model should confirm the following goals:

- The process model assists to identify potentially negative or unneeded functions of an application in an early phase of a development process and allows changes in product development.

- It measures the technology acceptance before entering the market as a final (and thus hardly changeable) product and helps to identify marketing measures for a successful market entry.

For Ubicomp application development it is critical to be able to change and adjust an application during the development process without the risk of losing significant investments in infrastructure (sunk costs). The process model connects various stages of prototypes with adequate evaluation and analysis methods. The process model will be tested using three artifacts from case studies. It serves as a utility theory for this analysis.

This chapter employs theory to develop the process model. First, the challenges related to developing Ubicomp applications are outlined to serve as the groundwork of the model (Chapter 4.1). Then the systematic processes related to evaluating Ubicomp applications will be described (Chapter 4.2), before laying out an initial a-priori process model (Chapter 4.3). Chapter 4.4 describes how the model will be tested with a selection of case studies and why the corresponding case studies were chosen.

4.1 Ubiquitous Computing Application Development

In the previous chapters (see chapter 2.2), several challenges of Ubicomp applications were described: First, creating consumer awareness of applications presents problems. Second, high initial investments in infrastructure makes widespread adoption and quick development of Ubicomp applications almost impossible. Third, the difficulty to develop Ubicomp applications based on current knowledge is limiting the number of current applications available. Section 3.1.1 highlighted additional constraints for humans and their complex patterns in an Ubicomp world. Taking these factors into account, developing applications in a Ubicomp world differs from developing applications that require less *physical* presence. In order to shed light on Ubicomp application development, section 4.1.1 describes the importance of non-functional requirements in Ubicomp systems and the differences related to traditional systems. Section 4.1.2 elaborates on the challenges of describing Ubicomp application requirements and why prototypes are helpful in this task. Section 4.1.3 emphasizes the importance of integrating the end user in the development of products or applications. Section 4.1.4 follows with an explanation of how prototypes can provide solutions to integrating the end user. Section 4.1.5 ends by explaining the relationship between system engineering and prototyping.

4.1.1 Determining Initial Requirements

To avoid the pitfalls related to developing Ubicomp applications, determining the necessary functional requirements for developers is needed at an early stage. Davis states three reasons that make obtaining a correct and complete set of requirements difficult (Davis 1982, 5):

- The constraints on humans as information processors and problem solvers.

- The variety and complexity of information requirements.

- The complex patterns of interaction among users and analysts in defining requirements.

The Institute of Electrical and Electronics Engineers (IEEE) defines requirements as "a condition of capability needed by a user to solve a problem or achieve an objective" (standard IEEE 610.12) in (IEEE 1990, 1998). Requirements are usually defined in early stages of system development to specify what should be implemented (Kotonya/Sommerville 1998, 6). It is important to prescribe only those requirements that cover what users expect, are implementable, and can be validated (Bjorner 2006, 368-370). Requirements engineering uses systematic and repeatable techniques to determine, document, and maintain a set of requirements (Eide/Stålhane 2005). Requirements are divided into system requirements which apply to the system as a whole. According to the IEEE document (IEEE 1998), systems requirements were traditionally regarded as a document for communicating user requirements to the technical community. The collection acts as a bridge between the two groups. There are several models that help support a systems and requirements engineering process (Bjorner 2006; Kotonya/Sommerville 1998; Pomberger/Blaschek 1993, 1997).

For many types of information systems it is impossible to distinguish the requirements of the software from broader requirements of the system[14] as a whole. Ubicomp systems range from small embedded systems to large scale infrastructures, making it almost impossible to gain information on detailed software requirements at an early stage. In particular the user-

---

[14]   The distinction between system, application, and software is again relevant to an overall understanding of this thesis. Here, the range of ubiquitous computing building blocks—more of an eco-system—is described as a system that contains all the relevant parts for shaping the development of the application (see definition in chapter 2.1.1).

centered focus of Ubicomp requires a more detailed examination of system requirements than in classic command and control systems.

A requirements specification includes both functional and non-functional requirements. A functional requirement specifies a function that a system or system component must be able to perform (IEEE 1990). Most commonly they are written in documents and use cases in different structural form (Ebert 2005; Eide/Stålhane 2005). Non-functional requirements are all other types of requirements beyond functional requirements. Functional requirements describe the characteristics of specific functionalities while non-functional requirements detail the constraints of various function attributes (ISO/IEC 2004). Non-functional requirements are also the non- also defined as the non-obvious features and functions that do not serve a particular purpose, instead they are quality attributes. Examples are modifiability, reliability, security, etc.; There are several taxonomies of non-functional requirements (Ebert 2005; Eide/Stålhane 2005; ISO/IEC 2004; McCall/Richards/Walters 1977). The "Volere" taxonomy from Robertson (Robertson/Robertson 1999) includes look and feel, usability (ease of use), performance, operationality, and maintainability and portability. Furthermore they add security, cultural and political and legal.

In Ubicomp, non-functional requirements are particularly interesting. In looking back at the HCI chapter (Chapter 3.1), there are many requirements for Ubicomp applications (such as visibility, conceptual model, etc.) that do not specify a function or a use case that can later be *implemented* in the application—they are instead integral parts of a successful infrastructure. These requirements express qualitative attributes (*haptic feedback*) and non-obvious features (*everyday task specifics*). For an application development process, these requirements are a basis for all applications used during and refined throughout the process.

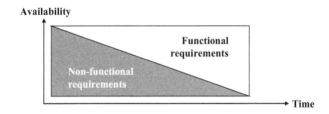

Fig. 40: The relation of functional and non-functional requirements over time

Fig. 40 shows that at the beginning of any Ubicomp application development process, a high availability of non-functional requirements exist. These might be for example requirements of usability and security, e.g. the ease of use of NFC. Functional requirements are generated over time as an application is evaluated, tested, and refined. The presence of non-functional requirements is high before the application development starts, while actual functions and use-cases might be determined later in the process.

4.1.2 Challenges

The costs of Ubicomp hardware and software infrastructure are high due to (Reilly et al. 2005):

• a lack of standards.

• a lack of know-how.

• a need to use expensive and emerging technologies, and

• the fact that they are still mostly available in laboratories only.

Ubicomp applications require costly tangible and non-physical components. The challenge lies in enabling requirement analysts to identify and prioritize requirements at an early stage in development to avoid wasting investments or incuring expensive system changes. But classic software engineering has only had to model "architectural" systems thus far, not the "physical" or "intentional" systems of ubicomp scenarios (Zambonelli/Parunak 2002a; Zambonelli/Parunak 2002b). Ubicomp has many attributes: contextuality, user-centered focus on privacy, data security, and technological limits (Abowd/Mynatt 2000). These challenges are best tackled by taking a systematic approach to what applications will look like in the future. Sandner et. al. define three layers of an Ubicomp application (Sandner/ Leimeister/Krcmar 2006):

• *Consumer World:* The consumer views the real world as the user environment that includes one or more users, interfaces, and items. The user can touch, hear, and see these components. Real world user actions control the Ubicomp application.

• *Product World:* So that the Ubicomp application is perceived by the customer, the physical product includes sensors, actuators, and interfaces (such as screen, speakers, terminals, mobile phones, etc)

• *Information World:* The virtual world includes all intangible (non-physical) components that are based on soft-ware, databases, algorithms, etc

For each layer there are different ways and methods for integrating the consumer in the product and service development process for identifying system requirements early on. Ubicomp requirement engineering needs to take these various *worlds* into account to build systems that support the eco-system of technologies. This means that if an Ubicomp application is tested by end-users, it should incorporate aspects of all the *worlds* in order to make it possible for the end user to evaluate the system as it will be introduced to markets later. To do so, an early integration of the end-user is helpful. With this, the requirements are specified and aligned from a user perspective. Early end user integration facilitates communication between users and developers, and helps to validate the interconnection between the different worlds in terms of physical and intentional systems. Early integration allows an end user to experience the system physically (haptically) and to gain a full appreciation of its functions and implications (Resatsch et al. 2007a).

4.1.3 End-User Integration

To lower the high failure rates of new products (Gourville 2006), companies strive to identify market and consumer needs right from the start. A common way for determining these needs is to involve consumers in the development process (Gruner/Homburg 2000). According to Nambisan (Nambisan 2002), customers can be involved in generating ideas for new products, co-creating these products, testing finished products, and providing end user support. Including customers in new product development impacts time to market and development costs. There are two concepts in the area of user integration: (1) lead users and (2) participatory design.

(1) Lead users: The extent to which customers can optimize the process varies significantly, therefore von Hippel proposed what are known as *lead users* to provide some insight (von Hippel 1986, 1988, 2001, 2005). Von Hippel put forward *user toolkits for innovation* with which users can actively create preliminary designs, simulate or construct prototypes, evaluate functions, and then improve the design (von Hippel 2001). *Lead users* face specific needs months and years before the mass market jumps on the wagon. Solving these needs is very important to the lead users—thus they are internally motivated to assist in new product development (von Hippel 1986; Urban/von Hippel 1988). Furthermore lead users can fulfill an important function in the pre-launch phases of a product and fuel the diffusion process in the post-launch phase as opinion leaders (Morrison/Roberts/Midgley 2000; Urban/von Hippel 1988).

Lead users have an opinion leadership with their peers and are networked at a certain level (Morrison/Roberts/Midgley 2000). Establishing word-of-mouth and other marketing measures, as well as identifying and utilizing lead users to influence opinion is difficult at this state in the development of Ubicomp where the technologies are too new to the market and applications are not yet available in markets. The potential to integrate a user or future customer in the process can help support Ubicomp product development.

For two reasons this analysis focuses on prototypes as a first step in the development process: First, given that Ubicomp is currently only at an early stage of its development, people are unaware of the concept's purported potential. Ubicomp technology might satisfy the needs of lead users, however in order to explain its potential, even tech-savvy lead users need something to experience. Second, the complexity of building a Ubicomp system cannot be done by lead users and tool kits in the first step. On the other hand prototyping technologies have traditionally supported artifact design, and developers typically accept a prototype as a physical prop of design (Abowd et al. 2005).

(2) Participatory design: Another popular approach for integrating users is *participatory design* (Muller 1993; Muller et al. 1991). Participatory design is a set of practices, theories, and studies related to end-users as participants in the development of software and hardware computer products and computer-based activities (Greenbaum/Kyng 1992; Muller 2003). It also involves collaboration between users and developers in the design process. The concept has unresolved issues, such as the participation with a non-organized workforce or the need for visual and hands-on techniques, which violates the requirements of universal availability (Muller 2003). Visual and hands-on techniques are also difficult in the case of Ubicomp technology because of its intrinsically complex technological nature. Another weakness of participatory design concerns formal evaluations and data. A study for measuring success would require that a product is implemented and marketed twice—once with participation, once without (Muller 2003). This is almost impossible because of the high costs and huge effort involved. According to Blomberg (Blomberg/Henderson 1990), the process of participatory design should be about targeting improving the quality of the user's work life, using collaborative development, and creating an iterative process. These tenets may also serve as guidelines for developing an Ubicomp specific process.

Participatory design commonly uses low-tech prototypes to create new relationships between people and technology. The end-user may reshape the low-tech materials in a *design-by-doing* process ((Bødker/Grønbæk/Kyng 1995), cf. (Muller 2003)). This low-tech approach has produced a range of benefits including enhanced communication and understanding, enhanced incorporation of new ideas, better working relations, and practical applications with measured success.

In addition various prototypes make it possible to identify design constraints and the contextual grounding of the design earlier on in the development process (Muller 2003). They also allow users to experiment with the technology and the concept of the prototypes. Different approaches have also been more successful in developing products when co-development with prototypes was integrated into the actual process (Anderson/Crocca 1993).

4.1.4 Prototypes

Prototypes have been a common component of software development methodology (Floyd 1983, 1989). Prototyping is a way to incorporate communication and feedback in software development. A distinction is made between *vertical prototypes* and *horizontal prototypes*. In *vertical prototypes* the system's functions are implemented, and selected functions are included in an evaluation. In *horizontal prototypes* there is no detailed implementation of functions—it is more of a demonstration tool [Floyd '83]. Which prototype is more relevant to Ubicomp is the subject of discussion for the next sections.

The emphasis must be placed on evaluating prototypes, because this makes it possible to define the functional selection and determines further use. Bleek, Jeenicke et al. (2002) claimed that *traditional* prototyping is only partially valid for the development of web-based applications, because of the diversity and complexity of web-projects [Bleek, Jeenicke et al. '02]. To what extent this is also valid for Ubicomp is not clear. To help future users fully understand the potential of Ubicomp applications, the use of experimental aspects can help them in an active way (Buchenau/Suri 2000). Buchenau and Suri (2000) describe the use of experience prototypes to evaluate how users experience new products. They recreate and study simulated experiences, but do not conduct these in real life situations—a step that is necessary to wholly understand the consequences of Ubicomp (see also section 3.1.1.3).

To overcome this aspect, Abowd, Hayes et al. (2005) recognized early on a need to take a different approach to Ubicomp prototyping and developed what are known as *paratypes* as a way of experience prototyping (Abowd et al. 2005). The paratype leverages real life situations (Iachello et al. 2006). The authors developed a set of pre-conditions for evaluation: It must be unobtrusive, gathering only essential information when evaluating the prototype, be compatible with the participant's expected cognitive load in the use situation, and be compatible with the physical environment. The paratypes combine event-contingent experience sampling with experience prototyping. Therefore they are used for evaluating high-level or implicit interactions where real life references are needed (Iachello et al. 2006). Besides this meta differentiation, there are usually four different kinds of prototypes used in practice (Davis 1982; Kranz/Schmidt 2005):

•   *Paper-prototyping*: paper sketch of a user interface with enough detail to make design decisions and usability evaluations. The evaluation can be conducted with usability inspections, focus groups, or simple user tests (see also story boarding as a support (Truong/Hayes/Abowd 2006)).

•   *Mock-up prototyping*: refers to *low-fidelity prototypes*, such as paper illustrations, screenshots, or simple configurations of screens with limited interaction.

•   *Wizard of Oz prototyping*: This technique requires users to interact with an interface in which the responses are being generated by a human, not a computer.

•   *Video prototyping*: Visualizing the interactive behavior of a system using video animation.

It is important that—also according to the findings in chapter 3.1 (HCI)—e.g. when talking about a haptic interface, only a physical prototype is subject to a formal evaluation. There are various ways of dealing with prototype development in the case of physical prototypes (Davis 1982; Kranz/Schmidt 2005):

•   *Create one-time throw-away prototypes:* the prototype is built and tested and thrown away after evaluation.

•   *Create incremental prototypes:* the final system is partitioned into smaller systems which are integrated and built step by step into the final version.

•   *Create evolutionary prototypes*: each prototype serves as basis for the next generation of prototypes.

The paradigm of ubiquitous computers and the particularities of inter-weaving the user in everyday computational scenarios make for a very close interrelation of potential users with software development. A poorly managed dialogue between users and developers might lead to unwanted results (Schrage 1996, 3). There is a difference in innovation culture between a specification-driven innovation and a prototype-driven one. Specification-driven cultures need market-research data before they can move concepts into the prototyping cycle. In prototyping cultures, the prototype is used to elicit market feedback before heading on to production (Schrage 1996, 3). In Ubicomp, where the market is yet to be defined, a *prototyping culture* is needed. It is then important to align the various described forms of prototypes with adequate evaluation methods.

4.1.5 System Engineering and Prototyping

This chapter started by describing both the difficulties of Ubicomp application development and its challenges. These can be overcome by integrating the end-user according to how he experiences Ubicomp applications with prototypes. As Abowd (1999) mentioned, applications that motivate users are an important part of ubiquitous computing (Abowd 1999). Therefore figuring out what is *motivating* about an application is a way to determine the usage potential of Ubicomp. A possible process model should start with an initial vision. This vision is then introduced into a system engineering and prototyping process in order to develop a product with an expected market acceptance (see Fig. 41).

Fig. 41: From vision to market

The previous sections addressed the middle part of requirement engineering as a part of system engineering and the role of prototypes in Ubicomp. Early user integration plays an important role in Ubicomp. We will use the term *customer* as the end user who might purchase a product or service in the final stage. The final product will have customer acceptance if the market accepts the product and enough units are sold[15] (see Fig. 42).

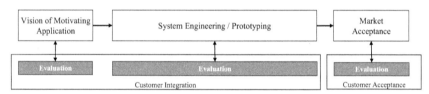

Fig. 42: Evaluation phases

As described in previous chapters Ubicomp is directed toward everyone and not only tech-savvy people. For this reason, the evaluation should be conducted not with lead users, but with average users who are likely to become customers in the future. For market entry, the lead user concept can be introduced at a later stage—but not for the development phase. The result is a system of company-customer integration (Wikström 1996; Milgrom/Roberts 1990).

These chapters have laid the foundation of the process model by defining a starting point (the vision of a motivating application), then the system engineering process with prototypes, followed by a market view (market acceptance). These processes are emphasized in various evaluation phases, and the steps they produce should be analyzed. How this can be achieved is discussed in the following chapter.

---

[15]   Of course, this is a trivial simplification on what makes a product successful and how to measure this. This idea should show an additional process path after the development.

4.2 Evaluating Ubicomp Applications

Compared to standard software and technology, the Ubicomp concept is determined to a large extent by its physical aspect, which requires the user to interact with computers in a different way. The challenges to analyzing and evaluating such systems are detailed in section 4.2.1. The prototyping evaluation is outlined in section 4.2.2, and finally, differences in the evaluations of specific prototype phases are explained in section 4.2.3.

4.2.1 Challenges

As described in chapter 2.2.2 people tend to prefer what they already know and Ubicomp is a rather unknown concept for most people. It is difficult to judge technology based on unknown procedures (such as touch-based interaction) without actually being able to interact with it. The difficulties of evaluating Ubicomp applications were discussed early on by Scholtz et.al. (Scholtz et al. 2002) and Abowd et. al. (Abowd/Mynatt/Rodden 2002) and have also been discussed in the area of mobile applications (Holmquist et al. 2002). As Carter and Mankoff (2004) explain: the "difficulty is due to issues like scale and ambiguity, and a tendency to apply Ubicomp in ongoing, daily life settings unlike task and work oriented desktop systems." (Carter/Mankoff 2004, 1). They also conclude that evaluating Ubicomp in an early stage of design is difficult, making it hard to develop later applications with a focus on user needs (Carter/Mankoff 2004). The following challenges arise when evaluating Ubicomp applications:

* *People are not aware of the technology and its potentials.* Therefore they tend to value the solely idea of a future system different to their statements when they actually try out an application. Ubicomp applications need to be seen in action. It requires understanding and measuring how people perform tasks or engage in activities where computing only makes up part of the user experience (Scholtz et al. 2002).

* *Technology acceptance* cannot be tested with only few users at a very early stage, since in order to run a valid analysis a larger sample size is needed.

* *Building a working prototype and implementing it in the field can cause massive costs* (Infrastructure, setup costs, handset costs, etc). Therefore evaluating such a prototype requires at least the ability to make pre-qualification of the application and the impact on users. But Ubicomp systems are ubiquitous by definition, and therefore require a certain overall presence. If this is not possible, working prototypes need to simulate this ubiquitousness in at least limited areas.

* *The evaluation needs real users, not laboratory settings* (see also (Scholtz et al. 2002)) which makes using grad students difficult.

Based on these challenges in evaluating Ubicomp applications, a first approach is to begin with evaluating small low-tech prototypes (see previous sections). Prototypes build a basis for user experience, especially in the forms of pre-prototypes or paratypes as explained by (Davis/Venkatesh 2004; Abowd et al. 2005). This method fully complies to design research approaches, where the artifact (Simon 1980; Simon 1996) can be the later prototype.

4.2.2 Evaluating Prototypes

Davis and Venkatesh (1989) used the Technology Acceptance Model (TAM) as a basis for their research on early user integration with pre-prototype testing and their findings suggested that users' expectations about a system, captured using reliable measures on key expectations, were accurate even before hands-on use of a prototype system (Davis 1986; Davis 1989; Davis/Bagozzi/Warshaw 1989). Davis' original setup model had five stages: Initial idea, low-fidelity prototype, initial working prototype, refined prototype, and final product.

In Fig. 43, the time frame for developing an IS is depicted on the horizontal axis, the vertical axis shows the magnitude of development time, cost, and effort as they increase during the project. At the time of the Low Fidelity Prototype, sufficient information is available to describe to potential users how a system is about to perform and to state the requirements of the application. Davis' (2004) findings were positive that user acceptance could already be determined at this point of time. Stimuli in the form of non-interactive pre-prototypes could yield good approximations of user perceptions after weeks of direct interaction with the system (Davis/Venkatesh 2004). The acceptance should be evaluated already in the first stages and is therefore closely related to the previous steps. The model was tested in an organizational innovation setting based on TAM constructs.

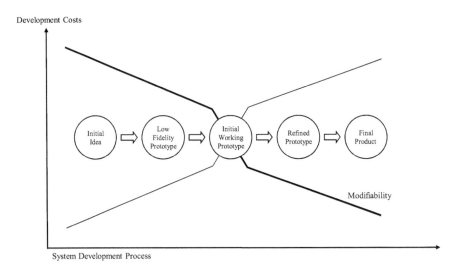

Fig. 43: Preprototype user acceptance testing
Source: (Davis/Venkatesh 2004)

Davis and Venkatesh show that user acceptance can be explored and tested earlier in the system development process than is done traditionally. This would help companies to make *go/ no-go* decisions (see Fig. 43). By the time functional requirements are fixed (typically after the low-fidelity prototype phase), less than 25% of the total cost has typically been incurred (Davis/Venkatesh 2004). Furthermore the functions can be better matched onto user needs. As Ubicomp might need a huge set of non-functional requirements to match the application with user needs, it is even more important to determine early on the level of technology acceptance. The original model had five stages, of which four can be significantly differentiated (Davis/Venkatesh 2004):

• *Initial idea:* The vision, or the first draft of a future application. Requirements in this stage are mainly drawn from previous information or experiences. The initial idea needs to be visualized somehow to show the customer a stable concept (paper-prototype as one time throw away prototype).

• *Low-fidelity prototype:* The low-fidelity prototype, or hands-on pre-prototype is a horizontal prototype in which future functions are shown, but not implemented in the whole spectrum. Requirements can be tested and the whole concept can be discussed in this stage.

• *Initial working prototype:* Extends the low-fidelity prototype to a degree in which most functions are fully implemented, making it almost a final product.

• *(Refined prototype):* In Davis' paper the refined prototype is not clearly distinguished from the other phases. It can be assumed that it is an improved working prototype and subsume it in the *initial working prototype* phase with an iteration.

• *Final product:* The final product is the entire application on the market.

These stages build the ground for an evaluation connected to application development. To make refining of the outcome of the relevant phase possible, a *refine* phase is implemented in between each of the phases (see Fig. 44) in order to allow for adjustments in the requirements and specification for the next stage of development.

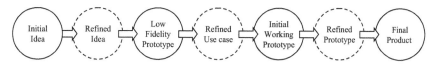

Fig. 44: Davis' approach extended

Whereas Davis used the TAM to measure progress, a different approach needs to be taken in the early phases given the amount of effort required in a standard TAM measurement procedure (see Chapter 3.2.3.3): a company would need to include a sizeable number of participants and enough time to make interpretations and changes. To facilitate this step, the next section takes a look at evaluation approaches that match up with the early phases in this process.

4.2.3 Evaluation in Specific Prototype Phases

IS research can be done either quantitatively or qualitatively (see Table 14):

Research paradigm	Methods
Quantitative	Non-empirical research (analytical, such as formal methods (econometrics), numerical methods (mathematical modelling)), survey methods, experimental
Qualitative	Action research, case study research, ethnography, grounded theory

Table 14: Classification of research methods
Source: (Myers 1997)

For an overview of various research methods and the underlying philosophical perspectives, see Myers (Myers 1997). Case study research is the most common qualitative method in IS (Orlikowski/Baroudi 1991; Myers 1997). For evaluating prototypes, an analysis of research approaches in relation to the possibility of using it for prototypes and its outcome in the specific phases is needed (see Table 15).

Name of approach	Roots	Description	Common literature examples
Non-empirical research (Analytical)	Conceptual thinking, psychology	Examples are theorem proof (formal methods to mathematical abstractions), simulation (formal model of a complex environment, in order to perform experimentation not possible in a real-world setting), conceptual research (opinion and speculation, and comprises philosophical and argumentative/dialectic analysis), futures research, scenario-building, review of existing literature	Most thesis' include parts of these approaches (see (Clarke 2001))
Experimental research	Biology and physics	The researcher has strong control over the environment being observed. This requires an artificial or semi-artificial environment in order to control variables. Variables are manipulated over time, numeric data collection takes place and models are tested through statistical analysis.	(Darley/Latane 1968; Latane/Nida/Wilson 1981; Roethlisberger/Dickson 1939)
Survey research	Economy and sociology	The researcher has analysed a considerable sample that permits quantitative evaluation. Survey research is applied to validate models or hypotheses.	(Ainlay/Singleton Jr/Swigert 1992; Wechsler et al. 1994; Stier/Lewin-Epstein 2003)
Case research	Business	An analysis of cases is used to build up or validate models or theories. Analysis can be done by the collection of textual data via interviews, story-telling, focus groups or online surveys. It is the most commonly used method in IS (Orlikowski/Baroudi 1991; Yin 2002)	(Ferratt et al. 1995; Sacco 1994; Markus 1983)
Grounded theory	Socio-psychology	A research method that seeks to develop theory that is grounded in data systematically gathered and analyzed (Myers 1997).	(Orlikowski 1993)

Ethnographic research	Social and cultural anthropology	Ethnographic research requires the researcher (ethnographer) to spend a significant amount of time in the field. They seek to place the phenomena studied in their social and cultural context (Myers 1997).	(Hughes/Randall/Shap iro 1992; Pettigrew 1985; Preston 1991)
Action research	Socio-psychology	Intention is to improve the participating organisation (client organisation) and the generation of knowledge. The researcher has typically less control over the environment but is expected to apply interventions.	(Olesen/Myers 1999; Lindgren/Henfridsson/ Schultze 2004)

Table 15: Overview on research approaches in information systems

These various forms of research come with different efforts and results. To consider are the ease of administration, time to administer, the clarity of results, cost, reliability and data availability (Fraenkel/Wallen 1990, 120-125). As for integration into the various phases of the process model, the following research methods are discussed:

- *Non-empirical research* will help to determine the various *worlds* (see section 4.1.2) of a Ubicomp application. It can be used to conceptualize applications and determine initial ideas It can also be used in its mathematical formulation as a tool for a market evaluation in a very late stage after the product has been successfully launched in markets.

- *Experimental research* is an option if the research controls the setting. This control is difficult to achieve in Ubicomp due to the ubiquity of the technology and the various entry points required to use it. It may be suitable in a late stage of the application.

- *Survey research* is suitable, but in its quantitative form also costly and time-consuming, if basic rules of data validity are followed. Qualitative surveys, such as interviews or storytelling methods, can be cheaper and less time-consuming—they are suitable in earlier phases of prototype research.

- *Case research* is suited as a research method to treat every artifact as its own case study. For the course of this analysis, the case studies represent the framing of the artifact in its environment. The analysis uses a combination of case research with other research methods to improve validity of measures.

- *Grounded theory* is focused on theory development, which is not a direct goal for product development with prototypes in Ubicomp.

- *Ethnographic research* requires the researcher to stay in the field. This is particularly interesting if the Ubicomp technology is available in the field. This is not yet the case, therefore the possible research questions are rather limited to existing technologies such as mobile phones. Due to the amount of time required, this method is particularly ill-suited for the quick iteration of prototyping as mentioned above.

- *Action research* is not a valid instrument because it aims primarily to improve an organisation. Ubicomp targets primarily the individual end-user in which different forms of evaluation are better suited.

This leaves survey research as a method and case research. Case studies are used to test the process model. Within the cases, several variances of survey methods are used. Table 16 matches the discussed phases of the process model with potential methods of research based on the maximal effort put into the prototype to reach the goal of the evaluation in the respective phase.

Prototype stage	Detail of prototype	Goal of evaluation	Restrictions of the prototype	Potential methods	Requirement for research method	Conceptionally rec. nethod
Initial idea	Paper-based concept description	Understand general problem, Conceptual tests, initial requirements	In this early phase the effort of building a full application is too high (especially with Ubicomp technology). With a paper version, not many users can be questioned.	Storytelling, storyboards, paper-based interviews, expert interviews, Non-empirical research (literature based)	Quick to pursue, very explorative, based on existing idea to demonstrate	Expert interview / Personal interviews
Low fidelity Prototype	Hands-on pre-prototype with basic use cases implemented	Generate general system requirements, learn about the system and technology acceptance	Although general requirements can be derived from the initial concept tests, the effort for a fully working prototype is too high. Also, asking too many users with a not fully functional prototype could lead to a misperception.	Focus-groups, interviews, surveys	More detailed, evaluate services.	Focus-groups
Initial Working prototype	Working prototype - most functions are fully implemented	Evaluate technology acceptance on a broad level	The prototype must now work in the field with more real users to test it. The effort put in the prototype is higher due to a complete implementation based on the requirements drawn from the previous phases.	Interviews, Survey	Technology acceptance can be measured according to the previous chapters by a survey. However, it needs quite a large sample to draw conclusions.	Survey & Usage data

Final product	Final product in market after launch	Improve product on market numbers	The product is not a prototype, and is therefore dependent on market power and consumer acceptance.	Non-empirical research, Statistics, Market research	Companies must draw conclusions on product improvement without changing the whole product.	Market research based on market data

Table 16: Prototype stages and suggested research methods

The starting point is a technology trigger for generating an initial idea that provides a basis for the process. The vision of the motivating application can be discussed based on a literature review and ideas. In this case it is NFC as a part of Ubicomp applications. According to the table above various possible forms of research match the process. Fig. 45 aligns the potential research methods with the proposed process.

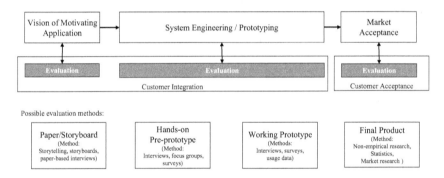

Fig. 45: Possible evaluation methods

Since NFC services are not yet available on a large scale (Resatsch et al. 2007a), a reframing of user acceptance testing to develop a final product that includes the ideas of early evaluation cycles are shown in Fig. 46 (Resatsch et al. 2008):

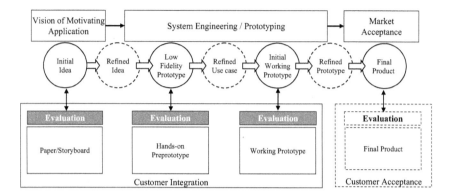

Fig. 46: Extended approach

Any initial ideas concerning *motivating applications* (Abowd 1999) need to be discussed with colleagues based on an actor, technology, product and service and strategy outlook model (Sandner/Leimeister/Krcmar 2006) which uses the various worlds as discussed in section 4.1.2. This leads to a stable concept of the application that can be shown on papers to users who participate in an interview. But, since most people outside the research area are not familiar with Ubicomp applications and their potential, valid system engineering is needed to build low-fidelity prototypes (also referred to as *hands-on preprototypes* (see also (Abowd et al. 2005))) that can explain how the applications will work in one or two use cases. As discussed by Davis and Venkatesh (Davis/Venkatesh 2004), paper evaluation succeeded in determining the later acceptance of intra-organizational tools. However, within Ubicomp— and outside of organizational contexts—imagination alone might not be sufficient to clarify peoples' questions and for asking about a later usage of the system. With the low-fidelity or hands-on preprototype, built according to the *paratype* ideas of Abowd et al. (Abowd et al. 2005), we seek to properly understand the future users' issues and demands for the desired application.

This evaluation includes actor-based technology acceptance research (Davis/Bagozzi/ Warshaw 1989) and previous practices, user felt needs/problems, innovativeness, and social systems' norms according to Rogers (Rogers 1995). The evaluation could be conducted with focus groups. The results build the basis for an initial working prototype. The key facts of ubiquitous computing software, such as situatedness, openness, locality in control, and locality in interactions are planned at this stage (Zambonelli/Parunak 2002a).

The initial working prototype extends the low-fidelity prototype to an almost final product with all use cases implemented following the non-functional and functional requirements. This prototype should/has to be evaluated on a broader scale, for example with a survey among designated test users in the field. Based on this version, the last stage is another iteration toward a final product. This includes the actor (target group), technology (ecosystem), product and services, and finally the strategy of the product (business case). The final step is the acceptance of the product which is simply measured by numbers of units sold and available market data.

4.3 A-priori: The Ubiquitous Computing Application Development and Evaluation Process Model (UCAN)

The previous sections developed step-by-step a theoretical process model. This chapter outlines the "Ubiquitous Computing Application Development and Evaluation Process Model (UCAN)". It is the underlying utility theory of this work (see Fig. 47).

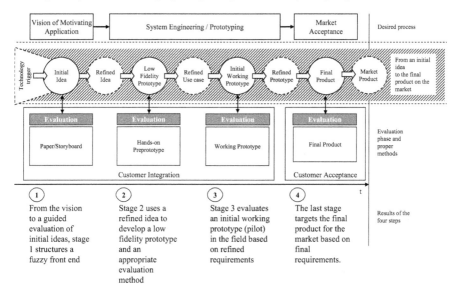

Fig. 47: Development and evaluation of Ubicomp applications (UCAN)

Based on the comprehensive phases in which the vision of a motivating idea is the starting point, leads to the system engineering and prototyping phase and finally on to the product, the UCAN process consists of four stages.

Stage 1 transforms the fuzzy front end generated by the technology trigger into an initial idea. Stage 2 takes a refined idea and develops a low fidelity prototype and evaluates it according to the method suitable to that stage of the prototype. Stage 3 evaluates an initial working prototype (pilot) in the field with larger numbers of test user. The last stage (4) targets the final product for the market. The evaluation methods in the lower section are selected to match the status of the prototype development in the respective phase. The initial idea and its respective paper prototype is tested with interviews, while the second may use focus groups or interviews. The working prototype in the field is evaluated according the UTAUT technology acceptance model (see section 3.2.3.6 - Unified Theory of Acceptance and Use of Technology (UTAUT) and section 3.2.3.7).

The general problem space of the utility theory will be the directed development and evaluation of IS applications based on NFC technology. The process model intends to generate improvements in this various phases of development by introducing evaluation methods from behavioral sciences and apply these to specific phases of the process.

This process model will be tested in various phases with three case studies in order to propose possible development and evaluation strategies for NFC-based Ubicomp applications. From the results of the case studies design guidelines for NFC applications are developed. In this book special frameworks for evaluation will not be developed, rather existing (and approved) evaluation frameworks in various phases of the evolution of an Ubicomp application will be used and mapped. Furthermore the focus of the evaluation is on the outcome of the process model and its artifacts.

4.4 Selection of Case Studies

This chapter explains how the artifacts and the case studies were selected for different phases of the UCAN process based on NFC technology: in section 4.4.1 NFC applications are specified and their market status quos are determined. Section 4.4.2 includes the selection criteria in order to identify the motivation for conducting these cases (Section 4.4.3). Section 4.4.4 describes how the case studies were conducted, before providing an overview of the selected case studies in section 4.4.5.

4.4.1 NFC Applications

There are usually two forces that affect a market: *business opportunities* and *technology advances* (Scott-Morton 1991). The rather classic approach speaks of *technology-push* and *market-pull*, in which either the technical opportunity raises entrepreneurial efforts or an increase in demand leverages the inventive activity (Schmookler 1966). Which effect is stronger is often debated (Goldenberg/Lehmann/Mazursky 2001; Astebro/Dahlin 2005), however it helps to categorize applications in the IS domain using the example of NFC. Fig. 48 shows push vs. pull services in NFC.

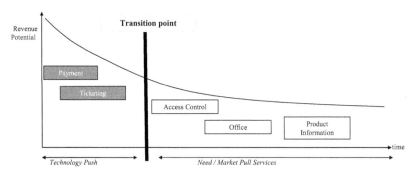

Fig. 48: Push vs. Pull services
Source: adapted from (Vilmos 2008)

For a basic overview of technology-push and market-pull, Fig. 48 shows revenue potential based on the amount of transactions possible and the potential global customer base. Revenue potential is limited by the required NFC infrastructure investments, availability of NFC handsets, and number of partners and standards needed for interoperability. These factors may change over the course of time. As a result the horizontal axis indicates time from the market introduction of NFC to a widespread availability of NFC services.

4.4.1.1 Technology Push

Certain applications have a good potential for generating high revenue and a solid customer base. Payment and ticketing are examples of areas that are capable of generating significant revenues given the high number of similar transactions. The application of NFC in payment transactions promises a solid future customer base as long as a demand exists for combining mobile phone and NFC-based credit card transactions (ABIResearch 2007). In the beginning payment application is limited due to closed loop solutions, in which geographical coverage is low, security requirements are not matched, and interoperability is not given between operator networks, credit card providers, handset manufacturers, and banks.

Only large global service providers can utilize both services given the underlying set of operating standards that must be met, the technical parameters set by partners, interoperability rules, as well as financial resources to build the infrastructure. Because of these limitations, only large mobile network operators and large transport associations are able to implement these kinds of applications (NFCForum 2007c).

Since customers hesitate to use different applications for the same service, the applications and underlying sources need to be accepted unconditionally and available globally. Most customers, especially in the payment area, are tied to one bank. In order to create a widely available, interoperable system, an enormous up-front effort is required to develop the proper standardization procedures. This can only be recouped if customers are then transferred to the new system. Therefore payment and ticketing are considered technology push services.

4.4.1.2 Market Pull

On the other hand, there are many applications with less revenue potential but a large overall combined customer base that makes for a market pull effect. First, there are business to business applications, such as access control systems or office-related applications based on NFC that are lower in reach and revenue potential. Then there are applications, such as product information, that may need an even higher penetration of NFC infrastructure. This can only be the case at a later point in time when market need for the product has increased in that NFC is available on a greater number of handsets, and is known as a technology that benefits customers.

Based on this distinction, the case studies conducted for this analysis were selected according to the availability of NFC services.

4.4.2 Selection Criteria

Various selection criteria determined which case studies were conducted. The UCAN process model was the basis for selection in the three phases: initial idea, low-fidelity prototype, and initial working prototype (see chapter 4.3). Three selection criteria were chosen upfront: (1) the temporal aspect of technology push/market pull, (2) availability of services, and (3) author involvement.

(1) Time: The three case studies were selected according to the already described temporal difference between technology push and market pull. Since the UCAN process describes application development from a very early stage to the final product, the case studies in the early phases (initial idea, low-fidelity prototype) are considered to be introduced further away in the future. This made it possible to test the usability of the process and for achievable results from an early stage onwards.

(2) Availability of services: At the time of the analysis, first mobile phones with NFC were available, so were the NFC tags. These components were used for the initial idea and the low-fidelity prototype.

(3) Author involvement: The author was involved in the development of two case studies, while in the third case, the author participated in the research efforts of the company..

In addition to these three aspects, a further aspect was the level of product performance required by the average user. Norman describes the transition point at which the level of product performance required by the average users is met by the technology. NFC is still in the technology domination phase. The level of performance required by average users is not met given limited interoperability and lack of NFC handsets on the market.

Three case studies have then been selected: *Easymeeting*, a meeting room management system, the *Mobile Prosumer*, a smart product information system, and *Public Transport Company*, an NFC-based mobile phone ticketing system for use in public transportation systems (see Fig. 49).

Case study name	Description
easymeeting	Meeting room management system
Mobile Prosumer	Smart product information system at the Point of Sale for consumers
Public Transport Company	NFC-based mobile phone ticketing system in public transport

Fig. 49: Case study overview

The case studies were selected in the technology domination area before reaching the transition point, i.e. the point at which the technology matches average users needs (see Fig. 50).

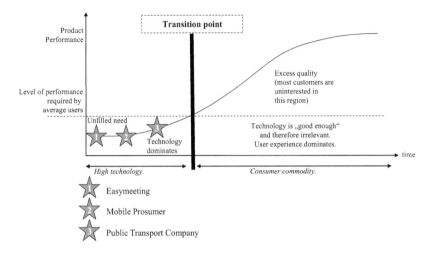

Fig. 50: Selection of case studies

The case studies in Fig. 50 depict the phases over time. Easymeeting as a first case study was developed at a very early stage of NFC component availability. In contrast the second case study, the Mobile Prosumer, was developed when the first market phones were released. The public transport company case was conducted at the point when NFC phones were already available to the average consumer.

4.4.3 Motivation

The UCAN process as described in chapter 4 demands a certain vision for a motivating application. For all three cases, this vision will be described using existing literature:

- *Easymeeting:* Easymeeting is designed to be a *smart* office solution, based on existing Ubicomp technologies (Near Field Communication). From the early Xerox PARC (Weiser/Gold/Brown 1999) research, many Ubicomp prototypes focused on office settings such as the 1992 active badge location system by Want et al. (Want et al. 1992; Want et al. 1995). Further work focused on location tracking (Elrod et al. 1993; Petzold et al. 2005; Ward/Jones/Hopper 1997) of workers, visual support (Abowd et al. 1998; Pinhanez 2001), and human-computer interaction (Poupyrev/Okabe/Maruyama 2004; Ballagas et al. 2003). Clearly office work is part of everyday life for many people and therefore a relevant field in which to continue working on the original Ubicomp vision.

- *Mobile Prosumer:* The Mobile Prosumer is a smart product information service for consumers. While consumers use the Internet as an easily accessible source of product information at home or at work, this information is not easily accessible at purchase time. In part, this is because many purchases are ad hoc, that is, made after searching for something else that closely matches a perceived need or made on impulse. Thus, the consumer must rely on the expertise, skill, and trustworthiness of sales assistants to provide relevant product information at the Point of Sale (PoS). Lack of knowledge and information about a product can make this purchase decision difficult (Kaas 1994;

Bettmann 1973; Mitchell 1992; Mitchell/Boustani 1994; Aßmann 2003). Useful information, such as user-generated product ratings, product reviews, or opinions from friends and family would be a great help at purchase time. Radio Frequency Identification (RFID) could be a solution to this problem since it can be configured to bridge offline and online worlds. The recent increase in RFID implementations enables the development of user-centered ubiquitous computing (Ubicomp) applications—by merging physical products and information products into so-called "smart products" (Loebbecke/Palmer 2006; Mattern 2005b; Maass/Filler 2006). "Smart products" and smart product information services are sought to help lower negative influences on purchase decisions, such as uncertainty and making shopping a more positive experience.

• *Public Transport Company:* Ubicomp brings together a wide range of disparate technological areas in focusing on a common vision (Bell/Dourish 2007). Especially in the area of public transport, a wide range of Ubicomp technologies is embedded in information technology systems: GPS-Tracking of buses[16], a live messaging service on bus arrival times[17], data on large display systems, and total surveillance with video cameras[18] (all using the example of Berlin, Germany). Furthermore it is already possible to buy tickets with a mobile phone in most German cities (Berlin, Frankfurt, and Munich). Even though a Ubicomp infrastructure already exists, people still deal with inaccessible ticket vending machines and overcrowded stations and trains. A way to work around these negative effects is to introduce smart card systems to public mass transit. However uniting smart cards and mobile phones is another way to further integrate public transport systems into the fabric of everyday life. The third case study takes this into account and focuses on the implications of mobile phone ticket purchasing with NFC.

4.4.4 Conducting the Case Studies

A *case study* is an empirical way to investigate contemporary phenomenon within a real-life context, especially when the boundaries between phenomenon and context are not clearly evident (Yin 1984, 13). Case studies possess five research design components that Yin considers important: a study's question, its propositions, its unit of analysis, the logic linking the data to the propositions, and the criteria for interpreting the findings. The next chapters use these components to explain the impact of Ubicomp applications according to prototypes. The method also allows researchers to understand the complexity of the process taking place and to gain valuable insights into new topics. Each case study was conducted according to the relevant phase in the UCAN process. Every case study provides the name, a short description,

---

[16]   Source: http://www.bvg.de/index.php/en/Bvg/Detail/folder/526/id/1879/nb/1/name/Real-Time+Information – accessed 2008-05-24

[17]   Source: http://www.bvg.de/index.php/de/Bvg/Detail/folder/301/rewindaction/Index/archive/1/year/2004/id/39632/name/Jetzt+kommen+Stra%DFenbahn+und+Bus+aufs+Handy – accessed 2008-05-24

[18]   Source: http://www.tagesspiegel.de/berlin/Polizei-Justiz-Raub;art126,2536004 – accessed 2008-05-24

the study's core question related to Ubicomp, the propositions, the unit of analysis, and the goal of the study (Yin 1984, 2002).

4.4.5 Overview

Fig. 51 shows the case studies as placed in the UCAN process.

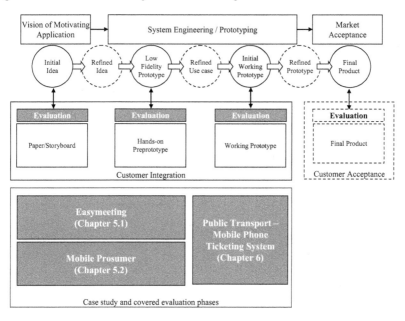

Fig. 51: Case studies and UCAN process model

Easymeeting and the *Mobile Prosumer* are relatively far away from realization (see section 4.4.1.2), therefore they can only be researched in the early phases of the UCAN process. The public transportation company working prototype (*PTC*) was ready to be evaluated in the field (see section 4.4.1.1) and served as an initial working prototype in the process model.

For this analysis the technology trigger for entering the UCAN process is the introduction of RFID in mobile phones as *Near Field Communication*. NFC is considered a valid Ubicomp technology (see section 2.1.5), which fulfils most of the requirements demanded by HCI from section 3.1.3. All developed artifacts and the case studies addressed are built upon NFC technology.

The goal of the case studies is to

*   Improve and theorize about the developed process model (UCAN).

*   Extend the domain knowledge in Ubicomp using the example of Near Field Communication (NFC) —determine design guidelines of NFC-based Ubicomp applications.

The goal of chapter 5 is to describe the first two case studies: Easymeeting and Mobile Prosumer—both were developed as artifacts and evaluated according the suggested structure of the UCAN process. Chapter 6 describes the third case study with a public transport company.

5 From Initial Idea to Low-Fidelity Prototype: Easymeeting and the Mobile Prosumer

This chapter presents two case studies: *Easymeeting*, a meeting room management system (in chapter 5.1), and the *Mobile Prosumer*, a smart product information system at the point of sale (in chapter 5.2). These case studies represent two different methods for evaluating and theorizing about the first two stages of the process model (initial idea and low-fidelity prototype). The findings from the case studies are used to establish a set of guidelines for designing NFC-based Ubicomp applications according to the research questions of the work.

Both case studies are presented according to the *ubiquitous computing application development and evaluation process model* (UCAN) (see chapter 4.3). Based on this model, application development and evaluation first begin by outlining the initial idea for a motivating application. This idea is then built as a paper-based prototype. The prototype is evaluated, refined, and developed into a low-fidelity prototype. The low-fidelity prototype is subjected to the same process but evaluated at this stage according to the selected method. Based on these evaluation findings, a refined use case is developed. Each chapter concludes with a more detailed examination of the benefits and limitations of the UCAN process, an analysis of the respective evaluation method, and finally a presentation of a set of application design guidelines that add to the growing Ubicomp body of knowledge.

5.1 Easymeeting: Meeting Room Management System

The goal of the Easymeeting case study was to better understand how people perceive NFC-based applications in an office setting. The general non-functional requirements as described in chapter 3 were used to develop the framework for this study. Table 17 presents a brief overview.

Case study name	Easymeeting
Short description	Meeting room management system
Unit of analysis	Individuals in two organizations

Table 17: Case study description

The first two phases of the UCAN process were used to evaluate Easymeeting. Fig. 52 shows the applied evaluation methods.

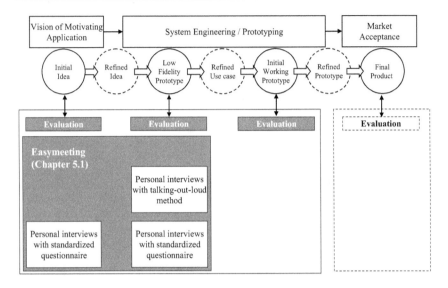

Fig. 52: Easymeeting evaluation within UCAN

Table 18 shows relevant research frameworks and methods:

Case study	Phase in UCAN process	Research Framework	Used evaluation method
Easymeeting	Initial idea	Quantitative survey	Personal interviews with standardized questionnaire
	Low-fidelity prototype	Quantitative survey	Personal interviews with standardized questionnaire
	Low-fidelity prototype	Qualitative analysis	Personal interviews with talking-out-loud method

Table 18: Evaluation methods of Easymeeting in the UCAN process

As explained in chapter 4, the UCAN process starts by describing an idea for a (user) motivating application. In this chapter this process will be presented as follows: description of the initial idea (Section 5.1.1), outline of the general problem (Section 5.1.2), in depth description of the initial idea (Section 5.1.3), and evaluation of the initial idea (Section 5.1.4). Then in section 5.1.5 the refined idea is introduced, which is used for designing a low-fidelity prototype as presented in section 5.1.6. This is followed in section 5.1.7 with an explanation of the research methodology, samples, and the data collection methods used in evaluating the low-fidelity prototype according the phases in the UCAN process model. In section 5.1.8 the evaluation findings are presented, a refined use case is introduced in section 5.1.9, and in section 5.1.10 the findings are summarized.

5.1.1 Vision of a Motivating Application

Easymeeting was designed as a meeting room management system. The system incorporates a range of components currently in use at various organizations. These components assist individuals attending meetings with easy-to-use functions. The emphasis is placed on an unobtrusive use of technology, because meetings have a personal and social character. The office system makes it possible to order beverages during a meeting or to notify the assistant about several actions that occur within the meeting room. The close proximity of a potential means for communication, which allows the user to silently communicate with the outer office environment on a high priority level, is new to the field. This was the idea for a motivating application, and therefore the starting point for the UCAN process.

In developing and evaluating Easymeeting using this process, creative individuals and students from the institute at the University of Arts Berlin were asked to participate in the study.

5.1.2 General Problem: Ubiquitous Computing in a Work Environment

An office infrastructure is packed with technology, e.g. desktop PC, video conferencing, telephones, time management systems, etc. Therefore, introducing Ubicomp applications into this environment should help to facilitate workers' daily processes and everyday tasks, provide additional benefits to the worker, and obviate the need for training in order to be able to use yet another new tool. Being in a competitive setting, the benefit of using the application should justify the implementation and deployment costs as well as possibly provide additional savings. With this in mind, the following hypotheses were outlined before conducting the evaluation process:

* H1. Users will positively perceive an NFC-based application as a means of office support—even if they are not aware of the underlying technology.

* H2. Future users will positively receive an NFC-based application if designed according to the general non-functional requirements (see chapter 3.1).

Based on these hypotheses, an initial idea was developed.

5.1.3 Initial Idea

The initial idea of a meeting management system based on Ubicomp technologies arose after moving the university institute into another office building with two meeting rooms in very separate parts of the office. After holding many meetings with research and industry partners, we sought a solution for improving the activities that are part of a meeting, such as calling a taxi after the meeting, ordering coffee during the meeting, or needing assistance to operate projectors etc. The meeting rooms and the assistant were located too far away from one another for it to be convenient, and calling out for the assistant was considered inappropriate during meetings. A first workshop was set up to discuss the issue with colleagues. It turned out that NFC could be a very cheap and effective way to enable colleagues to quickly manage meetings outside of the meeting room.

5.1.4 Evaluation of the Initial Idea

To better understand the possible functions of a ubiquitous computing meeting room management system, an initial phase of interviews among colleagues in one organization (O1

- N=22) was conducted. They were asked to describe what they considered most important during a meeting and what their rating on a Likert-scale from 0 = not important to 5 = very important would be.

Fig. 53 shows the results: most important was having a projector, followed by presentation printouts, and paper for jotting down memos. Coffee was important as well as assistance with operating equipment.

Things needed during meetings (O1)

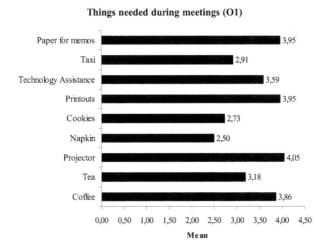

Fig. 53: Interview results on things needed during meetings (N=22)

A projector, paper for memos, and printouts are physical aspects that an assistant should provide before the meeting begins. This might also include cookies, napkins, coffee, and tee, but these might also run out during a meeting and need to be replenished. Calling for taxis and assistance with office equipment are modes of communication that address people. Based on these findings a refined idea was created.

5.1.5 Refined Idea

Instead of trying to cover all of these aspects, the focus was on the three of the most important ones affecting most meetings. The need to refresh the coffee (or tea, cookies, napkins, etc.), the need to ask for tech support and call a taxi were seen as things that affect most meetings and are likely to be important to meeting attendees. Another suggestion came from colleagues who used the meeting room quite often: a check in/check out functionality and the possibility to extend the blocked time in any meeting room management system.

In getting started, the application made use of the set of general non-functional system requirements as described in the summary of section 3.1.3. In order to keep the cognitive load low, only a few choices beyond the single top-level choice were offered. This led to three requirement sets each of which included the following: Requirement Set 1 (R1) refers to designing Ubicomp applications for the everyday, Requirement Set 2 (R2) refers to context-aware applications, and finally Requirement Set 3 (R3) lists Ubicomp principles (see Fig. 54).

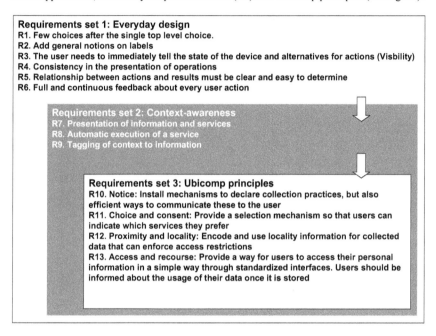

Requirements set 1: Everyday design
R1. Few choices after the single top level choice.
R2. Add general notions on labels
R3. The user needs to immediately tell the state of the device and alternatives for actions (Visbility)
R4. Consistency in the presentation of operations
R5. Relationship between actions and results must be clear and easy to determine
R6. Full and continuous feedback about every user action

Requirements set 2: Context-awareness
R7. Presentation of information and services
R8. Automatic execution of a service
R9. Tagging of context to information

Requirements set 3: Ubicomp principles
R10. Notice: Install mechanisms to declare collection practices, but also efficient ways to communicate these to the user
R11. Choice and consent: Provide a selection mechanism so that users can indicate which services they prefer
R12. Proximity and locality: Encode and use locality information for collected data that can enforce access restrictions
R13. Access and recourse: Provide a way for users to access their personal information in a simple way through standardized interfaces. Users should be informed about the usage of their data once it is stored

Fig. 54: Initial design criteria of Ubicomp applications
Source: (Resatsch et al. 2007c)

All of these non-functional requirements are to be implemented in the low-fidelity prototype system and serve as basic design elements of the artifact. Each of the requirements was implemented according to the suggestions in chapter 2 and 3. The first requirements R1 "Few choices after the single top level choice" was implemented by a line up similar to Norman's suggested shallow decision tree. Each time the user touched (or tapped) on of the tags, each tag had one function (see Fig. 55 – F1, F2,.... ,FX-1,FX) that started one process in the backend system. If a function required more than one single user adjustment (in Fig. 55 see F5), it was split into several tags, each tag has its own single attribute.

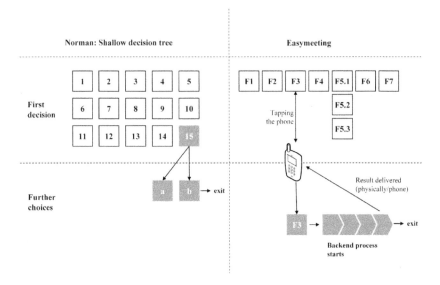

Fig. 55: Non-functional requirements on the example of R1

The linear arrangement of the NFC tags on the wall was supposed to help people easily understand the functions. Table 19 describes how the remaining requirements were implemented.

Requirement	Implemented via
R1. Few choices after the single top level choice.	Shallow decision tree—arrangement of NFC tags on wall
R2. Add general captions on labels	Captions below the tag were generalized and placed below the interaction field
R3. The user needs to immediately tell the state of the device and alternatives for actions	Mobile: Integrated into the NFC-phone was a vibration alarm Web: Personalized status reports, liveticker, Email updates
R4. Consistency in the presentation of operations	Similar icons on the front-end, known software to use the application
R5. Relationship between actions and results must be clear and easy to determine	Each tag had exactly one service.
R6. Full and continuous feedback about every user action	Feedback was incorporated largely by the status emails.
R7. Presentation of information and services	Any available information was clearly stated while using the application
R8. Automatic execution of a service	After touching the tag, the service execution had to be confirmed once.
R9. Tagging of context to information	Due to knowing the precise location of the NFC tags, any information could be tagged to an exact location.

R10. Notice: Install mechanisms to declare collection practices, but also efficient ways to communicate these to the user	Not implemented—the setting was an evaluation of a low-fidelity prototype. The data collection practice was obviously not intended.
R11. Choice and consent: Provide a selection mechanism so that users can indicate which services they prefer	Selection mechanism was given by the choice of services via the NFC tags—touch and use.
R12. Proximity and locality: Encode and use locality information for collected data that can enforce access restrictions	Both requirements were fulfilled by the application through the use of NFC as a technology. The data was not encoded for the low-fidelity prototype
R13. Access and recourse: Provide a way for users to access their personal information in a simple way through standardized interfaces. Users should be informed about the usage of their data once it is stored	The admin interface allowed users to see and delete their personal information.

Table 19: Non-functional requirements and their implementations in Easymeeting

These requirements served as the basis of the low-fidelity prototype.

5.1.6 Low-Fidelity Prototype

With the information gathered during the initial and refined idea stages, a low-fidelity prototype could be built. For the low-fidelity prototype, the then available Nokia 3220i with NFC shell, nine standard 13,56MHz passive tags, a sms2e-mail gateway service and Microsoft™ Exchange was used.

Our prototype was installed in a common conference room. Fig. 56 shows the initial low fidelity prototype and the tags mounted on paper backing attached to the wall in the conference room. In accordance with requirement 1 (R1) the tags are arranged on a shallow level to reduce the cognitive load of the meeting organizer.

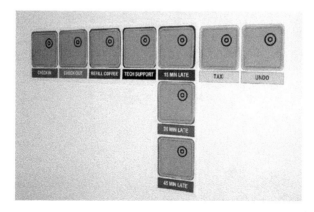

Fig. 56: Easymeeting low-fidelity prototype with NFC tags on the wall
Source: (Resatsch et al. 2007c)

Every tag incorporated a function based on the previously described mini-survey of most-wanted functions in meeting rooms:

• *Refill coffee*

• *Tech support*

• *15 Min late* (to indicate that the room should be blocked out for a longer period of time and to extend the duration if possible), *30 min late*, and *45 min late*

• *Taxi* (to call a cab when leaving the conference room)

• *Undo button* (to undo the last process, if possible)

Furthermore real-time functions were added:

• *Check in* (to indicate the room is now occupied).

• *Check out* (to facilitate communication with adjacent meetings and their organizers).

Colors describing the relevant function were used as background for the tag title, for example the tag *Taxi* was yellow, and the tag *Refill coffee* obviously brown. Every tag triggers one single pre-defined process. During the low-fidelity prototype phase the taxi tag was not connected to the taxi call center. All other tags used internal processes. The use cases are very simple and apply to mainly small and medium sized companies with less sophisticated conference management systems. A meeting organizer may now easily communicate unobtrusively from within the room (see Fig. 57).

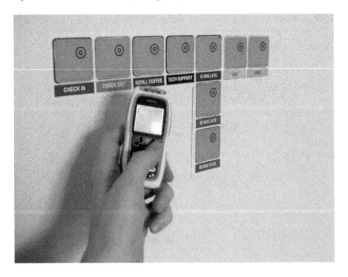

Fig. 57: Application transmits IDs to the system via mobile phone
Source: (Resatsch et al. 2007c)

The pre-arranged text on the tag includes an ID number for the meeting room (example: ROOM01) and a code for the action to execute, e.g. COFFEE. The text ROOM01 is used to identify the tag and for selecting the proper mail-template. After touching the tag, the user (meeting organizer) needs to confirm the operation once before the text is sent in the form of a text message with the short message system (SMS) of the mobile carrier.

The above-mentioned text message is received by the gateway in the form of an SMS from the *telephone number of initiator* with the text ROOM01 COFFEE, which is the code for *Please refill coffee in meeting room 1*. Now the gateway will convert the SMS into an e-mail and forward it to a pre-defined receiver. When the message arrives at the internal network, it will be delivered as a standard text-mail to the internal mail server. It then uses different mailboxes, each for one recipient according to the task description. One mailbox must behave according to the respective rules. This is the system mailbox with rule-based functions. One mailbox is for the assistant to receive incoming tasks that have been previously assigned to the rule mailbox. The process is also shown on a website (Fig. 58).

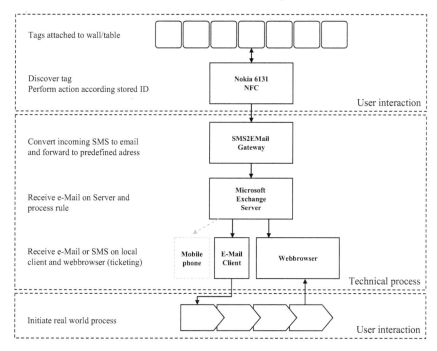

Fig. 58: Architectural overview of Easymeeting
Source: (Resatsch et al. 2007c)

A *live-ticker* was also installed in order to be able to view all actual events taking place in real time. The live-ticker could be shown on a TV screen in front of a meeting room or be accessed as a website by all employees in the organization. To check for changes and administer potentially discreet meetings, a very simple administrative interface was implemented. Access was granted to the management personnel at the institute. The admin interface listed all actual events. The administrator could then delete any event at a later point in time. Furthermore it can be attached to the major functionalities of professional conference management tools. An advantage to this solution is price. Using cards or buttons would require a costly infrastructure in meeting rooms, whereas the NFC tag solution is very inexpensive.

Easymeeting was designed according to the general requirements as described in the previous section. Furthermore, Easymeeting can be viewed as an everyday application because it addresses a process that many people in organizations experience regularly. The cognitive load needed to use the application is very low, since only a few options are presented that require only making one decision. The UCAN process was used to determine and evaluate whether the requirements are useful for further development of the application.

5.1.7 Evaluation of the Low-Fidelity Prototype

The evaluation was conducted at two organizations: Organization 1 (O1) is an institute at the University of Arts in Berlin, Organization 2 (O2) is an information technology service provider for the federal state of Mecklenburg-Vorpommern in Germany. Both organizations deal with information technology. At O1, only the institute staff—not students—took part in the survey. At O2, also the staff participated in the voluntary study.

5.1.7.1 Research Methodology

We used a combination of personal interviews with a questionnaire plus a simple *talking-out-loud* methodology while testing the low-fidelity prototype.

The questionnaire used had three parts: in part one (1) one's actual knowledge of RFID/NFC was questioned, in part two (2) the prototype was presented (using a Nokia 3220i handset) and participants could test and play with the prototype, and in part three (3) examined questioned items from the technology acceptance framework (UTAUT) by Venkatesh (Venkatesh et al., 2003) (3).

(1): In part one, participants were asked whether they knew what the terms RFID and NFC mean. Then participants were asked whether they had been previously aware of having used an RFID or NFC application. Additionally, participants were allowed to subjectively rate what they considered to be their level of knowledge about RFID/NFC.

(2): Part two was based on the qualitative *talking-out-loud* methodology. As a somewhat academic concept, most users are both unaware of Ubicomp as well as the details of RFID and NFC technology. So that participants could actually experience the application a prototype was presented to them. Accordingly the questionnaire was designed based on the finding that people cannot judge RFID or NFC systems if they are unaware of having used one before.

The *talking-out-loud* method was briefly introduced and the participants eagerly offered their comments while using the prototype. Before the prototype was presented and handed over, the interviewer explained RFID/NFC to all participants—even if they claimed in part one to already know about it—and that the focus of the case study was on short distance RFID/NFC. The participant then was given a certain task: *Please order coffee for your meeting.*

(3): The third and quantitative part used the technology acceptance measurement items presented in the Unified Theory of Acceptance and Use of Technology (UTAUT) framework (Venkatesh et al. 2003). The UTAUT framework is the unified model that integrates elements of eight competing technology acceptance models[19] that were described in chapter 3.2.3. The categories used to measure the items in the questionnaire were: Performance Expectancy, Effort Expectancy, Attitude Toward Using Technology, Social Influence, Facilitating Conditions, Anxiety, and Behavioral Intention. All categories had items as statements in an interval 5-item-scale from strongly agree to strongly disagree.

5.1.7.2 Sample

Table 20 sums up the study data and research framework.

Research framework	Quantitative/qualitative survey
Method of data collection	Personal interview with questionnaire
Period	December 19th 2006 to February 6th 2007
Measuring method	Interval 5-item-scale
Universe	Two organizations with 25 employees (O1) and 300 employees (O2)
Sample type	Random
Sample number	n=37 with n1=22 (O1) and n2=15 (O2)

Table 20: Study data

Within the study, 35% of the participants were female and 65% were male. Overall, 59.5% were familiar with the abbreviation RFID, while 51.4% recognized the abbreviation NFC. Only 2.7% considered themselves to be very knowledgeable about RFID/NFC, while the majority of 24.3% knew nothing about RFID/NFC and 21.6% only very little. Within the analysis in a non-representative framework the sample type was random.

5.1.7.3 Data Collection and Data Coding

The study consisted of 37 interviews with n1=22 in O1 and n2=15 in O2 with voluntary participants. Each interview took between 20 minutes to an hour; the average duration was 30 minutes. The data was collected using paper-based questionnaires.

---

[19]   The eight models are: Technology Acceptance Model, Motivational Model, Theory of Planned Behavior, Model combining the Technology Acceptance Model and the Theory of Planned Behavior, the Model of PC Utilization, the Innovation Diffusion Theory, and the Social Cognitive Theory - from (Venkatesh et al. 2003) See section 3.2.3

5.1.8 Evaluation Results of the Low-Fidelity Prototype

The main research question was: Would people accept RFID Ubicomp technology in personal settings if the system follows the non-functional requirements as stated in the general requirement section?

5.1.8.1 Evaluation Results—Qualitative with "Talking out Loud" Method

During the qualitative part of the interview (talking-out-loud), most participants described the system as useful and interesting. They asked almost no questions regarding how to use the application—despite that 35% had no previous experience with RFID, and 67% had none with NFC. Ten participants had problems with the OK button on the mobile phone and others struggled with the internal Nokia screensaver. The Nokia handset has a built-in screensaver, once activated an accidental tag reading is ignored by the system. Since participants had to press any key on the phone to wake the phone up the screensaver seemed to confuse people. It reactivated quickly, and if the scanning process was not initiated fast enough, people were not able to read the tag.

Participants considered the phone's built-in haptic feedback helpful in determining whether a command was activated. Interestingly in O2 the main argument against future usage were the previously introduced Blackberry handsets without NFC. Participants of O2 stated that they used the Blackberry also as a private phone and would not want to use another handset. One participant thought of a stationary device to use the system. A clear strategy for designing future Ubicomp applications emerged during this intermediate phase: If an information systems infrastructure (incl. hardware, such as the Blackberry™ in O2) already exists, or has been preconfigured by the company or other associated constituents, applications need to either be designed around available pre-existing interfaces or represent enough potential benefits to the company to justify the expenses necessary to change the current system.

The prototype was attached to the wall in O1. Some said it would be better to place the tags on the table instead of the wall because it is less obtrusive. Placing it on the table avoids unnecessary walking around during meetings. In O2, the prototype was placed on the table. In O2 almost nobody recommended attaching it to the wall. Hence placing tags on the table represented one solution, whereas another recommendation was to split functions between the door and table, for example the check-in/check-out process.

The main problem for most users was device-related: the location of the reader and antenna within the phone. Although a little NFC sign indicated the spot on the back of the phone where the reader is located, most participants placed the device with the flat top of the phone to the tag. Due to the overly close proximity, this led to reading errors or illegible tags. After the first successful usage, people quickly picked up the antenna location and then considered it easy to use. New Nokia handsets, such as the 6131 NFC, feature improved antenna usability.

Most participants considered the system useful even if they only infrequently served as meeting organizer or participant.

5.1.8.2 Evaluation Results—Quantitative According UTAUT Items

The questions in the quantitative serction were based on the set of the UTAUT categories (see chapter 3.2.3.6). The results were based on descriptive measures since the sample size did not allow for structural equation modelling (SEM) or partial least squares (PLS) tests.

Based on Performance Expectancy, 32.4% found Easymeeting very useful for their work (strongly agree), and 29.7% agreed that Easymeeting was useful. Taken together 56.7% either strongly agreed or agreed that Easymeeting increases performance in organizing meetings, however, 27.0% strongly disagreed (13.5%) or disagreed (13.5%) with this opinion. This may be a result of the fact that some participants are not responsible for organizing their own meetings and therefore see less benefit to its implementation.

There was also a highly positive Effort Expectancy. On a scale of 1 (strongly disagree) to 5 (strongly agree), the mean of the statement rating *The touch interaction makes it very easy to use the system* was 4.51, with 92% of all participants agreeing or strongly agreeing. 83.7% enjoyed working with the system, and 70.3% strongly agreed that RFID/NFC interaction is easy.

Attitude Toward Using the Technology was also positive with 35.1% strongly agreeing with the statement *I like more applications such as Easymeeting* vs. 32.4% who agreed, and only 5.4% who strongly disagreed. This is only valid for the application using the design criteria.

Social Influence was also very high. 29.7% strongly agreed with the statement *My organization thinks rather positively about RFID/NFC*, while 48.9% agreed, and 21.6% were neutral. There were no disagreements. Both organizations are in the information technology (IT) business. It would be interesting to test the application in a non-IT related branch, such as retail.

Facilitating Conditions: Although most of the participants (See Fig. 59) rated their knowledge of RFID/NFC between 1 (= none at all) to 3 (= neutral), 78% felt capable of using the application. This shows that knowledge about RFID/NFC technology is unnecessary for being able to use a Ubicomp application but also implies that the design criteria used enforced simplicity.

Comparison of knowledge and ability to use application

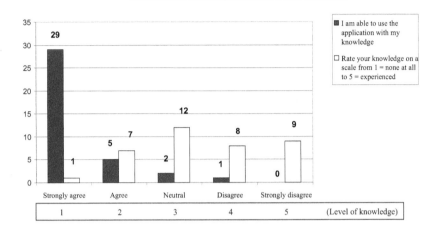

Fig. 59: Comparison of personal knowledge perception and ability to use (n=37)

The anxiety of using the application was very low. 83.8% strongly disagreed with the statement: *I am worried because of Easymeeting* and 51.4% were not afraid of being controlled by the application. The possibilities of the technology as shown were absolutely not intimidating for 62.2% and not intimidating for 27% of respondents. Most participants would not hesitate to use such an application because of privacy fears (67.6%) or data security concerns (54.1%). Privacy and security concerns played almost no role for the specific application, although it played a rather higher role in the overall rating.

According to the survey related to Behavioral Intention 56.8% would use Easymeeting in upcoming months. However, because of the early stage of the prototype, measuring use behavior of the actual system was not really possible. Therefore the Behavioral Intention needs to be evaluated at a later phase of the UCAN process with active users. With information only about behavioral intention, no company can make actual plans.

To sum up: Easymeeting proved to be a very simple and easy to design application that people were eager to use and understand from the start. Although user anxiety about RFID/NFC was present, people were not afraid to use a system that complies with the criteria of everyday applications. Therefore Easymeeting provided, as an artifact, a solution to the general problem. Participants rated the overall system as excellent—however the evaluation results cannot be applied directly to one or more of the non-functional requirements. It can only be assumed that combining the aforementioned requirements makes it possible for users to perceive the Easymeeting application in a highly positive way. More important is broad user acceptance. Because the system relies on user-initiated actions, the user's consent is assumed in performing a specific task. Additionally users are familiar with the environment of such an application. The system had no impact on the privacy concerns of end-users.

The shallow decision path, and its clear and easy human-computer interaction, both prove to be good strategies for designing and developing everyday Ubicomp applications. The outcome of the UTAUT based quantitative questionnaire was not helpful in clearly determining the subsequent steps for a refined use case due to the low number of participants.

To finalize the case study, the given hypotheses are qualitatively discussed:

• H1. Users will positively perceive an NFC-based application as a means of office support—even if they are not aware of the underlying technology.

This hypothesis is supported. Although the participants were not aware of NFC and RFID to a larger extent, they perceived the application as useful and had no further problems using it. The technology behind the service can diffuse into the background according to the Ubicomp principles.

• H2. Future users will positively receive an NFC-based application if designed according to the general non-functional requirements (see chapter 3.1).

There was no measurement of cause-and-effect relations between the non-functional requirements from chapter 3.1 and the user behaviour. Due to the overall very positive feedback, the hypotheses are also supported. Based on these results a refined use case was developed according the findings from the study.

5.1.9 Refined Use Case

The case study Easymeeting complies with the set of described non-functional system requirements of Ubicomp applications. In order to refine the use case, the requirements need to be sorted (Table 21).

Requirement	Details and relevance of requirements according to evaluation	Refined use case
R1. Few choices after the single top level choice.	According to participants, the application was clear and easy to understand. However people preferred the NFC tags on the table instead of the wall.	Tag splitting. Some functions are placed on the actual table, some on the wall (such as check in / check out).
R2. Add general captions on labels	According to participants, the captions made the tag function clear and understandable.	Captions remain the same.
R3. The user needs to immediately tell the state of the device and alternatives for actions	Due to the slow functionality of the early Nokia 3220i including the screensaver, users were not content with this.	This changed with the introduction of the new Nokia 6131 NFC. New phones are used in the refined use case.
R4. Consistency in the presentation of operations	The participants valued the application because of its clear presentation of operations.	The new NFC phones also allowed for a more detailed visualization of the functions.
R5. Relationship between actions and results must be clear and easy to determine	According participants, the application was clear and understandable.	Relationships remain the same.
R6. Full and continuous feedback about every user action	Users seemed to not necessarily have a problem with full feedback. Due to the extented usage of mobile phones, it was clear enough that some aspects were transferred by GSM technology and without direct feedback.	Continuous feedback needs to be implemented. Even with functions that physically are conducted in the office space, one needs to know about the stage of the action. Is someone taking care of the coffee call? Is the taxi really called? If these things are not clearly supported by status messages, a potential user might need to question a person thus making the whole thing obsolete.
R7. Presentation of information and services	According to participants, the application was clear and easy to understand.	Presentation remain the same, they might be integrated into the office space more seamlessly.
R8. Automatic execution of a service	Some users had problems with the OK key of the mobile phone.	This is a learning process and is kept the same.
R9. Tagging of context to information	According participants, the application was clear and understandable.	Contextualized information could be further added to support more functions.

R10. Notice: Install mechanisms to declare collection practices, but also efficient ways to communicate these to the user	Because of the deployment in rather known settings with a high value of trust, this was not demanded.	In the next phase (working prototype) this is an issue. The data collection practice needs to be visible and agreed upon before usage.
R11. Choice and consent: Provide a selection mechanism so that users can indicate which services they prefer	Users saw a high relevance in the touch as a new form of interaction to show choice and consent.	The proximity of NFC allowed for choice (functions) and consent (no accidental use), therefore the mechanism is valid.
R12. Proximity and locality: Encode and use locality information for collected data that can enforce access restrictions	Was not questioned by the participants	This might be interesting for security relevant operations in different offices (door services, etc.).
R13. Access and recourse: Provide a way for users to access their personal information in a simple way through standardized interfaces. Users should be informed about the usage of their data once it is stored	Was not questioned by the participants	See R10. Users can use the user interface in the next iteration to see their log and statistical data. They need to be able to manipulate parts of it, if demanded.

Table 21: Non-functional system requirements and their implementation

As a low-fidelity prototype the Easymeeting system implemented the given requirements. The whole set of requirements can be consolidated since some requirements have shown to have no particular impact on whether the system is accepted. Some requirements were essential according to the talking-out-loud evaluation results:

•   R1. Few choices after the single top-level choice.

•   R2. Add general captions on labels.

•   R3. The user needs to be able to immediately tell the state of the device and alternatives for actions.

•   R5. Relationship between actions and results must be clear and easy to determine.

•   R9. Tagging of context to information.

•   R11. Choice and consent: Provide a selection mechanism so that users can indicate which services they prefer.

These requirements could now serve as a basis for the next step in the UCAN process: the following initial working prototype. Because Easymeeting would need to be implemented in an office space, and large enough to test it with larger samples, it was not possible to develop the system into a working prototype.

The previously specified requirements have not been tested with this variation of the evaluation setup—they were taken as a basis for the development and are used as a set of guidelines for future Ubicomp developments.

5.1.10 Summary of the Results—Easymeeting

The following sections present ways in which to improve the UCAN process model and theorize about its benefits and limitations. It also evaluates the set of guidelines for designing NFC-based ubiquitous computing applications.

5.1.10.1 Improve and Theorize about the Developed Process Model (UCAN)

The examination of the process model addresses: the (1) benefits of the process and the (2) limitations to the process in its current stage, and (3) an in depth look at the evaluation method.

(1) Benefits of the process: The UCAN-guided process helped to further refine the initial idea and determine relevant functions for the later low-fidelity prototype. First preparing a paper-based prototype, which was followed by the horizontal low-fidelity prototype, helped to keep the effort low in terms of invested human and financial resources. The UCAN process would be useful for developing early-stage market strategies, e.g. the Blackberry issue was not considered relevant in previous discussions, but would have significant implications for actually introducing such a concept. The use of non-functional requirements may have led to a positive valuation of the underlying technology. NFC proved to be simple and easy to use, therefore receiving a high level of overall acceptance in the interviews. Questioning the later users was helpful in determining actual office-related requirements. Many Ubicomp applications are oftentimes researched with fellow students. In this case, the UCAN process enabled a company to include *normal* people as well.

(2) Limitations of process: The research setup in the process had certain limitations. The results are explorative and not representative. The sample group surveyed was too small to generate a representative number of interviews. Furthermore it is based on only two organizations with only a few common attributes. The interview was conducted at information technology (IT)-based organizations, and the results might be different at other organizations. Further research should also focus on non-IT companies, or on a comparison of the impacts of organizational mind-sets. Testing the non-functional requirements as a basis for evaluation needs to be approached more rigorously in order to evaluate the application and map successful requirements onto further developments. As a negative aspect, the sample group surveyed was too small during the first phase of the paper-based prototype in order to help define the functions that would be interesting to users in a relatively fast and convenient way. The larger sample group surveyed with interviews at the low-fidelity prototype stage was not large enough to conduct a statistical model test including a path analysis (with Structural Equation Modeling (SME)), which would have been necessary for determining correlations in between factors and path significances between constructs in the UTAUT. The use of UTAUT items helped to structure the questionnaire but was of no real value for developing further iterations of the application at this stage of the process. These facts speak for the discussed phases of evaluation in which different methods are used.

(3) Evaluation: The choice of using personal interviews had several advantages and pitfalls in the respective categories of the evaluation. Table 22 differentiates between the organization phase—during which the questionnaire was developed, the interviewees were recruited, the prototype was installed, and the room was set up, etc.—and the execution phase, during which the interviews were conducted with participants, and finally the analysis phase, during which the interviews were transcribed, data was imported into the analysis tools (SPSS) and analyzed.

Phases of evaluation	Positive	Negative
Organization phase	There was no larger organizational setup necessary (as opposed to focus groups, which need a special set up room). The interviews were conducted in the office during working hours.	Recruiting participants was difficult due to daily business workload. Target number of participants in O2 was 50, only 15 actually participated in the study. Many previous talks were needed to convince senior management to back up and support the study in O2.
Execution phase with questionnaire	-	The questionnaires used the UTAUT items. However, people in a personal interview were surprised because some items are almost the same with only a small variation of the wording. Also in O1, the interviewer was personally known by the participants, potentially biasing results.
Execution phase with talking-out-loud	People were very excited about testing the low-fidelity prototype and had many more ideas that were suggested in the talking-out-loud session. The talks lasted in two cases almost an hour with good insights into working practice and the benefit of such an application. The one-on-one situation allowed deeper questioning of specific areas, such as privacy or where to place the NFC tag.	-
Analysis phase with questionnaire	The analysis with the questionnaires was straightforward and simple.	The small number of participants did not allow for a statistically interesting analysis (such as path analysis or structural equation modeling). Therefore the results operate on more of an intuitive level than they are based on real statistical figures. There are no clear recommendations for actions derived from this instantiation of the artifact. It is not possible to suggest further steps based on the results.

Analysis phase with talking-out-loud	The method provided more interesting and better insights into the application and user behavior itself.	The talking-out-loud method made transferring data more difficult—it is rather unstructured and it takes more time to derive measures from the data.

Table 22: Evaluating the evaluation

The measures from the quantitative tests did not provide much helpful information. The low-fidelity prototype test with the talking-out-loud method provided more insights into people's perception of the application and resulted in recommendations for actions. Table 23 sums up the evaluation of Easymeeting, the research framework, the evaluation method used, respective samples sizes and items used in relation to the effort needed to conduct the study, and whether it helped generate additional product iterations.

Case study	Phase in UCAN process	Research Framework	Used evaluation method	Sample size	Items used	Effort to conduct	Helpful to determine product related iterations
Easy-meeting	Initial idea	Quantitative survey	Personal interviews with standardized questionnaire	N=22		Low	Yes
	Low-fidelity prototype	Quantitative survey	Personal interviews with standardized questionnaire	N=37	UTAUT	Low	No
	Low-fidelity prototype	Qualitative analysis	Personal interviews with talking-out-loud method	N=37		Medium	Yes

Table 23: Summary of the Easymeeting evaluation

The table shows that evaluating an initial idea helped to improve and develop further iterations of the application for developing the low-fidelity prototype. In evaluating the low-fidelity prototype it became clear that the personal interviews were less useful than the talking-out-loud method in terms of improving and positively altering the application. Although conducting the talking-out-loud interviews required more effort, the results produced were more helpful in designing the next iteration of the application. The UCAN process itself is very closely related to its underlying evaluation methods. To compare interviews to an alternative evaluation method, the next case study uses focus groups to evaluate the artifact.

5.1.10.2 Preparing Design Guidelines

One goal of evaluating the artifact is to broaden the Ubicomp body of knowledge as it relates to Near Field Communication (NFC)—in other words to establish a set of guidelines for designing future applications that take into account how NFC positively and negatively impacts user acceptance. To sum up, the challenges involved in developing Easymeeting further were grouped based on the information systems overview from chapter 2.3 (see Fig. 16) in (1) NFC technology and application, (2) tag infrastructure, (3) human factors, and (4) device itself:

(1) NFC technology and application: Based on the findings related to NFC technology and its application, a detailed understanding emerged about Ubicomp in office settings using the example of Easymeeting:

- Easymeeting was considered an easy-to-use and interesting smart-office application.

- NFC technology is an already available Ubicomp technology and can help to realize smart-office apps. In particular the use of mobile phones—easily recognized everyday objects and known to most users—facilitated understanding the application.

- Technical implementation was based on internal MS Exchange and established scripts. This cannot be applied easily to larger scale implementations requiring interfacing with existing conference management systems. We consider this development process very important to any future implementation. A need exists for a customizable lightweight developmental framework. Then the system could be easily applied to additional scenarios in and around office buildings, such as vehicle fleet management, time recording, and cafeteria systems. Despite low implementation costs given its tag-only infrastructure, the presence of pre-negotiated large-scale mobile phone contracts is potentially problematic as well as the need of handset manufacturers to incorporate another antenna for NFC usage.

- NFC seems to have a low impact on privacy and data security concerns.

- In particular, the simplicity of everyday tasks affords an opportunity to start a grassroots initiative for tagging the world around us.

Designers of Ubicomp applications should focus on simplicity and user-centered development. The user should be involved at a very early stage of the development. The case study makes it clear that developers need to: understand how everyday tasks are structured, design applications so that they are easy to understand, and use consistent captions, graphic, interfaces, and actions.

(2) The findings also related to the tag infrastructure or placement in office contexts:

- Tag placement was subject to discussion—splitting up the tags between the wall and the table for various functions seemed to be the preferred solution.

(3) Human factors:

- In general people were positively impressed by NFC technology—privacy was not much of an issue over the course of the interviews.

(4) Some of the findings gave interesting insights about the devices itself (4):

- The NOKIA screensaver confused people—it was unclear when the system was actually ready to read tags.

•   The built-in haptic feedback was considered very positive.

•   If the NFC-device differs from the one people normally use, the handling (buttons) seems to present a challenge.

•   Different devices need to be considered as existing infrastructure (e.g. RIM™'s Blackberry).

•   Location for reader and antenna were unclear—a one time explanation is helpful. This is a reason for prototyping in which future users can test the device and try out the interaction.

This implies that handset modifications could potentially have a considerable impact on the use and acceptance of future applications. For the next step in the process, a variation of different devices should be integrated.

Easymeeting showed that is very easy to set up a cheap, simple, grassroots Ubicomp information system with currently available standard components. This enables industry and small- and medium-sized enterprises to try out approaches in the field of RFID/NFC, and other wireless technologies that may or may not assist everyday processes and tasks. A rigorous approach is required in order to implement an easy-to-use technology for companies. To test out other forms of evaluation and a different domain, the case study *Mobile Prosumer* was developed.

5.2 Mobile Prosumer: Smart Product Information System at the Point of Sale

The second case study was called *Mobile Prosumer* (MP). The MP is a smart product information system at the Point of Sale (PoS). To evaluate whether NFC services and applications at the consumer level—especially in the area of retail—arouse positive public interest and fulfill the needs of consumers, a second case study was conducted with the UCAN process. The actual artifact was a NFC-based prototype of a smart product information system (see Table 24).

Case study name	Mobile Prosumer
Description	Smart product information system at the Point of Sale for consumers
Unit of analysis	Individuals in two focus groups

Table 24: Case study description

The following figure (see Fig. 60) provides an overview of the evaluation methods of the Mobile Prosumer case study in the various phases of the UCAN process.

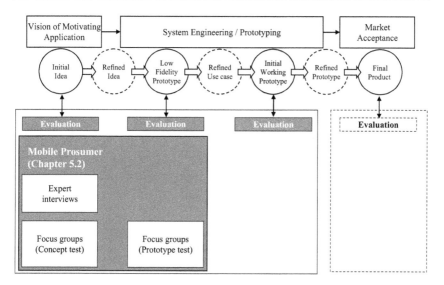

Fig. 60: Used evaluation methods of the Mobile Prosumer

Using the UCAN process, an initial idea was translated into the form of a paper-based evaluation and then developed into a low-fidelity prototype application, the *Mobile Prosumer* (MP)—a mobile phone application for delivering relevant product information at the PoS. Different to Easymeeting, the Mobile Prosumer targeted an existing infrastructure in retail (RFID-based). Therefore it was more important to deeply understand the general problem and formulate distinct research questions. Additionally the research instrument used moved from personal structured interviews to focus groups as a qualitative analysis. Table 25 shows the evaluation frameworks and methods used.

Case study	Phase in UCAN process	Research Framework	Used evaluation method
Mobile Prosumer	Initial idea	Qualitative analysis	Expert interviews
	Initial idea	Qualitative analysis	Focus groups (Concept test)
	Low-fidelity prototype	Qualitative analysis	Focus groups (Prototype test)

Table 25: Evaluation methods of the Mobile Prosumer in the UCAN process

Starting with the idea for a motivating application in section 5.2.1, section 5.2.2 helps to understand the general problem. In section 5.2.3 the initial idea is explained. An evaluation of the initial idea (Section 5.2.4) leads to a refined idea (Section 5.2.5). Based on the refined idea, the low-fidelity prototype is described and created in section 5.2.6. Section 5.2.7 states research methodology, sample and data collection to show the general evaluation results in section 5.2.8 and the low-fidelity evaluation results in section 5.2.9 The then refined use case is outlined in section 5.2.10. Section 5.2.11 sums up the results.

5.2.1 Vision of a Motivating Application

Most products and available information about them exist independently from one another. While consumers do use the Internet as an easily accessible source of product information at home or at work, they rely upon the expertise, skill and sometimes even moods of sales assistants in obtaining further product information at the Point of Sale (PoS). The gap between product and corresponding information makes coming to a significant independent decision about a purchase difficult and may increase the subjective feeling of uncertainty. Uncertainty is a result of trying to determine relevant product attributes before making a purchase (Kaas 1994; Bettmann 1973; Mitchell 1992; Mitchell/Boustani 1994; Aßmann 2003). Missing potentially useful product information, such as user-generated product ratings, testimonials, or opinions from friends and family at the PoS pose problems in the decision process of the consumer and may further increase uncertainty.

Radio Frequency Identification (RFID) could become a solution to this problem as it can bridge offline and online world and enhance products with additional information (see section 2.1.4). The recent increase in RFID implementations in also enables the development of user-centred ubiquitous computing (Ubicomp) applications—by merging physical products and information products into so-called "smart products" (Loebbecke/Palmer 2006; Mattern 2005b; Maass/Filler 2006). *Smart products* and *smart product information services* are sought in order to decrease negative factors such as uncertainty and to make shopping a positive experience. The MP aggregates content from various online sources for display on a mobile phone, using NFC.

Based on marketing literature (Meffert 2005, 103), it was conceptually determined which product information could be relevant to the consumer, and how improved access to product information may change the search and experience qualities, thus reducing uncertainty and facilitating purchasing decisions. The prototype was evaluated in two focus groups, one with consumers and one with professional sales personnel (Resatsch et al. 2008).

5.2.2 General Problem: Smart Products and Information Services

RFID was first introduced to retail in order to optimize logistics, solve out-of-stock problems and improve the supply chain (Fleisch/Christ/Dierkes 2005a; Fleisch/Mattern 2005; Fleisch/Mattern/Billinger 2004; Fleisch/Thiesse 2007; Mattern 2005b; Resatsch et al. 2007a; Murphy-Hoye/Lee/Rice 2005). Cost-benefit analysis show that RFID provides benefits for the supply-chain processes for manufacturer and stores, but also that competitive advantage might come from the use of RFID-generated data (Loebbecke/Palmer 2006). Once the infrastructure of RFID-tags is built, discussions around RFID also included applications for consumers, such as easy check out systems, cloak room services and as information source both for retailers and consumers alike (Novak 2005; Parkinson 2004). Here, the concept of Ubicomp enters the domain of retail and commerce (Weiser 1991, 1993; Loebbecke/Palmer 2006; Strüker/Sackmann/Müller 2004; Roussos 2005, 2006; Roussos/Moussouri 2004; Roussos et al. 2002). More RFID-equipped products could smooth the way for information services bringing additional information to the people at the PoS (see also the benefit circle in section 1.2). Furthermore, making the RFID infrastructure directly usable for consumers could yield understanding of the technology and increase a perceived value of such systems instead of focusing on the discussion of negative aspects such as privacy (Resatsch et al. 2007a). Yet, it is unclear if and how people like to obtain and use more information about a particular product in real shopping situations. To find an answer, it is important to first look at shopping differences between today's online and offline shopping (Resatsch et al. 2008).

5.2.2.1 Differences in Online and Offline Shopping

A shopping situation is characterized by many stress factors (Aylott/Mitchell 1998), such as time pressure, lack of response by retailers, crowd density, staff attitude and training, store layout/relocation, impulse purchasing pressure, location, product assortment, music, and lighting. These factors may influence the *feeling* people have, when using technology in a specific shopping situation. Definitions of shopping (Prus/Dawson 1991), as well as reasons why people shop (Tauber 1972), and influences on shopping-decisions (Cox/Rich 1964) have been investigated in many studies (Dowling/Staelin 1994; Punj/Staelin 1983). These studies had the consumer in the offline shopping world in mind. But offline shopping differs from online shopping for a variety of reasons. Degeratu et. al. (2000) indicate that brand names become more important online in some product categories, sensory search attributes, particularly visual cues about the product have lower impact on online choices, whereas factual information have a higher impact, and price sensitivity is also higher online (Degeratu/Rangaswamy/Wu 2000). Search costs are reduced online with different search dynamics for different goods (Alba et al. 1997; Shapiro/Varian 1999; Johnson et al. 2004). More factors such as ease of use, usefulness, and enjoyment, and exogenous factors like consumer traits, situational factors, product characteristics, previous online shopping experiences, and trust in online shopping play a role in the attitude of consumers to shop online (y Monsuwé/Dellaert/de Ruyter 2004). Chiang and Dholakia (2003) have defined search goods as goods for which full information on dominant attributes can be determined prior to the purchase and experience goods as those for which direct experience is necessary. Online shopping intention is higher for search goods than for experience goods (Chiang/Dholakia 2003). Similar to the difference of experience and search goods, particular purchases differ in search qualities, which can be determined before the purchase, experience qualities, known only after the purchase, and furthermore credence qualities that are difficult to judge even after the purchase (Adler 1996; Aßmann 2003; Darby/Karni 1973). Compared to online shopping, missing product information at the Point of Sale (PoS) in terms of search qualities and experience qualities pose problems in the decision process of the consumer— finally leading to higher uncertainty. Different products enquire different information services for adding an online or offline representation of the product (Levin/Levin/Heath 2003). Recent trends in increasing trust relationships and experience qualities through social networks, community systems and automatic recommendation systems add further possibilities to improve availability of experience qualities from one's peers (Eck et al. 2007; Heath/Motta/Petre 2007). These improvements support online shopping decisions, but are not available offline at the PoS until now.

5.2.2.2 Smart Products—Bridging the Gap of Offline and Online Information

Smart products—products that share information with consumers—are designed to combine the online and offline world. They give physical store operators in today's world of intense online shopping the possibility to compete with online retailers by providing direct access to the online information (Maass/Janzen 2007; Roussos 2005; Smith/Davenport/Hwa 2003). Smart products communicate with the consumer and also enable new ways of interaction (Fleisch/Christ/Dierkes 2005a). Whereas today's in-store products provide only static information, future smart products may provide information about their trip to their current location (e.g., multiple countries of origin), information about their ingredients (e.g., news articles on problems with a particular supplier) and possibly some embedded intelligence that determines the customer's needs (e.g., the types of difficulties others have had in assembling the product). Smart products can also act as a process interface and information source for retailers (e.g., how many times has the product been picked up by customers) (Fleisch/Thiesse 2007; Fleisch/Christ/Dierkes 2005a, 23).

A *smart product information service*, in this context, will be defined as an application that uses the data from the RFID-tagged product to provide Internet services related to the product via a mobile phone (NFC). Smart product information services, naturally, will provide, retrieve and display differing types of information depending on the product (Levin/Levin/Heath 2003). However, if such RFID-based smart products are to play a role in future retail scenarios, they must be technically feasible and provide a benefit to consumers.

The technical feasibility depends on availability of user devices to actually interact with products, software on both device and backend, availability of networks and relevant content. A middleware needs to further integrate the content sources and product information (Maass/Janzen 2007). With growing NFC penetration it is likely that information services based on automatic product identification become more relevant (ABIResearch 2007) (Kaasinen 2005; Välkkynen/Niemelä/Tuomisto 2006; Jalkanen 2005; Välkkynen et al. 2003; Rukzio 2007). Yet it is not known how the human resources in retail (e.g. sales personnel) will react to consumer information systems. Given the fact that smart products are in stores, the subject of sales personnel is also up for discussion.

In the area of pervasive retail systems, the RFID-based application myGrocer (Kourouthanassis/Roussos 2003), the mobile device and barcode-based AURA system (Smith/Davenport/Hwa 2003) and conceptual applications such as a consumer-support system for socially-conscious practices (Novak 2005) have been researched. No broad level usage of smart product information services is known so far, although additional data for products is widely available on the Internet.

Fig. 61 shows where smart product information services could potentially extent online shopping convenience to the PoS in terms of the aforementioned product qualities (Search, Experience, Credence).

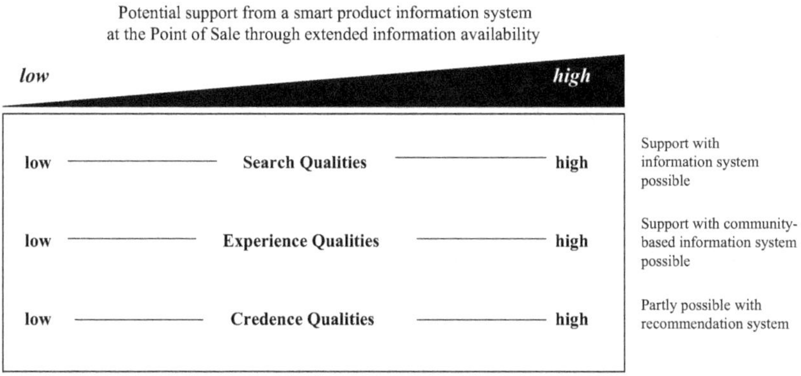

Potential support from a smart product information system
at the Point of Sale through extended information availability

low				*high*

low	——————— Search Qualities ——————— high	Support with information system possible
low	——————— Experience Qualities ——————— high	Support with community-based information system possible
low	——————— Credence Qualities ——————— high	Partly possible with recommendation system

Fig. 61: Product qualities and smart product information systems
Source: (Resatsch et al. 2008)

This potential extention adds on further importance to determine the user-side demand for RFID-based information services depending on the qualities of the products at the PoS.

5.2.2.3   Demand for RFID-based Information Services at the Point of Sale

For Ubicomp applications as product information services in retail, the following facts play a role (Resatsch et al. 2008):

• Most products and relevant information about them exist independent from one another (virtual world vs. physical world).

• While the Internet is usually used as an information source, consumers at the Point of Sale (PoS) rely upon the expertise, skill and even moods of sales assistants for obtaining relevant product information.

• The gap between product and related information makes purchase decisions difficult and may increase the perceived feeling of uncertainty.

• Information related to mainly experience qualities that may limit uncertainty are not available at the PoS.

These problems might cause stress for consumers and may lead to fewer purchases and limit the desired shopping experience. As a further prerequisite every PoS-application must support the needs (besides more sales) of retailers to be accepted in retail scenarios. The case study was deeper integrated into the UCAN process by clearly formulating several main research questions derived from the discussion about the general problem:

• What is considered relevant and useful information at the PoS to support search and experience qualities?

• Can consumers use any additional information services appropriately at the PoS?

- Do RFID-based information services have a perceived benefit to consumers?

- Do RFID-based information applications have a perceived benefit to sales assistants?

- Are smart product information services applications acceptable for consumers and sales assistants?

- Do perceived benefits of information services differ among different product categories?

- What is the overall acceptance of RFID/NFC technology at the PoS?

Using these questions, it becomes clear if an application such as the MP will have a chance in the market at all, what functions have the best impact on user perception, and what is the overall acceptance of the technology. To answer these questions, the UCAN process starts with the initial idea. With the answer of these questions, it might be possible to build the application according user needs (Resatsch et al. 2008).

5.2.3 Initial Idea

In 2006 we started the first discussions on a mobile product information system, aware of the rising potential to read barcodes with mobile phones and the then upcoming NFC technology (Resatsch/Karpischek/Michelis 2006). Fig. 62 shows the desired application overview including a connection to a EPCIS system. The user touches any NFC-tagged product with his NFC-enabled phone, a GSM/GPRS connection is established and from various content sources, data is aggregated about the touched product.

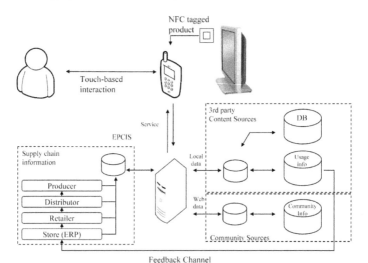

Fig. 62: Mobile Prosumer – conceptual application overview
Source: (Resatsch et al. 2008)

In a first workshop the initial idea targeted the consumer with an increased awareness about the goods they buy—whether these products may contain ecologically critical ingredients (e.g. genetically modified food) or the company produces products with questionable work ethics (e.g. child labor in third world countries). After the installation of such a product information application, the customer needed to select his preference profile according to his needs (e.g. ecological, allergy, low-fat, ethical profile). The allergy profile as an example contained ingredients, region of origin, nutritional value, and production methods. Using the mobile phone, the customer would retrieve product information, which is matched to the stored profile. In case of mismatches the application would turn red or green, giving information on ethics, health etc. with percentage scale and additionally shows further information on the scanned product.

5.2.4 Evaluation of the Initial Idea

According to the UCAN process, we first used expert talks to verify the initial idea (N=4). Quickly it was discovered that most decisions in that area were so-called *one-offs*. For instance, a person who wants to buy fair trade products, is aware of a number of brands in the organization social movement e.g. of fair trade[20] or can check the certification label on a product. Similar to ethical decisions, an allergy profile is difficult to establish for a variety of reasons. People are very aware of their allergies and may be too cautious to trust an electronic source if they can check with their doctor first—and also read the label. For these reasons, we iterated the initial idea to the possibility to obtain information on search and experience qualities.

5.2.5 Refined Idea

The refined idea focused on search and experience qualities (white goods, consumer electronics, media and groceries), products that may have an additional value to the user. Furthermore we refined the idea based on the degree of collective decision of a product (asking the friends & family about a purchase) and if there are existing purchase programs (a mind set that is generated automatically when buying the same product over and over again—one does not need to actually think about the purchase decision—think of toothpaste in this case). Online shopping provides significant benefits because of limited search costs and easier to obtain experience qualities via communities. With conceptual deduction of test product categories (see Fig. 63), the refined idea used the classification of Ruhfus as shown in Meffert (Meffert 2005, 103) and chose the example of wine as convenience good and example of a rather low degree of collective decision and available existing purchase program.

---

[20]   Sources are: www.fairtrade.net, www.fairtradefederation.org - accessed 09.12.2007

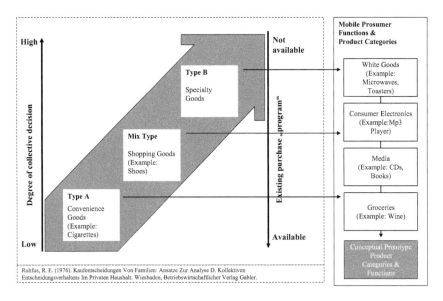

Ruhfus, R. E. (1976). Kaufentscheidungen Von Familien: Ansatze Zur Analyse D. Kollektiven
Entscheidungsverhaltens Im Privaten Haushalt. Wiesbaden, Betriebswirtschaftlicher Verlag Gabler.

Fig. 63: Deduction of test product categories (see also Ruhfus (1976)
Source: (Resatsch et al. 2008)

If a smart product information service would work for wine as a product it works for higher collective decision degrees and less available purchasing programs (Resatsch et al. 2008). The low fidelity prototype used wine partly as experience good and because of the corresponding information on the product available from various sources.

5.2.6 Low-Fidelity Prototype

The low fidelity prototype is outlined in Fig. 64 with a wine bottle and an NFC tag attached to it. The prototype had four use cases: A detailed product description, a recommendation system (*What your friends think*), an expert information display with a rating system (*Experts opinion*), and an order form (*Order larger amounts*). The product description use case follows rules about what additional product information needs to be provided (for example, if the product label is in another language) so that the product information is relevant and not redundant. The recommendation system use case provides recommendations based on similar purchases of others (search qualities). The expert information use case provides an evaluation of the product compared to other similar ones (experience qualities) and the order form use case provide price information and how the particular wine or other wines may be obtained.

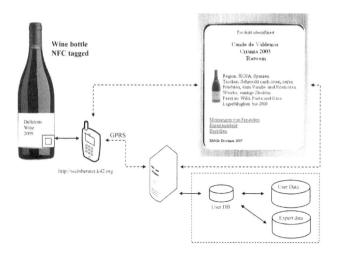

Fig. 64: Low-fidelity prototype of the Mobile Prosumer
Source: (Resatsch et al. 2008)

NFC Data Exchange Format (NDEF) messages are used to store an Electronic Product Code (EPC) on the NFC tag. According to the NFC Forum URI Record Type Definition we chose the URI Prefix urn:epc:id: (0x30) to store the EPC, in our example a SGTIN-96. The application now reads the URN from the NFC tag and resolves the EPC to a website URL. In a future step this resolving process can be done via an Object Naming Service (ONS) lookup according to the ONS specifications (EPCglobal 2005). The resolved URL is then used by the internal Web browser of the phone to show the information about a touched product, which is taken from any content source providing a web service. The content is sent back to the client and displayed on the mobile phone. The user can then access further information if provided (Resatsch et al. 2007b; Resatsch/Karpischek/Michelis 2006; Resatsch et al. 2008).

The refined use case, implemented on the example of wine as an experience good, would open the application to all goods with experience qualities, such as white goods, consumer electronics, groceries and media. According to the UCAN process, an evaluation is best when it determine how users perceive the benefit of such services in this stage of development to avoid high costs of software development later (Davis/Venkatesh 2004).

5.2.7 Evaluation of the Low-Fidelity Prototype

The intention in the evaluation of the Mobile Prosumer was not only to determine valuable insights into smart product information systems that can be used for Ubicomp applications in general, but also to determine if and how the use of focus groups helps to gain deeper understanding in the stage of low-fidelity prototypes. First the research methodology *focus groups* is described, then the description of the evaluation results.

5.2.7.1 Research Methodology

Focus groups are a form of group interviews using group interaction as part of the method. The method is useful for exploring people's knowledge and experiences. It can be used to examine what people think, how they think and why they think what they do (Kitzinger 1994; Kitzinger 1995). Focus groups allow gathering insights into people's shared understandings of everyday life and the ways in which individuals are influenced by others in a group situation. Focus group interviews are particularly suited for obtaining several perspectives about the same topic (Gibbs 1997). Depending on the area of research, sample size of focus groups ranges from six to ten, or as high as 15 (Kitzinger 1995; Powell/Single 1996). For the focus group, the sample consisted of ten people in each group.

Purposive sampling, multiple coding and respondent validation is added to the study set up (Barbour 2001) as proposed by Barbour, to improve the quality of the qualitative research approach within the MP case study:

- *Purposive sampling:* Qualitative research usually aims to reflect the diversity within a given population (Kuzel 1992)—as opposed to random sampling, a definition of user groups is important (Morgan 1998). Specific user groups are defined and during an intensive screening process, the participants are chosen carefully.

- *Multiple coding*: To avoid a bias of subjectivity, multiple coding involved cross checking of coding strategies and interpretation of data by independent researchers. The transcription documents of the focus groups were evaluated independently by two researchers and compared. In discussions the different viewpoints were contrasted and matched if applicable.

- *Respondent validation:* The moderator of the groups tried to cross-check views with the participants via continuous asking if he understood it right. Furthermore the statements were validated out of different points of view (Consumers and sales personnel).

Table 26 shows the research methodology and gives an overview on the study set up.

Research framework	Qualitative analysis/focus group
Method of data collection	Two focus groups with moderator
Period	September– 120 minutes for each focus group
Duration	Transcription and word count
Measuring method	Video recording, transcription and evaluation
Universe	Consumers (group 1) and sales assistants (group 2)
Sample type	Telephone pre-test questionnaire and screening. Buyers and sellers of groceries, consumer electronics, white goods (example given: toaster, washing machine), and media (especially books and CDs).
Sample size	n=20 (10/10)

Table 26: Research Methodology

Each focus group was recorded on video and transcribed afterwards. The sales personnel group was asked the same questions and showed the same material/prototype. The discussions of all groups were recorded in audio and video with the permission of the participants. During the discussion, a moderator led the talks. Afterwards, transcripts were analyzed.

5.2.7.2 Sample

Two focus groups were conducted in total; both on one day and each group consisted of 10 people. Participants in both groups were selected based on a rigorous screening and recruiting process on the telephone: *group 1 with consumers* and *group 2 with sales personnel*.

The consumer sample ranged in age from 18 to 25 (Digital Natives—young people who grew up with modern technology and the Internet) and 40 to 60 (Digital Immigrants—people who came into contact with information technology at a later point in live) with a half/half distribution (Prensky 2001a) (see also section 3.1.1). Digital Natives (DN) were of interest, because they learned to interact with new media from a very young age and are used to interaction with digital media. Digital Immigrants (DI) however needed to adjust to modern technologies and may perceive the benefits differently (Prensky 2001a, 2001b). Every group consisted of 50% males and 50% females.

All participants were fully employed or self-employed with a regular monthly income, or students. Sales personnel participants were selected according a product category scheme or products they directly sell in their store. Desired product groups were wine, do-it-yourself, consumer electronics, media, and white goods. A criterion for the consumer group was that every potential participant should have bought at a minimum two to three of four product categories in the last 12 weeks. They are active mobile phone users and use the Internet. The mixture was defined via life situations and marital status. Ten participants were finally selected and invited to the consumers focus group and to the sales personnel group (see Table 27).

Participant attributes	Group 1: Consumer (n=10)	Group 2: Sales personnel (n=10)
Sex	Five male, five female	Five male, five female
Details of group definition	- Digital Natives (Age:18 to 25 / n=5) - Digital Immigrants (Age: 40 to 55 / n=5)	- Fulltime employees in larger stores - At least 2 years of sales experience
Product categories	Previously bought products within the last 6 months included - Groceries (Wine) - Consumer Electronics (MP3 Player) - White Goods (Toaster, Microwave) - Media (CD, Books)	Experts in - Groceries (Wine) - Consumer Electronics (MP3 Player) - White Goods (Toaster, Microwave) - Media (CD, Books) - DIY
Media Usage	- Mobile phone users - Internet users	- Mobile phone users - Internet users
Briefing	The invited participants were not briefed in advanced or aware of the underlying discussion subject.	

Table 27: Consumers and sales personnel screening criteria

Group 2 of the sales assistants did not target digital natives and immigrants for two reasons: a) it was very difficult in the screening process to motivate the needed number of participants in that age ranges and b) it is clear that people in between the age groups also provide relevant information based on their experience. Both sexes were equally numbered. All designated participants were supposed to work fulltime and use a mobile phone, either a personal one belonging to themselves or a business one. Group 2 participants were selected according to a product group scheme or products they directly sell or are in charge of in their store. Desired product groups were wine, do-it-yourself, consumer electronics, media, and white goods.

5.2.7.3 Data Collection and Data Coding

The focus groups were conducted in a room with a one-way mirror covering the entire wall. Each focus group was recorded on video and transcribed afterwards. Fig. 65 shows the timeline of the focus groups and the discussed sections: First an introduction was given (warm-up), and then experiences and attitudes towards shopping were discussed, before a paper-based prototype was shown. To avoid a bias of opinions about the prototype, especially as it showed one product only, the study followed the UCAN process model: The low fidelity prototype was shown after a paper-based concept test with a handout. This combined both evaluations, the refined initial idea and a low fidelity prototype.

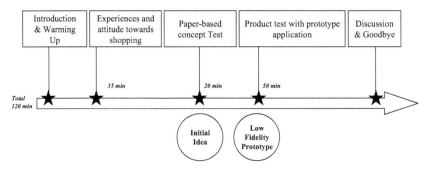

Fig. 65: Timeline of both focus groups

Both group discussions were divided in 8 sections, each with different content, questions and hypotheses according the preliminary findings (see Appendix for details). Each focus group lasted 120 min.

5.2.8 General Evaluation Results

The transcriptions were then evaluated according to the categories from the previously stated three categories: (1) experiences and attitudes towards shopping itself, a (2) paper-based concept test, and (3) finally the low-fidelity prototype.

5.2.8.1 Experiences and Attitude towards Shopping

In general, participants felt that shopping is often stressful because of an overwhelming range of products to choose from, difficulties in finding the right product, and unsatisfying checkout situations. Limited time, too many people, and high temperatures were also considered stress factors. The consumers disliked the insufficient number, availability, qualifications, and expertise of sales clerks. These findings are similar to those mentioned in the study of (Aylott/Mitchell 1998), although Aylott and Mitchell focused on grocery shopping. Non-food shopping was perceived as more stressful to the participants, whereas shopping for food happens as a matter of routine and is considered less stressful. Consumers said that they typically shop at the same collection of stores and usually know where to find grocery products (Resatsch et al. 2008).

The study found evidence that consumers are not happy with their overall shopping experience, but content with the current shopping process. They regard additional information on products as beneficial only to a certain extent and consider this information to be highly dependent on the particular product group. Uncertainty and information overload play a role, however, these deficits seem to be different for each product category. Online research was common among all participants and used to increase knowledge about price and availability of products before purchase (Resatsch et al. 2008).

To sum up, food and smaller white goods are routinely bought and consumers felt that the amount of money involved in their purchase is not high enough to warrant additional information searches. In contrast, consumer electronics are intensively researched online, but final decisions are also made because of the look and feel of the product. Difference between digital natives and digital immigrants was evident, with the digital natives actively using online recommendation systems and collaborative filtering systems. It was easy to imagine digital natives conducting such searches at PoS. Between the group of consumers and the group of sales assistants; it became obvious that there are deeply rooted differences in perceptions. Sales personnel perceived themselves as very knowledgeable and capable of providing good service, whereas all consumers claimed that sales personnel are rarely there when needed and, even if available, some are not helpful. Because of this perceptual gap between the two groups, it seems likely that a smart product information system could address these problems (Resatsch et al. 2008).

5.2.8.2 Evaluating the Initial Idea—Paper-based Concept Test

Following the collection of the participant's experiences and attitudes towards shopping, a paper-based concept evaluation took place. Supported by a slide that briefly introduced a smart product information service coupled to a mobile phone, both focus groups first discussed the concept (see Fig. 66).

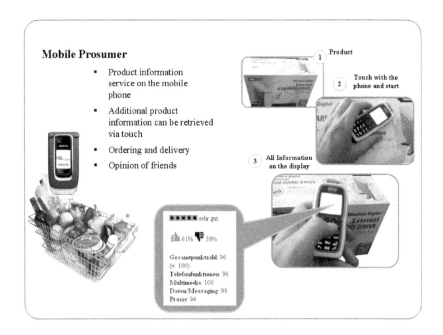

Fig. 66: The paper-based concept explanation on a power point slide

Immediately after a positive reaction, concerns arose around the trustworthiness of the information: It was not clear to the focus group which providers of information would be selected for the phone displays. Up-to-datedness of the information especially when it involved prices was also treated skeptically. Skepticism was stronger among the DIs. All consumers indicated that price comparisons were a useful service.

Although the use of RFID technology has been heavily discussed in the news media in terms of issues regarding privacy and data security (Resatsch et al. 2007a), participants had no major concerns about privacy threats. Some consumers were more concerned that the products would become more expensive when equipped with the RFID tag. Overall, both men and digital natives were more attracted by the Mobile Prosumer concept.

Apparently sales persons do not want consumers to have the possibility to gain too much information. They were afraid of becoming unnecessary. Furthermore they expected that clients will be even more insecure if they have more information. Finally, it became clear that a bad consumer review in a recommendation system available online will make it very difficult for sales persons to sell a product. But on the other hand there then is a chance in the bad rating: the vendor can try to convince consumers to buy a more expensive product.

The paper-based concept test did not show a clear benefit to the consumers. Contrary to our expectations, in which additional product information has an immediate value to consumers, the participants did not rate the service shown on paper as very valuable. It is not easy to understand what product information systems can provide, leading to less acceptance with consumers. Consumers need to feel, see, and understand the RFID technology to value their benefits (Resatsch et al. 2008).

5.2.9 Low-Fidelity Prototype Evaluation

The actual prototype was considered more valuable to the consumers than the paper based concept. Participants used a Nokia 6131 NFC-enabled phone with the Mobile Prosumer (MP) application and a wine bottle with NFC tag attached to it. The low-fidelity prototype was tested among the consumers (*focus group 1*) and among the sales assistants (*focus group 2*).

5.2.9.1 Low-Fidelity Prototype Evaluation—Focus Group 1: Consumers

The MP was perceived to be a reasonable support for purchasing high-quality products by some of the consumer respondents. They saw a benefit only if all products were equipped with the NFC/RFID tags. The success and practicability of the MP clearly depends on the amount of information available on the Internet. Contrary to the expectations that the example would indicate the value of providing price and product quality data, the focus group participants responded differently. They questioned both the validity and credibility of the information sources used in the low fidelity prototype. However the relevance of information (if believed) to product purchase was considered very important.

Other findings were:

- A general concern from consumers that sales personnel might become obsolete.

- Privacy was of no concern to participants except for one respondent.

- The NFC technology was considered innovative, very easy to use and a good way to retrieve information about products.

- A product information system should be available for all products in a product group.

- The product information service must be highly trustworthy.

In addition, digital native participants tended to understand the information power of the MP more than their digital immigrant counterparts. Overall, the comprehension of the basic capabilities of the MP was higher after the demonstration with the low fidelity prototype and the general acceptance of the system was higher (Resatsch et al. 2008).

5.2.9.2 Low-Fidelity Prototype Evaluation—Focus Group 2: Sales Assistants

The sales assistants group considered the MP appropriate for providing simple information— sort of an instrument of pre-selection. It could assist to avoid frequently asked questions. This is positive for consumers who do not want sales personnel interaction anyway.

For a merchant information system the group considered RFID technology highly useful. A system used by sales personal to determine whether an item is out-of-stock was considered more useful than the consumer oriented MP.

For both groups it was clear that a technological solution will not substitute expert knowledge from a sales assistant. Technological solutions further lead to information overflow, except for solutions that show only relevant information—a fact that is tough to realize in the real world (Resatsch et al. 2008).

5.2.10 Refined Use Case

The results of the evaluation enabled us to further detail the use case. The idea of the UCAN process is to eliminate potential misleading ideas in the process and adapt a future product to the user needs. For the refined use case, Fig. 67 maps the study results on the purchase decision model. For products with a higher degree of collective decision and fewer available purchase programs, the need for smart product information systems increases. Not all, but some specialty goods and also mix types are more promising areas. This includes experience products, as well as products that are not purchased regularly.

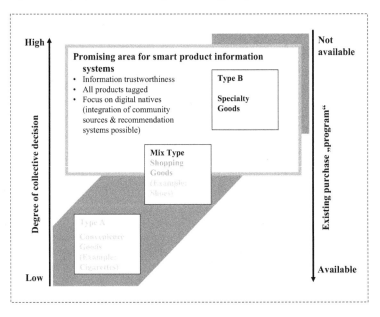

Fig. 67: Mapping the study results on the purchase decision model
Source: (Resatsch et al. 2008)

Although the search qualities are researched previously by consumers on the Internet before a purchase, the availability of products in shops may be different. A fact that increases the need to also provide information on search qualities in stores. A combination of these items in a factor such as product value attributes combined with an axis of existing purchase programs or behavior would make possible an evaluation of the value of a smart product information system for certain products for consumers. Fig. 68 shows that the most promising area for smart product information systems among the tested four categories is products with high product value attributes (life span, degree of collective decision, information intensity) and no available purchase program.

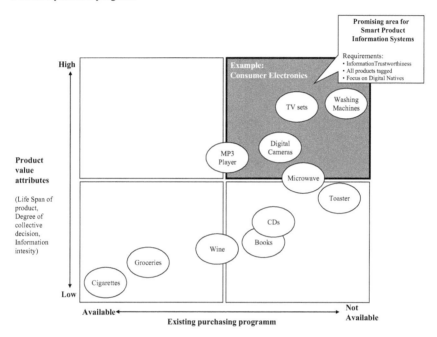

Fig. 68: Proposed product value – purchase behaviour – matrix (PVPB)
Source: (Resatsch et al. 2008)

The implications of this research on future product information services for smart products are important for further developments of B2C and user-centered applications and application development in the area of retail business. First and most important is to determine relevant information for different consumer types in each relevant product category. The relevance of information differs between digital natives and digital immigrants. Retail information systems may need to provide different services for these target groups. Decision support systems (Kindberg/Fox 2002; Shim et al. 2002) and semantically supported information systems (Maass/Filler 2006) help to determine the right information. Another challenge is the design of IT-supporting components, be it on the organizational (operator, business model, etc.) or technical level (certificates, etc.) to assure validity and credibility of information sources. This poses a challenge to implementing concepts for trustworthiness of information (3rd party provider).

The results allowed answering the initially targeted research questions within the case study (see Table 28). These questions would help to further refine the use case in order to build a working prototype.

What is considered relevant and useful information at the PoS to support search and experience qualities?	Reports of product experience were questioned many times in the study. Participants, especially the Digital Immigrants, thought that many people think differently and therefore the benefit of a product report for one's own purchases is limited. The concept of firsthand reports on products was seen as useful only for pricy, long-term used products, such as washing machines. Interestingly the participants explained the concept of collaborative filters and agreed that it would be useful, nevertheless, they denied its benefits when named directly. The benefit was regarded higher, if the people who wrote the report were known contacts— friends and family.
Can consumers use any additional information services appropriately at the PoS?	Sales personnel considered the cognitive load of too many products already as too high for average consumers. Likewise, consumers felt overwhelmed by the excess of products. Further information could add to the confusion and needs to be limited. Again, younger consumers seem to have no problem with information processing. The case of what exactly is *relevant* product information at the PoS needs to be further deepened and quantitatively evaluated.
Do RFID-based information services have a perceived benefit to consumers?	The various prototypes and iterations show that that RFID-based product information services can have a perceived benefit to consumers, but only if several basic principles are applied: • Only relevant, valid and trustworthy information • Targeting younger user groups • Tag all possible products and enable all services (even those that hurt – price comparison) Particularly the last aspect is difficult to realize in retail business. These principles act as requirements for the next stage in the UCAN process.
Do RFID-based information applications have a perceived benefit to sales assistants?	From the sales assistant perspective, the tested prototype was not considered to be a benefit. Sales persons do not want consumers to have the possibility to gain too much information—unless the MP only shows *Frequently Asked Questions*. The sales assistants were afraid of becoming unnecessary in the future. Furthermore they expected that clients will be even more insecure if they have more information. On the other hand, a system that targets the needs of sales personnel, such as stock-information or updated producer information would be of interest.
Do perceived benefits of information services differ among different product categories?	Generally, within the group of experience goods there is a gap between products used in long-term and products with shorter life-cycles. Toaster and microwaves trigger less of an information need than the washing machine. Consumer electronics incorporate an intensive online/offline behavior and are less routinely bought, thus are more valid for smart product information services to bring a benefit than for groceries (Food/Non-food).
Are smart product information services applications acceptable for consumers and sales assistants?	Technology-wise the application was accepted by the users. The use of NFC as an interaction technology was considered very easy and simple. Although the benefit was not clear to everyone, broad acceptance was given.

What is the overall acceptance of RFID/NFC technology at the PoS?	Contrary to the expected discussion of privacy aspects and fear of data security, this was not an issue for any of the groups. Privacy issues need to be addressed (Galanxhi/Nah 2005), however in our case they were not in the centre of discussions. Only when directly asked, both groups indicated minor concerns.

Table 28: Answering the case study research questions
Source: (Resatsch et al. 2008)

The initial question for this case study, if ubicomp applications [can] be used to meet individual information needs was not clearly answered with the instantiation of this evaluation and the smart product information service artifact. The ability to compare prices and access other opinions on a product are part of an overall product purchase decision, but these problems are now solved with prior Internet searches and by querying sales assistants. In those cases when shopping is routine, additional information was not regarded as needed or beneficial. The MP system provided more perceivable benefits for the technically savvy individuals. Others stated that they would use the MP because they felt that the introduction of mobile phones reading RFID tags was an unstoppable development. The primary stressors in offline shopping were those of physical discomfort, e.g., high or low temperatures, crowds, etc. maybe a starting point for a variation of classic shop concepts. Some participants stated that they would only use a smart product information service in specific cases, e.g., when buying expensive products—but only if all products are tagged (Resatsch et al. 2008).

For these reasons, smart products definitely target younger generations, need to be quick and easy to use, and should be introduced into specific product segments only. For the course of the next iteration stage these information proved to be more useful than in the Easymeeting case.

5.2.11 Summary of the Results – Mobile Prosumer

Compared to Easymeeting, the MP had a time frame of almost two years to be developed and researched. Easymeeting was conducted in only three months. This indicator shows that it is rather difficult to set up such a process including the prototyping. This section will sum up the results of the MP case study insofar as it theorizes about the UCAN process and the contribution to Ubicomp.

5.2.11.1 Improve and Theorize about the Developed Process Model (UCAN)

This paragraph describes the (1) benefits of the process, the (2) limitations, and sums up (3) the research instrument focus groups.

(1) Benefits of the process: The approach with the UCAN process showed that the opinions of participants about the paper-based concept test and actual product test with a prototype were different contrary to the quantitative findings of Venkatesh (2004), the extended user acceptance framework for Ubicomp applications based on the ideas of Venkatesh and Abowd is capable to first let users discuss paper-based concepts and then test the prototype to determine a difference between conceptual idea and experiment, and the findings also show the benefit of the research approach and delivers new insights for the design of smart products in retail in general.

The case study used two ways to evaluate the initial idea: with a concept test and expert interviews. These two worked out well in the distinction of a very early initial idea, which can be discussed among colleagues and experts, and the initial idea tested with a larger focus group to assure that the concept itself is interesting to the group participants. In the process, the concept test can then be evaluated at the same place and time as the low-fidelity prototype.

Using the UCAN process aside from the requirement engineering into a more product design aspect helped to find out the most likely instantiation of the artifact that targets user needs best.

(2) Limitations of the process: An obvious first step to take a closer look was in the UCAN methodological area. Is the finding, that the perception of the service was different between paper-based and actual prototype a singular event or is this the case in other Ubicomp settings as well? The study setup itself had also several limitations during the process. The prototype test was done one by one, some users might have been afraid to make a mistake and hesitated to test it because of the group dynamic. When the first people already discussed the system, the others had not tried the prototype yet, thus some comments were made before actual system use. An integration of the talking-out-loud methodology could help in the case. Furthermore there was no control for cultural background / factors influencing the respondents.

(3) Evaluation: Contrary to using personal interviews as in the first case study (Easymeeting), the case study used focus groups—starting with expert interviews to discuss the initial idea. Again the use and outcome of the instrument in the three phases of the evaluation was evaluated.

The case study was useful to evaluate a smart information product system with an existing prototype and real consumers, as well as sales personnel to strengthen internal validity and backup the findings. The focus groups allowed a better understanding of soft factors that determine user perception. From the first initial idea to the next iteration, the focus groups were very helpful and gave better recommendations than the interviews in the previous case study.

The findings based on the adapted pre-prototype approach are significantly different to what was expected based on current literature and that what a single paper concept test would have revealed. This again shows the importance to test a future Ubicomp system with real users outside the research laboratories and student groups. Few Ubicomp prototypes have been tested outside student environment (Välkkynen/Niemelä/Tuomisto 2006), while most were tested in the research lab environment or with fellow researchers. In the case of the Mobile Prosumer it became clear that a test with only digital natives grad students could have led to too positive results, showing the importance of real user participants.

Compared to the instrument interviews, the focus group findings were more dynamic and more helpful to determine application changes (see Table 29). However, it was less possible to really test for requirements in this phase, because the focus groups were only partially structured and depended on the moderator more than the interviewer.

Phases of evaluation	Positive	Negative
Organisation phase	-	It took a lot of effort to recruit the participants for the focus groups. Also the use of the special room was very expensive and only possible with the support and help of TNS Infratest.
Execution phase	It took only 4 hours in total to actually conduct the whole focus group.	-
Analysis phase	The focus groups led to very good results to improve the application.	Efforts were high, because one had to first transcribe the whole video and then the analysis took a long time because of the many replies.

Table 29: Evaluation instrument: Focus Groups

Overall (see Table 30) the field of smart products is very promising for both research and practice, but it needs much more research attention to shed light into these and many more related areas.

Case study	Phase in UCAN process	Research Framework	Used evaluation method	Sample size	Effort to conduct	Helpful to determine product related iterations
Mobile Prosumer	Initial idea	Qualitative analysis	Expert interviews	N=4	Low	Yes
	Initial idea	Qualitative analysis	Focus groups (Concept test)	2*N=10	Medium	Yes
	Low-fidelity prototype	Qualitative analysis	Focus groups (Prototype test)	2*N=10	Medium	Yes

Table 30: Summary of the Mobile Prosumer evaluation

The next section describes the design guidelines that can be prepared from the study.

5.2.11.2 Preparing Design Guidelines

The contributions are clustered again in: (1) NFC technology and application, (2) tag infrastructure, (3) human factors, and (4) the device itself:

(1) NFC technology and application:

• It may be good for retailers to focus on applications targeting sales personnel, because they are cheaper to implement with connections only to internal databases, easier to set up the system (limited), the penetration of user devices is manageable and the information needs of sales personnel can be clearly determined (feedback channel, more product information updates). Also, there is no problem of trustworthiness if the publisher of information is the company itself.

• The major drivers for customers satisfaction is—of course—not the technology itself, not only to limit current stressors (temperature, crowd density), but to make the shopping experience as pleasurable and easy as possible with better product selection.

In the overall context of Ubicomp it is the human being, the user, who is in the middle of things—a fact even more important for application developers and a good reason to use pre-, proto- and para-types in an early development stage.

• NFC seems to have had none to only low impact on privacy and data security concerns.

(2) Tag infrastructure:

• It became clear that either all products in total or at least all products within a specific product group need to be tagged to provide visible benefit for the consumers—this is difficult to realize in the real business environment.

• Tag placements were of no concern to the participants (shelf level or product level)

(3) Human factors:

• Using the very easy to use NFC technology as way of interaction has had a perceived positive influence on the acceptance of the system. It could not be measured to what extent the easy usage of the mobile phone NFC system has added to a positive evaluation of the overall system, but it can be assumed that this might have an effect on user intentions to use an innovative information system at the PoS—similar in the way prior research has shown for hedonic information systems (van der Heijden 2004).

• All non-functional requirements from Easymeeting case study were applicable to the Mobile Prosumer as well. Shopping is clearly an everyday activity and has certain limitations for consumers—for example there should be no high cognitive load to make shopping easy and simple. This interaction component can be done by the introduction of NFC.

There were no **(4) device** related results in this variation of the study setup. This might be due to the different handset used (Nokia 6131 NFC vs. Nokia 3220i) or to the different explanations given.

To finalize the UCAN process model, the last phase needs to be researched with its own case study in the next chapter.

6   Working Prototype: An NFC-based Mobile Phone Ticketing System

This chapter describes the case study to theorize about and test the last stage of the UCAN process model (working prototype). It is tested with a method used for evaluating technology acceptance. Also case study findings are presented in offering design guidelines for NFC-based Ubicomp applications. This chapter covers the mobile phone ticketing system of a public transportation company.

The two previous case studies provided a better understanding of Ubicomp in domain specific settings (office and retail), however the use of technology acceptance models is subject to discussion for the next stage: the initial working prototype. The initial working prototype is supposed to be conducted in the field—and therefore involves more potential participants taking part in the study. With more participants the possibility is presented to conduct a technology acceptance study involving a larger sample size for necessary statistical model tests.

In section 4.4.1 demonstrates that ticketing applications are based on technology-push strategies. Changing existing ticketing solutions may lead to infrastructural changes (*technology side*), and to behavioral changes (*human side*). To evaluate the impact of NFC on ticketing solutions, this case study examines technology acceptance of a newly introduced NFC ticketing solution. The technology acceptance models from 3.2.3 provide the basis for evaluating the UCAN process. Table 31 shows the overall description of the case study.

Case study name	Public Transport Company (PTC)
Description	NFC-based mobile phone ticketing system in public transport
Unit of analysis	Individuals in an online survey

Table 31: Case study description

This chapter begins by first outlining the step from the initial idea to the working system prototype (Chapter 6.1). Then the initial working prototype is described (Chapter 6.2), followed by an evaluation of sample, research design, and data collection and data processing (Chapter 6.3). Then the data analysis, and the results of the evaluation are presented, followed by interpretation and analysis (Chapter 6.4). The chapter ends with the summary of the results within the UCAN process (see Chapter 6.5 and Fig. 69).

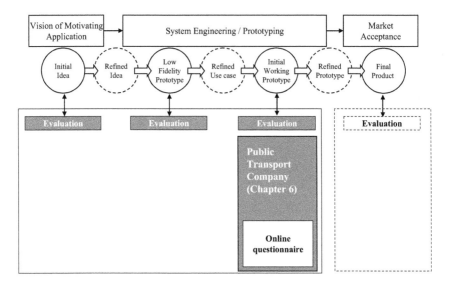

Fig. 69: Used evaluation method in the PTC case

Table 32 shows the research framework and subsequent evaluation method used in the course of the case study according to the phase in the UCAN process.

Case study	Phase in UCAN process	Research Framework	Used evaluation method
PTC	Working prototype	Quantitative survey	Online questionnaire

Table 32: Evaluation methods for PTC in the UCAN process

The chapter differentiates between the Mobile Phone Ticketing System as such, abbreviated with MPTS (the initial idea) and the NFC-based mobile phone ticketing system, abbreviated with MPTS NFC (the working prototype).

6.1 From the Initial Idea to the Working Prototype

Contrary to the first two case studies (Easymeeting and Mobile Prosumer), in which the author was able to follow the development from the motivating application vision to the low-fidelity prototype, the PTC had been started in 2004. The working prototype that was examined during the analysis was already in existence and therefore not taken through all stages of the UCAN process. Given this limitation it was not possible to determine if different functions or usability issues would have been triggered in the previous phases of UCAN. Similar to the UCAN, the PTC employed other versions before launching the working prototype. This section describes the path from the initial idea to the initial working prototype. Several previous trials and pilots had already been set up for the PTC prior to actually conducting the NFC working-prototype pilot test.

An early trial took place from 2005 to 2006 using a bonus card with NFC functionality. A second pilot that provided the basis for the final NFC application ran from 2006 to 2007. This trial was turned into a productive system in early 2008.

The initial idea was to determine the technical feasibility and user acceptance of a mobile phone that can be used as a smart card, and compare it with a contactless smart card scheme that has been in use for several years. Thus the first 10-month trial was arranged with 155 participants in a city with 95.000 residents. The trial used a Nokia 3220 NFC phone (see also Fig. 14) that functioned as a loyalty card (smart card mode) and a public transportation ticket. The previously available smart cards were still used in parallel with the NFC enabled phones.

It quickly became evident that the major problem in building a system with fixed reader systems had to do with the enormous infrastructure-related costs. Fig. 70 shows the amount of investments in fixed infrastructure versus an infrastructure that consists of passive RFID tags. The fixed infrastructure is called a terminal-based, check-in check-out solution (CICO), because terminals with implemented logical functions are needed in the bus or train. By comparison, the NFC-tag based CICO solution incorporates the logic on the mobile phone with no extra terminals needed. Check-in takes place when users enter the bus and touch an NFC tag. The whole original system is converted—from a technical point of view. The figure shows that the cost of deploying a NFC-tag based CICO solution is cheaper than the terminal-based solution.

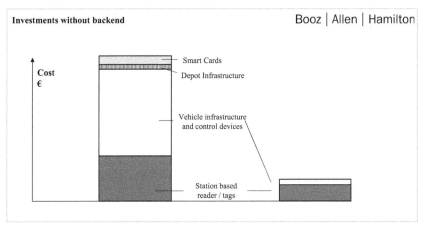

Fig. 70: Investments (without backend costs) necessary to build ticket system
Source: PTC, BAH 2007

These considerations and pilot results led to the plans to introduce a NFC-based solution. To further facilitate usage, a mobile phone check-in-only (CI) solution was preferred – in which the system determines (or the user enters) the starting point of the journey. To migrate from the existing systems, the public transportation company first introduced a Java-based ticketing system as a mobile client solution for most available mobile phones. On a technological basis, the system used a J2ME smart client without network restriction. The registration was Internet-based and included payment information to assure payments. The system included single-trip tickets or daily passes for the pilot area. Starting in May 2006 the system also served as the basis for the later NFC trial. Approximately 5,700 users currently use the Java-based application. In order to further differentiate between the NFC-based solutions, Fig. 71 shows the process of the Java-based mobile phone ticketing system (MPTS).

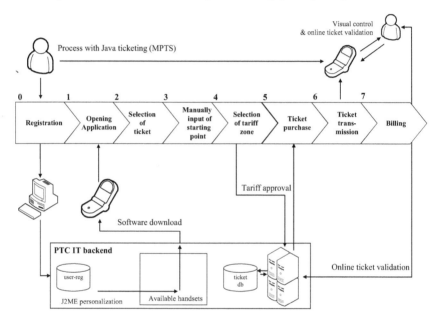

Fig. 71: Java ticketing overview (MPTS)

Seven process steps are needed to buy a ticket including: registration, manually opening the application, choosing the ticket, entering the starting point, selecting the correct tariff zone, final purchase, and receiving the ticket. Billing is the final process step, although the system does not necessarily indicate that billing occurs directly after the ticket is sent to the user. The control of tickets is visual, whereas the controller must check online tickets manually.

After one year of experience with the system a small consumer study was used to research the initial MPTS. The sample size was n=625 of all PTC MPTS for Java-basis users. This research serves as a foundation for the initial working prototype. The results showed that the main driver behind MPTS use was the desire to facilitate ticket purchases by avoiding the hassle associated with ticket vending machines, to use a cash free system, and to have flexibility in when to buy tickets. Out of all participants 10.2% mentioned that easier entry of starting points would be beneficial (n=392 – all users with suggestions for improvements).

To summarize, the main improvement potential of ways in which the MPTS could be improved according to users included:

•   Technical facilitation of installations and easier input of starting position.

•   Metropolitan area-wide coverage.

The challenges to implementing a NFC-based MPTS included:

•   The wide-spread tag infrastructure.

•   Technical facilitation of system usage.

•   Extension over the greater metropolitan area (reach).

•   Know more about the technology acceptance of the customers.

•   Research tag placements and device issues.

The next step was an the initial working prototype with NFC functionality. Thus the PTC introduced a Java-based midlet that was enhanced with a NFC reader functionality. All inner-city public transport stops (bus/subway stops) where equipped with passive RFID tags. The following chapters will focus on this trial set up—the case study is considered the initial working prototype in the UCAN process.

6.2 Working Prototype

This chapter describes the setup of the initial working prototype of the MPTS NFC case study as it appeared in the field.

The MPTS NFC case study with the initial working prototype was conducted from July 2007 until November 2007. The built application connected a virtual ticketing system with a physical location by using a NFC (RFID) tag. The physical location was either a bus stop pole or a ticket vending machine in a subway station (see Fig. 72).

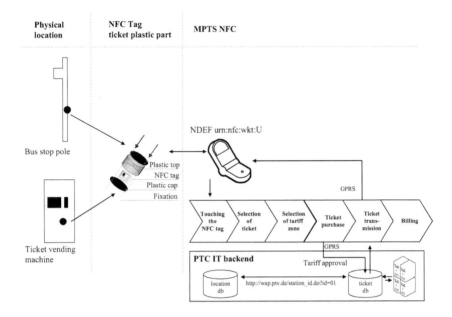

Fig. 72: Working prototype setup of MPTS NFC application

The application was built on the Java midlet that also included a NFC reader function. Instead of the previous solution, in which the user manually entered the starting point of the journey, the functionality of NFC allowed the user to wave his phone in front of the NFC-touch point (tag) to locate himself. The starting point was then read into the system and distributed to the backend. The rest of the ticket purchasing process was rather similar to the process as described above with the Java only application (see Fig. 71). Fig. 73 compares Java ticketing to Java plus NFC ticketing in a process flow chart. Having to manually enter the starting point was the only step saved in the process.

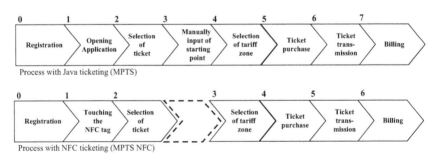

Fig. 73: Comparison of NFC-based ticket purchases with Java ticketing

Although covering only one process step, this process step of manually opening the application and entering the starting point is also the most time-consuming. Therefore, NFC technology should be implemented in order to reduce ticket-buying times and to provide customers greater convenience. The MPTS NFC application took this finding into account by providing the necessary NFC tag infrastructure to avoid the manually entering process step.

The MPTS NFC application used NFC tags embedded in a plastic case. The plastic case securely covered the underlying NFC tag. An adhesive layer on the back of the plastic case made it possible to attach the tags to all ticket machines and station polls at relatively low cost.

All NFC tags used are write protected. For updates, all tags can be opened with the individual tag keys. Each tag stores an NDEF message with 2 NDEF records. The second record contains the URL for accessing web information:

NDEF urn:nfc:wkt:U
(URL of station - e.g. http://wap.ptc.de/station_id.do?id=01)

The working prototype used in the case study covered 59 NFC-enabled bus stops and subway station ticket vending machines. To cover the entire area, several thousand NFC-enabled stations would be needed. The next chapter describes the evaluation of this working prototype.

6.3 Evaluation of the Working Prototype

This chapter describes the evaluation of the working prototype of the NFC-based mobile phone ticketing system. The research questions of this chapter are based on the finding that UTAUT and technology acceptance can help further the development of Ubicomp applications. The research question to be answered is:

Will the UTAUT model help to explain the acceptance of NFC technology in the public transportation field, and will it provide recommendations for developing the application further?

If using a standard unified model, such as the UTAUT, allows companies to determine technology acceptance and improve the tested application, the effort to use it can be justified by the results. If the results do not provide recommendations for application development the use of technology acceptance evaluations needs to be reconsidered. This evaluation makes use of the standard UTAUT constructs and their items, adapts these to the Ubicomp scenario, and analyses the working prototype. Fig. 74 explains the process of the evaluation according to the suggested social research process described in (and adapted from (Singleton/Straits 2005)):

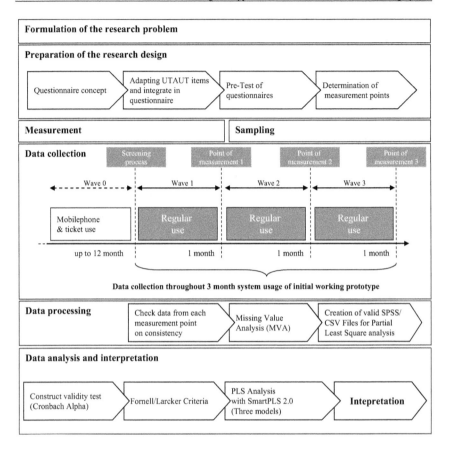

Fig. 74: Overview of research methodology
Source: adapted from (Singleton/Straits 2005)

First, the research problem was formulated. Then, the research design was prepared. This included a questionnaire with general questions. Furthermore the standard UTAUT items were adapted to the specifics of the MPTS NFC case study. This was pre-tested to ensure that the question set would run smoothly. Finally, in the preparation phase, several measurement points were defined in order to measure changes over time. Measurement and sampling are further described in the next paragraph. The data collection phase included a preliminary screening process and three measurement points with the same target users (panel survey). Data processing followed the data collection with consistency checks, a missing value analysis, and the creation of valid SPSS/.csv files for the following Partial Least Square (PLS) analysis. In the analysis phase, the constructs were built and checked, then analyzed with PLS, followed by the final interpretation of the results. The next paragraph begins by detailing the sample used in the study.

6.3.1 Sample

The Public Transport Company (PTC) had previously introduced a mobile phone ticketing system in 2004 with approx. 5000 users (see initial idea description). For the case study measuring technology acceptance, participants were selected from users who had agreed to be contacted for additional research purposes. The screening process of the participants was conducted with an online questionnaire. The goal of the screening process was to determine basic attitudes towards media usage in general, mobile services, and public transportation.

All users received an email to apply for the pilot test with the initial working prototype. Furthermore, companies located in the area of the pilot test received an email to forward it to potentially interested candidates for the prototype evaluation. In this screening process, 600 people responded. From the initial 600 respondents, 250 participants were selected to be part of the study based on gender, their previous media usage, and how frequently they used public transportation (see Table 33). The quantitative survey used three online questionnaires at three different measuring points.

Research framework	Quantitative survey
Method of data collection	Three online questionnaires at three different measuring points.
Language of questionnaire	German
Period	September 2007 to December 2007
Measuring method	Interval 5-item-scale
Universe	Public transportation users in German city with 663.000 inhabitants
Sample type	Pre-screening based on demographic data, media usage and frequency of public transportation use
Sample number wave 0 (pre-selection of participants)	N = 600
Sample number wave 1	N = 217
Sample number wave 2	N = 214
Sample number wave 3	N = 211
Sample number – participants participating in all three waves including answering UTAUT related items in at least two waves	N = 179
Sample number – participants participating in at least two waves including answering all UTAUT related items plus at least 1 NFC ticket purchase (= N for the final PLS analysis)	N = 148

Table 33: Sample

Although a greater number of female participants were sought for the study, the actual male to female ratio of participants did not represent the average group of public transportation users. The sample is therefore not representative. The participants are mainly male, which is an indication of the general male interest in technology. Participants that were selected received a brand new Nokia 6131 NFC phone as an incentive. They were allowed to keep the phone after the pilot test.

In Wave 1, 217 people filled out the online questionnaires properly, in Wave 2, 214 people, and in Wave 3, 211 people answered all questions. Two reasons were behind the different sample sizes in the table: the questionnaires included exactly the same set of UTAUT items. Over all three measurement points, the UTAUT items had to be answered at least twice—i.e. at three measurement points with complete UTAUT sets the respondents needed to fill out all items at least twice. Only 179 participants filled out the UTAUT items at least twice completely. From the 179 participants, excluded were those who never actually used the system (they never bought a ticket with the NFC-tag), although they obviously answered the questionnaire. All participants who actually bought one or more NFC tickets with the system were included in the final sample (N=148). This number of people was used for the PLS model tests (*People who bought at least 1 ticket via NFC*).

6.3.2 Preparing the Research Design

Research design preparation included developing the questionnaire concept and adapting the UTAUT standard constructs.

6.3.2.1 Questionnaire Concept

The three questionnaires were split into two parts. Part one included overall questions concerning the prototype, while part two was conceptually similar with UTAUT constructs and its adapted items. The overall questions addressed: public transportation usage frequency, satisfaction with PTC and the service, and ticket usage.

Participants had one week to fill out the online questionnaire form. If the number of completed survey forms fell below 200 after one week, a reminder was sent out and the deadline was extended for an extra week. After three months of the pilot study Wave 1 was conducted with a total sample size of N=217. Wave 2 took place after four months of the pilot study with N=214 participants, and Wave 3 after the pilot was finished with N=211 participants.

The questionnaire statements were adapted from the original questionnaire items by Venkatesh et. al. (2003) and the UTAUT items (see chapter 3.2.3.6). The statements were adapted to the NFC context of the study. The participants were asked to rate their level of agreement on a five-point Likert scale (1=*completely disagree* to 5=*completely agree*). The questionnaire was conducted in German. To test for translation errors, the adapted UTAUT items were translated into German, and then re-translated back into English to check for significant deviations from the original texts.

6.3.2.2 Adaptation of Original UTAUT Constructs

The original UTAUT constructs in (Venkatesh et al. 2003) were based on various studies of organizational contexts (e.g. financial services or retail electronics). In the case of the working prototype the constructs were applied to the daily lives of users voluntarily experiencing a completely new technology, independent of any organizational context. Because of this, the original UTAUT constructs and items needed to be specifically adapted to NFC technology. The next sections briefly describe the original constructs and how they were modified for the purpose of the case study. Based on the idea that a technology acceptance model should be easily adapted to a new case, the PTC case adapted the existing constructs of the original UTAUT study. UTAUT still needs to be researched to determine whether it can be generally adapted to other settings. Following the description of the constructs and how they have been adapted, the hypothesis applied to the case study have been borrowed from Venkatesh et. al. (2003).

The following constructs were adapted and applied to our study: (1) Performance Expectancy (PE), (2) Effort Expectancy, (3) Social Influence, (4) Attitude Towards Using Technology (ATUT), (5) Facilitating Conditions, (6) Self-Efficacy, (7) Anxiety, (8) Behavioral Intention, and (9) Use Behavior:

(1) Performance Expectancy (PE): Performance Expectancy (PE) as used by Venkatesh (2003) is a root construct based on various constructs from other models. Its items include perceived usefulness (Davis 1989; Davis/Bagozzi/Warshaw 1989), extrinsic motivation (Davis/Bagozzi/Warshaw 1992), job-fit (Thompson/Higgins/Howell 1991), relative advantage (Moore/Benbasat 1991), and outcome expectations (Compeau/Higgins/Huff 1999; Compeau/Higgins 1995b).

In studies by Venkatesh et. al., PE was the strongest predictor of intention and remained significant at all points of measurement in voluntary and mandatory settings (Venkatesh et al. 2003). Previous studies focused on the organizational setting in measuring the construct. In this type of context, job performance bears directly on how quickly the job gets done, whether managers acknowledge one's efforts, and whether one improves job-related output. The main difference between the organizational setting and the consumer setting in Ubicomp is that for the consumer setting *job* performance does not exist. While everyday activities may share similarities with jobs, they take place in an environment outside the workplace (Norman 1988). For this reason the PE construct needed to be adapted to the voluntary setting of public transportation mobile services featuring NFC technology.

In Davis (1992), defines *extrinsic motivation* as the inclination of the user to perform an activity because the activity makes it easier to achieve desired outcomes that are distinct from the activity itself. This might be increased job performance, pay, or promotions. Similarly, Moore and Benbasat (1991 define the *relative advantage* construct as the perception that using an innovation will provide greater benefits than using its precursor. Compeau and Higgins (1995) also target outcome expectations as a function of behavioral consequences (Compeau/Higgins 1995a; Davis/Bagozzi/Warshaw 1992; Moore/Benbasat 1991).

Thus, in terms of the NFC application, a relevant line of investigation is to find out the system's usefulness in daily life (Resatsch et al. 2007c). It is also important to determine whether users perceive the combining of mobile phones and a (new) enabling front-end (the NFC tags) as useful to their everyday life. Since no *job* is to be done, the process of buying a ticket is used as the underlying improvement potential. Two items are used to determine if the user thinks that, with the help of NFC, he can buy tickets faster (task performance) and more easily (usability). The ability to save time represents another important aspect in daily life. Two items examine the system and the NFC mobile phone to determine if they are potential time savers (see Table 34).

Performance expectancy	
PE1	I would find the system useful in my daily life
PE2	I would find the combination of NFC tags plus NFC mobile phone ticketing useful in my daily life
PE3	Using the NFC mobile phone ticketing enables me to buy my tickets easier
PE4	Using the NFC mobile phone ticketing enables me to buy my tickets faster
PE5	The system makes public transport more efficient
PE6	I save time using the system
PE7	I save time using the NFC Mobile Phone

Table 34: Adapted construct performance expectancy (PE)

Since PE plays a major role in explaining behavioral intention in previous studies, the first hypothesis is adapted from the PE scenario:

H1: Performance expectancy has a significant influence on behavioral intention.

Moderators, such as gender and age, defined the construct in other studies (Park/Yang/Lehto 2007). In our study, the female gender was under-represented, therefore the moderator gender was not tested. The mean age was 32 years with low variation. The moderator age was also not used.

(2) Effort Expectancy (EE): Effort Expectancy (EE) refers to a system's ease-of-use. Ubicomp systems, especially NFC, are considered extremely easy to use (Kranz/Schmidt 2005; Rukzio et al. 2006a; Rukzio et al. 2006b). The root construct by Venkatesh (2003) combines three constructs with highly similar items: perceived ease-of-use (Davis 1989; Davis/Bagozzi/Warshaw 1989), complexity (Thompson/Higgins/Howell 1991), and Moore's ease-of-use (Moore/Benbasat 1991).

The EE construct loses its significance over periods of extended and sustained usage (Venkatesh et al. 2003) since it applies more to the early stages of new behavior. EE concerns process issues—knowing how to operate the technology—that need to be mastered. Hence for NFC in general, and for the public transportation case in particular, touching something with a mobile phone is integral to using the NFC application and must be performed at least once in order to understand the new behavior (Resatsch et al. 2007c). The useful and complementary *touch* paradigm is a key element of NFC and has been researched and compared to other forms of interaction by several authors (Välkkynen/Niemelä/Tuomisto 2006; Välkkynen et al. 2003; Rukzio 2007; Riekki/Salminen/Alakärppä 2006).

Table 35 shows the adapted EE items. The system registration process was critical since it involved installing the mobile phone client. Furthermore focus was placed on the "touch-based" interaction with NFC phone and tags, and on the efforts required to learn how to operate the system.

Effort expectancy	
EE1	Registering for the system did not bother me
EE2	I would find the system easy to use
EE3	You need to touch the NFC tags with your NFC-enabled mobile phone. This touch-based interaction is clear and easy to understand.
EE4	I would find touch-based interaction easy to use
EE5	Learning to operate the system is easy to me

Table 35: Adapted construct effort expectancy (EE)

For EE the hypothesis is:

H2: **Effort Expectancy** has a significant influence on behavioral intention.

(3) Social influence (SI): Social Influence (SI) is related to the terms "social factors", "subjective norm" (Thompson/Higgins/Howell 1991) and "social norm" (Ajzen 1985; Ajzen 1991). Subjective norm comes from early technology acceptance research by (Ajzen 1991; Ajzen/Fishbein 2005; Fishbein/Ajzen 1975) and is also used in (Taylor/Todd 1995). All these aspects describe the importance of a reference group's subjective culture on the individual subject. The innovation's image and how the innovation enhances the status of the individual within a social system pertains to this construct (Moore/Benbasat 1991).

None of the construct items measured in the above studies played significant roles in voluntary settings. In mandatory settings, social influence appears to be important only in the early stages of an innovation, and becomes non-significant with sustained usage (Venkatesh/Davis 2000). Individuals are more likely to conform to other's opinions when others have the ability to reward the behavior or punish non-behavior (Barki/Hartwick 1994), especially in early stages (Agarwal 2000). This normative pressure decreases over time because of the increasing experience (Venkatesh et al. 2003).

The usage of NFC technology in the context of the public transportation study was voluntary. The participant could also choose to buy a ticket with cash or other forms of payment. The adapted social influence items (see Table 36) show the influence of social perceptions on mobile phone ticketing in general and on NFC technology in particular. Both are important factors in the adaptation of the NFC-ticket system.

Social influence	
SI1	People who are important to me think positive about mobile phone ticketing
SI2	People who are important to me think positive about NFC technology

Table 36: Adapted construct social influence (SI)

The next hypothesis:

H3: Social influence has a significant influence on behavioral intention.

(4) Attitude Towards Using Technology (ATUT): Attitude Towards Using Technology (ATUT) is defined "as an individual's overall affective reaction to using a system" (Venkatesh et al. 2003). It consists of the ideas underlying four constructs used in other models: attitude toward behavior (Davis/Bagozzi/Warshaw 1989; Fishbein/Ajzen 1975; Taylor/Todd 1995), intrinsic motivation (Davis/Bagozzi/Warshaw 1992), affect towards use (Thompson/Higgins/Howell 1991), and affect (Compeau/Higgins/Huff 1999; Compeau/ Higgins 1995a, 1995b).

Venkatesh (2003) mentions that attitude constructs can be significant over different time periods, and are the strongest predictor of behavioral intention in certain cases. In other cases they are not significant at all. It seems that attitude constructs are only significant when performance expectancy and effort expectancy are not included in the model. Attitude constructs tap into an individual's liking, enjoyment, and pleasure associated with technology use. This is part of intrinsic motivation (Deci 1975; Ryan/Deci 2000).

Ubicomp systems target everyday life (Resatsch et al. 2007c). Daily life is rather boring conceptually (Norman 1988). To test whether users perceive Ubicomp technology as *fun*, users could rank the system both in terms of *like* as well as *fun* in the study items. Questions related to process improvement and understanding the desire for more NFC-based applications were also included (Table 37). Finally the attitude towards the technology itself was questioned in seeking to determine the preference of NFC-technology over the alternative paper tickets.

Attitude towards using technology	
ATUT1	I like using the system
ATUT2	Using the system is fun
ATUT3	Using NFC-Technology with a mobile phone is fun
ATUT4	The system improves traveling with public transport
ATUT5	I would like to have more NFC-application such as the PTC Mobile Phone Ticket System
ATUT6	I prefer buying NFC tickets than paper tickets

Table 37: Adapted construct attitude towards using technology (ATUT)

The ATUT hypothesis is:

H4: **Attitude towards NFC devices /services** will **not** have an influence on behavioral intention.

(5) Facilitating conditions (FC): Facilitating Conditions (FC) describe the degree to which an individual believes that an organizational and technical infrastructure exists to support the use of the system. In the UTAUT, constructs underlying the facilitating conditions were combined from perceived behavioral control (Ajzen 1991; Taylor/Todd 1995), facilitating conditions (Thompson/Higgins/Howell 1991), and compatibility (Moore/Benbasat 1991).

Table 38 shows the items used in the study. The technical infrastructure is reflected in item FC2 and FC3: the amount of NFC tags available in the city and at the stations. In the German version of the questionnaire, *resources* was translated into a term that referenced the NFC-tags used in the test—this was communicated to study participants in advance. The first item was used to test if the knowledge needed to use the ticketing system was available to individual subjects (Ajzen 1991). Finally, the *switching cost* of changing a mobile phone brand in order to have an NFC-enabled phone were considered as part of an infrastructure related issue (Lee/Lee/Feick 2001).

Facilitating conditions	
FC1	I have the necessary knowledge about NFC to use the PTC Mobile Phone Ticket System
FC2	There are enough resources (NFC tags) in the city
FC3	There are enough resources at the stations
FC4	I would change my mobile phone brand in order to own a NFC-enabled mobile phone

Table 38: Adapted construct facilitating conditions (FC)

For FC two hypothesizes are used from the original set of hypothesizes

H5: Facilitating Conditions will **not** have a significant influence on behavioral intention.

H6: Facilitating Conditions have a significant influence on use behavior.

(6) Self-Efficacy (SE): Self-Efficacy (SE) refers to how one perceives one's own ability to use a technology for accomplishing a particular job or task. SE is conceptually different from *effort expectancy* (EE) (Venkatesh 2000). In the original UTAUT item set, two items pertained to the availability of technical assistance (request help if stuck or use the built-in help facility for assistance). The items in the public transportation study were adapted to the wish of users to have a direct contact person available at the PTC and the possibility to call someone if the ticket purchase does not work (see Table 39).

Self-Efficacy	
SE1	I would like to have a direct contact person at the PTC
SE2	I would appreciate it, if I could call someone for help if I got stuck with buying a ticket.

Table 39: Adapted construct self-efficacy (SE)

For SE it is hypothesized:

H7: Self-Efficacy will **not** have a significant influence on behavioral intention.

(7) Anxiety (ANX): Anxiety (ANX) is the sense of unease or insecurity that performing a particular action evokes. The introduction of Ubicomp brought many privacy and data security issues to the fore (Spiekermann 2005; Bohn et al. 2004; Juels 2006; Galanxhi/Nah 2005; Jensen/Potts/Jensen 2005; Iachello et al. 2005; Langheinrich 2002). However a discrepancy often exists between what is perceived and any actual threat (Jensen/Potts/Jensen 2005; Resatsch et al. 2007a). Because of the importance of privacy and data security in Ubicomp systems, several items pertaining to privacy and security concerns were included in the study (see Table 40).

An item on health risk was included on behalf of the Public Transport Company.

Anxiety	
ANX1	I am worried about using the system
ANX2	It scares me that the PTC knows exactly the location I have been to
ANX3	I hesitate to use the system for fear of making mistakes I cannot correct
ANX4	The system is somewhat intimidating to me
ANX5	I hesitate to use a system such as the NFC PTC Mobile Phone Ticket System, because of privacy concerns
ANX6	I hesitate to use a system such as the NFC PTC Mobile Phone Ticket System, because of data security concerns
ANX7	I fear other aspects of NFC technology besides ticketing
ANX8	I think there are no health risks of NFC usage

Table 40: Adapted construct anxiety (ANX)

The hypothesis as taken from the original source will be:

H8: **Anxiety** will **not** have a significant influence on behavioral intention.

(8) Behavioral Intention (BI): Behavioral Intention (BI) consists of three items that are geared toward estimating future usage of the application (See Table 41). BI was not adapted since its purpose is to measure future usage.

Behavioral intention	
BI1	I intend to use the system in the next six months
BI2	I predict I would use the system in the next 12 months
BI3	I plan to use the system in the next 12 months

Table 41: Behavioral intention (BI)

BI has directly influenced system usage measurements in previous studies. This represents the core the technology acceptance models. If the construct BI has a significant influence on system usage and use behavior, a forecast of actual usage is possible. This is very important for companies wanting to adjust their applications to market demands with the use of technology acceptance models.

For BI, the hypothesis is

H9: **Behavioral Intention** will have a significant positive influence on system use.

(9) Use behavior: Use Behavior refers to how the user uses the system. Common measures of system usage found in the literature are: subjective, self-reported measures, and objective, computer-recorded measures (Straub/Limayem/Karahanna-Evaristo 1995). Straub (1995) reflects on the methodological problems of subjective, self-reported measures. In a study by (Rice/Borgman 1983) evidence was found that the discrepancy was wide between reported answers to sociometric questions and actual system use. Also in (Ettema 1985) the self-reported frequency of use of a prototype system did not correspond significantly with the number of uses monitored by the system. Self-reports may also be biased by a tendency to report socially desirable behaviors (Ajzen 1988). This leads to the conclusion that using the internal system capability of the NFC-based working prototype information backend system to automatically determine system use might be a stronger indicator than self-reported usage..

As (Burton-Jones/Straub 2006) state, there is no accepted definition of *system usage* in IS literature. They conclude that evaluation constructs, such as quality of use (Auer 1998) and appropriate use (Chin/Gopal/Salisbury 1997) do not measure system usage, instead they measure the degree to which one's usage corresponds with another construct such as expected use or system "spirit" (Chin/Gopal/Salisbury 1997). They clearly conclude that system usage needs quantification. Burton-Jones et al. distinguish between (two) lean and (various levels of) rich usage measures. Whereas lean measures attempt to track the activity in an overall measurement of use/non use, duration of use, or extent of use, rich measures incorporate the nature of the usage activity. The authors recommend taking a rich measurement approach for determining system usage. Rich measurements indicate the extent to which a system was used (breadth of use/number of features), the extent to which the user employs the system (cognitive absorption), the extent to which the user is used to carry out the task (variety of use/number of subtasks), and the extent to which the user employs the system to carry out the task (Burton-Jones/Straub 2006).

For the purpose of this case study evaluation, a lean measure is used: the number of purchased tickets with NFC. This was done for three reasons: First, the goal of the study is to determine the relationship between actual NFC use vs. the intention to use NFC. The NFC system combines a Java-based mobile phone application with the notion of physical touch. Therefore the task *to buy a ticket* is obviously reflected in the actual *touch*. This differs from more complex office application environments where the number of available functions potentially changes how the user employs the system.

The number of purchased tickets via NFC is a clear measurement of NFC system usage. Second, the number of available features during the test was limited to the purchase of two different tickets and a timetable, and therefore there was no need to measure breadth of use. Last, cognitive absorption, variety of use and the extent to which the user employs the system to carry out the task, could have been measured by a combination of NFC use in different areas. This was not possible in the study set up. Therefore system usage is measured primarily by the number of tickets purchased via the NFC phone and NFC tag.

Other papers in the UTAUT used the following measures (see Table 42):

Paper source	Measure used	Scale
(Carlsson et al. 2006)	Self report the degree of current usage: • Do you use MMS? • Do you use search services? • Do you use ring tones?	5-point-scale from 1 = "never used" to 5 = "use daily"
(Park/Yang/Lehto 2007)	Not measured	Not measured
(Wang/Yang 2005)	Not measured	Not measured

(He/Lu 2007)	Use behavior as a construct was used, but it is not mentioned what exactly was measured.	In the limitations, the authors state that the behavior was claimed by the respondents, but not drawn from actual usage.
(Pu Li/Kishore 2006)	Frequency (usage pattern) of using "Weblogs" as claimed by respondents.	4-item-scale: Seldom, At least once a month, At least once a week, Once a day
(Keller/Hrastinski/Carlsson 2007)	Self report the degree of current usage:	Not mentioned
(Garfield 2005)	Not measured	Not measured

Table 42: Use behavior measured in various publications

Based on the comparison table in (Gefen/Straub 2000b) even in the TAM context, real usage was seldom employed as a measure of system use. It is not easy to measure the real usage, because of the stage in which technology acceptance models are commonly applied. An already working and deployed prototype is needed to measure the actual system use. In (Moore/Benbasat 1991) and (Thompson/Higgins/Howell 1991), real PC utilization and adoption were used. In the original work by Davis (Davis 1989), he used self-reported usage in study 1, and intended use in study 2. Also in (Fenech 1998; Karahanna/Straub/Chervany 1999; Straub/Keil/Brenner 1997; Hendrickson/Collins 1996; Igbaria et al. 1997; Taylor/Todd 1995; Keil/Beranek/Konsynski 1995; Adams/Nelson/Todd 1992; Straub 1994) self-reports are used to determine system use. In other TAM based publications, the intention to use was the core construct (Chau 1996; Szajna 1996; Mathieson 1991).

To avoid a methodological bias, since only one of the proposed measures in literature was used, we also added self-report use to our questionnaire. Although measuring self-reported system use may lead to unacceptable *artifacts*, the value of perceived measures maybe tenable (Straub/Limayem/Karahanna-Evaristo 1995). Straub (1995) suggested to reformulate system use as two entirely separate constructs, i.e. perceived system use vs. actual system use. Therefore two *perceived system use* items were included in all three available measurement points in addition to the *actual system use* of the system:

•   Self-reported use with NFC: *To buy tickets with your NFC-enabled mobile phone you touch the NFC tag with your phone. How many times are you using this NFC-function with the NFC-tag to buy your tickets?*

•   Self-reported use without NFC: *The ticket purchase is also possible without touching the NFC-tag. In this case you have to manually open the PTC ticketing application and enter your starting point into the phone. How many times are you using this function without the NFC-tag to buy your tickets?*

The comparison between both questions makes one believe that participants in the study used the NFC-option more than the manual option in purchasing tickets. Ticket usage also differed between participants: whereas some were heavy users, others bought no tickets at all.

During the survey period people bought an average of 23 tickets, almost double the amount purchased during the period before the survey. In the case of NFC-based ticket purchases, 31 people purchased no tickets at all. These participants were excluded from the technology acceptance measurement since without actual use they lacked the authority to comment on the system.

6.3.2.3 Summary of Items and Constructs

Table 43 lists all items that were adapted from the standard UTAUT constructs to the needs of NFC and Ubicomp as discussed in previous sections:

Performance Expectancy	
PE1	I would find the system useful in my daily life
PE2	I would find the combination of NFC tags plus NFC mobile phone ticketing useful in my daily life
PE3	Using the NFC mobile phone ticketing enables me to buy my tickets easier
PE4	Using the NFC mobile phone ticketing enables me to buy my tickets faster
PE5	The system makes public transport more efficient
PE6	I save time using the system
PE7	I save time using the NFC Mobile Phone
Effort Expectancy	
EE1	Registering for the system did not bother me
EE2	I would find the system easy to use
EE3	You need to touch the NFC tags with your NFC-enabled mobile phone. This touch-based interaction is clear and easy to understand.
EE4	I would find touch-based interaction easy to use
EE5	Learning to operate the system is easy to me
Attitude Towards Using Technology	
ATUT1	I like using the system
ATUT2	Using the system is fun
ATUT3	Using NFC-Technology with a mobile phone is fun
ATUT4	The system improves traveling with public transport
ATUT5	I would like to have more NFC-application such as the PTC Mobile Phone Ticket System
ATUT6	I prefer buying NFC tickets than paper tickets
Social Influence	
SI1	People who are important to me think positive about mobile phone ticketing
SI2	People who are important to me think positive about NFC technology
Facilitating Conditions	
FC1	I have the necessary knowledge about NFC to use the PTC Mobile Phone Ticket System
FC2	There are enough resources (NFC tags) in the city
FC3	There are enough resources at the stations
FC4	I would change my mobile phone brand in order to own a NFC-enabled mobile phone

Self –Efficacy	
SE1	I would like to have a direct contact person at the PTC
SE2	I would appreciate it, if I could call someone for help if I got stuck with buying a ticket.
Anxiety	
ANX1	I am worried about using the system
ANX2	It scares me that the PTC knows exactly the location I have been to
ANX3	I hesitate to use the system for fear of making mistakes I cannot correct
ANX4	The system is somewhat intimidating to me
ANX5	I hesitate to use a system such as the NFC PTC Mobile Phone Ticket System, because of privacy concerns
ANX6	I hesitate to use a system such as the NFC PTC Mobile Phone Ticket System, because of data security concerns
ANX7	I fear other aspects of NFC technology besides ticketing
ANX8	I think there are no health risks of NFC usage
Behavioral Intention	
BI1	I intend to use the system in the next six months
BI2	I predict I would use the system in the next 12 months
BI3	I plan to use the system in the next 12 months
Use behavior	
Use behavior A1	Actual system use during the 3 months of the study with NFC ticket purchases
Use behavior A2	Actual system use during the 3 months of the study overall ticket purchases
Use behavior Q1	Self-reported use behavior during phase 1
Use behavior Q2	Self-reported use behavior during phase 2
Use behavior Q3	Self-reported use behavior during phase 3

Table 43: Items used in estimating UTAUT

These items were incorporated into all three questionnaires. Several pre-tests took place with people from the research institution and the PTC.

6.3.2.4 Determining Measurement Points

To increase the quality of data the survey was conducted in three waves. This meant three questionnaires at three measurement points in time (see Fig. 75).

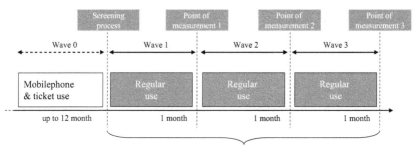

Data collection throughout 3 month system usage of initial working prototype

Fig. 75: Determination of measurement points

The questionnaires were conceptually similar with UTAUT items in all three main waves. Participants received an email with the link to the online questionnaire. In between measurement points, 1 month of regular use took place.

6.3.3 Data Collection

Participants received an email with the link to the online questionnaire. The study data was collected via an online survey system.

The participants were asked to rate their level of agreement on a five-point Likert scale (*1=completely disagree* to *5=completely agree*). Respondents who took too long to fill out any of the questionnaires were deleted in the final sample. Most respondents were between 30 and 39, mean age was 32 in Wave 1 (see Table 44). There were far more male participants (85%) than female (15%).

Gender	Male	85 %
(n = 217)	Female	15 %
Age	<19	9,2 %
(n = 217)	20-29	24,0 %
	30-39	41,5 %
	40-49	20,3 %
	50-59	3,7 %
	> 60	1,4 %

Table 44: Overall sample descriptive statistics wave 1

The majority of participants had university degrees and were currently employed (see Table 45). The large number of males indicates a non-representative sample. Also the age distribution was not representative.

Education (n = 216)	
University	48 %
University of applied science	16 %
Apprenticeship	15 %
Abitur (Diploma from German secondary school qualifying for university admission or matriculation)	9 %
Realschule (Secondary School)	6 %
Lehre	4 %
Ph.D.	2 %
Hauptschule	1 %
Current employment (n = 217)	
Employee	75 %
Self-employed	14 %
School, Apprenticeship, University	5 %
Retiree	1 %
Homemaker	1 %
Other	4 %

Table 45: Education and current employment

The sample consisted of a technology-savvy group of mostly male, employed, highly educated people. As already mentioned the sample was not representative.

6.3.4 Data Processing

To test the technology acceptance model, a partial least squares regression is used to find the relations between the model constructs. According to Chin et al. (Chin/Marcolin/Newsted 2003) the Partial Least Squares (PLS) approach has several advantages over a covariance fitting approach. The component-based PLS avoids the problems of inadmissible solutions and factor indeterminacy. PLS and related software works better for smaller samples (Ringle 2004; Jahn 2007) than e.g. AMOS (Scholderer/Balderjahn 2006). Furthermore, the data set must not necessarily be in a multivariate normal distribution because PLS has no distribution assumptions.

Chin (Chin 1998a) recommends reporting information clearly on the following aspects:

- The population from which the data sample was obtained.

- The distribution of the data to determine the adequacy of the statistical estimation procedure.

- The conceptual model to determine the appropriateness of the statistical models analyzed.

- Statistical results to corroborate the subsequent interpretation and conclusions.

The population of this analysis was clearly identified, and distribution statements were made clear in the previous section.

The path values of the results were calculated with Partial Least Square analysis (PLS) with the software SmartPLS2.0 (Ringle/Wende/A. 2005). The SPSS data from the study was saved as *.por file, a format in which long variable names and other SPSS-specific entries are deleted. The file was then saved as *.xls, opened with MS Excel and saved as *.csv file. An import into SmartPLS2.0 provided the basis for the results.

SmartPLS2.0 settings were: path weighting scheme, data metric mean 0, var 1, maximum number of iterations 300, the abort criterion set to 1.0E-5 and initial weights were 2.0. As missing value algorithm, mean replacement based on a pre-configured data file with missing values set to -999 was used. T-values were calculated with Bootstrapping, individual sign changes, 148 cases and 2000 samples.

6.4 Data Analysis and Interpretation

This chapter first shows the PLS results (see section 6.4.2). The next sections describe the findings of the various constructs.

6.4.1 Data Analysis

For a data analysis of UTAUT, the first test was for the quality of the constructs with Cronbach's alpha, the convergent validity with factor loadings and the discriminant validity based on Fornell/Larcker (see Appendix).

The central constructs of the UTAUT were formed by using a principal component factor analysis with Varimax rotation. After this explorative factor analysis, Cronbach's alpha was tested to determine the internal consistency of the summated scale variables and thus the reliability. All factors with an alpha value above the agreed cut-off point 0.7 (Nunnally/Bernstein 1994) were included in the further analysis. Also according to Hair, Anderson, Tatham, and Black (1998), the generally agreed upon lower limit for Cronbach's is 0.70, although it may decrease to 0.60 in exploratory research (Hair et al. 1998; Hair Jr et al. 1995).

Reliability analysis tests were run for different criteria to determine whether a single item can be used for the total test. Similar to a pre-test, useful items are aggregated, whereas useless statements are excluded from the test. Cronbach's alpha measures the reliability of a scale by the correlations between and the absolute number of single variables. Each of the measurement points will also show reliability and validity indicators based on (Chin 1998a, 1998b) and (Ringle 2004).

Chin calls the coefficient of determination (r2) of latent endogenous variables as substantial (0.67), medium (0.33), and weak (0.19). Based on this categorization the coefficient of determination is shown in each Figure (see Appendix).

There are no common indices of fit possible with PLS (Hulland/Richard Ivey School of 1999), such as the Goodness of Fit (GOF), usable with AMOS. To check for model validity the strength of the f2 effect of a latent exogenous variable of the dependant endogenous variable is calculated. A value of about 0.02 is considered small, values above 0.15 medium, and values over 0.35 are considered large. F2 is calculated as

$$f^2 = \frac{R^2_{included} - R^2_{exluded}}{1 - R^2_{included}} \tag{1}$$

(1) was calculated only for the complete UTAUT model.

Finally the construct cross-validated redundancy (Q2) is calculated using PLS. It should be above 0 (Ringle 2004; Ringle/Wende/A. 2005). The Q2 is the Stone-Geisser criteria and is calculated using the Blindfolding procedure by SmartPLS (Ringle/Wende/A. 2005).

Several constructs did not meet these criteria in the different questionnaires and were excluded or changed after the validation processes (see Appendix for tables and details):

In Q1, PE, SI, FC, SE and BI no items were excluded. However, FC had an alpha value below the lower limit of 0.7 and was deleted as a factor (See also (Park/Yang/Lehto 2007)). EE_1 and ATUT_6 were deleted because of a higher Cronbach alpha after deletion. ANX loaded to two factors, after deletion of ANX_8 one factor with squared loadings of 49.035% was reached.

A similar picture to Q1 could be seen in Q2. No items were deleted in factors SI, FC, SE, BI. FC was not included because of a Cronbach Alpha below 0.7. In PE, item PE_1 was deleted because of factor loadings. EE_1 and ATUT_6 were not included in analysis to improve Cronbach Alpha. For ANX, two items were excluded: ANX_8 and ANX_3.

At time Q3, PE, EE, SI, FC, SE and BI saw no changes. ATUT_6 was excluded because of factor loadings. This is different to previous measurement points, when ATUT_6 was excluded because of a lower alpha value. ANX had the same pattern as in previous points of measurement, where ANX_8 and ANX_3 were excluded.

6.4.2 PLS Analysis

This section looks at the PLS analysis. The analysis was conducted with SmartPLS (Ringle/Wende/A. 2005). The level of significance is indicated by asterisks in the figures (see Table 46).

Level of significance					
*	p<=0.1	Low	***	p<=0.01	Strong
**	p<=0.05	Moderate	****	p<=0.001	Extremely Strong

Table 46: Significance levels

Fig. 76 shows the results of the PLS-analysis for the first wave of the survey (questionnaire 1).

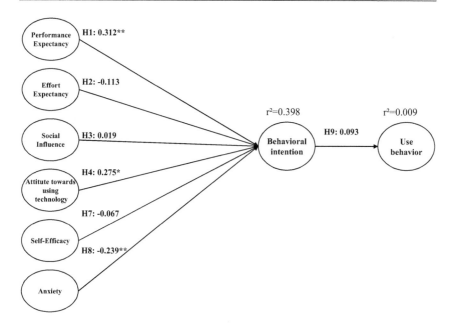

Fig. 76: PLS results questionnaire 1 (Q1)

Questionnaire 1 shows only three significant paths: ANX to BI, PE to BI and ATUT to BI. PE has the strongest path coefficient, with ANX following closely on a negative scale. R^2 is rather low with 39.8% of the variance explained by the constructs. There is no significant path from BI to Use behavior. R^2 of Use behavior is very low with only 0.9%.

Fig. 77 pictures the results in Wave 2 (questionnaire 2).

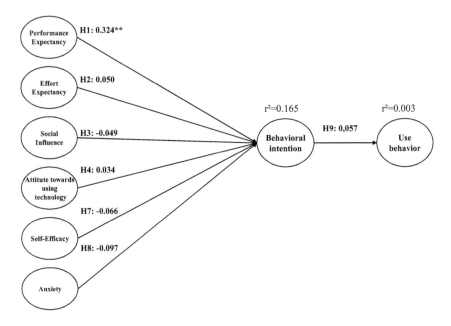

Fig. 77: PLS results questionnaire 2 (Q2)

In Q2, the picture was different to Q1 with only one significant path from PE to BI. R^2 dropped half in both cases BI and Use behavior.

In Fig. 78, the results of Wave 3 (questionnaire 3) of the PLS analysis are shown.

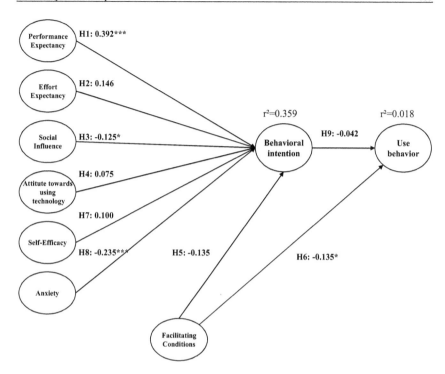

Fig. 78: PLS results questionnaire 3 (Q3)

In Q3 the model worked better. PE to BI was significant and rather strong with 0.392. SI was significant and also ANX again had a significant (negative) impact on BI. FC were included in this model with FC to Use behavior showing a significant (negative) path.

Finally a last model was tested with all available data from Q1, Q2, to Q3 in a combined measurement model (see Fig. 79).

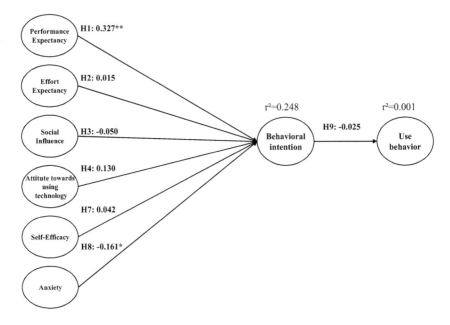

Fig. 79: PLS results combined measurement model (Q1+Q2+Q3)

The combined measurement model (Q1+Q2+Q3) behaves similarly to the other models with PE showing a significant path, low and very low R²s, and ANX with significant path.

The model of Q3 had more significant constructs than previous models. An explanation could be that with extended usage of the system, people built a rather valid opinion of the system. This is very relevant for other research in which a model was measured at only one point in time. The next section looks at the hypotheses and discusses the evaluation results.

First the original UTAUT hypotheses were tested according to the literature in Table 47. In case the construct itself has had no significant impact, the model without non-significant path values was used.

#	Hypotheses	Supported/Not supported			
		Q1	Q2	Q3	Combined Measurement Model
H1	Performance expectancy has a significant influence on behavioral intention.	**Supported**	**Supported**	**Supported**	**Supported**
H2	Effort expectancy has a significant influence on behavioral intention.	Not supported	Not supported	Not supported	Not supported
H3	Social influence has a significant	Not	Not	**Supported**	Not

	influence on behavioral intention.	supported	supported		supported
H4	Attitude towards NFC devices /services will not have an influence on behavioral intention.	Not supported	**Supported**	**Supported**	**Supported**
H5	Facilitating conditions will not have a significant influence on behavioral intention.	Not included	Not included	**Supported**	Not included
H6	Facilitating conditions have a significant influence on use behavior.	Not included	Not included	**Supported**	Not included
H7	Self-efficacy will not have a significant influence on behavioral intention.	**Supported**	**Supported**	**Supported**	**Supported**
H8	Anxiety will not have a significant influence on behavioral intention.	Not supported	**Supported**	Not supported	Not supported
H9	Behavioral intention will have a significant positive influence on system use.	Not supported	Not supported	Not supported	Not supported

Table 47: Hypothesis tests

H1 was accepted for all three phases as well as the combined measurement model. In our study, H2 (EE) was rejected for all measurement points. H3 was only supported in Q3, while H4 was supported in three cases. FC was not included in three of the four measurement models, however in one case H5 and H6 were supported. H7 was supported at all four measurement points. H8 was contrary to other UTAUT research, since it was not supported in three cases—meaning that ANX had a significant influence on BI. The non-supported H9 bears several interesting questions for interpretation. This study was one of the first to measure actual system usage in UTAUT models in voluntary settings in three phases. The next section interprets the results.

6.4.3 Interpretation

The next sections interpret the findings from the various constructs. The interpretation first examines the most important construct BI, followed by the other constructs PE, EE, SI, ATUT, SE, and ANX.

6.4.3.1 Behavioural Intention

It is interesting to see how the mean between the three measurement points decreases. To see if this decrease was significant, we used a paired samples t-test with each of the items in the BI construct throughout the three measurement points (e.g. BI item 1 Q1 with BI item 1 Q3, BI item 2 Q1 with BI item 1 Q3, BI item 1 Q1 with BI item 1 Q2) resulting in nine possible pairs (3x3). The paired samples t-test compares the means of two variables for a single group, in other words, it assesses differences between a pair of linked variables. It calculates the differences between values of the two variables for each case and tests whether the average differs from zero. There was a significant difference in the mean scores of all Behavioral Intention items from Q1 to Q3, and from Q1 to Q2 as well (see Table 48).

Paired Samples Test									
		Paired Differences							
		Mean	Std. Devia tion	Std. Error Mean	95% Confidence Interval of the Difference		t	df	Sig. (2-tailed)
					Lower	Upper			
Pair 1 Q2->Q3	I intend to use the system in the next six months	.014	.735	.063	-.109	.138	.232	137	.817
Pair 2 Q2->Q3	I predict I would use the system in the next 12 months	.015	.883	.075	-.135	.164	.194	136	.847
Pair 3 Q2->Q3	I plan to use the system in the next 12 months	.058	.931	.079	-.099	.214	.729	138	.467
Pair 4 Q1->Q3	I intend to use the system in the next six months	.159	.704	.058	.043	.274	2.713	144	.007
Pair 5 Q1->Q3	I predict I would use the system in the next 12 months	.172	.819	.068	.038	.307	2.534	144	.012
Pair 6 Q1->Q3	I plan to use the system in the next 12 months	.205	.778	.064	.078	.333	3.190	145	.002
Pair 7 Q1->Q2	I intend to use the system in the next six months	.153	.737	.063	.029	.278	2.436	136	.016
Pair 8 Q1->Q2	I predict I would use the system in the next 12 months	.176	.851	.073	.032	.321	2.418	135	.017
Pair 9 Q1->Q2	I plan to use the system in the next 12 months	.182	.925	.079	.026	.339	2.308	136	.022

Table 48: Paired Samples Test (t-values (t), degrees of freedom (df), significance (sig.))

The difference between Q2 and Q3 was not significant. However, the mean decrease especially from Q1 to Q3 shows that a regret effect occurred in relation to people's original expectations of the system. This is primarily a function of what people were told or learned about the system before taking part in the study and using the system. A possible interpretation is that the marketing material initially communicated to test participants should not overstate system benefits. In introducing new technology systems only clear concrete uses should be stated.

Another relevant finding was the *non-existence of a significant path value between BI and use behavior* in all three models and the combined measurement model (see PLS charts above). This could mean that although people were indeed very positive about the study system with high means in the intention to use the system after the trial ended, this was not reflected in real and self-reported system usage.

The interpretation could be that the previous ticket purchase behavior did not change during the study. Participants either still bought tickets with pocket money or with their mobile phone Java application directly. Another possibility is an overconfidence of the participants about the intention to use the system. The participants might be answering they would use the system in the future, but they did not actively pursue this intent in terms of actual NFC system usage. Potential reasons are discussed below. Without a significant path between these two constructs (measured with self-reported use and actual use behavior) it is not possible to forecast the extent of real usage after the study. The UTAUT measurement instrument did not generate relevant information in this case.

Another interpretation of the missing path: In the study setting, NFC tags were placed either on the ticket machine or the bus stop pole. Overall participants appeared satisfied with the number of tags placed around the city (see Fig. 80) – the FC.

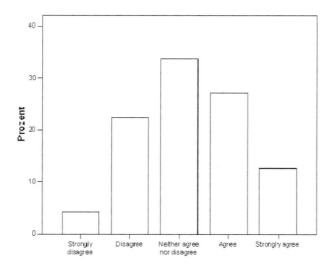

Fig. 80: Participants opinion on amount of tags placed throughout the city

Some participants mentioned that NFC tags for purchasing tickets should be located at every platform entrance. To avoid creating a situation where people would expect others to cut ahead of them in line, they suggested placing the tag on the side of the ticket machine or in autonomous locations. Table 49 shows other tag placements named by participants. Participants had to respond to an open question in answering where they most wanted the NFC tags to be.

Location	Occurrences
On the trains/busses	25,27%
Ticket machines	15,38%
Escalator	14,29%
Entrance area	8,79%
Bus stop pole	7,69%
Platform	7,69%
Staircase	6,59%
Train schedule tables	5,49%
Bus stop	3,30%
Close to the ticket machine	2,20%
SOS-telephone	2,20%
At cooperation partners (Shops)	1,10%
Total percentage of answers	100,00%

Table 49: Suggested NFC tag placement by participants (in percent)

In tallying up the occurrences it emerged that people want NFC tags placed at locations with the highest integration in current processes—a fact that further underscores the positive PE influence. But there are reasons that speak against a placement in the best process flow: A good reason for not placing the tags near escalators or staircases was that people buying tickets would become obstacles to others *in the flow* of purchasing tickets.

That respondents would like to have NFC tags more directly integrated into the process of purchasing a ticket might also explain the missing significance in the path. Given the high mean values in terms of behavioral intention this might be interpreted as evidence of a favorable view of the technology, but that improvements in actual implementation—e.g. the positioning of the NFC tags—would result in greater usage. The presence of suggestions for NFC tag placements supports this interpretation. The highest value was recorded with a tag inside the trains and busses. However, a different tag placement could also present problems in finding the tag: 93% mentioned that they found the tag quickly when it was attached to the ticket vending machine, but only 69% found it quickly at the bus stop pole. This indicates that a tag should be visible and have an easy to recognize layout and caption.

6.4.3.2 Performance Expectancy

The total value still showed an overall impact of PE on BI and use behavior, indicating that PE is the strongest predictor of both. This compares with findings by (Venkatesh et al. 2003) and various others (Carlsson et al. 2006; Park/Yang/Lehto 2007) in similar fields. PE has the strongest impact on behavioral intention. In the original context, PE describes the degree to which an individual believes that using a system will help him or her to increase job performance. This held true for mandatory as well as voluntary settings.

In the study, the setting was voluntary and the gains related to improvements in time and effort to buy a ticket. PE has a stronger correlation to BI than to the actual Use behavior. PE was the strongest predictor of BI at all three measurement points, which means that the convenience to buy tickets is most important. However, it seems that the people expected more of the backend system than the actual use was considered beneficial. This means that further improvements in the system should be based on software or process-based changes in the backend infrastructure.

6.4.3.3 Effort Expectancy

With increased usage, the effect of EE grew over time from a negative value -0,113 (Q1), to 0,050 (Q2) up to 0,146 (Q3). However, the significance level of the path was very low and therefore not counted. EE results from the model are very interesting in terms of what is often-claimed as NFC's ease-of-use. At all three points of measurement, no significant correlation existed between EE and BI. The items used in the EE construct were all related to the theoretically defined ease-of-use referring to the NFC technology.

This might be interpreted as evidence of the fact that ease-of-use belongs to the user's basic expectations of a system. Nevertheless, in a further test in Q3, relating EE directly to use behavior, the negative path value demonstrated a significant correlation between EE and actual use behavior. This effect might be interpreted as evidence of people's expectation that the system be easy to use, but it was in fact not as easy to use as expected, thus leading to a negative path. These findings may represent the tipping point of NFC. The promotion of NFC mostly concerns the ease-of-use aspect of the technology. But after using it once the wow-effect decreases quickly, and people just expect the actual system (i.e. the application) to work properly. Systems should be easy to use.

The ease-of-use of NFC can be a door opener for marketing purposes, but it needs to work flawlessly if it is to replace already existing systems'. From a communication perspective, the ease-of-use can be communicated, but there should also be information on the service behind the notion of *touch* of NFC. Furthermore, there is more to the *ease-of-use* than the *touch* concept only. The tag placement and device related issues add on to the total user experience of the NFC system. Actual system usage might also be increased if more NFC tags are placed in different locations than was the case during the case study evaluation.

6.4.3.4 Social Influence

Interestingly, in Q1 SI had the largest *direct* influence on use behavior (0,196, T-Value=2,080), and in Q3, it still recorded strong values (0,194, T-Value=2,245). The influence on behavioral intention was negative in Q1 to Q3, and was only significant in Q3. This means that SI influenced the intention to use the system only in Q3, but that real usage was influenced in Q1 and Q3. ANX was a moderator of SI on BI. People who are less reluctant to use the system (tested with the item *I hesitate to use [...] because of data security* and *I hesitate to use [...] because of privacy*) are closely connected with friends or family. This might partly be a function of the concept of the "Locus of Control" (Rotter 1966). The *locus of control* refers to how the individual views the root causes of events in his own life. The *external* Locus of Control indicates that an individual thinks his life is guided by fate, luck, or other external circumstances. Within the *internal* Locus of Control the individual believes that his behavior is guided by personal decisions and efforts. People with a higher internal locus of control tend to be more self-controlled and try to achieve more. In the case of the study, there is evidence to suggest that people with a higher internal locus of control see fewer problems with data security and privacy. This could lead to potential problems when introducing the system to mass markets. People who tend to scare more easily tend to ask their friends and family members for advice—people who might not be aware of the scope of positive privacy and data security measures. It is important to communicate the positive attributes of NFC on a broad scale.

6.4.3.5 Attitude towards Using Technology

ATUT had high path coefficients and included a significant path in Q1. ATUT might play a different role in voluntary settings in which the fun aspect has higher relevance for behavioral intention. At the first Q1, the fun aspect might have been more important to the user than at later measurement points. Similar to the wow-effect described within the EE construct, this might be interpreted as evidence that the system is fun and that participants rate this fact high during the first weeks of usage. After that it is more important that the service works and fulfills its intended function—purchasing a ticket—rather than being *fun*.

6.4.3.6 Self Efficacy

SE had very low path coefficients and had no significance for any of the models tested. The hypothesis stated that it would not have a significant influence on BI. This hypothesis can be supported. This fact is important for companies introducing such systems. It indicates that people feel generally confident in using the system and worry little about having to contact a company representative for clarification. This is subject to change if errors crop up or if the system malfunctions. During the case study evaluation only several calls concerning mostly minor problems were fielded.

6.4.3.7 Anxiety

Contrary to the original UTAUT hypotheses and the results derived from an organizational perspective, ANX had a significant influence on BI in three cases. The ANX constructs worked in a way that was similar with previously published Internet privacy studies (see adapted items description ANX in section 6.3.2.2). If users felt their data would be used in a malicious way they hesitated using the system, but because it was a field study and they appeared to trust the PTC, they planned on using the system frequently. Privacy and data security are important issues but have no real influence on user behavior or behavioral intention. This is an interesting finding for marketing campaigns—in the most significant cases ANX apparently impacted BI in a relatively highly negative way. Although privacy and data security concerns were addressed in the marketing packet handed out to participants, the ANX construct still played a relevant role for respondents. The marketing of future NFC systems needs to actively address ANX.

6.4.3.8 Facilitating Conditions

The effect of FC only showed up in questionnaire 3. This may have been the result of the way in which the questions were ordered in the questionnaire. Two questions addressed the availability of NFC tags throughout the city, while the other two concerned participant's knowledge of a particular mobile phone brand and whether they were aware of the costs of switching carriers or services. After calculating Cronbach's Alpha for both items these two were excluded. Therefore FC only measured the availability of NFC tags in the city. The hypothesis was supported in Q3. This shows that the underlying infrastructure and its perception has an influence on the behavioral intention of participants. This impacts the overall tag infrastructure as long as the need exists for a significant number of tags to be visibly recognized by users.

6.4.4 PLS Multi-Group Comparisons

According to Chin (Chin 2000, 79) a multi-group comparison is made by bootstrapping the various constructs and treat the standard error estimates from each re-sampling in a parametric sense via t-tests (see Table 50).

$$t = \frac{Path1 - Path2}{\sqrt{\frac{(m-1)^2}{(m+n-2)} \cdot S.E.1^2 + \frac{(m-1)^2}{(m+n-2)} \cdot S.E.2^2} \cdot \left(\sqrt{\frac{1}{m} + \frac{1}{n}}\right)} \quad (2)$$

(2) Multi-group comparison

	BI			Use Behavior		
	Q1 -> Q2	Q2 -> Q3	Q1 -> Q3	Q1 -> Q2	Q2 -> Q3	Q1 -> Q3
PE	-0.05	-0.42	0.48			
EE	-1.06	-0.65	-1.90*			
SI	0.59	0.61	1.40			
ATUT	1.29	0.29	1.03			
SE	-0.01	-0.81	-1.45			
ANX	-1.16	-1.72*	-0.02			
BI				1.28	0.03	1.51

Table 50: Multi-group comparison

(* Significance Level: * = 0.1, ** = 0.05, *** = 0.01)

The multi-group tests compared Questionnaire 1 with Questionnaire 2 (Q1 -> Q2), Q2 -> Q3, and Q1 -> Q3. Table 50 shows the results. The participants did not change their minds significantly during the study, apart from two cases. The influence of the constructs on behavioral intention does not vary significantly. EE varied from Q1 to Q3 while ANX varied from Q2 to Q3. The change of ANX could indicate a variation in the perception of privacy and data security risk over the course of the pilot test.

6.4.5 Further Results

If NFC simplifies the ticket purchasing process, relatively quicker ticket purchase times, compared to standard paper-based ticket purchases, it should result in greater customer satisfaction. Fig. 81 shows the answers to the question *How satisfied are you with the speed of buying a ticket using NFC*:

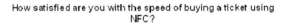

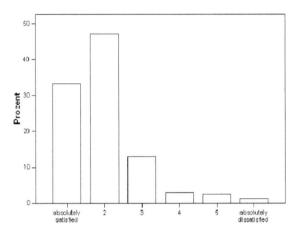

Fig. 81: Satisfaction level with speed of ticket purchases with NFC

Compared to these answers, the next question referred to paper-based ticket purchase (see Fig. 82):

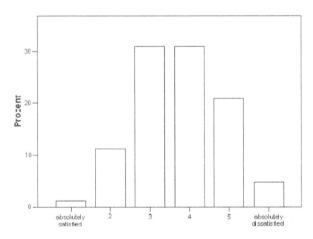

Fig. 82: Satisfaction level with speed of ticket purchases with paper based tickets

Comparing satisfaction values from both tables showed a two-tailed significance level (p<.000). However, when comparing experience with NFC usage to the level of satisfaction with the speed of purchasing tickets with NFC, the value was negligible (see Table 51).

	Experience with NFC usage*	N	Mean	SD	SE
3 - 1. How satisfied are you with the MPTS NFC in Frankfurt?	1.00	68	2.24	.900	.109
	3.00	60	1.75	.600	.077
2 - 1. How satisfied are you with the MPTS NFC in Frankfurt?	1.00	64	2.42	.887	.111
	3.00	56	1.98	.774	.103
1 - 1. How satisfied are you with the MPTS NFC in Frankfurt?	1.00	68	2.54	1.043	.126
	3.00	60	2.12	.922	.119

* 1 = High Experience (heavy user), 3 = Low Experience (slow user)

Table 51: Cross table satisfaction of NFC buying speed with experience

Cross table comparison of PTC MPTS values, with NFC and without NFC, based on the level of experience. A very small correlation exists between the experience and the satisfaction with the system based on questionnaire 3 (in Table 52).

Crosstabling user preferences					
		Experience with NFC usage			Total Number
		Low	Average	High	
What do you like better: the PTC MPTS with NFC tag or without NFC tag (with manually opening the program)	With NFC tag	44	38	52	134
	Without NFC tag	6	3	0	9
	Same	14	9	7	30
	I cannot rate that	4	1	1	6
Sample		68	51	60	N=179

*Table 52: Manual start of program * Experience with NFC usage (Crosstable)*

A high number of participants stated that they would prefer having the NFC tag as an interaction component compared to having to manually open the application. Interestingly, this was also stated by participants who had little prior experience with NFC technology (19 cases in the low experience group failed to purchase even one NFC tag-based ticket)— another case of overconfidence in the sample.

Among participants who actually used the system satisfaction was high. Overall usage could be improved if more people knew about the system, and if a market need were created.

6.4.6 Direct Limitations

The process of conducting the case study and evaluating its artifact has been directly restricted by several limitations from outside the UCAN process model. This section interprets these limitations. First, Wilde et al. provides an effective overview of problems typically associated with technology acceptance studies (Wilde et al. 2008). To discuss the limitations of the case study, three problems specific to the study are addressed: (1) the problem of internal validity, (2) the problem of the theoretical basis, and (3) the problem of the sample.

(1) Problem of internal validity: The problem of internal validity refers to the testing of a certain technology with a prototype vs. a description-only approach. In the case of Wilde et al. this did not produce different results, however in our study, the respondents were actually testing the system—no comparison was made to the description-only approach. Using three different points of measurement helps to overcome this limitation—especially since the results were very similar at all three points of time.

(2) Problem of the theoretical basis: The problem of the theoretical basis refers to how theory was used to adapt the study items to serve the underlying NFC technology. Theory from the research field was used to adapt the study items to NFC. Whether the items could have been more closely adapted to the specifics of NFC should be a part of future research. Changes in the theoretical bases of items are potentially immense, within Ubicomp settings it is still limited.

(3) Problem of the sample: According to Wilde et al. (2008) the major problem was the sample itself—i.e. that in some studies so-called convenience samples are used. Most trials sample the opinions of technologically savvy students or grad students—a fact that deforms the results. For our study a convenience sample was not used, instead we focused on real users in the field. But the sample itself was not representative since it contained too many male participants. This may have produced a bias in the findings.

In terms of how the case study was set up, it largely avoided the limitations described by Wilde et al. (2008). However there were other limitations: First, the way in which the constructs were assembled (1), second the number of items per construct (2), third the translation from UTAUT items into German (3), and fourth the way in which the participants were provided incentives (4).

(1) Constructs: The UTAUT constructs were developed from the basic questionnaire set found in (Venkatesh et al. 2003) and adapted to the specifics of NFC technology. This option was chosen because if—as the research questions implied—UTAUT can be easily adapted to other settings, and can help recommend which actions companies should take, then the items would also be easy to apply in this case and generate fruitful recommendations. The items were adapted according to Ubicomp theory—however the extent to which the notion of Ubicomp actually drives the perception of NFC remains unknown. Ubicomp is a complex concept and it is unclear if all NFC specifics apply to the notion of Ubicomp—although NFC fits the definition of Ubicomp and the basic ideas behind it. The findings are thus primarily valid for one single domain or industry: public transportation—not for Ubicomp in general. It is not clear if and how these may be generalized to other Ubicomp settings. For example, the difference in user perception between NFC and RFID has not been clearly evaluated. NFC seems to have a better reputation among participants, but it was not really compared. Furthermore, in previous UTAUT studies only one piece of software was evaluated. In our case we had a system, consisting of NFC phones, NFC tags, Java application, etc; in the questionnaires it was referred to as *the system* or *the technology*. This may have led to a different understanding among the participants as to what exactly was being questioned. For

Ubicomp, in order to understand in detail where technology acceptance applies to the system, the questions must refer to exactly one single aspect of the overall system.

(2) Number of items per construct: There should be more than two items per construct. This strengthens internal validity and makes it possible to substitute or delete an item without losing data quality in the factor analysis. In the case of SI and SE, only two items were used. This had mostly to do with the fact that other adaptations to the UTAUT could not be based on Ubicomp literature without distorting the model as is.

(3) Translation from UTAUT items into German: The adaptation and translation of the UTAUT item set was not clear enough. Some questions in the constructs have a high similarity—i.e. are too similar to the original items. For example ANX_5 and ANX_6 are very similar, PE_3 und PE_4 as well. In the rather complex NFC system environment a participant might not have properly understood the distinction between variations. This may have led to misperceptions and varying results. Furthermore, the actual translation—although conducted as recommended—may have given participants a different impression than what the questions intended.

(4) Incentives for participants: Participants received a free mobile phone during the study that they were allowed to keep afterwards. This rather expensive reward for participation might have distorted the behavioral intention item. BI was rated very high, while the actual use behavior did not correspond to the BI. It might be interpreted that participants were to a certain extent grateful and wanted to rate their intention higher.

These limitations can be avoided in future research by varying the study setup.

6.5 Summary of the Results

Both previous case studies (Easymeeting and Mobile Prosumer) went from the initial idea of an Ubicomp application to a low-fidelity prototype with different evaluation methods. The PTC case was based on an initial working prototype—the last phase before the final product is developed and sent to markets. The particular phase of the PTC case allowed in-depth analysis with a common technology acceptance model (UTAUT). The next section describes the benefits and limitations of the UCAN process as well as the outcomes for Ubicomp research.

6.5.1 Improve and Theorize about the Developed Process Model (UCAN)

The UCAN process suggested evaluating the prototype during the initial working prototype phase with a quantitative survey (see Chapter 4). The UTAUT technology acceptance model provided the basis for the survey (see Chapter 3.2). This section explains whether the outcome was successful in turning an initial working prototype into a final product.

6.5.1.1 Benefits of the Process

The quantitative survey revealed ways in which technology acceptance applied to the application that were not clear before the survey was conducted.

The PTC case study began with the initial working prototype, therefore researching the overall development process from initial idea, to low-fidelity prototype, and finally to working prototype was not part of the study. However, the UCAN process would still be beneficial since even a relatively late evaluation of an initial working prototype saves time and efforts in earlier stages. The product (the NFC ticketing solution) is now on the market—but there was no further evaluation of this during the course of this thesis.

6.5.1.2 Limitations of the Process

The quantitative survey revealed facts that have nothing to do with the actual implementation of the information system. Some of the results were more related to marketing materials, showing that it is possible to potentially improve a market entry with the UTAUT methodology. Companies are supposed to conduct the UCAN process. For the purpose of a quantitative survey with UTAUT items, including the necessary PLS tests, a statistically experienced person is required. Set-up costs to conduct the survey are extremely high given the intrinsic complexity of the models used. Test results are limited compared to the amount of effort put into the research model. Although a standard model (UTAUT) was used, the study only produced a few recommendations for possible actions. Finally, the UCAN process was designed to start with an initial idea. In the case of the PTC, the case study was already in the working prototype phase, which made evaluating the early phases (initial idea, low-fidelity prototype) impossible to the same extent as Easymeeting and Mobile Prosumer.

6.5.1.3 Evaluation of the Research Instrument: Quantitative Survey

Contrary to the use of interviews, as in the first case study (Easymeeting), and focus groups, as in the second case study (Mobile Prosumer), the third case study was evaluated with an online survey (in Table 53).

Phases of evaluation	Positive	Negative
Organization phase	-	The organisational setup for the amount of participants plus the incentive in the form of a mobile phone is very high and costly. Sponsors are needed.
Execution phase	Easy-to-use software exists for executing such studies.	The total workload related to several measurement points during the study was high.
Analysis phase	The analysis produced interesting results. However these did not really translate into action items for the PTC. The results are rather soft and changes come late in the process—when an initial prototype is closer to the final product and further away from being able to change functions.	The data sample was too small to run full statistical tests with Structural Equation Modelling (SEM), which provides more insights than PLS. Although the sample size was decent compared to other studies, a sample size of 500 to 1000 is recommended. Samples in this range make such a study very expensive and seem impractical to conduct—especially in this case, in which the mobile handsets (the Ubicomp technology) were not broadly available on the market and were provided to participants.

		Without an expert in PLS within the company it is very difficult to evaluate the samples. This is more than what is usually done in market research departments in companies, thus making it difficult for companies to use this evaluation model.

Table 53: Evaluation instrument: Quantitative survey with online questionnaire

The evaluation setup was limited in several ways by the UCAN process. First, although participants were pre-selected, many of those who participated were technologically savvy. This runs counter to the stipulation that the evaluation be conducted with *normal* users. The sample was selected from the previous group of MPTS users. One can assume that these people are early adopters and have high expectations of certain technologies. This might have biased the results in unknown ways. In order to integrate the UCAN process at a future point, a different cross section of the population should be selected as the sample group.

Also, participants were given marketing information about the project beforehand. Study data reveals that this might have influenced their point of view. The working prototype should be evaluated without any pre-supplied information.

Apart from these biases and limitations, the results of the survey would suggest making a few changes including modifying the working prototype or the next iteration phase. Table 54 provides an overview on the evaluation method used.

Case study	Phase in UCAN process	Research Framework	Used evaluation method	Sample size	Items used	Effort to conduct	Helpful to determine product related iterations
PTC	Working prototype	Quantitative survey	Online questionnaire	N=149	UTAUT with PLS-tests	High	Yes

Table 54: Overview of the evaluation methods

The next section sums up the findings to determine design guidelines.

6.5.2 Preparing Design Guidelines

The device—as given to participants—was a basis of the last case study and not questioned. However, since some of the participants never actually bought an NFC ticket via the telephone, it can be inferred that the device itself experienced certain issues.

As in previous sections, the results produced by design guidelines pertain to (1) NFC technology and application, (2) tag infrastructure, (3) and human factors. Device (4) was not researched in this setting.

(1) NFC technology and application:

- By using the system people significantly improved a daily process-based action. NFC helps to improve these process-based actions, because it can facilitate and speed up a certain process.

- The working prototype was not as easy to use as expected (perhaps due to the tag placement)

(2) Tag infrastructure was highly relevant for the participants:

- Participants wanted tags to be located within the progress flow rather than at the ticket vending machine. This is similar to the finding that states that the greatest potential for optimization the NFC application lies in the modifying the process.

- On the other hand, more people preferred having the tag at the ticket vending machine than at the bus stop pole. This preferential difference might speak to the need to design the tag differently to make it more visible.

- Overall system satisfaction had a (small) correlation with the amount of NFC tags placed throughout the study. The more tags and the easier they are to locate the better. This conflicts with the notion of lower infrastructural costs.

(3) Human factors: some findings pertaining to soft factors (non-functional requirements) were produced over the course of the study:

- Convenience in buying public transportation tickets is most important to users—buying tickets is an everyday activity, therefore the various requirements for everyday activities (such as keeping the cognitive load low) are important to keep in mind for designing future NFC systems.

- A regret effect related to behavioral intention emerged during the study. The initial excitements decreased, showing the importance of the service behind the NFC solution. Not only the ease-of-use aspects are important, but also the overall system behaviour.

- An overconfidence effect relating to system usage was present—potentially because of the study sample.

- Ease-of-use is an expected part of a system—not a function itself. Promotion and communication of NFC should focus on the functions behind NFC.

- Privacy and data security concerns are important and prevalent. Anxiety has had a negative path to behavioral intention—making the communication of a trustworthy service important.

These results help further understand the PTC case study. The next step in the UCAN process would be to develop another iteration of the product development application that would integrate findings from this study. It was not possible to perform this step over the course of this thesis. Finally the next chapter draws conclusions and provides a future outlook.

7 Conclusion, Limitations, and Future Research

The aim of this thesis was twofold: research three NFC-based artifacts in case studies to design a *process model* for developing and evaluating Ubicomp applications, and propose a set of *design guidelines* based on the results of the case study evaluations.

The analysis combined research from the fields of social sciences and computer science in order to shed light on the nature of *Ubiquitous Computing*. This approach is new to the field and provides relevant findings for the design of future Ubicomp applications.

The three case studies conducted were *Easymeeting* (Chapter 5.1), the *Mobile Prosumer* (Chapter 5.2) and *Public Transport Company* (Chapter 6). Each case study represented the combination of an artifact that was designed and built, and an evaluation method that explained and evaluated the artifact according to the design science methodology (Chapter 1.4). A utility theory was used to address the case studies and embedded artifacts in order to design a process model as described in chapter 4. This process model was based on the design science methodology explained in section 1.4. Chapter 2 and 0 provided the necessary theoretical background in order to develop the utility theory, the required knowledge needed to develop and build the artifacts, and the proper theory and methods to evaluate the artifacts. Chapter 5 described the case studies Easymeeting and MP, and Chapter 6 focused on the PTC. Over the course of the research the case studies were tested and refined, and the *benefits* and *limitations of the process* were explained in detail. The findings of the case studies were added to the sections concerning the preparation of *design guidelines* for NFC-based Ubicomp applications.

This chapter summarizes the findings from the case studies, provides answers to the research questions, describes what this work contributes to the field, and deduces a set of design guidelines for introducing future Ubicomp applications with the help of a guided process. Finally a recommendation for future research is provided.

To begin, the conclusions from the case studies and the artifacts are summarized.

7.1 Conclusion

In this analysis three case studies were conducted in three different domains: office (Easymeeting), retail (Mobile Prosumer), and transport & ticketing (PTC). The selection of the case studies and their related artifacts produced a range of findings from improving the UCAN process, identifying domain specific knowledge, to coming to general conclusions about NFC. This chapter sums up the findings in the following order: evaluation of the case studies (Section 7.1.1), comparison of the technology of the three case studies (Section 7.1.2), suggestions for improving the UCAN process model (Section 7.1.3), design guideline proposals for NFC-based Ubicomp applications (Section 7.1.4), and finally what this thesis contributes to the field (Section 7.1.5).

7.1.1 Evaluation of the Case Studies

The length of each case study research process—from the initial idea, to the start of an evaluation, to the final analysis—varied from five months (Easymeeting) to ten months (Mobile Prosumer), and to more than 18 months for the PTC case. Fig. 83 shows the different lengths of the phases divided into organizing the evaluation (including development of the prototype), the execution phase, and finally the analysis phase.

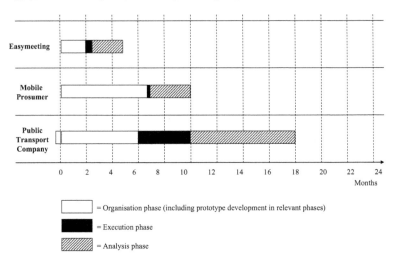

Fig. 83: Duration of the case studies

Easymeeting was developed in approximately two months. This entailed setting up the infrastructure, finding and convincing participants to take part in the study, obtaining the approval of management in both organizations, and designing the study, etc. The actual execution of the study required one day in both organizations, including travel time. Another two months were required to analyze the questionnaires and the talking-out-loud method results.

The Mobile Prosumer case study took slightly longer, especially in the organization phase. Setting everything up—the research proposal, the study design and recruiting participants—required extra time. The actual focus groups were conducted within four hours. Transcription and analysis was completed in approximately two and a half months.

The basis of the PTC application was developed in advance of the actual case study. At least six months before the start of the evaluation, the working prototype was built including the infrastructural components. The execution phase lasted four months with one screening point and three measurement points. The analysis required almost eight months to complete—mostly because of the sample size and the analysis program that was used.

A complete UCAN development and evaluation process can take up to two years. With adequate funding and a pre-determined setting for the process the amount of time can be radically reduced—additional human resources can also help in this regard. However this fact may prevent small start-ups and innovative smaller companies from engaging in this process. Only large organizations will have the time and resources to actually conduct all phases necessary to proper UCAN evaluation. However the situation might be improved for smaller companies if various evaluation methods were integrated in a shorter period of time with a fixed set of participants.

7.1.2 Technological Comparison

The case studies employed three different types of information systems with different levels of information system complexity. The case studies will be compared according to the architectural layers of the information system illustrated in Fig. 84.

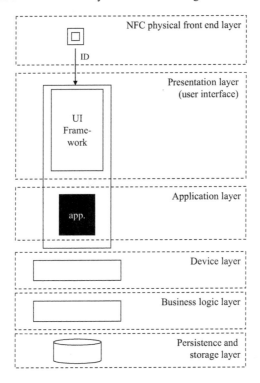

Fig. 84: Information system architectural overview

The primary layer is the NFC physical front-end layer. This layer includes different tags, packaging, and identification schemes. The presentation layer—or user interface front-end—features a designed GUI. In the mobile business world, the commonly used approach is to use a thin or a smart client, or to display all content via pre-installed applications such as the mobile phone browser. The application layer is on the phone deck. The next layer is the device layer that covers various devices. The business logic layer includes the back office logic—and if implemented also the various APIs to other systems. The final layer is the persistence and storage layer. The various layers are either connected wirelessly (e.g. in between the application layer and business logic) or within an IT system. Table 55 shows the overview and a comparison between the various technological architectures of the case studies.

	Easymeeting	Mobile Prosumer	Public Transport Company
NFC front end layer: "Tag"	The tag stored a text message with telephone number in a SMS format. A pre-defined NFC action was used: Sending a text message after touching the tag. The txt message included a case number.	The EPC is stored in Unique Resource Identifier (URI) format in an NFC Data Exchange Format (NDEF) message, according to the NFC Forum standard specification Record Type Definition (RTD) for URIs. Touching the tag resulted in opening the internal mobile web browser.	The tag saved an internal code in Unique Resource Identifier (URI) format in an NFC Data Exchange Format (NDEF) message, according to the NFC Forum standard specification Record Type Definition (RTD) for URIs. The tag initiated two different events in the phone. If the application is installed, the tag opened an application—if it is not installed, the tag opened the browser. For this comparison the client version is described.
Presentation layer (user interface)	The user only confirmed sending the text message – therefore a mobile phone internal system message is shown.	The mobile phone browser was used to display the content.	The user interface was based on a client realized with J2ME.
Application layer	An internal NFC application was used. No extra client software was installed on the phone.	Same as Easymeeting	Mobile client.
Device layer	Since the application layer uses an internal NFC application, any NFC-enabled mobile phone can be used for the Easymeeting application.	Same as Easymeeting	The client was programmed for the Nokia 6131 only—a series 40 telephone.

Business logic layer	The SMS2Email Gateways selected the actions and an email was send to the MS Exchange Server.	The server-side of the application is a web application with a standard web server and a data backend. For the prototype, the application was implemented using PHP. In a production environment the server application would be connected to a gateway server, which gets its data from the company's ERP system.	The business logic was webbed into the ticketing system and added upon the existing "Handy Ticket" solution.
Persistence and storage layer	A mySQL database was used to save the events.	A mySQL database was used to save the events.	The internal ticketing system database was used for the system.
Integrated Development Environment	Development framework: none. Programming on the device: Internal NFC settings. Programming on the server: Visual Basic. The SMS2Email gateway was set up online.	Development framework: Zend Programming on the device: Internal NFC settings. Programming on the server: PHP	Development framework: Eclipse, Nokia 6131 NFC SDK, Carbide.j Programming on the device: J2ME, Java, JSRs. Programming on the server: n.n.

Table 55: Overview of technologies and architecture of the case studies

The three case studies implied different levels of technological developments. The case studies can be compared using the mobile infrastructure graphic in section 2.1.5.2. In the first two case studies—according the UCAN process—a rather simple and quick development approach was used. On the device side in the case of Easymeeting, only internal mobile phone resources were used, such as the operating system, the contactless interface, and the mobile browser as application. In the case of Mobile Prosumer, a service provider layer was emulated using the described technologies. The public transport system used variations of the contactless service management platform. Easymeeting used a phone only setup— according the prototype principles—, while the Mobile Prosumer integrated more components (low-fidelity prototypes). The largest and most complex application was used in the PTC case study (initial working prototype). Each of the artifacts were built to solve the general problem mentioned in the respective sections. This complied with the design science methodology.

7.1.3 Improving UCAN

While the benefits and limitations of the UCAN development process were described in the three case study chapters, this section deals with the overall evaluation of the UCAN development process model as described in chapter 4. The main goal was to minimize the *insecurity* felt by application providers in response to so many Ubicomp options, and to increase *application availability* with shorter development cycles (see Chapter 2.3).

A development process model was proposed that would be capable of directing prototype evaluation—this was achieved in the case of UCAN. It was designed to measure technology acceptance before the final Ubicomp product enters the market. The acceptance model used was the UTAUT. The development process model would also enable a corporation to change the functions of the application according to evaluation results produced during the process. Finally the UCAN development process took the specifics of Ubicomp into account—such as everyday processes, importance of interfaces, understanding the technology, etc.

The UCAN development process employed various evaluation methods over the course of the case studies. The question is: Which methods proved more beneficial than others? To facilitate the comparison, Table 56 describes the transitions between process phases.

	Easymeeting	Easymeeting	Mobile Prosumer	Mobile Prosumer	PTC
Initial idea – evaluation method used	Personal interviews (Standardized questionnaire)	-	Expert interviews (Questionnaire guideline)	Focus group (Concept test)	-
How did it help to get from initial idea to low-fidelity prototype?	The structured interviews with consumers helped to define the functions of the software. They did not help to increase the user's understanding of the system.	-	The interviews revealed specifics about the application, i.e. that an mobile software that acts as an allergy counsel would make no sense. However, they can only serve as a starting point.	The focus group was most helpful for ascertaining user thoughts and for understanding which changes in the system were necessary as a result of the findings.	-

Low-fidelity prototype – evaluation method used	Personal interviews (Standardized questionnaire)	Personal interviews (Talking-out-loud method)	Focus groups (Prototype test)	-	-
How did it help to get from the low-fidelity prototype to the initial working prototype?	The standardized questionnaire with the UTAUT items showed what people actually thought about the system. It did not help to create further iterations of the application.	The talking-out-loud method helped to ascertain the application's weak spots. It could be integrated into a part of the focus group.	The focus group prototype test helped, but was too confusing in terms of group testing. People speaking first prevented others from testing the application from a neutral point of view.		
Initial working prototype – evaluation method used	-	-	-	-	**Online questionnaire**
How did it help to get from the initial working prototype to the product?	-	-	-	-	Although the online questionnaire helped in determining general issues, the UTAUT model did not help to finalize the product as was expected.

Table 56: Comparison of UCAN success between the case studies

The focus groups led to better results in the domain itself and in the application area. Therefore the UCAN process should be adapted to take advantage of focus groups—despite taking longer—for the early phases of prototype development.

The findings in the last case study raised the question whether UCAN should be using UTAUT as a technology acceptance model. This section aims at the demanded theoretical "tweaking" (Venkatesh/Davis/Morris 2007) to the research of Technology Acceptance and research an Ubiquitous Computing topic from a practitioners point of view. The tweaking comes from adding NFC-based constructs to the UTAUT framework in a voluntary setting. However, the lack of a connection between the otherwise significant relationship of behavioral intention to use behavior (see Chapter 6.5) raises a central question: Are the constructs used in the case study powerful enough to predict behavioral intention and to forecast use behavior given the voluntary aspect of testing consumer applications, and, if not, what would the alternatives be?

An popular alternative method for measuring preferences or simulating purchase decisions is the Conjoint Analysis (Green/Srinivasan 1978) which has been used commercially for a long time (Wittink/Vriens/Burhenne 1994). It identifies the importance of product related attributes to a person's overall preferences (Perrey 1996). The Conjoint Analysis is based on the assumption that all participants will definitely decide to buy the simulated product at a later point. This assumption does not necessarily apply to the case of new products where stated preferences sometimes vary from actual purchase decisions (Voeth 1998). Given the limited information surrounding the future market share of a simulated product, Voeth introduced the Limit-Card enhanced Conjoint Analysis (Limit-Conjoint Analysis) (Voeth 1998) to supplement the standard Conjoint Analysis. The Limits-Card concept lets participants not only rank products, but also state the ranking at which they would buy the product. This concept divided the set of products into two groups: one in which the respondent would buy the product in the future, and another in which the respondent is not willing to pay for the product and therefore not buy the product in the future. For UCAN case studies, the Limit-Conjoint Analysis could be a blueprint to determine the actual usage behavior or the purchase behavior of an NFC phone. In the case study PTC, respondents were given a free phone to test with free unlimited data rates in order to measure behavioral intention. This might have biased the behavioral intention of participants. By actually simulating real-life pricing and purchasing of a NFC phone (where one usually pays for a phone and traffic), future usage of the product would be better estimated. This allows to show how respondents intended to use the product in the future in a way that was not reflected by actual system usage and self-reported usage behavior. Besides the aforementioned reasons, taking a different approach to measuring behavioral intention could lead to a more thorough prediction of actual use behavior.

Although the UCAN process model can only be used in hindsight for understanding what could have been done better—but also for designing the final product—one could also use it, for instance, to make recommendations in marketing and communication areas. Given the detailed nature of the results functions or requirements cannot be directly adjusted or changed. Here a separate requirement engineering process would be helpful. The process itself was evaluated and analyzed theoretically during the course of this study. Chapter 1.4 described the proceeding from theorizing about an utility theory.

Fig. 85 shows the adapted UCAN evaluation process in relation to the findings about applicability of evaluation methods.

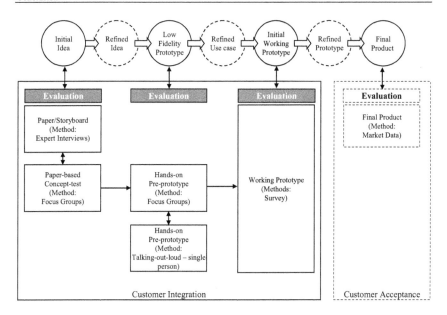

Fig. 85: Adapted and refined UCAN process model (Evaluation phase)

Compared to the original process, the adapted and refined UCAN process model has different evaluation methods that are adapted to the referring process stage: The initial idea is now being evaluated with a) expert interviews in a very early stage, followed by b) a paper-based concept test in a focus group. This procedure makes it easier to arrive at a refined idea. The low-fidelity prototype is evaluated with a) a focus group and an adapted b) talking-out-loud test with all participants in the focus group (in one-on-one meetings). The initial working prototype may be evaluated with a survey. The actual acceptance model needs to be refined and adapted in future research.

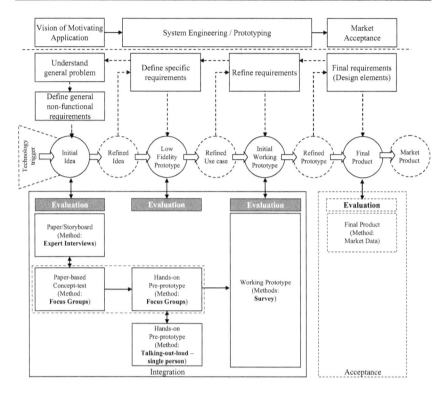

Fig. 86: Final proposed UCAN process model

Fig. 86 shows the final UCAN process model. Based on a visionary idea, the general problem is defined. Non-functional requirements in the specific domain are selected (see section 3.1.3 for a set of Ubicomp related non-functional requirements). The evaluation phases are taking place according to the aforementioned phases. An iterating requirement engineering process will help to control the non-functional and functional application requirements. The final requirements (design elements) are ready with the final product. With this process, companies can be assured to follow design rules and integrate functions as desired by the user. This increases the probability of designing a successful product.

Product changes in late stages come with high costs, especially in the case of Ubicomp because an infrastructure of *tags* is needed. With the help of structured application development costs and early user integration, UCAN is capable of reducing the risk of wasted investment costs by avoiding applications with little or no user acceptance. The following sub-goals were part of the model and were discussed if the goals were met by the instantiation and variation of the UCAN process model.

• **The process model helps to identify potentially negative or unnecessary application functions in an early phase of a development process and allows changes in product development.**

Because of the structure of the UCAN process, it is possible to determine unneeded and even unwanted functions in a very early phase with the initial idea and the low-fidelity prototype. Both phases come with minimal costs and allow for easy changes in developing further iterations of the application. It allows for changes in the latter stages and is appropriate for designing Ubicomp applications.

• **It measures acceptance of the technology before it enters the market as a final—hence nearly unchangeable—product and helps to identify marketing strategies for successful market entry.**

The UCAN process uses the initial working prototype as the second last step before entering final product stage. The used UTAUT model helped to determine—despite several disadvantages—proper marketing materials, and to further improve the application. The UCAN met all requirements of the desired development and application evaluation.

Furthermore it allows people to touch and feel Ubicomp technology at an early stage. The participants can try out and perform tasks or engage in activities. The technology acceptance is measured at a later stage when the prototype is in a more mature phase. Using the later prototype with higher functionality, a larger distribution in the field and larger sample sizes are possible. Therefore valid analysis can be conducted.

The pre-qualification of the application and the impact on the user is more directed towards a closer analysis of end-user perception of the application. The UCAN process also targeted the challenge to include real users, not in laboratory settings, but in daily life situations with Ubicomp technology.

All challenges are met with this implementation of the UCAN process. The next section will now sum up the devising of design guidelines from the three case study chapters.

7.1.4 Design Guidelines for NFC-based Ubiquitous Computing Applications

The idea behind the case studies was to find out more about people's *awareness* and *attitude* towards the technological potential of *NFC mobile phone and tag infrastructure* (see Chapter 2.3). For that reason the primary information systems structure (see Chapter 2.1.6) and relevant findings are stated in this chapter in order to derive design guidelines for future NFC-based Ubicomp applications.

The first initial requirements are to create NFC applications on a non-functional requirement basis, (see Table 57). These requirements were tested in the first case study Easymeeting.

Requirements	Design guideline
Few choices after the single top level choice.	NFC is a rather new concept. The technology easily confuses people if complex navigation structures are employed. The first non-functional requirement is based on Norman's (1999) notion of a shallow structure. In addition to the single top-level choice, only a few other function choices are important in terms of NFC tag usage. Every tag should trigger only one function or at least limit the functions shown on the mobile phone to a few options. Once NFC becomes well known it might be possible to alter this.
Add general captions on labels	Despite advances in logos and trademarks for NFC, the tag should clearly state which function it triggers in text form or in symbols or icons. These general captions should be placed on the tag and avoid the use of technical jargon. The RFID-specific word "tag" is itself largely unknown to people.
The user needs to immediately tell the state of the device and alternatives for actions	With haptic feedback from the telephone the user can clearly tell the current status of the information system. Haptic feedback should be turned on as standard. On the mobile front end, any data transaction should be stated clearly with a progress bar or similar status indicators.
Relationship between actions and results must be clear and easy to determine	NFC exists in the physical world, not only on a screen. This media break is difficult to understand. The relationship between tag (as initiator) and action (mobile service) should be clear insofar as the action suggested by the tag leads to the expected service. If that is not the case, confidence in the system will quickly be lost.
Tagging of context to information	A NFC tag is related to a certain context. This can be a public space, an underground station, a park, a shop, etc.; A tag needs to be situated and placed in a certain environment in which people are accustomed to use-services. A tag for payments should be either located close to the cashier or in a process flow, e.g. when leaving the sales floor.
Choice and consent: Provide a selection mechanism so that users can indicate which services they prefer	The active behavior to touch a tag and start a service implies certain consent. If there are more tags available at a site, the user can easily choose his service as a simple selection mechanism. The number of tags placed in our environment will be limited. Thus offering the relationship of one service to one tag will not be realistically possible. Important however is establishing a close relation between choice and consent.

Table 57: Key non-functional requirements for NFC-based Ubicomp applications

Some of the less critical challenges might vary in different domains or industries. These challenges may also contradict one another and should be researched. For example, requiring full coverage tagging of all objects may increase infrastructural start-up costs, thus heightening financial risks.

Fig. 87 shows the findings from the studies based on the four categories used throughout the evaluations: (A) NFC technology and application, (B) Tag infrastructure, (C) Human factors (also non-functional requirements), and (D) Device, all based on Fig. 16.

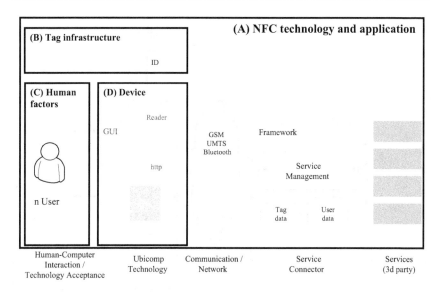

Fig. 87: Thesis information systems structure and findings

The following tables list combined and overall findings from the three case studies in the four areas (A) NFC technology and application (Table 58), (B) Tag infrastructure (Table 59), (C) Human factors (also non-functional requirements) (Table 60), and (D) Device (Table 61).

Finding	Interpretation of finding	Design Guideline
NFC is related to process efficiency.	NFC can be used to improve existing processes that require a greater degree of efficiency. These might include public transport ticketing, entry management, fleet management, parking tickets, etc. in which companies look to speed up process times in order to generate a greater number of transactions possible or to satisfy customers by reducing waiting times. The important relationship between NFC and processes implies that developers tailor the application to an existing process, not tailor the process according to the possibilities of NFC.	Design for the process, not for NFC.

An NFC application is usually considered very easy to use, but the wow-effect decreases quickly.	This finding has implications for marketing strategies. Campaigns marketed to future consumers needs to fulfill several NFC-related requirements: - This means that NFC ease-of-use should not be the sole focus of any marketing and promotional campaign. Ease-of-use drops in significance over periods of extended and sustained usage. - NFC tag processes or functions are extremely relevant and should not be overstated. Marketing should communicate that NFC makes a process faster or more convenient to the user (task performance). The "wow"-effect mentioned in chapter 3.1.1.4 describes how stimuli tend to fade after repeated action. A communication of only the "wow"- effect would lead to misperceptions at consumer and frustration after longer usage.	Focus in communicating the benefits of the application, not the technology.
An NFC application is usually considered very easy to use, but the wow-effect decreases quickly.	This finding has implications for marketing strategies. Campaigns marketed to future consumers needs to fulfill several NFC-related requirements:	Focus in communicating the benefits of the application, not the technology.
Issuing party needs to be trustworthy	In the PTC study participants expressed issues concerning NFC privacy and security. In the other studies these issues were not relevant. This indicates that, when questioned anonymously, the mass public still has concerns—in the other case an interviewer or moderator was present. Moreover, the average user is insecure about information provided via a mobile service. In particular, an NFC-based application provider should go to the necessary lengths to create a trustworthy image or to acquire the relevant certificates from issuing parties, such as VeriSign™, etc.—in the NFC world this is also conducted with Trusted Service Managers—at least for the payment area.	Design trustworthy applications with clear terms of services for privacy and security.
Implementation to existing systems is a crucial factor.	The NFC application should be adapted to existing systems. Each company has fixed IS processes and existing information systems—NFC could be used to add on an easier entry point to the process, but this point has to be attached as a mobile service. This demands valid frameworks and middleware to easily implement needed application interfaces – especially concerning the tag infrastructure, the identification scheme, the backend solution to transfer the IDs to a service, etc.; A customizable lightweight development framework is required.	Design NFC to map existing systems.
An NFC information system should be available for all products in a product group or all objects in an object group.	If tags are placed on multiple products and objects, it is crucial to provide the relevant services matching each product and object. Starting with full implementation is recommended rather than providing only a few services. Each product, object or location, and each tag should provide a specific service that the user wants or expects in a certain usage situation.	Design relevant and specific services for all products, objects or locations.

Table 58: (A) NFC technology and application

Finding	Interpretation of finding	Design guideline
Tag placement is important in relation to the process.	Tag placement is one of the most important issues in NFC-based Ubicomp applications. NFC tags should be integrated as seamlessly as possible into current processes. NFC tags are small in scale, thus hard to find if they do not have the right color, caption, or shape (see also tag shape). The evaluation should also test the placement in real life situations. To increase and simplify usage and to increase adoption rates, maintain the same process and integrate NFC into the *flow*.	Place the tags in the current process flow.
Tag shape, caption and placement is important in relation to the desired function of the tag.	The shape, caption, and placement should be easily identifiable in terms of what function is triggered by touching the tag. Because NFC is very new to the market, it is not clear to the average user what to do with an NFC tag. The touch-based interaction with a mobile phone is new. To avoid confusion, the industry needs to establish European wide tag-appearance standards. Currently only a few logos made available by organizations such as the NFC Forum exist—none of which has been applied widely. Depending on tag context, bright colors and self-explanatory symbols need to be added.	Design a tag that is self-explanatory for the normal user (use captions, icons, colors).
NFC tags should be available for all products in a product group or all objects in an object group.	Similar to the availability of information services, a tag should be easy to locate. This is important since NFC tag infrastructures are built around existing physical objects and, at times, within a limited amount of space. To facilitate usage, a tag has to be placed on all products or objects of a product or object category to avoid disappointing customers if usage is only applicable in certain areas. Limited products, limited locations, and limited objects within a group featuring NFC tags will confuse users. Consequently the user cannot adopt the service due to a lack of reliability when needed. The more tags, and the easier they are to find, the better.	Furnish all objects, locations, or products with tags.

Table 59: (B) Tag infrastructure

Finding	Interpretation of finding	Design guideline
Tagging target group is digital natives.	The digital natives target group responded best in two cases to several tagging scenarios. This group supposedly has an affinity for technology and is most likely to quickly adopt the service (see also Chapter 3.1.1.1. in which it was assumed that digital natives have different characteristics). More research needs to be done considering that digital immigrants also responded very positively to NFC in other studies.	Design first for digital natives.
Low impact of NFC to privacy and data security concerns.	Although privacy and security concerns were low (see also NFC technology), they need to be considered. However, participant's overall positive opinion of NFC indicates that companies should not hesitate introducing NFC-based Ubicomp applications.	See above.
Simplicity	Simplicity is a very soft factor, but directly corresponds to application success. If NFC makes processes more efficient and greatly improves ease of use, simplicity will continue to convince users of the service. Keeping complexity out of the application means that the ease of use of the touch-based interaction should also be reflected in the actual implementation of the service. The conceptual model must be simple.	Design simple applications.
Keep cognitive load low.	Understanding the Ubicomp concept is not easy. To make Ubicomp applications useful, the application design needs to take into consideration our limits of understanding. The clear communication of what happens after a tag is touched is crucial to the service acceptance. In keeping the cognitive load low, the guidelines as shown by Norman (1998) help build the services.	Design the application according Norman's guidelines.
Stick to known and existing process.	What people already know about using electronic systems needs to be taken into account. Changing the process from the ground up is not the right way. NFC only aids in simplifying service initiation, rather than in initiating process changes. For example in ticketing. NFC should not be introduced to change the ticketing process.	Design for existing processes.
Social influence is an important factor.	Social influence has an impact on user perceptions about new technologies. To create initial positive influences in adoption rates, it is important to either use a lead user strategy or viral marketing.	Design with lead users.

Table 60: (C) Human factors

Finding	Interpretation of findings	Design guidelines
Haptic feedback in a mobile device is considered positive for usage.	Haptic feedback after touching an NFC tag helped people to understand when the RF transmission took place. An NFC-enabled phone should have the haptic feedback turned on by default to ensure users that touching the tag results in an action.	Use haptic feedback as default.
Existing device infrastructure needs to be considered	Existing infrastructures are difficult to change. In the mobile phone industry, RIM™'s Blackberrys and recently Apple™ iPhones are produced without NFC. These phones will dominate the market in certain business or leisure segments making changes almost impossible. Market demand factors are needed to build NFC into phones.	Build NFC in Smartphones first.
NFC reader location needs to be clearly identifiable.	Study participants had problems locating the antenna when using the phone for the first time. Even if an introductory explanation helped people in this regard, users who do not have the benefit of expert instruction must be able to easily identify the reader's location. With simple touch symbols, first usage becomes easier and the barrier to try services decreases.	Clearly indicate where the reader is placed.

Table 61: (D) Device

A better understanding of Ubicomp prototypes was achieved in the three case studies. Some of the findings applied to all case studies while some were specific to one or two studies. The following table (Table 62) lists the most relevant findings and the case study in which they occurred in the four categories device, tag infrastructure, NFC technology and application, and soft factors:

Findings	Easy-meeting	MP	PTC	Design Guideline
(A) NFC technology and application				
NFC is related to process efficiency.	X		X	Design for the process, not for NFC.
An NFC application is usually considered very easy to use, but the wow-effect decreases quickly.	X	X	X	Focus in communicating the benefits of the application, not the technology.
Issuing party needs to be trustworthy.		X		Design trustworthy applications with clear terms of services for privacy and security.
Implementation to existing systems is a crucial factor.	X	X	X	Design NFC to map existing systems.
An NFC information system should be available for all products in a product group or all objects in an object group.		X	X	Design relevant and specific services for all products, objects or locations.

(B) Tag Infrastructure				
Tag placement is important in relation to the process.	X	X	X	Place the tags in the current process flow.
Tag shape, caption and placement is important in relation to the desired function of the tag.	X		X	Design a tag that is self-explanatory for the normal user (use captions, icons, colors).
NFC tags should be available for all products in a product group or all objects in an object group.		X	X	Furnish all objects, locations, or products with tags.
(C) Human factors (non-functional requirements)				
Tagging target group is digital natives.		X		Design first for digital natives.
Low impact of NFC to privacy and data security concerns.	X	X		See above.
Simplicity	X			Design simple applications.
Keep cognitive load low.	X	X		Design the application according Norman's guidelines.
Stick to known and existing process.	X		X	Design for existing processes.
Social influence is an important factor.	X		X	Design with lead users.
(D) Device				
Haptic feedback in a mobile device is considered positive for usage.	X	X		Use haptic feedback as default.
Existing device infrastructure needs to be considered	X	X	X	Build NFC in Smartphones first.
NFC reader location needs to be clearly identifiable.	X	X		Clearly indicate where the reader is placed.

Table 62: Findings and number of occurrences in the case studies

These guidelines are a first start for designing NFC applications according user needs and perceptions. They may help companies to better plan and design their NFC applications.

These design guidelines will give companies an overview of important questions around NFC-technology and application, device specifics, tag placement and human factors.

7.1.5 Contributions of the Analysis

The thesis developed a process model and a set of design guidelines that assist the development and evaluation of Ubicomp applications using the example of NFC. The research aimed to answer three research questions:

- **RQ1: What are the defining elements of RFID- and NFC-applications (information systems) and what specific challenges are implied by the development of these applications?**

This research question was addressed at various points throughout the analysis: The Ubicomp technologies used were introduced in section 2.1.4 (RFID) and in section 2.1.5 for (NFC).

The application elements are specified in section 2.1.6. Development challenges are based on the results of chapter 2.2 and 2.3, and are integrated into the process model in section 4.1. These considerations lay the foundation for later chapters.

- **RQ2: Which technology acceptance models and which evaluation methods support the development of Ubicomp applications?**

Existing technology acceptance models and corresponding evaluation methods were described in chapter 3.2, based on the consolidated findings in chapter 3.1, and sections 3.1.2, as well as sections 3.1.3. Section 3.2.4 summed up the innovation adoption and technology acceptance sections, while in chapter 4.2 the evaluation methods are mapped to the process of application development as described in chapter 4.1. The research question has been answered by the foundation of the process model described in chapter 4.3.

- **RQ3: How can companies develop successful Ubicomp applications in a directed process and what are the design guidelines for these applications?**

The three case studies and the underlying artifacts in chapter 5 and 6 were selected according to chapter 4.4 and used to theorize about and test the process model developed in chapter 4.3. The findings in the course of the analysis indicated that a process model can be used to better explain the development process and create design guidelines for the applications (see sections 5.1.10.2, 5.2.11.2, and 6.5.2). The process model can be used as a basis to answer the research question. Furthermore the Ubicomp technology examined in this analysis was Near Field Communication, thus the guidelines developed apply for NFC only. However, the process model and its evaluation phases made it possible to determine various design guidelines that can be used in future studies to further improve NFC applications. The results of the analysis are mentioned in chapter 7.1 and its limitations in 7.2.

The contributions of the analysis are:

1.   To describe the theoretical background that is necessary for an understanding of the characteristics of Ubiquitous Computing technology

The research for chapter 2 concentrated on currently available literature in the field Ubiquitous Computing. It defined Ubicomp and its applications in a working definition, described available technologies and attributes, and proposed an initial information systems overview, which was later used to allocate the findings of the work. Furthermore the chapter looked at the current state of RFID in order to draw conclusions about end-user related Ubicomp technologies for NFC and RFID. The chapter provided the theoretical and technological background needed for understanding other aspects of the work.

2.   To state initial requirements based on human-computer interaction theory for NFC-based applications

Chapter 3.1 proposed a set of requirements based on human-computer interaction by describing Ubicomp's human aspects specific to everyday user actions. In addition it described the necessities of employing a human-computer interface for comparing interaction possibilities and compiling the set of requirements. This set provided the initial design guidelines for developing the first theoretically grounded Ubicomp applications.

3.   To integrate technology acceptance models to be used in Ubicomp settings

Chapter 3.2 presented an overview of Ubicomp related to the end-user, explained the innovation adoption process, and its influence upon Ubicomp. A comparison of technology acceptance models helped to critically assess the various models, and to conclude that the empirically tested consolidation in the forming of the UTAUT model provides a basis for the Ubicomp setting. Furthermore it showed how the UTAUT model was used in a large-scale online study in conjunction with a working prototype in the field.

4.   To use existing theory to develop a process model as a utility theory for the development and evaluation of Ubicomp applications

Chapter 4 used prototyping and technology-acceptance related theories to develop a utility theory process model (UCAN). In creating the process model the challenges of developing Ubicomp applications are first outlined. This is followed by a declaration of Ubicomp evaluations. To test the model, a selection of artifacts embedded within case studies is introduced, and the selection criteria of the case studies are stated. The process model provided a basis to further theorize and to elaborate upon them.

5.   To theorize about and test the process model with different evaluation methods and use the findings of the cases to prepare design guidelines for NFC-based Ubicomp applications.

Chapters 5 and 6 used the case studies and its artifacts as a basis for evaluating them according the process model stated in chapter 4 and to test the model and artifacts. Different evaluation methods were used in the process (from interviews, talking-out-loud, focus groups, to online surveys). The findings of the evaluations were compared and design guidelines extracted in the sections of the case studies. Finally this chapter (Chapter 7) summarized the results and suggested improvements to the UCAN process as well as defined a set of design guidelines for future NFC-based Ubicomp applications.

The challenges for companies discussed in this study are (1) the justification of high initial investments in infrastructure, (2) unknown user technology acceptance, (3) unknown technology among future users (RFID/NFC) and (4) the need of consumers to experiment with NFC to determine its values. To overcome these barriers and challenges, the thesis determined a process model—called UCAN—that helps companies develop applications and evaluate these accordingly in early stages (Table 63).

Challenges	Process model UCAN support
(1) high initial investments in infrastructure	UCAN helps to determine and optimize tag amounts, tag placements, tag captions, and the probability that a user will accept an application. Therefore initial investment in infrastructure can be kept to a minimum. Within the various UCAN process steps, it becomes clear where users want to have their tags, how many they need, etc.—with this information, an optimum of tags can be placed in the real world.
(2) unknown user technology acceptance	UCAN allows a company to determine interesting application functions from the start with a paper-based concept. With a more mature initial working prototype, technology acceptance becomes measurable. Technology acceptance is known and allows the company to change the application or the marketing.

(3) unknown technology among future users (RFID/NFC)	UCAN helps to build marketing materials and exposes study participants to the technology, information that can also be relayed to friends and family. The evaluation has a positive impact on word-of-mouth marketing and assist in developing appropriate marketing concepts.
(4) the need of consumers to experiment with NFC to determine its values	As early as in the (low-cost) low-fidelity prototype UCAN stage, the company allows future consumers to experiment with NFC and determine its value. With this process step, the future user can better express his thoughts about the NFC-based application than is possible in single point-in-time measurements.

Table 63: Support of the UCAN process model for the various challenges

The research problem was solved through a variation of a technology acceptance approach and by developing several design guidelines. The design guidelines help to further improve application technology acceptance and to facilitate addressing the factors A, B, C, and D in the table above.

With the variation of the UCAN process model and the developed design guidelines, the three research questions were answered.

The analysis contributed to the Ubiquitous Computing body of knowledge by a) describing design guidelines (non-functional requirements) of NFC-based Ubicomp applications, b) researching potential evaluation methods that support the successful development of Ubicomp applications and c) providing a guided process that allows for early application evaluation and a reduction of costs..

All of the results bear several limitations and suggest possible avenues for future research.

7.2 Limitations and Future Research

The analysis bears limitations and provides suggestions for future research in the area of Ubicomp. Section 7.2.1 states the general limitations, and section 7.2.2 describes future research opportunities.

7.2.1 Limitations

The research setup of this analysis had certain limitations: (1) the selection of the case studies, (2) the extent of the research process, and (3) the addition of further methodologies.

(1) Selection of the case studies: The case studies were selected according to time to market, availability, and author involvement. This resulted in case studies in three domains. To compare the cases, it would have been better to select cases within the same domain. The use of a utility theory as process model should be defined by effectiveness, efficacy, and efficiency. For this research, only the effectiveness of the results of the evaluations methods was tested. There was no research setting to directly compare the methods and suggest different setups for improving effectiveness or efficacy. As the artifacts improve over the course of development, thus providing a better solution to the general problem they are designed to solve, their effectiveness, efficacy, and efficiency increases. So does the UCAN process as a utility theory itself. The final version will be better able to measure technology acceptance, however there needs to be more built-in measures in order to determine the value of UCAN for companies (e.g. will product development be able to release more successful products due to UCAN?).

The findings are primarily valid for a single domain or branch. It is not clear if and how these might be generally applied to other Ubicomp settings. For example, the difference in user perception between NFC and RFID has not been clearly evaluated. NFC seems to have a better reputation among the participants, but it was not directly compared in a single study.

(2) Extent of the research process: The research process of UCAN was never fully conducted from initial idea to final product. It can therefore only be used as a foundation for future research in the area. Similar to the problem of participatory design, it is practically impossible to measure the success of such a process model since this would require developing and evaluating the product twice—once with participation, once without. Without the final measure of product success, the results of this study need to be taken with caution.

(3) Addition of further methodologies: There was no comparison between different user integration methods, such as participatory design as a whole, lead-user-integration, etc.; However, this was not the focus of this work given its stated intention of presenting a potential process model for prototyping Ubiquitous Computing product development. The selection of the methods used was not complete. Storytelling and others were not used to learn more about the application. The use of prototypes as a basis can be varied in another study.

7.2.2 Future Research

Future research needs to further detail (also quantitative) approaches on user-centered design and acceptance models for Ubicomp applications. Is the UCAN approach meeting the needs of Ubicomp application developers and does it enhance the development process?

Using various evaluation methods might lead to different results. An interesting future research area is a test of the various TAM derivates (UTAUT, TAM2) for comparing the results of this work. Furthermore the UTAUT itself is a part of future research. The question is, how the model itself can be modified to improve its forecast value for product development.

The UCAN process model needs to be enhanced with business engineering methods, such as an early business case evaluation—the UCAN model only targeted user acceptance and soft measures of product development and software engineering. Especially in the early phases, the business models need to be evaluated thoroughly. From an information systems and computer science perspective, the requirement engineering aspect needs to be further discussed in such a process. The question is, if requirement engineering can be adapted to a rigorous technology acceptance measurement process.

Finally the introduction to consumer markets of a technology such as Near Field Communication or RFID is shaped by a multiplicity of factors influencing consumer decisions (marketing, design), in comparison to the more financially driven decision making of companies, so that it remains unclear which factors will actually help NFC become the leading mobile technology of the 21st century. The design guidelines presented in this work are a first start for actually introducing NFC to markets and for understanding how NFC will gain momentum during the first years. Therefore the design guidelines need to be tested and also present a future research opportunity in providing a basis for determining how they influence NFC adoption.

Bibliography

AbiResearch (2007): Near Field Communication (Study). ABI Research 2007.

Abowd, G.D. (1996): Ubiquitous Computing: Research Themes and Open Issues from an Applications Perspective (GVU Technical Report (GIT-GVU-96-24)). Graphics, Visualization & Usability Center, Georgia Institute of Technology, 1996.

Abowd, G.D. (1999): Software Engineering Issues for Ubiquitous Computing. Paper presented at the ICSE, Los Angeles, CA, p. 75-84.

Abowd, G.D.; Atkeson, C.; Essa, I. (1998): Ubiquitous Smart Spaces. Paper presented at the DARPA, Atlanta.

Abowd, G.D.; Atkeson, C.; Essa, I.; Ramachandran, K. (1998): Development of a Large-Scale Ubiquitous Computing Interface, 1998.

Abowd, G.D.; Hayes, G.R.; Iachello, G.; Kientz, J.A.; Patel, S.N.; Stevens, M.M.; Truong, K.N. (2005): Prototypes and paratypes: designing mobile and ubiquitous computing applications. In: Pervasive Computing, Vol. 4, 4, pp. 67-73.

Abowd, G.D.; Mynatt, E., D.; Rodden, T. (2002): The human experience [of ubiquitous computing]. In: Pervasive Computing, Vol. 1, 1, pp. 48-57.

Abowd, G.D.; Mynatt, E.D. (2000): Charting Past, Present and Future Research in Ubiquitous Computing. In: ACM Transactions on Computer-Human Interaction, Vol. 7, 1, pp. 30ff.

Adams, D.A.; Nelson, R.R.; Todd, P.A. (1992): Perceived Usefulness, Ease of Use, and Usage of Information Technology: A Replication. In: MIS Quarterly, Vol. 16, 2, pp. 227-247.

Adelmann, R.; Langheinrich, M.; Flörkemeier, C. (2006): Toolkit for Bar Code Recognition and Resolving on Camera Phones - Jump Starting the Internet of Things. Paper presented at the Informatik 2006, Dresden.

Adler, J. (1996): Informationsökonomische Fundierung von Austauschprozessen, Wiesbaden 1996.

Agarwal, R. (2000): Individual Acceptance of Information Technologies. In: Framing the Domains of IT Management: Projecting the Future ... Through the Past. Ed.: Zmud, R.W. Pinnaflex Education Resources Inc. 2000, pp. 85-104.

Agarwal, R.; Prasad, J. (1998): A Conceptual and Operational Definition of Personal Innovativeness in the Domain of Information Technology. In: Information Systems Research, Vol. 9, 2, pp. 204-215.

Aiken, M.W.; Sheng, O.; Vogel, D.R. (1991): Integrating Expert Systems With Group Decision Support Systems. In: ACM Transactions on Information Systems, Vol. 9, 1, pp. 75-95.

Ainlay, S.C.; Singleton Jr, R.; Swigert, V.L. (1992): Aging and Religious Participation: Reconsidering the Effects of Health. In: Journal for the Scientific Study of Religion, Vol. 31, 2, pp. 175-188.

Ajzen, I. (1985): From intentions to actions: A theory of planned behavior. In: Springer series in social psychology. Ed.: Kuhl, J.; Beckmann, J. Springer Berlin 1985, pp. 11-39.

Ajzen, I. (1988): Attitudes, personality, and behavior, Open University Press Milton Keynes 1988.

Ajzen, I. (1991): The theory of planned behavior. In: Organizational Behavior and Human Decision Processes, Vol. 50, pp. 179-211.

Ajzen, I.; Fishbein, M. (2005): The influence of attitudes on behavior. In: The handbook of attitudes. Ed.: D. Albarracín, B.T.J., & M. P. Zanna Erlbaum, Mahwah, NJ 2005, pp. 173-221.

Alba, J.; Lynch, J.; Weitz, B.; Janiszewski, C.; Lutz, R.; Sawyer, A.; Wood, S. (1997): Interactive Home Shopping: Consumer, Retailer and Manufacturer Incentives to Participate in Electronic Markets. In: Journal of Marketing, Vol. 61, pp. 38-53.

Anderson, J.E.; Schwager, P.H. (2004): SME Adoption of Wireless Lan Technology: Applying the UTAUT Model Paper presented at the Proceedings of the 7th Annual Conference of the Southern Association for Information Systems (SAIS), Savannah, p. 39-43.

Anderson, W.L.; Crocca, W.T. (1993): Engineering practice and codevelopment of codevelopment of product prototypes. In: Communications of the ACM, Vol. 36, 6, pp. 49-56.

Archer, L.B. (1965): Systematic Method for Designers, Council of Industrial Design, HMSO 1965.

Arnall, T. (2005a): The address book desk. http://www.elasticspace.com/2005/12/address-book-desk, accessed July 7, 2006.

Arnall, T. (2005b): A graphic language for touch. http://www.elasticspace.com/2005/11/graphic-language-for-touch accessed

Asif, Z.; Mandviwalla, M. (2005): Integrating the supply chain with RFID: A technical and business analysis. In: Communications of the Association for Information Systems, Vol. 15, 24, pp. 393–426.

Aßmann, J. (2003): Der Einfluss computeranimierter Produktpräsentationen auf die Validität von Konzepttests. Eine informationsökonomische Analyse alternativer Präsentationsformen., Wissenschaftlicher Verlag, Berlin 2003.

Aßmann, J.; Resatsch, F.; Schildhauer, T. (2006): Ubiquitous Computing im Wissensmanagement - Die Bedeutung allgegenwärtiger Informationsstrukturen auf das Wissensmanagement. In: i-com Zeitschrift für interaktive und kooperative Medien, Vol. 5, 2, pp. 11-16.

Astebro, T.B.; Dahlin, K. (2005): Opportunity Knocks. HEC Paris.

Auer, T. (1998): Quality of IS use. In: European Journal of Information Systems, Vol. 7, 3, pp. 192–201.

Auto-ID-Center (2003): Technology Guide. Auto-ID Center MIT, 2003.

Aylott, R.; Mitchell, V.-W. (1998): An exploratory study of grocery shopping stressors. In: International Journal of Retail & Distribution Management, Vol. 26, 9, pp. 362-373.

Baars, B.J.; McGovern, K. (1996): Cognitive views of consciousness: What are the facts? How can we explain them? In: The Science of Consciousness: Psychological, Neuropsychological, and Clinical Reviews. Ed.: Velmans, M. Routledge, London 1996.

Ballagas, R.; Borchers, J.; Rohs, M.; Sheridan, J.G. (2006): The Smart Phone: A Ubiquitous Input Device. In: Pervasive Computing Vol. 5, 1, pp. 70-77.

Ballagas, R.; Ringel, M.; Stone, M.; Borchers, J. (2003): iStuff: A Physical User Interface Toolkit for Ubiquitous Computing Environments. Paper presented at the CHI 2003, Ft. Lauderdale, Florida, USA, p. 537-544.

Bandura, A. (1977a): Self-efficacy: Toward a unifying theory of behavioral change. In: Psychological Review, Vol. 84, 2, pp. 191-215.

Bandura, A. (1977b): Social learning theory, Prentice Hall, Englewood Cliffs, NJ 1977b.

Bandura, A. (1986): Social foundations of thought and action: A social cognitive theory, Prentice-Hall, Englewood Cliffs, NJ 1986.

Bandura, A. (1989): Human agency in social cognitive theory. In: American Psychologist, Vol. 44, 9, pp. 1175-1184.

Barbour, R.S. (2001): Checklists for improving rigour in qualitative research: a case of the tail wagging the dog? In: BMJ, Vol. 322, 7294, pp. 1115-1117.

Barki, H.; Hartwick, J. (1994): Measuring User Participation, User Involvement, and User Attitude. In: MIS Quarterly, Vol. 18, 1, pp. 59-82.

Baude, P.F.; Ender, D.A.; Kelley, T.W.; Haase, M.A.; Muyres, D.V.; Theiss, S.D. (2003): Organic semiconductor RFID transponders. In: Electron Devices Meeting, 2003. IEDM'03 Technical Digest. IEEE International, pp. 8.1.1- 8.1.4.

Beckwith, R. (2003): Designing for Ubiquity: The Perception of Privacy. In: Pervasive Computing, Vol. 3, pp. 40-46.

Bell, G.; Dourish, P. (2007): Yesterday's tomorrows: notes on ubiquitous computing's dominant vision. In: Personal and Ubiquitous Computing, Vol. 11, 2, pp. 133-143.

Belt, S.; Greenblatt, D.; Häkkilä, J.; Mäkelä, K. (2006): User Perceptions on Mobile Interaction with Visual and RFID Tags. Paper presented at the MobileHCI 2006 Workshop Mobile Interaction with the Real World Espoo, Finland.

Bettmann, J.R. (1973): Perceived Risk and Its Components: A Model and Empirical Test. In: Journal of Marketing Research, Vol. 10, pp. 184-190.

BITKOM (2005): RFID Technologie, Systeme und Anwendungen (White Paper). Bundesverband Informationswirtschaft, Telekommunikation und neue Medien e.V., 2005.

Bjorner, D. (2006): Software Engineering 3, Springer 2006.

Blackler, A.; Popovic, V.; Mahar, D. (2003): The nature of intuitive use of products:an experimental approach. In: Design Studies Vol. 24, 6, pp. 491-506.

Bleecker, J. (2005): A Manifesto for Networked Objects — Cohabiting with Pigeons, Arphids and Aibos in the Internet of Things. (Vol. 1).

Blomberg, J.L.; Henderson, A. (1990): Reflections on participatory design: lessons from the trillium experience. Paper presented at the Proceedings of the SIGCHI conference on Human factors in computing systems: Empowering people, p. 353-360.

Bødker, S.; Grønbæk, K.; Kyng, M. (1995): Cooperative design: techniques and experiences from the Scandinavian scene. In: Human-computer interaction: toward the year 2000. Ed. Morgan Kaufmann Publishers Inc., San Francisco, CA, USA 1995, pp. 215-224

Boff, K.R.; Kaufman, L.; Thomas, J.P. (1986): Handbook of perception and human performance, Wiley New York 1986.

Bohn, J.; Coroamă, V.; Langheinrich, M.; Mattern, F.; Rohs, M. (2004): Living in a World of Smart Everyday Objects – Social, Economic, and Ethical Implications. In: Human and Ecological Risk Assessment, Vol. 10, 5, pp. 763-785.

Boudreau, M.C.; Robey, D. (2005): Enacting Integrated Information Technology: A Human Agency Perspective. In: Organization Science, Vol. 16, 1, pp. 3-18.

Brancheau, J.C.; Brown, C.V. (1993): The management of end-user computing: status and directions. In: ACM Computing Surveys (CSUR), Vol. 25, 4, pp. 437-482.

Buchenau, M.; Suri, J.F. (2000): Experience prototyping. Paper presented at the DIS 2006, New York City, New York, United States, p. 424-433.

Burkhardt, J.; Henn, H.; Hepper, S.; Rindtorff, K.; Schaeck, T. (2001): Pervasive Computing, Addison Wesley 2001.

Burton-Jones, A.; Straub, D. (2006): Reconceptualizing System Usage: An Approach and Empirical Test. In: Information Systems Research, Vol. 17, 3, pp. 228-246.

Carlsson, C.; Carlsson, J.; Hyvonen, K.; Puhakainen, J.; Walden, P. (2006): Adoption of Mobile Devices/Services - Searching for Answers with the UTAUT. Paper presented at the 39th Hawaii International Conference on System Sciences (HICSS), Hawaii p. 132a-132a.

Carter, S.; Mankoff, J. (2004): Challenges for Ubicomp Evaluation (Technical Report). Computer Science Division, University of California, 2004.

CCC (2006): Scannt Eure Tickets, ehe es wer anders tut! http://www.ccc.de/updates/2006/rfid-tickets-fuer-berlin?language=de, accessed July 7, 2006.

Chan, S.-C.; Lu, M.-t. (2004): Understanding Internet Banking Adoption and Use Behavior: A Hong Kong Perspective. In: Journal of Global Information Management, Vol. 12, 3, pp. 21-43.

Chappell, G.; Durdan, D.; Gilbert, G.; Ginsburg, L.; Smith, J.; Tobolski, J. (2002): Auto-ID on Delivery: The Value of Auto-ID Technology in the Retail Supply Chain (Report). Auto-ID Center MIT, 2002.

Chau, P.Y.K. (1996): An empirical assessment of a modified technology acceptance model. In: Journal of Management Information Systems, Vol. 13, 2, pp. 185-204.

Chiang, K.P.; Dholakia, R.R. (2003): Factors Driving Consumer Intention to Shop Online: An Empirical Investigation. In: Journal of Consumer Psychology, Vol. 13, 1, pp. 177-183.

Chin, W. (2000): Partial least squares for IS researchers: an overview and presentation of recent advances using the PLS approach. Paper presented at the International Conference on Information Systems: Proceedings of the twenty first international conference on Information systems, p. 741-742.

Chin, W.W. (1998a): Issues and Opinion on Structural Equation Modeling. In: MIS Quarterly, Vol. 22, 1.

Chin, W.W. (1998b): The partial least squares approach to structural equation modeling. In: Modern Methods for Business Research. Ed.: Marcoulides, G.A. Mahwah: Lawrence Erlbaum Associates 1998b, pp. 295-336.

Chin, W.W.; Gopal, A.; Salisbury, W.D. (1997): Advancing the theory of adaptive structuration: The development of a scale to measure faithfulness of appropriation. In: Information Systems Research, Vol. 8, 4, pp. 342-367.

Chin, W.W.; Marcolin, B.L.; Newsted, P.R. (2003): A Partial Least Squares Latent Variable Modeling Approach for Measuring Interaction Effects: Results from a Monte Carlo Simulation Study and an Electronic-Mail Emotion/Adoption Study. In: Information Systems Research, Vol. 14, 2, pp. 189-217.

Christensen, C.M. (1997): The Innovator's Dilemma. (Reprint 2003 HarperCollins Publishers Ed.), Harvard Business School Press 1997.

Christensen, C.M. (2003): The Innovator's Solution. Creating and Sustaining Successful Growth., Harvard Business School Press 2003.

Chwelos, P.; Benbasat, I.; Dexter, A.S. (2001): Research Report: Empirical Test of an EDI Adoption Model. In: Information Systems Research, Vol. 12, 3, pp. 304-321.

Clarke, R. (2001): Appropriate Research Methods for Electronic Commerce. http://www.anu.edu.au/people/Roger.Clarke/EC/ResMeth.html accessed Nov 20, 2006.

Compeau, D.; Higgins, C.A.; Huff, S. (1999): Social Cognitive Theory and Individual Reactions to Computing Technology: A Longitudinal Study. In: MIS Quarterly, Vol. 23, 2, pp. 145-158.

Compeau, D.R.; Higgins, C.A. (1995a): Application of social cognitive theory to training for computer skills. In: Information Systems Research, Vol. 6, 2, pp. 118-143.

Compeau, D.R.; Higgins, C.A. (1995b): Computer Self-Efficacy: Development of a Measure and Initial Test. In: MIS Quarterly, Vol. 19, 2, pp. 189-211.

Cox, D.F.; Rich, S.U. (1964): Perceived Risk and Consumer Decision-Making: The Case of Telephone Shopping. In: Journal of Marketing Research, Vol. 1, 4, pp. 32-39.

Csikszentmihalyi, M. (1991): Design and Order in Everyday Life. In: Design Issues, Vol. 8, 1, pp. 26-34.

Darby, M.R.; Karni, E. (1973): Free Competition And The Optimal Amount Of Fraud. In: The Journal of Law and Economics, Vol. 16, pp. 67-88.

Darley, J.M.; Latane, B. (1968): Bystander intervention in emergencies: diffusion of responsibility. In: J Pers Soc Psychol, Vol. 8, 4, pp. 377-83.

Davis, F.D. (1986): A Technology Acceptance Model for Empirically Testing New End-User Systems: Theory and Results. Ph.D. dissertation, Massachusets Institute of Technology 1986.

Davis, F.D. (1989): Perceived Usefulness, Perceived Ease of Use, and User Acceptance of Information Technology. In: MIS Quaterly, Vol. 13, pp. 319 - 339.

Davis, F.D.; Bagozzi, R.P.; Warshaw, P.R. (1989): User acceptance of computer technology: a comparison of two theoretical models. In: Management Science, Vol. 35, 8, pp. 982-1003.

Davis, F.D.; Bagozzi, R.P.; Warshaw, P.R. (1992): Extrinsic and Intrinsic Motivation to Use Computers in the Workplace. In: Journal of Applied Social Psychology, Vol. 22, 14, pp. 1111-1132.

Davis, F.D.; Venkatesh, V. (2004): Toward preprototype user acceptance testing of new information systems: implications for software project management. In: IEEE Transactions on Engineering Management, Vol. 51, 1, pp. 31-46.

Davis, G.B. (1982): Strategies for Information Requirements Determination. In: IBM Systems Journal, Vol. 21, 1, pp. 4-30.

Deci, E.L. (1975): Intrinsic Motivation. (1 Ed.), Plenum Press, New York 1975.

Degenhardt, W. (1986): Akzeptanzforschung zu Bildschirmtext. Methoden und Ergebnisse, München 1986.

Degeratu, A.M.; Rangaswamy, A.; Wu, J. (2000): Consumer choice behavior in online and traditional supermarkets: The effects of brand name, price, and other search attributes. In: International Journal of Research in Marketing, Vol. 17, 1, pp. 55-78.

Dey, A.K. (2001): Understanding and Using Context. In: Personal and Ubiquitous Computing, Vol. 5, 1, pp. 4-7.

Dishawa, M.T.; Strong, D.M. (1999): Extending the technology acceptance model with task-technology fit constructs. In: Information & Management, Vol. 36, 1, pp. 9-21.

Dowling, G.R.; Staelin, R. (1994): A Model of Perceived Risk and Intended Risk-Handling Activity. In: The Journal of Consumer Research, Vol. 21, 1, pp. 119-134.

Dressen, D. (2004): Considerations for RFID technology selection. In: Applications journal, 3, pp. 45-47.

Ebert, C. (2005): Systematisches Requirements Engineering - Anforderungen ermitteln, spezifizieren, analysieren und verfolgen, dpunkt.verlag, Heidelberg 2005.

Eck, D.; Lamere, P.; Bertin-Mahieux, T.; Green, S. (2007): Automatic Generation of Social Tags for Music Recommendation. Paper presented at the Advances in Neural Information Processing Systems (NIPS).

ECMA-340 (2004): Near Field Communication Interface and Protocol (NFCIP-1), 2004.

Eekels, J.; Roozenburg, N.F.M. (1991): A methodological comparison of the structures of scientific research and engineering design: their similarities and differences. In: Design Studies, Vol. 12, 4, pp. 197–203.

Eide, P.L.H.; Stålhane, T. (2005): Quantification and Traceability of Requirements (TDT4735 Software Engineering Depth Study). NTNU, 2005.

Elrod, S.; Hall, G.; Costanza, R.; Dixon, M.; Des Rivières, J. (1993): Responsive office environments. In: Communications of the ACM, Vol. 36, 7, pp. 84-85.

EPCglobal (2005): Object Naming Service (ONS) Version 1.0 (Technical Specification). EPCglobal 2005.

Ettema, J.S. (1985): Explaining Information System Use With System-Monitored vs. Self-Reported Use Measures. In: The Public Opinion Quarterly, Vol. 49, 3, pp. 381-387.

Fenech, T. (1998): Using perceived ease of use and perceived usefulness to predict acceptance of the World Wide Web. In: Computer Networks and ISDN Systems, Vol. 30, 1-7, pp. 629-630.

Ferratt, T.W.; Lederer, A.L.; Hall, S.R.; Krella, J.M. (1995): Information technology and competitors: a case for collaborative advantage. Paper presented at the SIGCPR conference on Supporting teams, groups, and learning inside and outside the IS, Nashville, Tennessee, United States, p. 139-147.

FIFA (2004): 2006 FIFA World Cup OC agrees deal with CTS. http://fifaworldcup. yahoo.com/06/en/040816/1/203i.html, accessed July 7, 2006.

Fine, C.; Klym, N.; Tavshikar, M.; Trossen, D. (2006): The Evolution of RFID Networks (Paper 224). MIT Sloan School of Management - MIT Communications Futures Program (CFP) Research Network Cambridge University Communications 2006.

Fishbein, M.; Ajzen, I. (1975): Belief, Attitude, Intention, and Behavior: An Introduction to Theory and Research, Addison-Wesley, Reading, MA 1975.

Fleisch, E. (2004): RFID – Technologie: Neuer Innovationsmotor für Logistik und Industrie? http://www.ecin.de/mobilebusinesscenter/rfidtechnologie/, accessed March 2, 2009.

Fleisch, E.; Christ, O.; Dierkes, M. (2005a): Die betriebswirtschaftliche Vision des Internets der Dinge. In: Das Internet der Dinge. Ed.: Fleisch, E.; Mattern, F. Springer-Verlag, Berlin 2005a, pp. 3-37.

Fleisch, E.; Christ, O.; Dierkes, M. (2005b): Die betriebswirtschaftliche Vision des Internets der Dinge. In: Das Internet der Dinge. Ed.: Fleisch, E.; Mattern, F. Springer-Verlag 2005b.

Fleisch, E.; Mattern, F. (2005): Das Internet der Dinge - Ubiquitous Computing und RFID in der Praxis: Visionen, Technologien, Anwendungen, Handlungsanleitungen, Springer, Berlin 2005.

Fleisch, E.; Mattern, F.; Billinger, S. (2004): Betriebswirtschaftliche Applikationen des Ubiquitous Computing. Beispiele, Bausteine und Nutzenpotentiale. http://www.vs.inf.ethz.ch/ publ/papers/BW_ApplUbicomp.pdf, accessed 10.Januar, 2005.

Fleisch, E.; Thiesse, F. (2007): On the Management Implications of Ubiquitous Computing: An IS Perspective. Paper presented at the Fifteenth European Conference on Information Systems, St. Gallen, p. 1929-1940.

Floerkemeier, C.; Mattern, F. (2006): Smart Playing Cards - Enhancing the Gaming Experience with RFID. Paper presented at the Proceedings of the Third International Workshop on Pervasive Gaming Applications - PerGames 2006 at PERVASIVE 2006, Dublin, Ireland.

Floyd, C. (1983): A Systematic Look at Prototyping. Paper presented at the Approaches to Prototyping, Namur, p. 1-18.

Floyd, C. (1989): Softwareentwicklung als Realitätskonstruktion. In: Informatik-Fachberichte, Vol. 212, pp. 1-20.

FoeBUD (2006): WM-Tickets absurd. http://www.foebud.org/rfid/wm-tickets-absurd, accessed July 7, 2006.

Foley, J.D.; Wallace, V.L.; Chan, P. (1984): The human factors of computer graphics interaction techniques. In: IEEE Computer Graphics and Applications, Vol. 4, 11, pp. 13-48.

Fraenkel, J.R.; Wallen, N.E. (1990): How to design and evaluate research in education, McGraw-Hill Companies 1990.

Galanxhi, H.; Nah, F.F.-H. (2005): Privacy Issues in the Era of Ubiquitous Commerce. Paper presented at the Proceedings of the Americas Conference on Information Systems (AMCIS 2005), Omaha, Nebraska, USA, p. 1926 - 1934.

Garfield, M.J. (2005): Acceptance of Ubiquitous Computing. In: Information Systems Management, Vol. 22, 4, pp. 24-31.

Gefen, D.; Straub, D. (2000a): The Relative Importance of Perceived Ease of Use in IS Adoption: A Study of E-Commerce Adoption. In: Journal of the Association for Information Systems, Vol. 1, 8, pp. 1-28.

Gefen, D.; Straub, D. (2000b): The Relative Importance of Perceived Ease of Use in IS Adoption: A Study of E-Commerce Adoption. In: Journal of the Association for Information Systems Vol. 1, 8, pp. 1-28.

Gershenfeld, N.; Krikorian, R.; Cohen, D. (2004): The Internet of Things. In: Scientific American, pp. 76-81.

Gibbs, A. (1997): Focus Groups. In: Social Research Update, Vol. 19.

Gillert, F.; Hansen, W.-R. (2007): RFID - Für die Optimierung von Geschäftsprozessen, Carl Hanser Verlag München 2007.

Goldenberg, J.; Lehmann, D.R.; Mazursky, D. (2001): The Idea Itself and the Circumstances of Its Emergence as Predictors of New Product Success. In: Management Science, Vol. 47, 1, pp. 69-84.

Goldkuhl, G. (2004): Design Theories in Information Systems–A Need for Multi-Grounding. In: Journal of Information Technology Theory and Application, Vol. 6, 2, pp. 59-72.

Golledge, R.G.; Stimson, R.J. (1997): Spatial Behavior: A Geographical Perspective, Guilford, New York 1997.

Goodhue, D.L. (1995): Understanding user evaluations of information systems. In: Management Science, Vol. 41, 12, pp. 1827-1844

Goodhue, D.L.; Thompson, R.L. (1995): Task-Technology Fit and Individual Performance. In: MIS Quarterly, Vol. 19, 2, pp. 213-236.

Gourville, J.T. (2006): Wann Kunden neue Produkte kaufen. In: Harvard Business Manager, pp. 45-53.

Graafstra, A. (2006): RFID Toys: 11 Cool Projects for Home, Office and Entertainment Wiley Publishing Indianapolis, Indiana 2006.

Green, P.E.; Srinivasan, V. (1978): Conjoint Analysis in Consumer Research: Issues and Outlook. In: Journal of Consumer Research, Vol. 5, 2, pp. 103.

Greenbaum, J.; Kyng, M. (1992): Design at work: cooperative design of computer systems, Lawrence Erlbaum Associates, Inc. Mahwah, NJ, USA 1992.

Greenhalgh, T.; Robert, G.; Bate, P. (2004): A systematic review of the literature on diffusion, dissemination and sustainability of innovations in service delivery and organisation. National Coordinating Centre for Service Delivery and Organisation, 2004.

Gregor, S. (2006): The nature of theory in information systems. In: MIS Quarterly, Vol. 30, 3, pp. 611-642.

Gruner, K.E.; Homburg, C. (2000): Does Customer Interaction Enhance New Product Success? In: Journal of Business Research, Vol. 49, 1, pp. 1-14.

GSM-Association (2006): Membership and Market Statistics. GSM Association, 2006.

GSM-Association (2007): Mobile NFC Technical Guidelines 2007.

GSMAssociation (2007): Mobile NFC Technical Guidelines 2007.

Günther, O.; Spiekermann, S. (2005): RFID And The Perception of Control: The Consumer's View. In: Communications of the ACM, Vol. 48, 9, pp. 73-76.

Hagenhoff, S.; Kaspar, C.; Resatsch, F. (2008): Basic Concepts of Mobile Radio Technologies. In: Encyclopedia of Multimedia Technology and Networking. Ed.: Pagani, M., (2.Ed.), Hershey, USA 2008, pp. 113-120.

Hainbuchner, C. (2005): Technology Acceptance of Complex Products and Systems - The Case of Terrestrial Trunked Radio (TETRA). Dissertation, Wirtschaftsuniversität Wien 2005.

Hair, J.F.; Anderson, R.E.; Tatham, R.L.; Black, W.C. (1998): Multivariate Analysis, Upper Saddle River, NJ: Prentice Hall 1998.

Hair Jr, J.F.; Anderson, R.E.; Tatham, R.L.; Black, W.C. (1995): Multivariate data analysis: with readings, Prentice-Hall, Inc. Upper Saddle River, NJ, USA 1995.

Hallnäs, L.; Redström, J. (2002): From use to presence: on the expressions and aesthetics of everyday computational things. In: ACM Transactions on Computer-Human Interaction, Vol. 9, 2, pp. 11-12.

Hansmann, U.; Merk, M.; Nicklous, M.; Stober, R. (2003): Pervasive Computing Handbook. (2nd Ed.), Springer-Verlag 2003.

He, D.; Lu, Y. (2007): Consumers Perceptions and Acceptances Towards Mobile Advertising: An Empirical Study in China. Paper presented at the Wireless Communications, Networking and Mobile Computing (WiCom 2007), p. 3770-3773.

Heath, T.; Motta, E.; Petre, M. (2007): Computing Word-of-Mouth Trust Relationships in Social Networks from Semantic Web and Web2. 0 Data Sources. Paper presented at the Workshop on Bridging the Gap between Semantic Web and Web 2.0 - 4th European Semantic Web Conference (ESWC2007).

Heinrich, C.E. (2005): RFID and Beyond: Growing Your Business Through Real World Awareness, Wiley 2005.

Hendrickson, A.R.; Collins, M.R. (1996): An Assessment of Structure. In: The DATA BASE for Advances in Information Systems, Vol. 27, 2, pp. 61.

Heng, S. (2006): RFID Funkchips. Deutsche Bank Research 2006.

Henseler, W. (2001): Interface Agenten. Der Wandel in der Mensch-Objekt-Kommunikation oder Von benutzungsfreundlichen zu benutzerfreundlichen Systemen. In: Der digitale Wahn. Ed.: Bürdek, B.E. edition suhrkamp, Frankfurt am Main 2001.

Herstatt, C.; Lettl, C. (2000): Management of "technology push" development projects. Technology and Innovation Management at the Technische Universität Hamburg-Harburg, 2000.

Hevner, A.R.; March, S.T.; Park, J.; Ram, S. (2004): Design Science in Information Systems Research. In: MIS Quarterly, Vol. 28, 1, pp. 75-105.

Hewett, T.; Baecker, R.; Card, S.; Carey, T.; Gasen, J.; Mantei, M.; Perlman, G.; Strong, G.; Verplank, W. (1992): ACM SIGCHI Curricula for Human-Computer Interaction. accessed Nov 22, 2006.

Hofstede, G. (2001): Culture's consequences: Comparing values, behaviors, institutions and organizations across nations . Beverly Hills. CA: Sage.

Holmquist, L.E.; Höök, K.; Juhlin, O.; Persson, P. (2002): Challenges and Opportunities for the Design and Evaluation of Mobile Applications. Paper presented at the Workshop - Main issues in designing interactive mobile services, Mobile HCI.

Hughes, J.A.; Randall, D.; Shapiro, D. (1992): Faltering from ethnography to design. In: Proceedings of the 1992 ACM conference on Computer-supported cooperative work, pp. 115-122.

Hulland, J.; Richard Ivey School of, B. (1999): Use of Partial Least Squares (PLS) in Strategic Management Research: A Review of Four Recent Studies. In: Strategic Management Journal, Vol. 20, 2, pp. 195-204.

Iachello, G.; Smith, I.; Consolvo, S.; Chen, M.; Abowd, G.D. (2005): Developing privacy guidelines for social location disclosure applications and services. Paper presented at the Proceedings of the 2005 symposium on Usable privacy and security, Pittsburgh, Pennsylvania, p. 65-76.

Iachello, G.; Truong, K.N.; Abowd, G.D.; Hayes, G.R.; Stevens, M.M. (2006): Prototyping and sampling experience to evaluate ubiquitous computing privacy in the real world. Paper presented at the Proceedings of ACM Conference on Human Factors in Computing Systems (CHI 2006), Montréal, Québec, Canada, p. 1009-1018.

IEEE (1990): IEEE Std 610.12-1990, IEEE Standard Glossary of Software Engineering Terminology., 1990.

IEEE (1998): IEEE Guide for Developing System Requirements Specifications, 1998.

Igbaria, M.; Zinatelli, N.; Cragg, P.; Cavaye, A.L.M. (1997): Personal Computing Acceptance Factors in Small Firms: A Structural Equation Model. In: MIS Quarterly, Vol. 21, 3, pp. 279-305.

Informationsforum-RFID (2006a): Angesagt in jeder Saison.
http://rfidabc.de/artikel/ freizeit/008_veranstaltungen/index.html, accessed Nov 10, 2006.

Informationsforum-RFID (2006b): Ihr Steak. Erkennen Sie's wieder?
http://rfidabc.de/artikel/shoppen/034_tierzucht1/index.html, accessed Nov 10, 2006.

Ishii, H.; Ullmer, B. (1997): Tangible Bits: Towards Seamless Interfaces between People, Bits, and Atoms. Paper presented at the CHI, Atlanta, Georgia p. 234-241.

ISO/IEC (2004): ISO/IEC TR 9126-4:2004, 2004.

Jahn, S. (2007): Strukturgleichungsmodellierung mit LISREL, AMOS und SmartPLS - Eine Einführung (WWDP 86/2007). Technische Universität Dresden, 2007.

Jalkanen, J. (2005): User-initiated context switching using NFC. Paper presented at the Proceedings of the IJCAI05 Workshop on Modeling and Retrieval of Context (MRC2005), Edinburgh, Scotland.

Jensen, C.; Potts, C.; Jensen, C. (2005): Privacy practices of Internet users: Self-reports versus observed behavior. In: International Journal of Human-Computer Studies, Vol. 63, 1-2, pp. 203-227.

Johnson, E.J.; Moe, W.W.; Fader, P.S.; Bellman, S.; Lohse, G.L. (2004): On the Depth and Dynamics of Online Search Behavior. In: Management Science, Vol. 50, 3, pp. 299-308.

Jones, J.W. (1989): Personality and epistemology: Cognitive social learning theory as a philosophy of science. In: Zygon, Vol. 24, 1.

Juels, A. (2006): RFID security and privacy: a research survey. In: IEEE Journal on Selected Areas in Communications, Vol. 24, 2, pp. 381- 394.

Kaas, K.P. (1994): Ansätze einer institutionenökonomischen Theorie des Konsumentenverhaltens, Forschungsgruppe Konsume und Verhalten, München 1994.

Kaasinen, E. (2005): User acceptance of mobile services – value, ease of use, trust and ease of adoption. Doctoral Thesis, Tampere University of Technology 2005.

Kahol, K.; Tripathi, P.; McDaniel, T.; Panchanathan, S. (2005): Modeling Context in Haptic Perception, Rendering and Visualization. In: LECTURE NOTES IN COMPUTER SCIENCE, Vol. 3665, pp. 102.

Karahanna, E.; Straub, D.W.; Chervany, N.L. (1999): Information Technology Adoption Across Time: A Cross-Sectional Comparison of Pre-Adoption and Post-Adoption Beliefs. In: MIS Quarterly, Vol. 23, 2, pp. 183-213.

Karaiskos, D.; Kourouthanassis, P.; Giaglis, G. (2007): User Acceptance of Pervasive Information Systems: Evaluating an RFID Ticketing System. . Paper presented at the Fifteenth European Conference on Information Systems, St. Gallen, p. 1910-1921.

Keil, M.; Beranek, P.M.; Konsynski, B.R. (1995): Usefulness and ease of use: field study evidence regarding task considerations. In: Decision Support Systems, Vol. 13, 1, pp. 75-91.

Keller, C. (2006): Technology acceptance in academic organisations: implementation of virtual learning environments. Paper presented at the Fourteenth European Conference on Information Systems (ECIS), Goteborg, p. 1128-1135.

Keller, C.; Hrastinski, S.; Carlsson, S. (2007): Students` Acceptance of E-Learning Environments: A Comparative Study in Sweden and Lithuania. Paper presented at the Fifteenth European Conference on Information Systems (ECIS), St. Gallen, p. 395-406.

Kindberg, T.; Fox, A. (2002): System Software for Ubiquitous Computing. In: Pervasive Computing, Vol. 2, pp. 70-81.

King, W.R.; He, J. (2006): A meta-analysis of the technology acceptance model. In: Information & Management, Vol. 43, 6, pp. 740-755.

Kitzinger, J. (1994): The methodology of focus groups: the importance of interactions between research participants. In: Sociology of Health and Illness, 16, pp. 103-121.

Kitzinger, J. (1995): Qualitative Research: Introducing focus groups http://bmj.bmjjournals.com/cgi/content/full/311/7000/299, accessed 14-08, 2006.

Knebel, U.; Leimeister, J.M.; Krcmar, H. (2006): Strategic Importance of RFID – The CIO Perspective; An Empirical Analysis in Germany. Paper presented at the Americas Conference on Information Systems, Acapulco, Mexico.

Kommandur, B. (2004): Exploration of disruptive technologies for low cost RFID manufacturing, Massachusetts Institute of Technology 2004.

Kotonya, G.; Sommerville, I. (1998): Requirements engineering, Wiley 1998.

Kourouthanassis, P.; Roussos, G. (2003): Developing consumer-friendly pervasive retail systems. In: Pervasive Computing, Vol. 2, 2, pp. 32-39.

Kranz, M.; Schmidt, A. (2005): Prototyping Smart Objects for Ubiquitous Computing. Paper presented at the International Workshop on Smart Object Systems in Conjunction with the Seventh International Conference on Ubiquitous Computing.

Krcmar, H. (2005): Informationsmanagement (4 Ed.), Springer, Berlin 2005.

Kuzel, A.J. (1992): Sampling in qualitative inquiry. In: Doing qualitative research, Vol. 3, pp. 31-44.

Landt, J. (2005): The history of RFID. In: Potentials, IEEE, Vol. 24, 4, pp. 8-11.

Langheinrich, M. (2002): A Privacy Awareness System for Ubiquitous Computing Environments. Paper presented at the Ubicomp 2002, p. 237–245.

Latane, B.; Nida, S.; Wilson, D. (1981): The Effects of Group Size on Helping Behavior. In: Altruism and Helping Behavior: Social, Personality, and Developmental Perspectives. Ed.: Rushton, P.J.; Sorrentino, R.M. Lawrence Erlbaum Associates, Hillsdale, NJ 1981, pp. 287–313.

Lee, C.-P. (2006): An Empirical Study of Organizational Ubiquitous Computing Technology Adoption: The Case of Radio Frequency Identification in the Healthcare Industry Dissertation Mississippi State University 2006.

Lee, J.; Lee, J.; Feick, L. (2001): The impact of switching costs on the customer satisfaction-loyalty link: mobile phone service in France. In: Journal of Services Marketing, Vol. 15, 1, pp. 35-48.

Leimeister, J.M.; Krcmar, H. (2005): Das Internet der Dinge. In: Menschen und Informationstechnik (m&it), Vol. 3, pp. 39-41.

Lender, F. (1991): Innovatives Technologie-Marketing: Grenzen der konventionellen Marktforschungskonzepte und Ansätze zur methodischen Neugestaltung, Vandenhoeck & Ruprecht Göttingen, Göttingen 1991.

Leonard-Barton, D.; Deschamps, I. (1988): Managerial Influence in the Implementation of New Technology. In: Management Science, Vol. 34, 10, pp. 1252-1265.

Levin, A.M.; Levin, I.P.; Heath, C.E. (2003): Product Category Dependent Consumer Preferences for Online and Offline Shopping Features and Their Influence on Multi-Channel Retail Alliances. In: Journal of Electronic Commerce Research, Vol. 4, 3, pp. 85-93.

Lindgren, R.; Henfridsson, O.; Schultze, U. (2004): Design Principles for Competence Management Systems: A Synthesis of an Action Research Study. In: MIS Quarterly, Vol. 28, 3, pp. 435-472.

Littlefield, L. (2004): Psychosocial aspects of mobile phone use among adolescents. The Australian Psychological Society, 2004.

Loebbecke, C.; Palmer, J.W. (2006): RFID in the Fashion Industry: Kaufhof Department Stores AG and Gerry Weber International AG, Fashion Manufacturer. In: MIS Quarterly Executive, Vol. 5, 2, pp. 15-25.

Louho, R.; Kallioja, M.; Oittinen, P. (2006): Factors Affecting the Use of Hybrid Media Applications. In: Graphic Arts in Finland, Vol. 35, 3.

Lubrin, E.; Lawrence, E.; Zmijewska, A.; Navarro, K.F.; Culjak, G. (2006): Exploring the Benefits of Using Motes to Monitor Health: An Acceptance Survey. Paper presented at the International Conference on Networking, International Conference on Systems and International Conference on Mobile Communications and Learning Technologies, p. 208-208.

Luk, J.; Pasquero, J.; Little, S.; MacLean, K.; Levesque, V.; Hayward, V. (2006): A role for haptics in mobile interaction: initial design using a handheld tactile display prototype. Paper presented at the SIGCHI conference on Human Factors in computing systems, Montréal, Québec, Canada, p. 171-180

Lumsden, J.; Brewster, S. (2003): A paradigm shift: alternative interaction techniques for use with mobile & wearable devices. Paper presented at the Proceedings of 13th Annual IBM Centers for Advanced Studies Conference CASCON, p. 97-110.

Maass, W.; Filler, A. (2006): Towards an Infrastructure for Semantically Annotated Physical Products. Paper presented at the Workshop: Vom M-Business zum W-Business? Geschäftstätigkeit im Wireless Internet und in Mobilfunknetzen (Informatik 2006), Dresden.

Maass, W.; Janzen, S. (2007): Dynamic Product Interfaces: A Key Element for Ambient Shopping Environments. Paper presented at the Proceedings of 20th Bled eConference eMergence: Merging and Emerging Technologies, Processes, and Institutions (Bled 2007), Bled, Slovania.

Maeda, J. (2006): The laws of simplicity, MIT Press 2006.

Mantyjarvi, J.; Paternò, F.; Salvador, Z.; Santoro, C. (2006): Scan and Tilt – Towards Natural Interaction for Mobile Museum Guides. Paper presented at the MobileHCI 2006, Espoo, Finland.

March, S.T.; Smith, G.F. (1995): Design and natural science research on information technology. In: Decision Support Systems, Vol. 15, 4, pp. 251-266.

Markus, M.L. (1983): Power, politics, and MIS implementation. In: Communications of the ACM, Vol. 26, 6, pp. 430-444.

Markus, M.L.; Majchrzak, A. (2002): A Design Theory For Systems That Support Emergent Knowledge Processes. In: MIS Quarterly, Vol. 26, 3, pp. 179-212.

Mathieson, K. (1991): Predicting User Intentions: Comparing the Technology Acceptance Model with the Theory of Planned Behavior. In: Information Systems Research, Vol. 2, 3, pp. 173-191.

Mathieson, K.; Peacock, E.; Chin, W.W. (2001): Extending the technology acceptance model: the influence of perceived user resources. In: ACM Special issue on adoption, diffusion, and infusion of IT, Vol. 32, 3, pp. 86-112

Mattern, F. (2002): The Vision and Technical Foundations of Ubiquitous Computing. accessed 15.05.2005,

Mattern, F. (2003a): Die technische Basis für das Internet der Dinge, ETH Zürich 2003a.

Mattern, F. (2003b): Total vernetzt - Szenarien einer informatisierten Welt, Springer, Berlin 2003b.

Mattern, F. (2003c): Vom Verschwinden des Computers – Die Vision des Ubiquitous Computing. In: Total Vernetzt. Ed.: Mattern, F. Springer-Verlag 2003c, pp. 1-41.

Mattern, F. (2004): Allgegenwärtige Informationstechnik – Soziale Folgen und Konsequenzen für die Menschenrechte.

Mattern, F. (2005a): Die technische Basis für das Internet der Dinge. In: Das Internet der Dinge – Ubiquitous Computing und RFID in der Praxis. Ed.: Fleisch, E.; Mattern, F. Springer, Berlin 2005a, pp. 39-66.

Mattern, F. (2005b): Ubiquitous Computing: Schlaue Alltagsgegenstände. Die Vision von der Informatisierung des Alltags. http://www.vs.inf.ethz.ch/publ/papers/mattern2004_sev.pdf, accessed 15.Januar, 2005.

McCall, J.A.; Richards, P.K.; Walters, G.F. (1977): Factors in Software Quality, NTIS 1977.

McCullough, M. (2004): Digital Ground - Architecture, Pervasive Computing, and Environmental Knowing, MIT Press, Cambridge, Massachussetts 2004.

McIlraith, S.A.; Zeng, T.C.H. (2001): Semantic Web services. In: Intelligent Systems, IEEE [see also IEEE Intelligent Systems and Their Applications], Vol. 16, 2, pp. 46-53.

Meffert, H. (2005): Marketing - Grundlagen marktorientierter Unternehmensführung. (9 Ed.), Gabler Verlag, Wiesbaden 2005.

Melone, N.P. (1990): A Theoretical Assessment of the User-Satisfaction Construct in Information Systems Research. In: Management Science, Vol. 36, 1, pp. 76-91.

Merriam-Webster (2006a): Definition of calm In.

Merriam-Webster (2006b): Definition of end user. http://www.m-w.com/dictionary/end%20user, accessed Nov 9 2006.

Merriam-Webster (2006c): Definition of pervasive In.

Merriam-Webster (2006d): Definition of ubiquitous http://www.m-w.com/dictionary/ubiquitous, accessed Nov. 9, 2006.

Michelis, D.; Nicolai, T.; Resatsch, F.; Schildhauer, T. (2005): The Disappearance of the Screen - Research on Audible Interfaces in the Ubiquitous Computing Environment. Paper presented at the ICMB 2005, Sydney.

Milgrom, P.; Roberts, J. (1990): Rationalizability, Learning, and Equilibrium in Games with Strategic Complementarities. In: Econometrica, Vol. 58, 6, pp. 1255-1277.

Mitchell, V.-W. (1992): Understanding Consumers' Behaviour: Can Perceived Risk Theory Help? In: Management Decision, Vol. 30, 3, pp. 26-31.

Mitchell, V.-W.; Boustani, P. (1994): A Preliminary Investigation into Pre- and Post-Purchase Risk Perception and Reduction. In: European Journal of Marketing, Vol. 28, 1, pp. 56-71.

MLR (2006): The Mobile Life Report 2006. The Carphone Warehouse, 2006

Moore, G.A. (2002): Crossing the Chasm, HarperCollins Publishers 2002.

Moore, G.C.; Benbasat, I. (1991): Development of an instrument to measure the perceived characteristics of adopting an information technology innovation. In: Information Systems Research, Vol. 2, 3, pp. 192-222.

Morgan, D.L. (1998): Planning focus groups, Sage 1998.

Morrison, P.D.; Roberts, J.H.; Midgley, D.F. (2000): Opinion Leadership Amongst Leading Edge Users. In: Australasian Marketing Journal, Vol. 8, 1, pp. 5-14.

Muller, M. (1993): PICTIVE: Democratizing the Dynamics of the Design Session. In: Participatory Design: Principles and Practices, pp. 211-237.

Muller, M.J. (2003): Participatory Design: The Third Space in HCI, Erlbaum, Mahway, NJ, USA 2003.

Muller, M.J.; Blomberg, J.L.; Carter, K.A.; Dykstra, E.A.; Madsen, K.H.; Greenbaum, J. (1991): Participatory design in Britain and North America: responses to the "Scandinavian Challenge". Paper presented at the SIGCHI conference on Human factors in computing systems: Reaching through technology, New Orleans, Louisiana, United States p. 389-392.

Murphy-Hoye, M.; Lee, H.L.; Rice, J.B.J. (2005): A Real-World Look at RFID. In: Supply Chain Management Review, pp. 18-26.

Myers, M.D. (1997): Qualitative Research in Information Systems. In: MIS Quarterly, Vol. 21, 2, pp. 241-242.

Nambisan, S. (2002): Designing virtual customer environments for new product development: Toward a theory. In: The Academy of Management review, Vol. 27, 3, pp. 392-413.

NFCForum (2006a): NFC Data Exchange Format (NDEF) - NDEF 1.0 (Technical Specification NFCForum-TS-NDEF_1.0). NFC Forum, 2006a.

NFCForum (2006b): NFC Record Type Definition (RTD) - RTD 1.0 (Technical Specification NFCForum-TS-RTD_1.0). NFC Forum, 2006b.

NFCForum (2006c): Smart Poster Record Type Definition - SPR 1.1 (Technical Specification NFCForum-SmartPoster_RTD_1.0). NFC Forum, 2006c.

NFCForum (2006d): Text Record Type Definition - RTD-Text 1.0 (Technical Specification NFCForum-TS-RTD_Text_1.0). NFC Forum, 2006d.

NFCForum (2006e): URI Record Type Definition - RTD-URI 1.0 (Technical Specification NFCForum-TS-RTD_URI_1.0). NFC Forum, 2006e.

NFCForum (2007a): Near Field Communication in the real world – part II: Using the right NFC tag type for the right NFC application. NFCForum, 2007a.

NFCForum (2007b): Near Field Communication in the real world – part III: Moving to System on Chip (SoC) integration. NFCForum, 2007b.

NFCForum (2007c): Near Field Communication in the real world: Turning the NFC promise into profitable, everyday applications, 2007c.

Nicolai, T.; Resatsch, F.; Michelis, D. (2005): The Web of Augmented Physical Objects. Paper presented at the International Conference on Mobile Business (ICMB 2005), Sydney, Australia, p. 340-346.

NIST (2001): Pervasive computing is a term for the strongly emerging trend. http://www.nist.gov/pc2001, accessed March 31st, 2006.

Norman, D.A. (1988): The design of everyday things. Basic Books 1988.

Norman, D.A. (1999a): Affordance, conventions, and design. In: interactions, Vol. 6, 3, pp. 38-41.

Norman, D.A. (1999b): The Invisible Computer, MIT Press, Cambridge, MA 1999b.

Novak, J. (2005): Ubiquitous Computing and Socially-Aware Consumer - Support Systems in the Augmented Supermarket. Paper presented at the Proceedings of the First International Workshop on Social Implications of Ubiquitous Computing (UbiSoc 2005), Portland, Oregon, USA.

Nunamaker, J.F.; Chen, M.; Purdin, T. (1991): Systems development in Information systems research. In: Journal of Management Information Systems, Vol. 7, 3, pp. 89-106.

Nunnally, J.C.; Bernstein, I.H. (1994): Psychometric Theory. (3rd Ed.), McGraw-Hill, New York 1994.

o.V. (2006): The Netsize Guide 2006 Edition - Small Screens Global Vision Netsize, 2006.

Olesen, K.; Myers, M.D. (1999): Trying to improve communication and collaboration with information technology - An action research project which failed. In: Information Technology & People, Vol. 12, 4, pp. 317-332.

Öquist, G. (2006): Multimodal Interaction with Mobile Devices: Outline of a Semiotic Framework for Theory and Practice. Paper presented at the Proceedings of Wireless Networks and Systems Setubal, Portugal, p. 276-283.

Orlikowski, W.J. (1993): CASE Tools as Organizational Change: Investigating Incremental and Radical Changes in Systems Development. In: MIS Quarterly, Vol. 17, 3, pp. 309-341.

Orlikowski, W.J.; Barley, S.R. (2001): Technology and institutions: What can research on information technology and research on organizations learn from each other. In: MIS Quarterly, Vol. 25, 2, pp. 145-165.

Orlikowski, W.J.; Baroudi, J.J. (1991): Studying Information Technology in Organizations: Research Approaches and Assumptions. In: Information Systems Research, 2, pp. 1-28.

Paolucci, M.; Kawamura, T.; Payne, T.R.; Sycara, K. (2002): Semantic Matching of Web Services Capabilities. In: Proceedings of the 1st International Semantic Web Conference (ISWC), Vol. 348.

Park, J.K.; Yang, S.J.; Lehto, X. (2007): Adoption of Mobile Technologies for Chinese Consumers In: Journal of Electronic Commerce Research, Vol. 8, 3, pp. 196-206.

Parkinson, J. (2004): RFID: U.S. consumer research findings. Paper presented at the Workshop on RFID, Washington, D.C., USA.

Pentland, A. (2000): Perceptual intelligence. In: Communications of the ACM, Vol. 43, 3, pp. 35-44.

Perrey, J. (1996): Erhebungsdesign-Effekte bei der Conjoint-Analyse. In: Marketing ZFP, Vol. 18, 2, pp. 105-116.

Pettigrew, A.M. (1985): Contextualist research and the study of organizational change processes. In: Research Methods in Information Systems, pp. 53-78.

Petzold, J.; Bagci, F.; Trumler, W.; Ungerer, T. (2005): Next Location Prediction Within a Smart Office Building. In: 1st International Workshop on Exploiting Context Histories in Smart Environments (ECHISE'05) at the 3rd International Conference on Pervasive Computing, Munich, Germany, May.

Pfaff, D.; Skiera, B. (2005): Ubiquitous Computing - Abgrenzung, Merkmale und Auswirkungen aus betriebswirtschaftlicher Sicht. In: Wirtschaftsinformatik: Der Mensch im Netz- Ubiquitous Computing. Ed.: Britzelmaier, B.; Geberl, S.; Weinmann, S. Teubner-Reihe Wirtschaftsinformatik, Leipzig 2005.

Pfeffers, K.; Tuunanen, T.; Gengler, C.E.; Rossi, M.; Hui, W.; Virtanen, V.; Bragge, J. (2006): The Design Science Research Process: A Model for Producing and Presenting Information Systems Research. Paper presented at the First International Conference on Design Science Research in Information Systems and Technology, Claremount, California, USA, p. 84-147.

Pinhanez, C. (2001): The Everywhere Displays Projector: A Device to Create Ubiquitous Graphical Interfaces. Paper presented at the 3rd international conference on Ubiquitous Computing, Atlanta, Georgia, USA, p. 315-331.

Pinto, H.; Jos, R. (2006): Activity-centered ubiquitous computing support to localized activities. Paper presented at the Conference on Mobile and Ubiquitous Systems : proceedings of the Conference on Mobile and Ubiquitous Systems (CMUS 2006), Guimarães, p. 119-128.

Pomberger, G.; Blaschek, G. (1993): Software Engineering, Hanser, München 1993.

Pomberger, G.; Blaschek, G. (1997): Object-Orientation and Prototyping in Software Engineering. In: ACM SIGSOFT Software Engineering Notes, Vol. 22, 2, pp. 102.

Porter, M.E. (1998): Competitive Strategy: Techniques for Analyzing Industries and Competitors. (1 Ed.), Free Press 1998.

Poupyrev, I.; Okabe, M.; Maruyama, S. (2004): Haptic feedback for pen computing: directions and strategies. Paper presented at the CHI '04 extended abstracts on Human factors in computing systems, Vienna, Austria, p. 1309-1312.

Powell, R.A.; Single, H.M. (1996): Focus groups. In: International Journal of Quality in Health Care, Vol. 8, 5, pp. 499-504.

Prensky, M. (2001a): Digital Natives, Digital Immigrants. In: On the Horizon, Vol. 9, 5.

Prensky, M. (2001b): Digital Natives, Digital Immigrants, Part II:Do They Really Think Differently? In: On the Horizon, Vol. 6, 9.

Preston, A.M. (1991): The 'problem' in and of management information systems. In: Accounting, Management and Information Technologies, Vol. 1, 1, pp. 43-69.

Prus, R.; Dawson, L. (1991): Shop'til You Drop: Shopping as Recreational and Laborious Activity. In: Canadian Journal of Sociology/Cahiers canadiens de sociologie, Vol. 16, 2, pp. 145-164.

Pu Li, J.; Kishore, R. (2006): How Robust is the UTAUT Instrument? A Multigroup Invariance Analysis in the Context of Acceptance and Use of Online Community Weblog Systems. Paper presented at the ACM SIGMIS CPR conference on computer personnel research: Forty four years of computer personnel research: achievements, challenges & the future, Claremont, California, USA, p. 183-189.

Punj, G.N.; Staelin, R. (**1983**): A Model of Consumer Information Search Behavior for New Automobiles. In: The Journal of Consumer Research, Vol. 9, 4, pp. 366-380.

Raskin, J. (**2000**): The Humane Interface, Addison-Wesley/ACM Press, Reading, MA 2000.

Reilly, D.; Dearman, D.; Welsman-Dinelle, M.; Inkpen, K. (**2005**): Evaluating Early Prototypes in Context: Trade-offs, Challenges, and Successes. In: IEEE Pervasive Computing, Vol. 4, 44, pp. 42-50.

Resatsch, F.; Aßmann, J.; Schildhauer, T.; Michelis, D. (**2007a**): Start a grassroots RFID initiative! The relevance of communication and showcases on the success of RFID. Paper presented at the Wirtschaftsinformatik (WI 2007), Karlsruhe, p. 37-54.

Resatsch, F.; Karpischek, S.; Hamacher, S.; Sandner, U. (**2007b**): Mobile Sales Assistant - NFC for Retailers. Paper presented at the MobileHCI 2007, Singapore

Resatsch, F.; Karpischek, S.; Michelis, D. (**2006**): Mobile Prosumer. Paper presented at the Workshop Near Field Interactions With the Internet of Things (NordiCHI 06), Oslo, Norway.

Resatsch, F.; Sandner, U.; Leimeister, J.M.; Krcmar, H. (**2008**): Do Point of Sale RFID-Based Information Services Make a Difference? Analyzing Consumer Perceptions for Designing Smart Product Information Services in Retail Business In: Electronic Markets, Vol. 18, 3, pp. 216-231

Resatsch, F.; Sandner, U.; Michelis, D.; Hoechst, C.; Schildhauer, T. (**2007c**): Everyday Simplicity – The Implications of Everyday Tasks for Ubiquitous Computing Applications. Paper presented at the Americas Conference on Information Systems (AMCIS 2007), Denver, CO, USA.

Rezabakhsh, B.; Bornemann, D.; Hansen, U.; Schrader, U. (**2006**): Consumer Power: A Comparison of the Old Economy and the Internet Economy. In: Journal of Consumer Policy, Vol. 29, 1, pp. 3-36.

Rice, R.E.; Borgman, C.L. (**1983**): The Use of Computer-Monitored Data in Information Science and Communication Research. In: Journal of the American Society for Information Science, Vol. 34, 4, pp. 247-56.

Riekki, J.; Salminen, T.; Alakärppä, I. (**2006**): Requesting Pervasive Services by Touching RFID Tags. In: Pervasive Computing, Vol. 5, 1, pp. 40-46.

Ringle, C.M. (**2004**): Gütemaße für den Partial Least Squares-Ansatz zur Bestimmung von Kausalmodellen. Arbeitspapier Nr. 16, 2004.

Ringle, C.M.; Wende, S.; A., W. (**2005**): SmartPLS - Ver. 2.0].

Robertson, S.; Robertson, J. (**1999**): Mastering the requirements process, ACM Press/Addison-Wesley Publishing Co. New York, NY, USA 1999.

Roethlisberger, F.J.; Dickson, W.J. (**1939**): Management and the Worker. Cambridge, MA: Harvard University Press.

Rogers, E.M. (**1995**): The diffusion of innovations. (5 Ed.), Free Press, New York 1995.

Rogers, Y. (**2006**): Moving on from Weiser's Vision of Calm Computing: Engaging UbiComp Experiences. Paper presented at the Ubicomp 2006, Orange County, California, p. 404-421.

Rotter, J. (**1966**): Generalized expectancies for internal versus external control of reinforcements. In: Psychological Monographs, Vol. 80, 609.

Roussos, G. (**2005**): Consumers and Ubiquitous Commerce. Paper presented at the Ubiconf 2004, London, p. 2.

Roussos, G. (**2006**): Enabling RFID in Retail. In: Computer, Vol. 39, 3, pp. 25-30.

Roussos, G.; Moussouri, T. (**2004**): Consumer perceptions of privacy, security and trust in ubiquitous commerce. In: Personal and Ubiquitous Computing, Vol. 8, pp. 416-429.

Roussos, G.; Tuominen, J.; Koukara, L.; Seppala, O.; Kourouthanasis, P.; Giaglis, G.; Frissaer, J. (**2002**): A case study in pervasive retail. Paper presented at the Proceedings of the 2nd international workshop on Mobile commerce, Atlanta, Georgia, USA, p. 90-94.

Rukzio, E. (**2007**): Physical Mobile Interactions: Mobile Devices as Pervasive Mediators for Interactions with the Real World. Dissertation, Ludwig-Maximilians-Universität München 2007.

Rukzio, E.; Leichtenstern, K.; Callaghan, V.; Holleis, P.; Schmidt, A.; Chin, J. (**2006a**): An Experimental Comparison of Physical Mobile Interaction Techniques: Touching, Pointing and

234   Bibliography

Scanning. Paper presented at the Eighth International Conference on Ubiquitous Computing (Ubicomp 2006), California, USA.

Rukzio, E.; Paolucci, M.; Wagner, M.; Berndt, H.; Hamard, J.; Schmidt, A. (2006b): Mobile Service Interaction with the Web of Things. Paper presented at the 13th International Conference on Telecommunications (ICT 2006), Funchal, Madeira Island, Portugal.

Rukzio, E.; Schmidt, A.; Hussmann, H. (2004): Physical Posters as Gateways to Context-aware Services for Mobile Devices. Paper presented at the WMCSA, Cumbria, UK.

Ryan, R.M.; Deci, E.L. (2000): Intrinsic and Extrinsic Motivations: Classic Definitions and New Directions. In: Contemporary Educational Psychology, Vol. 25, pp. 54-67.

Sacco, J.F. (1994): Implementing microcomputers in local government: a case study of a loosely structured approach. Paper presented at the Computer personnel research conference on Reinventing IS: managing information technology in changing organizations, Alexandria, Virginia, United States, p. 261-271.

Sandner, U.; Leimeister, J.M.; Krcmar, H. (2006): Business Potentials of Ubiquitous Computing. In: Managing Development and Application of Digital Technologies. Ed.: Kern, E.-M.; Hegering, H.-G.; Brügge, B. Springer, Berlin 2006.

Saponas, T.S.; Prabaker, M.K.; Abowd, G.D.; Landay, J.A. (2006): The home: The impact of pre-patterns on the design of digital home applications. Paper presented at the DIS 2006.

Satyanarayanan, M. (2002): A Catalyst for Mobile and Ubiquitous Computing. In: IEEE Pervasive Computing, Vol. 1, 1, pp. 2-5.

Scheer, A.W.; Feld, T.; Göbl, M.; Hoffmann, M. (2002): Das mobile Unternehmen. In: Mobile Commerce. Ed.: Silberer, G.; Wohlfahrt, J.; Wilhelm, T. Gabler 2002, pp. 91-110.

Schmookler, J. (1966): Innovation and Economic Growth, Cambridge, Mass 1966.

Scholderer, J.; Balderjahn, I. (2006): Was unterscheidet harte und weiche Strukturmodelle nun wirklich. In: Marketing ZFP, Vol. 28, pp. 57-70.

Scholtz, J.; Arnstein, L.; Kim, M.; Kindberg, T.; Consolvo, S. (2002): User-centered evaluations of ubicomp applications (Technical Report IRS-TR-02-014. May). Intel Research 2002.

Schomaker, L. (1995): A Taxonomy of Multimodal Interaction in the Human Information Processing System. Esprit/BRA, NICI, 1995.

Schrage, M. (1996): Cultures of Prototyping. In: Bringing Design to Software, pp. 191–205.

Scott-Morton, M.S. (1991): The Corporation of the 1990s: Information Technology and Organizational Transformation, Oxford University Press, New York 1991.

Shapiro, C.; Varian, H.R. (1999): Information Rules, Harvard Business School Press, Boston, Massachusetts 1999.

Sheffi, Y. (2004): RFID and the Innovation Cycle. In: International Journal of Logistics Management, Vol. 15, 1.

Shim, J.P.; Warkentin, M.; Courtney, J.F.; Power, D.J.; Sharda, R.; Carlsson, C. (2002): Past, present, and future of decision support technology. In: Decision Support Systems, Vol. 33, 2, pp. 111-126.

Shneiderman, B. (1992): Designing the user interface: strategies for effective human-computer interaction, Addison-Wesley Longman Publishing Co., Inc. , Boston, MA, USA 1992.

Simon, H.A. (1980): The Newest Science of the Artificial. In: Cognitive Science, 4, pp. 33-46.

Simon, H.A. (1996): The Sciences of the Artificial. (3 Ed.), MIT Press, Cambridge, MA 1996.

Singleton, R.A.j.; Straits, B.C. (2005): Approaches to Social Research. (4 Ed.), Oxford University Press, New York 2005.

Smith, B.C.; Gerth, R.J. (2006): Key Factors that Enable Product Development: An Investigation of Creating "Cool" Products, 2006.

Smith, H.; Konsynski, B. (2003): Developments in Practice X: Radio Frequency Identification (RFID)-An Internet for Physical Objects. In: Communications of the AIS, Vol. 12, pp. 301-311.

Smith, M.; Davenport, D.; Hwa, H. (2003): AURA: A mobile platform for object and location annotation. Paper presented at the Fifth International Conference on Ubiquitous Computing (UbiComp 2003), Seattle, Washington.

Sousa, J.P.; Garlan, D. (2002): Aura: an Architectural Framework for User Mobility in Ubiquitous Computing Environments. Paper presented at the 3rd IEEE/IFIP Conference on Software Architecture, Montreal, Canada.

Spiekermann, S. (2005): Perceived Control: Scales for Privacy in Ubiquitous Computing, Humboldt Universität zu Berlin 2005.

Stier, H.; Lewin-Epstein, N. (2003): A Comparative Analysis of Preferences for Working Hours. In: Work and Occupations, Vol. 30, 3, pp. 302-326.

Stockman, H. (1948): Communication by Means of Reflected Power. Paper presented at the IRE, p. 1196-1204.

Straub, D.; Keil, M.; Brenner, W. (1997): Testing the technology acceptance model across cultures: A three country study. In: Information & Management, Vol. 33, 1, pp. 1-11.

Straub, D.; Limayem, M.; Karahanna-Evaristo, E. (1995): Measuring System Usage: Implications for IS Theory Testing. In: Management Science, Vol. 41, 8, pp. 1328-1342.

Straub, D.W. (1994): The Effect of Culture on IT Diffusion: E-Mail and FAX in Japan and the US. In: Information Systems Research, Vol. 5, 1, pp. 23-47.

Strüker, J.; Sackmann, S.; Müller, G. (2004): Case Study on Retail Customer Communication Applying Ubiquitous Computing. Paper presented at the Proceedings of the IEEE International Conference on E-Commerce Technology, Washington, DC, USA, p. 42-48.

Subramanian, V.; Chang, P.C.; Huang, D.C.; Lee, J.B.; Molesa, S.E.; Murphy, A.R.; Redinger, D.R.; Volkman, S.K. (2006): Progress Toward Development of All-Printed RFID Tags: Materials, Processes, and Devices. Paper presented at the 9th International Conference on VLSI Design (VLSID'06).

Sultan, F.; Farley, J.U.; Lehmann, D.R. (1990): A Meta-Analysis of Applications of Diffusion Models. In: Journal of Marketing Research, Vol. 27, 1, pp. 70-77.

Szajna, B. (1996): Empirical Evaluation of the Revised Technology Acceptance Model. In: Management Science, Vol. 42, 1, pp. 85-92.

Takeda, H. (1990): Modeling Design Processes. In: AI Magazine, pp. 37-48.

Tan, H.Z. (2000): Perceptual user interfaces: haptic interfaces. In: Communications of the ACM, Vol. 43, 3, pp. 40-41.

Tauber, E.M. (1972): Why Do People Shop? In: Journal of Marketing, Vol. 36, 4, pp. 46-49.

Taylor, S.; Todd, P.A. (1995): Understanding Information Technology Usage: A Test of Competing Models. In: Information Systems Research, Vol. 6, 23, pp. 144-176.

Thackara, J. (2000): The Design Challenge of Pervasive Interface - Keynote speech at CHI2000. The Hague

Thevenin, D.; Coutaz, J. (1999): Plasticity of User Interfaces: Framework and Research Agenda. Paper presented at the Interact, p. 110-117.

Thiesse, F. (2007): RFID-enabled shelf replenishment with case-level tagging: a simulation study. Paper presented at the AMCIS 2007, Keystone, Colorado.

Thompson, R.L.; Higgins, C.A.; Howell, J.M. (1991): Personal Computing: Toward a Conceptual Model of Utilization. In: MIS Quarterly, Vol. 15, 1, pp. 125-143.

Toye, E.; Sharp, R.; Madhavapeddy, A.; Scott, D. (2005): Using Smart Phones to Access Site-Specific Services. In: IEEE Pervasive Computing, Vol. 4, 2, pp. 60-66.

Truong, K.N.; Hayes, G.R.; Abowd, G.D. (2006): Storyboarding: an empirical determination of best practices and effective guidelines. Paper presented at the DIS 2006, University Park, Pennsylvania, USA.

Ullmer, B.; Ishii, H. (2000): Emerging frameworks for tangible user interfaces. In: IBM Systems Journal, Vol. 39, 3, pp. 915-931.

Urban, G.L.; von Hippel, E. (1988): Lead user analyses for the development of new industrial products. In: Management Science, Vol. 34, 5, pp. 569-582.

UsabilityFirst.com (2006): Affordance http://www.usabilityfirst.com/glossary/main.cgi? function=display_term&term_id=66, accessed Nov 23, 2006.

Utterback, J.M. (1971): The Process of Innovation: A Study of the Origination and Development of Ideas for New Scientific Instruments. In: IEEE Transactions on Engineering Management, Vol. EM-18, 4, pp. 124-131.

Vaishnavi, V.; Kuechler, B. (2004): Design Research in Information Systems. http://www.isworld.org/Researchdesign/drisISworld.htm, accessed Nov 21, 2006.

Välkkynen, P.; Korhonen, I.; Plomp, J.; Tuomisto, T.; Cluitmans, L.; Ailisto, H.; Seppä, H. (2003): A user interaction paradigm for physical browsing and near-object control based on tags. Paper presented at the Proceedings of the Physical Interaction Workshop on Real World User Interfaces (Mobile HCI '03), Udine, Italy, p. 31-34.

Välkkynen, P.; Niemelä, M.; Tuomisto, T. **(2006):** Evaluating touching and pointing with a mobile terminal for physical browsing. Paper presented at the Proceedings of the 4th Nordic conference on Human-computer interaction: changing roles, Oslo, Norway, p. 28-37

Vallerand, R.J. **(1997):** Toward a hierarchical model of intrinsic and extrinsic motivation. In: Advances in experimental social psychology, Vol. 29, pp. 271–360.

van der Heijden, H. **(2004):** User acceptance of hedonic information systems. In: MIS Quarterly, Vol. 28, 4, pp. 695-704.

Venable, J. **(2006):** The Role of Theory and Theorizing in Design Science Research. Paper presented at the Design Science Research in Information Systems and Technology, Claremount, California, US.

Venkatesh, V. **(2000):** Determinants of Perceived Ease of Use: Integrating Control, Intrinsic Motivation, and Emotion into the Technology Acceptance Model. In: Information Systems Research, Vol. 11, 4, pp. 342-365.

Venkatesh, V. **(2006):** Where To Go From Here? Thoughts on Future Directions for Research on Individual-Level Technology Adoption with a Focus on Decision Making. In: Decision Sciences, Vol. 37, 4, pp. 497-518.

Venkatesh, V.; Davis, F.D. **(1996):** A Model of the Antecedents of Perceived Ease of Use: Development and Test. In: Decision Sciences, Vol. 27, 3, pp. 451-481.

Venkatesh, V.; Davis, F.D. **(2000):** A Theoretical Extension of the Technology Acceptance Model: Four Longitudinal Field Studies. In: Management Science, Vol. 46, 2, pp. 186-204.

Venkatesh, V.; Davis, F.D.; Morris, M.G. **(2007):** Dead or Alive the Development, Trajectory and Future of Technology Adoption Research. In: În: Journal of the AIS, Vol. 8, 4, pp. 267-286.

Venkatesh, V.; Morris, M.G. **(2000):** Why Don't Men Ever Stop to Ask for Directions? Gender, Social Influence, and Their Role in Technology Acceptance and Usage Behavior. In: MIS Quarterly, Vol. 24, 1, pp. 115-139.

Venkatesh, V.; Morris, M.G.; Davis, G.B.; Davis, F.D. **(2003):** User acceptance of information technology: Toward a unified view. In: MIS Quarterly, Vol. 27, 3, pp. 425-478.

Venkatesh, V.; Speier, C. **(1999):** Computer Technology Training in the Workplace: A Longitudinal Investigation of the Effect of Mood. In: Organizational Behavior and Human Decision Processes, Vol. 79, 1, pp. 1-28.

Vilmos, A. **(2008):** Issuing and managing financial applications in NFC capable mobile handsets. Paper presented at the WIMA, Monaco, Monaco.

Voeth, M. **(1998):** Limit Conjoint Analysis - a modification of the traditional Conjoint Analysis. Paper presented at the 27th EMAC Conference "Marketing Research and Practice", Stockholm p. 315-331.

von Hippel, E. **(1986):** Lead Users: A Source of Novel Product Concepts. In: Management Science, Vol. 32, 7, pp. 791-805.

von Hippel, E. **(1988):** The sources of innovation, New York: Oxford University Press 1988.

von Hippel, E. **(2001):** User Toolkits for Innovation. In: Journal of Product Innovation Management, Vol. 18, 4, pp. 247-257.

von Hippel, E. **(2005):** Democratizing innovation, MIT Press 2005.

Walls, J.G.; Widmeyer, G.R.; El Sawy, O.A. **(1992):** Building an Information System Design Theory for Vigilant EIS. In: Information Systems Research, Vol. 3, 1, pp. 36-59.

Wang, H.I.; Yang, H.L. **(2005):** The Role of Personality Traits in UTAUT Model under Online Stocking. In: Contemporary Management Research, Vol. 1, 1, pp. 69-82.

Want, R. **(2006):** An Introduction to RFID Technology In: Pervasive Computing, Vol. 6, pp. 25-33.

Want, R.; Hopper, A.; Falcão, V.; Gibbons, J. **(1992):** The active badge location system. In: ACM Transactions on Information Systems (TOIS), Vol. 10, 1, pp. 91-102.

Want, R.; Pering, T.; Danneels, G.; Kumar, M. **(2002):** The Personal Server: Changing the Way We Think About Ubiquitous Computing. Paper presented at the UBICOMP 2002, p. 1-9.

Want, R.; Schilt, B.; Adams, N.; Gold, R.; Petersen, K.; Ellis, J.; Goldberg, D.; Weiser, M. **(1995):** The PARCtab ubiquitous computing experiment (Tech. Rep. CSL-95-1). XEROX Parc, 1995.

Ward, A.; Jones, A.; Hopper, A. (1997): A new location technique for the active office. In: Personal Communications, Vol. 4, 5, pp. 42-47.

Ward, M.; Kranenburg, R.v.; Backhouse, G. (2006): RFID: Frequency, standards, adoption and innovation. JISC Technology and Standards Watch, 2006.

Wechsler, H.; Davenport, A.; Dowdall, G.; Moeykens, B.; Castillo, S. (1994): Health and behavioral consequences of binge drinking in college. A national survey of students at 140 campuses. In: JAMA, Vol. 272, 21, pp. 1672-1677.

Weick, K.E. (1995): What Theory is Not, Theorizing Is. In: Administrative Science Quarterly, Vol. 40, 3, pp. 385-390.

Weiser, M. (1991): The Computer for the 21st Century. In: Scientific American, Vol. 265, 3, pp. 94-104.

Weiser, M. (1993): Some Computer Science Issues in Ubiquitous Computing. In: Communication of the ACM, Vol. 36, 7, pp. 74-84.

Weiser, M.; Gold, R.; Brown, J.S. (1999): The origins of ubiquitous computing research at PARC in the late 1980s. In: IBM SYSTEMS JOURNAL, Vol. 38, 4, pp. 693-696.

Westfall, R. (1999): An IS research relevancy manifesto. In: Communications of the AIS, Vol. 2, 14.

Wikström, S. (1996): Value Creation by Company-Consumer Interaction. In: Journal of Marketing Management, Vol. 12, 5, pp. 359-374.

Wilde, T.; Hess, T.; Hilbers, K.; Str, N. (2008): Akzeptanzforschung bei nicht marktreifen Technologien: typische methodische Probleme und deren Auswirkungen. Paper presented at the Multikonferenz Wirtschaftsinformatik (MKWI), p. 1031-1043.

Wilding, R.; Delgado, T. (2004): RFID Demystified: Company Case Studies. In: Logistics & Transport Focus, Vol. 6, 5, pp. 31-42.

Wittink, D.R.; Vriens, M.; Burhenne, W. (1994): Commercial Use of Conjoint Analysis in Europe: Results and Critical Reflections. In: International Journal of Research in Marketing, Vol. 11, 1, pp. 41-52.

Wray, R.; Chong, R.; Phillips, J.; Rogers, S.; Walsh, B. (2006): A Survey of Cognitive and Agent Architectures. http://ai.eecs.umich.edu/cogarch0/common/prop/closedloop.html, accessed July 9, 2006.

y Monsuwé, T.P.; Dellaert, B.G.C.; de Ruyter, K. (2004): What drives consumers to shop online? A literature review. In: International Journal of Service Industry Management, Vol. 15, 1, pp. 102-121.

Yayla, A.; Hu, Q. (2007): User Acceptance of E-Commerce Technology: A Meta-Analytic Comparison of Competing Models. Paper presented at the Fifteenth European Conference on Information Systems (ECIS 2007), St. Gallen, p. 179-190.

Yin, R.K. (1984): Case study research: Design and methods, Sage, Newbury Park, California 1984.

Yin, R.K. (2002): Applications of Case Study Research, Sage Publications 2002.

Zambonelli, F.; Parunak, H.V.D. (2002a): From design to intention: signs of a revolution. Paper presented at the Proceedings of the first international joint conference on Autonomous agents and multiagent systems: part 1, Bologna, Italy, p. 455-456.

Zambonelli, F.; Parunak, H.V.D. (2002b): Signs of a Revolution in Computer Science and Software Engineering. Paper presented at the Engineering Societies in the Agents World III, Madrid, Spain, p. 13-28.

Zhao, Q.-J.; Tu, D.-W.; Gao, D.-M.; Wang, R.-S. (2004): Human-Computer Interaction Models and their Application in an Eye-Gaze Input System. Paper presented at the Proceedings of the Third International Conference on Machine Learning and Cybernetics, Shanghai, China, p. 2274-2278.

Zmud, R.W. (1998): Conducting and Publishing Practice-Driven Research. Paper presented at the IFIP WG8.2 and WG8.6 joint working conference on Information Systems: Current Issues and Future Changes, Helsinki, Finland.

Appendix

Questionnaire „easymeeting"

QUESTIONNAIRE „EASYMEETING"

German Version / Version 2.0 (/FR)	Nr: ( )
Interviewer:	
Datum:	
RFID/NFC-Block – 1	

1) Was verstehen Sie unter der Abkürzung R.F.I.D.?

2) Was verstehen Sie unter der Abkürzung N.F.C?

3) Hatten Sie schon mal mit einem RFID System in irgendeiner Art und Weise zu tun?

□ Ja, einmal
□ Ja, mehrmals
□ Nein
□ Nein, sagt mir überhaupt nichts
□ Ich bin mir nicht sicher.

4) Hatten Sie schon mal mit einem Near Field Communication (NFC) System in irgendeiner Art und Weise zu tun?

□ Ja, einmal
□ Ja, mehrmals
□ Nein
□ Nein, sagt mir überhaupt nichts
□ Ich bin mir nicht sicher.

5) Wie schätzen Sie Ihre Kenntnis über NFC/RFID ein?	*Regie: Da NFC und RFID sehr ähnlich sind, fassen wir im folgenden beide zusammen.* *Interviewer: Skala vorlesen: Bitte bewerten Sie auf einer Skala von 1 „ich weiß überhaupt nichts über NFC/RFID" bis 5 „ich bin sehr vertraut mit RFID".*

Ich weiß überhaupt nichts über NFC/RFID   Ich bin sehr vertraut mit RFID

6) Bitte bewerten Sie folgende Statements:	*Interviewer: Skala vorlesen: Bitte bewerten Sie auf einer Skala von 1 „Stimme überhaupt nicht zu" bis 5 „Stimme voll und ganz zu".*

6a) „NFC/RFID ist eine Gefahr für die Privatsphäre und den Datenschutz"

Stimme überhaupt nicht zu   Stimme voll und ganz zu

6b) „Der Einsatz von NFC/RFID verbessert Ihre persönliche Lebenssituation bereits heute?"

Stimme überhaupt nicht zu   Stimme voll und ganz zu

6c) „NFC/RFID macht mir Angst?"

Stimme überhaupt nicht zu   Stimme voll und ganz zu

Meeting-Block

Meeting Organisator = Person die das Meeting organisiert, also für Raum, Kaffee, Technik, etc. sorgt.
Meeting Teilnehmer ist der reine Teilnehmer, der sich nicht um die Organisation kümmert.

7) Wie häufig nützen Sie Konferenzräume in der Rolle als Meeting-Organisator?

- ☐ Nie
- ☐ Täglich
- ☐ Mehrmals wöchentlich
- ☐ Mehrmals im Monat
- ☐ 1-mal im halben Jahr

8) Wie häufig nützen Sie Konferenzräume in der Rolle als Meeting-Teilnehmer?

- ☐ Nie
- ☐ Täglich
- ☐ Mehrmals wöchentlich
- ☐ Mehrmals im Monat
- ☐ 1-mal im halben Jahr

11) Bitte bewerten Sie folgende Statements für Konferenzraummanagementsysteme:	*Interviewer: Skala vorlesen: Bitte bewerten Sie auf einer Skala von 1 „Stimme überhaupt nicht zu" bis 5 „Stimme voll und ganz zu".*

11a) „Ein elektronisches System ist wichtig für die Buchung von Meetings"

Stimme überhaupt nicht zu   Stimme voll und ganz zu

11b) „Die bisherige Lösung der DVZ ist ausreichend"

Stimme überhaupt nicht zu   Stimme voll und ganz zu

11c) „Ich bin zufrieden mit der bisherigen Lösung"

Stimme überhaupt nicht zu   Stimme voll und ganz zu

11d) „Ich würde gerne genau wissen, wer, wann im Konferenzraum ist (Real-time)"

Stimme überhaupt nicht zu   Stimme voll und ganz zu

11e) „Mir fehlt meistens die Technik zur Durchführung des Meetings"

Stimme überhaupt nicht zu   Stimme voll und ganz zu

11f) „Ich habe Probleme beim Umgang mit/Bei der Bedienung der Technik"

Stimme überhaupt nicht zu   Stimme voll und ganz zu

LIVE_TEST Block (Talking out loud methode)

Interviewer: Das easyMeeting Konzept und Beschreibung Handy: easymeeting ist ein NFC System auf Basis von RFID. Es ermöglicht die direkte Steuerung eines elektronischen Buchungssystems mittels eines Handys und verschiedener RFID-Tags. Das wichtigste ist, das ein einfaches Berühren langt um die Anwendung zu nutzen!! Neben dem Handy nutzen wir auch einen Liveticker, der uns genau zeigt, wann der Konferenzraum besetzt ist und wann nicht.

12) Task: Bitte ordern Sie Kaffee für Ihr Meeting!

13) Rückfragen die im Gespräch kamen:

14) Meinung zum Prototyp

15) Sagen Sie mir Attribute, die Sie für die Interaktion des Berührens im Kopf hatten?

Meinung zur Nutzung

Vorab: easymeeting ist EIN RFID / NFC System (Begrifflichkeit klären)

16) Bitte bewerten Sie folgende Statements: *Interviewer: Skala vorlesen: Bitte bewerten Sie auf einer Skala von 1 „Stimme überhaupt nicht zu" bis 5 „Stimme voll und ganz zu".*

Wahrgenommener Nutzen

PE1: Ich finde easymeeting nützlich für meine Arbeit

Stimme überhaupt nicht zu   Stimme voll und ganz zu

PE2: easymeeting erleichtert mir die Arbeit

Stimme überhaupt nicht zu   Stimme voll und ganz zu

PE3: easymeeting erhöht meine Performance bei der Organisation von Meetings

Stimme überhaupt nicht zu   Stimme voll und ganz zu

PE4: easymeeting würde den Ablauf eines Meetings nicht stören

Stimme überhaupt nicht zu   Stimme voll und ganz zu

Wahrgenommene Bedienungsfreundlichkeit

EOU1: Die Interaktion mit dem RFID/NFC System ist klar und verständlich

Stimme überhaupt nicht zu   Stimme voll und ganz zu

EOU2: Die Interaktion des Berührens macht die Bedienung sehr einfach

Stimme überhaupt nicht zu   Stimme voll und ganz zu

EOU3: Das System easymeeting ist einfach zu bedienen

Stimme überhaupt nicht zu   Stimme voll und ganz zu

Einstellung gegenüber der Technologie

ATUT1: Ich arbeite gerne mit dem easymeeting System wie eben gezeigt

Stimme überhaupt nicht zu   Stimme voll und ganz zu

ATUT2-1: Es macht Spaß easymeeting zu bedienen

Stimme überhaupt nicht zu   Stimme voll und ganz zu

ATUT2-2: Es macht Spaß NFC/RFID Systeme mit dem Handy zu bedienen

Stimme überhaupt nicht zu   Stimme voll und ganz zu

ATUT3: Easymeeting macht Arbeiten interessanter

Stimme überhaupt nicht zu   Stimme voll und ganz zu

ATUT4-1: Ich hätte gerne mehr RFID/NFC Anwendungen bei der DVZ

Stimme überhaupt nicht zu   Stimme voll und ganz zu

ATUT4-2: Ich hätte gerne mehr RFID/NFC Anwendungen allgemein

Stimme überhaupt nicht zu   Stimme voll und ganz zu

Sozialer Einfluss
SI2: Die DVZ *(als Organisation)* gesamt denkt positiv über RFID/NFC

Stimme überhaupt nicht zu   Stimme voll und ganz zu

Vereinfachende Bedingungen
FC2: Ich fühle mich mit meinem Wissen über RFID/NFC in der Lage easymeeting zu nutzen

Stimme überhaupt nicht zu   Stimme voll und ganz zu

Angst/Befürchtung
ANX1: Ich mache mir Sorgen wegen easymeeting

Stimme überhaupt nicht zu   Stimme voll und ganz zu

ANX2: Ich befürchte andere können genau nachvollziehen, was ich wann mit easymeeting gemacht habe, ich fühle mich kontrolliert!

Stimme überhaupt nicht zu   Stimme voll und ganz zu

ANX3: Die Möglichkeiten der Technologie wie bei Easymeeting eingesetzt, wirkt einschüchternd

Stimme überhaupt nicht zu   Stimme voll und ganz zu

ANX4: Ich zögere ein RFID/NFC System wie easymeeting zu nutzen, weil ich Angst um meine Privatsphäre habe

Stimme überhaupt nicht zu   Stimme voll und ganz zu

ANX5: Ich zögere ein RFID/NFC System wie easymeeting zu nutzen, weil ich Angst um den Datenschutz habe

Stimme überhaupt nicht zu   Stimme voll und ganz zu

ANX6: Mehr Angst als das RFID/NFC macht mit der Liveticker im easymeeting

Stimme überhaupt nicht zu   Stimme voll und ganz zu

Intention zur Handlung
BI1: Ich würde easymeeting in den nächsten Monaten nützen

Stimme überhaupt nicht zu   Stimme voll und ganz zu

BI2: Ich plane ein RFID/NFC System in den nächsten Monaten zu nützen

Stimme überhaupt nicht zu   Stimme voll und ganz zu

17) Bitte bewerten Sie folgende Statements:

17a) „Wenn es NFC Handys auf dem Markt gäbe, würde ich mir sofort eins kaufen!"
Stimme überhaupt nicht zu   Stimme voll und ganz zu

17b) „Wenn es NFC Handys auf dem Markt gäbe, würde ich diese sicher nutzen!"
Stimme überhaupt nicht zu   Stimme voll und ganz zu

17c) „Die Verbindung RFID und Mobiltelefon (=NFC) erscheint mir nützlich"
Stimme überhaupt nicht zu   Stimme voll und ganz zu

17d) „Ich könnte mir vorstellen, weitere NFC Applikationen wie den Mobile Prosumer zu nützen"
Stimme überhaupt nicht zu   Stimme voll und ganz zu

17e) „RFID erschließt sich mir in der Form von NFC"
Stimme überhaupt nicht zu   Stimme voll und ganz zu

18) Bitte bewerte folgende Statements (Wiederholung zu vor dem Test):
18a) „NFC/RFID ist eine Gefahr für die Privatsphäre und den Datenschutz"
Stimme überhaupt nicht zu   Stimme voll und ganz zu

18b) „Der Einsatz von NFC/RFID verbessert Ihre persönliche Lebenssituation bereits heute?"
Stimme überhaupt nicht zu   Stimme voll und ganz zu

18c) „NFC/RFID macht mir Angst?"
Stimme überhaupt nicht zu   Stimme voll und ganz zu

Sozio-demographie

S1 Rolle innerhalb der DVZ
□ Praktikant
□ Studentischer Mitarbeiter
□ Freier Mitarbeiter
□ Fester Mitarbeiter
□ Leiter von „X" (Sachgebietsleiter, etc.)
□ Direktor, Vorstand, Geschäftsführung

S2 Geschlecht
□ Männlich
□ Weiblich

S3 Alter
□ < 18
□ 18-25
□ 26-30
□ 31-45
□ > 46

Mobile Prosumer Focus Group – Consumers

MOBILE PROSUMER FOCUS GROUP – CONSUMERS

1. Einführung	approx. 5 min
2. Warming up: Vorstellungsrunde der Teilnehmer	approx. 5 min

- Kurze Vorstellung der Teilnehmer
- Vorname, Familienstand, Beruf, Hobbies
- Ausblick auf das Thema: **Shopping**: persönliche Erfahrungen, Verbesserungsvorschläge etc. Total 10 Minuten

3. U & A Shopping Verhalten - Spontan	approx. 15 min

- Bitte erzählen Sie über Ihre Erfahrungen beim täglichen Einkaufen
  - Likes: Was gefällt Ihnen gut? Warum?
  - Dislikes: Was gefällt Ihnen nicht? Warum nicht?
  - Was fehlt Ihnen?

- Bitte erzählen Sie über Ihre Erfahrungen bei besonderen, nicht alltäglichen Einkäufen
  - Likes: Was gefällt Ihnen gut? Warum?
  - Dislikes: Was gefällt Ihnen nicht? Warum nicht?
  - Was fehlt Ihnen?

- Wer von Ihnen kauft auch online ein?
  - Wenn nicht, warum nicht?
  - Haben Sie irgendwelche Vorbehalte gegen online-shopping?
  - Welche Produkte kaufen Sie online?
  - Warum kaufen Sie diese Produkte online?
  - Was sind die Vorteile beim Kauf im Internet?
  - Was sind die Nachteile beim Kauf im Internet?

4. Shopping	approx. 20 min

[Bitte im Folgenden Fragen für die einzelnen Produktgruppen stellen]
Das Thema „Mangel an Produktinformationen" nicht erwähnen – heraushören, bei welchen Produkten ein Informationsdefizit empfunden wird.

1. Lebensmittel

- Wie kaufen Sie normalerweise Lebensmittel ein?
  - Nehmen Sie sich dafür Zeit, sind Sie in Eile?
- Wie empfinden Sie die Produktauswahl?
- Wo kaufen Sie normalerweise Wein?
- Stellen Sie sich vor Sie sind in einem großen Supermarkt und wollen eine Flasche Wein kaufen, wie machen Sie das?
  - Wie entscheiden Sie, welche Flasche Sie nehmen?
  - Woher wissen Sie, welcher der richtige Wein für Sie ist?
  - Wissen Sie schon, welchen Wein Sie kaufen?
  - Entscheiden Sie nach dem Preis, nach dem Etikett, nach Erfahrung (immer der gleiche Wein)?
[Heraushören: spielt Qualität eine Rolle? Woran wird die Qualität festgemacht?]
  - Fragen Sie Freunde, Verwandte, Bekannte nach einer Empfehlung?
  - Fragen Sie einen Mitarbeiter des Supermarktes/ einen Verkäufer?
    - Warum? Warum nicht?
    - Welche Erfahrungen haben Sie gemacht, wenn Sie einen Verkäufer gefragt haben?
- Welchen Eindruck haben Sie von der Qualität der Produkte, speziell Weine? Gibt es Unterschiede hinsichtlich der Qualität im Sortiment?
- Wie zufrieden sind Sie mit dem Weinkauf im Supermarkt?
- Was sollte Ihrer Meinung nach verbessert werden?
- Informieren Sie sich über Wein, bevor Sie Wein kaufen?
  - Wenn ja, wo, bei wem?
  - Wenn nein, warum nicht?

2. Consumer Electronics

• Wo kaufen Sie normalerweise kleinere Elektrogeräte?
• Stellen Sie sich vor Sie wollen einen MP3 Player kaufen, wie machen Sie das?
   • Wie gehen Sie da vor?
   • Ist das ein geplanter Einkauf oder ein Spontankauf?
   • Informieren Sie sich vor dem Besuch des Geschäftes (und suchen ganz gezielt ein Produkt) oder sehen Sie sich verschiedene Produkte im Geschäft an?
• Wie empfinden Sie die Produktauswahl?
• Stellen Sie sich vor Sie sind in einem Elektromarkt und wollen einen MP3 Player kaufen, wie machen Sie das?
   • Wie entscheiden Sie, welcher MP3 Player der richtige für Sie ist?
   • Woher wissen Sie, welcher der richtige MP3 Player für Sie ist?
   • Entscheiden Sie nach dem Preis, nach der Marke, nach Erfahrung mit einer Marke, nach Empfehlung von Tests oder Freunden und Bekannten?
[Heraushören: spielt Qualität eine Rolle? Woran wird die Qualität festgemacht?]
   • Fragen Sie einen Mitarbeiter des Elektromarktes/ einen Verkäufer?
      • Warum? Warum nicht?
      • Welche Erfahrungen haben Sie gemacht, wenn Sie einen Verkäufer gefragt haben?
• Welchen Eindruck haben Sie von der Qualität der MP3 Player? Gibt es Unterschiede hinsichtlich der Qualität im Sortiment?
• Wie zufrieden sind Sie mit dem Kauf eines MP3 Players im Elektromarkt?
• Was sollte Ihrer Meinung nach verbessert werden?
• Welches Gefühl haben Sie wenn Sie sich für den Kauf eines Produktes (MP3 Players) entscheiden haben?
   • Sind Sie sicher, das richtige Gerät gekauft zu haben?
   • Fühlen Sie sich unsicher, vielleicht ein Gerät gekauft zu haben, dass nicht Ihren Erwartungen entspricht?
[Wenn unsicher:]
   • Hängt das Gefühl der Unsicherheit mit dem Preis des Gerätes zusammen (z.B. je teurer, desto unsicherer?)
   • Was müsste verbessert werde, damit Sie das Gefühl haben, die richtige Entscheidung getroffen zu haben?

3. Medien

• Wie kaufen Sie normalerweise Bücher, CDs ein?
   • Wo kaufen Sie Bücher? Wo kaufen Sie CDs?
   • Nehmen Sie sich dafür Zeit, sind Sie in Eile?
• Stellen Sie sich vor Sie sind in einer großen Buchabteilung /Buchhandlung oder einer großen CD Abteilung und wollen ein Buch und eine CD kaufen, wie machen Sie das?
   • Wie entscheiden Sie, welches Buch / welche CD Sie nehmen?
   • Entscheiden Sie nach dem Preis, nach bekanntem Autor/ Interpret Etikett, nach Empfehlung (wenn ja von wem)?
[Heraushören: wie wird entschieden ob die CD, das Buch gefällt?]
   • Fragen Sie einen Mitarbeiter der Buchhandlung/ Buchabteilung/ CD Abteilung/ einen Verkäufer?
      • Warum? Warum nicht?
      • Welche Erfahrungen haben Sie gemacht, wenn Sie einen Verkäufer gefragt haben?
• Welchen Eindruck haben Sie von dem Buch, der CD?
• Sind Sie sicher, dass diese Ihnen gefallen werden?
• Wie zufrieden sind Sie mit dem Kauf von Büchern / CDs?
• Was sollte Ihrer Meinung nach verbessert werden?
• Informieren Sie sich über Bücher oder CDs bevor Sie diese kaufen?
   • Wenn ja, wo, bei wem?
   • Wenn nein, warum nicht?

4. Weiße Ware

• Wo kaufen Sie normalerweise weiße Ware [Mikrowelle, Toaster]?
• Stellen Sie sich vor Sie wollen eine Mikrowelle oder einen Toaster kaufen, wie machen Sie das?
   • Wie gehen Sie da vor?
   • Ist das ein geplanter Einkauf oder ein Spontankauf?
   • Informieren Sie sich vor dem Besuch des Geschäftes (und suchen ganz gezielt ein Produkt) oder sehen Sie sich verschiedene Produkte im Geschäft an?

- Fragen Sie Freunde, Verwandte, Bekannte nach einer Empfehlung?
- Gehen Sie anders vor, wenn Sie einen Kühlschrank oder eine Waschmaschine kaufen?
  - Was machen Sie da anders? Warum?
- Wie empfinden Sie die Produktauswahl bei Mikrowellen und Toastern?
- Stellen Sie sich vor Sie sind in einem Elektromarkt und wollen eine Mikrowelle oder einen Toaster kaufen, wie machen Sie das?
  - Wie entscheiden Sie, welches das richtige Gerät für Sie ist?
  - Woher wissen Sie, welches das richtige Gerät für Sie ist?
  - Entscheiden Sie nach dem Preis, nach der Marke, nach Erfahrung mit einer Marke, nach Empfehlung von Tests oder Freunden und Bekannten?
  [Heraushören: spielt Qualität eine Rolle? Woran wird die Qualität festgemacht?]
  - Fragen Sie einen Mitarbeiter des Elektromarktes/ einen Verkäufer?
    - Warum? Warum nicht?
    - Welche Erfahrungen haben Sie gemacht, wenn Sie einen Verkäufer gefragt haben?
- Welchen Eindruck haben Sie von der Qualität der Geräte? Gibt es Unterschiede hinsichtlich der Qualität im Sortiment?
- Wie zufrieden sind Sie mit dem Kauf eines Toasters/ einer Mikrowelle im Elektromarkt?
- Was sollte Ihrer Meinung nach verbessert werden?
- Welches Gefühl haben Sie wenn Sie sich für den Kauf eines Produktes (Mikrowelle/ Toaster) entscheiden haben?
  - Sind Sie sicher, das richtige Gerät gekauft zu haben?
  - Fühlen Sie sich unsicher, vielleicht ein Gerät gekauft zu haben, dass nicht Ihren Erwartungen entspricht?
  [Wenn unsicher:]
  - Hängt das Gefühl der Unsicherheit mit dem Preis des Gerätes zusammen (z.B. je teurer, desto unsicherer?)
  - Ist das Gefühl ein anderes, wenn Sie sich einen Kühlschrank oder eine Waschmaschine gekauft haben?
  - Was müsste verbessert werde, damit Sie das Gefühl haben, die richtige Entscheidung getroffen zu haben?

5. Konzept „Mobile Prosumer"   approx. 20 min
- Was würden Sie davon halten, wenn Sie im Geschäft mehr Informationen zu einzelnen Produkten bekommen könnten?
  - In welchen Situationen würden Sie das nutzen?
  - Bei welchen Produkten würden Sie das nutzen?
- Welche Informationen würden Sie gerne erhalten:
  - Lebensmittel: Wein – Welche Informationen fehlen Ihnen? Welche würden Sie gerne erhalten?
  - Consumer Electronics: MP3 Player – Welche Informationen fehlen Ihnen? Welche würden Sie gerne erhalten?
  - Weiße Ware: Mikrowelle, Toaster – Welche Informationen fehlen Ihnen? Welche würden Sie gerne erhalten?
  - Medien: Bücher, CDs – Welche Informationen fehlen Ihnen? Welche würden Sie gerne erhalten?
  [Bitte heraushören und ggf. nachfragen: informieren sich die Konsumenten permanent (über welche Themen/ Produkte) oder informieren sie sich punktuell, wenn notwendig?]
  → *Konzept des Mobile Prosumer auf einer PPT Folie an jeden Teilnehmer austeilen*
- Welchen Eindruck haben Sie von diesem Konzept?
- Was gefällt Ihnen gut? Was ist an diesem Service attraktiv?
- Was gefällt Ihnen weniger gut?
- Was ist unklar?
- Wer von Ihnen kann sich vorstellen diesen Service zu nutzen?
  - Warum würden Sie diesen Service nutzen?
    - Welchen Nutzen haben Sie davon?
    - Wie häufig würden Sie diesen Service nutzen?
  - Warum würden Sie diesen Service nicht nutzen?
  - Für welche Produkte erscheint Ihnen dieser Service geeignet?
  - Was halten Sie von diesem Service für folgende Produkte: **[bitte einzeln abfragen]** Wein/ Consumer Electronics/ Weiße Ware/ Medien?
  - Für welche Produkte ist dieser Service Ihrer Meinung nach noch / besser geeignet?

- Warum für diese Produkte?
- Welchen Nutzen haben Sie von diesem Service bei diesen Produkten?

6. Mobile Prosumer Testprodukt	approx. 50 min

[Bitte allen Teilnehmern die Gelegenheit geben das Testprodukt auszuprobieren – ca. 5 Minuten pro Teilnehmer]

- Was halten Sie von dem Service?
- Was gefällt Ihnen gut?
- Was gefällt Ihnen nicht gut?
- Welchen Eindruck haben Sie von der Bedienung des Gerätes?
  - Was gefällt Ihnen an der Bedienung gut?
  - Was gefällt Ihnen an der Bedienung weniger gut?

[Bitte im folgenden nicht nur über die Informationen zu Wein sprechen sondern auch auf die andern Produktgruppen übertragen]

- Welchen Eindruck haben Sie von den Informationen?
  - Sind die Informationen für Sie hilfreich?
  - Welche weiteren Informationen würden Sie sich wünschen?
  - Welche Informationen sind für Sie weniger interessant?
- Wären Sie bereit für diesen Service zu bezahlen?
- Was könnte Sie überzeugen diesen Service zu nutzen?
- Wo sollten die Tags angebracht sein? An jedem Produkt? An der (Um-)Verpackung? Am Regal?

7. Abschließende Diskussion und Bewertung	approx. 5 min

- Was ist Ihr Eindruck von diesem Angebot?
- Likes: was gefällt Ihnen an diesem Angebot?
- Dislikes: Was gefällt Ihnen an diesem Angebot nicht?
- Was ist unklar, unverständlich?
- Was fehlt diesem Angebot?
- Vorteile für den Kunden? Was überzeugt, was nicht?
- Wie relevant ist dieses Angebot für Sie?

8. Thank everyone and say goodbye	approx. 1 min

Mobile Prosumer Focus Groups – Sales Assistants

MOBILE PROSUMER FOCUS GROUP – SALES ASSISTANTS

1. Einführung	approx. 5 min
2. Warming up: Vorstellungsrunde der Teilnehmer	approx. 5 min

- Kurze Vorstellung der Teilnehmer
- Vorname, in welchem Geschäft sind Sie tätig, was sind Ihre Hauptaufgaben, welche Produkte verkaufen Sie hauptsächlich
- Ausblick auf das Thema: **Shopping**: persönliche Erfahrungen, Verbesserungsvorschläge etc. Total 10 Minuten

3. U & A Shopping Verhalten - Spontan	approx. 15 min

- Bitte erzählen Sie mir aus Ihrer professionellen Sicht und aus Ihren Erfahrungen mit Ihren Kunden:
  - Ganz generell: werden Ihnen von den Kunden Fragen zu den Produkten gestellt?
  - Welche Fragen stellen die Kunden? Was wollen die Kunden über Produkte wissen?
  - Hat sich das Verhalten und Informationsbedürfnis der Kunden in den letzten Jahren verändert? Wenn ja, wie?
- Können Sie den Kunden alle Informationen geben, die sie von Ihnen haben möchten?
- Welche Informationen würden Sie gerne Ihren Kunden geben können?
- Gibt es auch Informationen, die Sie den Kunden nicht weitergeben?
  - Wenn ja, welche Informationen sind das?
  - Warum wollen Sie diese Informationen nicht weitergeben?
- Müssen Sie die Kunden auch gelegentlich alleine lassen um anderswo Informationen zu besorgen? [Z.B.

nachsehen in welcher Größe ein Paar Schuhe noch auf Lager ist]
- Wie reagieren Ihre Kunden darauf?
- Würden Sie lieber beim Kunden bleiben und Informationen in Gegenwart des Kunden einholen?
- Haben Sie den Eindruck es ist für die Kunden frustrierend, alleine zurückbleiben zu müssen?

4. Shopping	approx. 20 min

[Bitte im Folgenden Fragen für die einzelnen Produktgruppen stellen]
Das Thema „Mangel an Produktinformationen" nicht erwähnen – heraushören, bei welchen Produkten ein Informationsdefizit empfunden wird.

1. Lebensmittel

- Wie kaufen Ihre Kunden normalerweise Lebensmittel ein?
  - Nehmen sie sich dafür Zeit, sind sie in Eile?
- Wie reagieren die Kunden auf die Produktauswahl?
- **Im Detail:** stellen die Kunden Fragen zu Lebensmitteln – besonders zu Wein?
  - Was fragen die Kunden beim Wein?
  - Was wollen die Kunden sonst noch wissen?
- Können Sie die Fragen der Kunden beantworten?
  - Welche Fragen können Sie beantworten?
  - Welche Fragen können Sie nicht beantworten?
  - Wie reagieren die Kunden darauf?
- Nach Ihrer Erfahrung, wonach entscheiden die Kunden, welchen Wein sie kaufen?
[Heraushören: spielt Qualität eine Rolle? Woran wird die Qualität festgemacht?]
- Wie zufrieden sind die Kunden mit dem Weinkauf im Supermarkt?
- Was sollte Ihrer Meinung nach verbessert werden?

2. Consumer Electronics

- Wie kaufen die Kunden normalerweise kleinere Elektrogeräte?
- Stellen Sie sich einen typischen Kunden vor, der einen MP3 Player kaufen möchte, wie macht er das?
  - Ist das ein geplanter Einkauf oder ein Spontankauf?
  - Sind die Kunden informiert (und suchen ganz gezielt ein Produkt) oder sehen sich die Kunden verschiedene Produkte im Geschäft an?
- Wie reagieren die Kunden auf die Produktauswahl?
- **Im Detail:** stellen die Kunden Fragen zu Consumer Electronics – beispielsweise zu MP3 Playern?
  - Was fragen die Kunden bei MP3 Playern?
  - Was wollen die Kunden sonst noch wissen?
- Können Sie die Fragen der Kunden beantworten?
  - Welche Fragen können Sie beantworten?
  - Welche Fragen können Sie nicht beantworten?
  - Wie reagieren die Kunden darauf?
- Nach Ihrer Erfahrung, wonach entscheiden die Kunden, welchen MP3 Player sie kaufen?
  - Entscheiden Kunden nach dem Preis, nach der Marke, nach Erfahrung mit einer Marke, nach Empfehlung von Tests oder Freunden und Bekannten?
[Heraushören: spielt Qualität eine Rolle? Woran wird die Qualität festgemacht?]
- Wie zufrieden sind die Kunden mit dem Kauf eines MP3 Players im Elektromarkt?
- Was sollte Ihrer Meinung nach verbessert werden?

3. Medien

- Wie kaufen die Kunden normalerweise Bücher, CDs ein?
  - Nehmen Sie sich dafür Zeit, sind Sie in Eile?
- Stellen Sie sich einen typischen Kunden in einer großen Buchabteilung /Buchhandlung oder einer großen CD Abteilung vor, wie kauft er ein Buch oder eine CD?
  - Ist das ein geplanter Einkauf oder ein Spontankauf?
  - Sind die Kunden informiert (und suchen ganz gezielt ein Produkt) oder sehen sich die Kunden verschiedene Produkte im Geschäft an?
- Wie reagieren die Kunden auf die Produktauswahl?
- **Im Detail:** stellen die Kunden Fragen zu Büchern oder CDs?
  - Was fragen die Kunden bei Büchern/ CDs?
  - Was wollen die Kunden sonst noch wissen?
- Können Sie die Fragen der Kunden beantworten?
  - Welche Fragen können Sie beantworten?
  - Welche Fragen können Sie nicht beantworten?

- Wie reagieren die Kunden darauf?
- Nach Ihrer Erfahrung, wonach entscheiden die Kunden, welches Buch / welche CD sie kaufen?
- Entscheiden Kunden nach dem Preis, nach bekanntem Autor/ Interpreten, nach Empfehlung von Zeitschriften oder Freunden und Bekannten?
- *[Heraushören: wie wird entschieden welches Buch / welche CD gefällt?]*
- Wie zufrieden sind die Kunden mit dem Kauf eines Buchs oder einer CD?
- Was sollte Ihrer Meinung nach verbessert werden?

4. Weiße Ware

- Wie kaufen die Kunden normalerweise weiße Ware (Toaster/ Mikrowelle)?
- Stellen Sie sich einen typischen Kunden vor, der einen Toaster / Mikrowelle kaufen möchte, wie macht er das?
  - Ist das ein geplanter Einkauf oder ein Spontankauf?
  - Sind die Kunden informiert (und suchen ganz gezielt ein Produkt) oder sehen sich die Kunden verschiedene Produkte im Geschäft an?
- Wie reagieren die Kunden auf die Produktauswahl?
- **Im Detail:** stellen die Kunden Fragen zu weißer Ware – beispielsweise zu Toaster / Mikrowelle?
- Was fragen die Kunden bei Toaster/ Mikrowelle?
- Was wollen die Kunden sonst noch wissen?
  - Stellen Kunden bei teureren Geräten (Kühlschrank oder Waschmaschine andere Fragen?
- Können Sie die Fragen der Kunden beantworten?
  - Welche Fragen können Sie beantworten?
  - Welche Fragen können Sie nicht beantworten?
  - Wie reagieren die Kunden darauf?
- Nach Ihrer Erfahrung, wonach entscheiden die Kunden, welchen Toaster /Mikrowelle sie kaufen?
- Entscheiden Kunden nach dem Preis, nach der Marke, nach Erfahrung mit einer Marke, nach Empfehlung von Tests oder Freunden und Bekannten?
- Wie ist as bei teureren Geräten?
- *[Heraushören: spielt Qualität eine Rolle? Woran wird die Qualität festgemacht?]*
- Wie zufrieden sind die Kunden mit dem Kauf eines Toasters /Mikrowelle im Elektromarkt?
- Was sollte Ihrer Meinung nach verbessert werden?

5. Konzept „Mobile Prosumer" und MSA   approx. 30 min

MOBILE SALES ASSISTANT:

- Was würden Sie davon halten, wenn Sie mehr Informationen zu einzelnen Produkten bekommen könnten um Kunden besser beraten zu können?
  - In welchen Situationen würden Sie das nutzen?
  - Bei welchen Produkten würden Sie das nutzen?
- *[➔ Konzept des Mobile Sales Assistant auf einer PPT Folie an jeden Teilnehmer austeilen]*
- Welchen Eindruck haben Sie von diesem Konzept?
- Was gefällt Ihnen gut? Was ist an diesem Service attraktiv?
- Was gefällt Ihnen weniger gut?
- Was ist unklar?
- Wer von Ihnen kann sich vorstellen diesen Service zu nutzen?
  - Warum würden Sie diesen Service nutzen?
  - Welchen Nutzen haben Sie davon?
- Für welche Produkte erscheint Ihnen dieser Service geeignet?
- Für welche Informationen erscheint Ihnen dieser Service geeignet?
- Was halten Sie von diesem Service für folgende Produkte: *[bitte einzeln abfragen]* Wein/ Consumer Electronics/ Weiße Ware/ Medien?
- Für welche Produkte ist dieser Service Ihrer Meinung nach noch / besser geeignet?
  - Warum für diese Produkte?
  - Welchen Nutzen haben Sie von diesem Service bei diesen Produkten?

MOBILE PROSUMER:

- Was würden Sie davon halten, wenn die Kunden im Geschäft mehr Informationen zu einzelnen Produkten bekommen könnten?
- Welche Informationen wären für Kunden relevant?
- Lebensmittel: Wein – Welche Informationen würden Kunden helfen?
- Consumer Electronics: MP3 Player – Welche Informationen würden Kunden helfen?
- Weiße Ware: Mikrowelle, Toaster – Welche Informationen würden Kunden helfen?

- Medien: Bücher, CDs – Welche Informationen würden Kunden helfen?
- *[➔ Konzept des Mobile Prosumers auf einer PPT Folie an jeden Teilnehmer austeilen]*
- Welchen Eindruck haben Sie von diesem Konzept?
- Was gefällt Ihnen gut? Was ist an diesem Service attraktiv?
- Was gefällt Ihnen weniger gut?
- Was ist unklar?
- Denken Sie die Kunden würden diesen Service nutzen?
  - Warum würden Kunden diesen Service nutzen?
    - Welchen Nutzen haben Kunden davon?
  - Für welche Produkte erscheint Ihnen dieser Service für Kunden geeignet?
  - Was halten Sie von diesem Service für folgende Produkte: *[bitte einzeln abfragen]* Wein/ Consumer Electronics/ Weiße Ware/ Medien?
  - Für welche Produkte ist dieser Service Ihrer Meinung nach noch / besser geeignet?
    - Warum für diese Produkte?
    - Welchen Nutzen haben Sie von diesem Service bei diesen Produkten?

6. Mobile Prosumer Testprodukt	approx. 40 min

[Bitte allen Teilnehmern die Gelegenheit geben das Testprodukt auszuprobieren]
- Was halten Sie von dem Service?
- Was gefällt Ihnen gut?
- Was gefällt Ihnen nicht gut?
- Welchen Eindruck haben Sie von der Bedienung des Gerätes?
  - Was gefällt Ihnen an der Bedienung gut?
  - Was gefällt Ihnen an der Bedienung weniger gut?
- Welchen Eindruck haben Sie von den Informationen?
  - Sind die Informationen für Ihre Kunden hilfreich?
  - Welche weiteren Informationen würden Sie sich wünschen?
  - Welche Informationen sind für Sie weniger interessant?
- Was könnte Sie überzeugen den MSA Service zu nutzen?

7. Abschließende Diskussion und Bewertung	approx. 5 min

- Was ist Ihr Eindruck von diesem Angebot?
- Likes: was gefällt Ihnen an diesem Angebot?
- Dislikes: Was gefällt Ihnen an diesem Angebot nicht?
- Was ist unklar, unverständlich?
- Was fehlt diesem Angebot?
- Welche Vorteile haben Sie von dem MSA?
- Welche Vorteile haben die Kunden? Was überzeugt, was nicht?
- Wie relevant ist dieses Angebot für Sie?

[Falls noch nicht angesprochen:]
- Sehen sie ein solches Konzept als Hilfe an?
- Wie bewerten Sie das Mobile Prosumer Tool?
- Wie bewerten Sie das MSA Tool?
- Haben Sie den Eindruck ein solches Konzept gefährdet Ihren Arbeitsplatz?
- Ist Ihnen die Nutzung dieser Technik aus Ihrem Unternehmen bekannt?
  - Wenn Ja, welche Erfahrungen haben Sie damit gemacht?

8. Thank everyone and say goodbye	approx. 1 min

Public Transport Company (PTC) – PLS Tests Additional Tables and Data Quality

The following table lists the items used in estimating UTAUT.

Performance expectancy	
PE1	I would find the system useful in my daily life
PE2	I would find the combination of NFC tags plus NFC mobile phone ticketing useful in my daily life
PE3	Using the NFC mobile phone ticketing enables me to buy my tickets easier
PE4	Using the NFC mobile phone ticketing enables me to buy my tickets faster
PE5	The system makes public transport more efficient
PE6	I save time using the system
PE7	I save time using the NFC Mobile Phone
Effort expectancy	
EE1	Registering for the system did not bother me
EE2	I would find the system easy to use
EE3	You need to touch the NFC tags with your NFC-enabled mobile phone. This touch-based interaction is clear and easy to understand.
EE4	I would find touch-based interaction easy to use
EE5	Learning to operate the system is easy to me
Attitude towards using technology	
ATUT1	I like using the system
ATUT2	Using the system is fun
ATUT3	Using NFC-Technology with a mobile phone is fun
ATUT4	The system improves traveling with public transport
ATUT5	I would like to have more NFC-application such as the PTC Mobile Phone Ticket System
ATUT6	I prefer buying NFC tickets than paper tickets
Social influence	
SI1	People who are important to me think positive about mobile phone ticketing
SI2	People who are important to me think positive about NFC technology
Facilitating conditions	
FC1	I have the necessary knowledge about NFC to use the PTC Mobile Phone Ticket System
FC2	There are enough resources (NFC tags) in the city
FC3	There are enough resources at the stations
FC4	I would change my mobile phone brand in order to own a NFC-enabled mobile phone
Self efficacy	
SE1	I would like to have a direct contact person at the PTC
SE2	I would appreciate it, if I could call someone for help if I got stuck with buying a ticket.
Anxiety	
ANX1	I am worried about using the system
ANX2	It scares me that the PTC knows exactly the location I have been to
ANX3	I hesitate to use the system for fear of making mistakes I cannot correct
ANX4	The system is somewhat intimidating to me
ANX5	I hesitate to use a system such as the NFC PTC Mobile Phone Ticket System, because of privacy concerns
ANX6	I hesitate to use a system such as the NFC PTC Mobile Phone Ticket System, because of data security concerns
ANX7	I fear other aspects of NFC technology besides ticketing

ANX8	I think there are no health risks of NFC usage
Behavioral intention	
BI1	I intend to use the system in the next six months
BI2	I predict I would use the system in the next 12 months
BI3	I plan to use the system in the next 12 months

Questionnaire 1 - Changes of constructs because of reliability tests in factor analysis

Construct	Items deleted	Cronbach Alpha* for factor after deletion
Performance Expectancy (PE)	None	0.884
Effort Expectancy (EE)	None from factor analysis – Cronbach showed a higher reliability without EE_1	0.833
Social Influence (SI)	None	0.906
Facilitating Conditions (FC)	**None**	**0.672**
Attitude towards using technology (ATUT)	None from factor analysis – Cronbach showed a higher reliability without ATUT_6	0.839
Self-Efficacy (SE)	None	0.751
Anxiety (ANX)	ANX_8 (Original set loaded to two factors -Extraction sums of squared loadings after deletion of ANX_8: 49,035%)	0.813
Behavioral Intention (BI)	None	0.964

* = List-wise deletion based on all variables in summary
In Q1, PE, SI, FC, SE and BI no items were excluded. However, FC had an alpha value below the lower limit of 0,7 and was deleted as a factor (See also (Park et al. 2007)). EE_1 and ATUT_6 were deleted because of a higher Cronbach alpha after deletion. ANX loaded to two factors, after deletion of ANX_8 one factor with squared loadings of 49,035% was reached.

The next sections report results of c^2-difference test and Fornell-Larcker criterion (Fornell et al. 1981; Jöreskog et al. 1982) to assess discriminant validity.

Fornell/Larcker Criteria and latent variable correlations – questionnaire 1

	AVE	ANX	ATUT	BI	EE	PE	SE	SI	Use Behavior
ANX	0.5062	**0.7115**	0.0000	0.0000	0.0000	0.0000	0.0000	0.0000	0.0000
ATUT	0.613	-0.2990	**0.7829**	0.0000	0.0000	0.0000	0.0000	0.0000	0.0000
BI	0.9342	-0.3967	0.5288	**0.9665**	0.0000	0.0000	0.0000	0.0000	0.0000
EE	0.6676	-0.4260	0.5892	0.3090	**0.8171**	0.0000	0.0000	0.0000	0.0000
PE	0.6017	-0.3404	0.7452	0.5608	0.4711	**0.7757**	0.0000	0.0000	0.0000
SE	0.237	0.1770	-0.1128	-0.1748	-0.0864	-0.1416	**0.4868**	0.0000	0.0000
SI	0.9141	-0.2566	0.4433	0.2680	0.2638	0.3049	0.0076	**0.9561**	0.0000
Use Behavior	1	0.0490	0.1572	0.0928	0.0383	0.0802	-0.0655	0.1952	**1.0000**

This is the matrix of correlations between constructs (latent variables), with the squared root of AVE in the diagonal. If this value is greater than the construct correlations, the constructs have discriminant validity, which is the case here.

Questionnaire 2 - Changes of constructs because of reliability tests in factor analysis

Construct	Items deleted	Cronbach Alpha* for factor after deletion
Performance Expectancy (PE)	PE_1 (Original set loaded to two factors -Extraction sums of squared loadings after deletion of PE_1: 64,038 %)	0.883
Effort Expectancy (EE)	None from factor analysis – Cronbach showed a higher reliability without EE_1	0.815
Social Influence (SI)	None	0.930
Facilitating Conditions (FC)	**None**	**0.687**
Attitude towards using technology (ATUT)	None from factor analysis – Cronbach showed a higher reliability without ATUT_6	0.833
Self-Efficacy (SE)	None	0.792
Anxiety (ANX)	ANX_8 ANX_3 (Original set loaded to two factors -Extraction sums of squared loadings after deletion of ANX_8 and ANX_3: 61,125 %)	0.859
Behavioral Intention (BI)	None	0.928

* = List-wise deletion based on all variables in summary
A similar picture to Q1 could be seen in Q2. No items were deleted in factors SI, FC, SE, BI. FC was not included because of a Cronbach Alpha below 0,7. In PE, item PE_1 was deleted because of factor loadings. EE_1 and ATUT_6 were not included in analysis to improve Cronbach Alpha. For ANX, two items were excluded: ANX_8 and ANX_3.

Fornell/Larcker Criteria and latent variable correlations – questionnaire 2

	AVE	ANX	ATUT	BI	EE	PE	SE	SI	Use Behavior
ANX	0.6057	**0.7783**	0.0000	0.0000	0.0000	0.0000	0.0000	0.0000	0.0000
ATUT	0.587	-0.2922	**0.7662**	0.0000	0.0000	0.0000	0.0000	0.0000	0.0000
BI	0.8768	-0.2096	0.2729	**0.9364**	0.0000	0.0000	0.0000	0.0000	0.0000
EE	0.6319	-0.3126	0.3998	0.2331	**0.7949**	0.0000	0.0000	0.0000	0.0000
PE	0.6359	-0.3019	0.6575	0.3800	0.4155	**0.7974**	0.0000	0.0000	0.0000
SE	0.5238	0.0427	-0.0251	-0.0747	-0.1665	0.0304	**0.7237**	0.0000	0.0000
SI	0.9347	-0.2797	0.4835	0.0851	0.1242	0.2837	0.1095	**0.9668**	0.0000
Use Behavior	1	-0.0416	0.1399	-0.0574	-0.0361	0.1363	-0.0395	0.2459	**1.0000**

Questionnaire 3 - Changes of constructs because of reliability tests in factor analysis

Construct	Items deleted	Cronbach Alpha* for factor after deletion
Performance Expectancy (PE)	None	0.901
Effort Expectancy (EE)	None	0.829
Social Influence (SI)	None	0.877
Facilitating Conditions	None	0.738

(FC)		
Attitude towards using technology (ATUT)	ATUT_6 (Original set loaded to two factors -Extraction sums of squared loadings after deletion of ATUT_6: 55,344 %)	0.858
Self-Efficacy (SE)	None	0.804
Anxiety (ANX)	ANX_8 ANX_3 (Original set loaded to three factors -Extraction sums of squared loadings after deletion of ANX_8 and ANX_3: 58,180 %)	0.849
Behavioral Intention (BI)	None	0.910

* = List-wise deletion based on all variables in summary

Fornell/Larcker Criteria and latent variable correlations – questionnaire 3

	AVE	ANX	ATUT	BI	EE	FC	PE	SE	SI	Use Behavior
ANX	0.505	**0.7106**	0.0000	0.0000	0.0000	0.0000	0.0000	0.0000	0.0000	0
ATUT	0.6372	-0.1934	**0.7982**	0.0000	0.0000	0.0000	0.0000	0.0000	0.0000	0
BI	0.8391	-0.2987	0.4576	**0.9160**	0.0000	0.0000	0.0000	0.0000	0.0000	0
EE	0.6194	-0.2432	0.5817	0.4041	**0.7870**	0.0000	0.0000	0.0000	0.0000	0
FC	0.4139	-0.2381	0.3161	0.1076	0.2531	**0.6434**	0.0000	0.0000	0.0000	0
PE	0.6339	-0.1340	0.7815	0.5252	0.5148	0.2303	**0.7962**	0.0000	0.0000	0
SE	0.8184	0.0653	0.0600	0.0617	-0.1202	0.0051	0.0263	**0.9047**	0.0000	0
SI	0.891	-0.2540	0.4813	0.1340	0.2582	0.2161	0.2793	0.1630	**0.9439**	0
Use Behavior	1	0.018	0.1487	-0.0482	-0.0333	0.1206	0.146	0.0563	0.2227	**1.0000**

At time Q3, PE, EE, SI, FC, SE and BI saw no changes. ATUT_6 was excluded because of factor loadings. This is different to previous measurement points, when ATUT_6 was excluded because of a lower alpha value. ANX had the same pattern as in previous points of measurement, where ANX_8 and ANX_3 were excluded.

Level of significance					
*	p<=0.1	Low	***	p<=0.01	Strong
**	p<=0.05	Moderate	****	p<=0.001	Extremely Strong

Questionnaire 1 – Results

UTAUT PLS values – questionnaire 1

Construct	Dependent Construct	Path	T-Value
PE	BI	0.312**	2.734
EE	BI	-0.113	1.478
SI	BI	0.019	0.493
ATUT	BI	0.275*	2.163
SE	BI	-0.067	1.211
ANX	BI	-0.239**	2.902
BI	Use Behavior	0.093	1.451

Tests: r2=0.398 (medium) for BI, r2=0.009, f2=0.07 (small, excluded PE), f2=0.01 (small, excluded EE), f2=0.00 (small, excluded SI), f2=0.04 (small, excluded ATUT), f2=0.01 (small, excluded SE), f2=0.07 (small, excluded ANX). The measurement model is weak. Q2 is substantial above 0 for all constructs, except SE and Use behavior.

Use behavior measured with self reporting – questionnaire 1

Construct	Dependent Construct	Path	T-Value
BI	Use Behavior	-0.044	0.812

Because of non-significance, the new model excluded EE, SI, SE and Use behavior and included PE, ATUT, and ANX.

Model tests without non-significant constructs – questionnaire 1

Construct	Dependent Construct	Path	T-Value
PE	BI	0.317***	2.786
ATUT	BI	0.227**	1.961
ANX	BI	-0.221***	2.712

r2 = 0.386 (medium)
To counter test, the original UTAUT with PE, EE, and SI, BI, and Use behavior are used as constructs. Use behavior was measured with absolute numbers.

Values of original UTAUT constructs – questionnaire 1

Construct	Dependent Construct	Path	T-Value
PE	BI	0.510***	5.431
EE	BI	0.041	0.604
SI	BI	0.102*	1.706
BI	Use Behavior	0.093	1.412

Contrary to the expected results (based on previous UTAUT studies), only PE and SI seemed to be significant in all cases.

Questionnaire 2 – Results

UTAUT PLS values – questionnaire 2

Construct	Dependent Construct	Path	T-Value
PE	BI	0.324**	2.710
EE	BI	0.050	0.650
SI	BI	-0.049	0.737
ATUT	BI	0.034	0.416
SE	BI	-0.066	1.266
ANX	BI	-0.097	1.308
BI	Use Behavior	-0.057	0.926

Tests: r2=0.165 (weak) BI. r2=0.003 (very weak) Use Behavior
f2=0,06 (small, excluded PE), f2=0,02 (small, excluded EE), f2=0,02 (small, excluded SI), f2=0,00 (small, excluded ATUT), f2=0,00 (small, excluded SE), f2=0,01 (small, excluded ANX). The measurement model is weak. Q2 is substantial above 0 for all constructs, except SE and Use behavior. Interestingly, a change from PE directly to Use behavior shows a positive (and significant) path.

Use behavior measured with self reporting – questionnaire 2

Construct	Dependent Construct	Path	T-Value
BI	Use Behavior	0.018	0.310

The result would be an almost non-existing model without EE, SI, ATUT, SE, ANX, Use behavior and only one path from PE -> BI.

Model tests without non-significant constructs – questionnaire 2

Construct	Dependent Construct	Path	T-Value
PE	BI	0.381***	4.548

r2= 0.145 (weak)

Values of original UTAUT constructs – questionnaire 2

Construct	Dependent Construct	Path	T-Value
PE	BI	0.350***	4.006
EE	BI	0.093	1.172
SI	BI	-0.025	0.488
BI	Use Behavior	-0.057	0.895

Similar to the previous test, only PE proved to be statistically significant.

Questionnaire 3 – Results

UTAUT PLS values – questionnaire 3

Construct	Dependent Construct	Path	T-Value
PE	BI	0.392***	3.423
EE	BI	0.146	1.664
SI	BI	-0.125*	1.825
ATUT	BI	0.075	0.801
SE	BI	0.100	1.522
ANX	BI	-0.235***	3.483
FC	BI	0.135	1.565
FC	Use Behavior	0.135*	2.115
BI	Use Behavior	-0.042	1.050

Tests: r2=0.359 (medium) BI, r2=0.018 (weak) Use Behavior, f2=0.08 (small, excluded PE), f2=0.02 (small, excluded EE), f2=0.02 (small, excluded SI), f2=0.00 (small, excluded ATUT), f2=0.01 (small, excluded SE), f2=0.08 (small, excluded ANX). The measurement model is again weak. Q2 is substantial above 0 for all constructs. The data of this measurement point has the best relevance of all measurement points. Measured with self-reporting behavior did not change the results.

Questionnaire 3 test without construct BI

Construct	Dependent Construct	Path	T-Value
PE	Use Behavior	0.321***	3.314
EE	Use Behavior	-0.301**	2.368
SI	Use Behavior	0.204**	2.508
ATUT	Use Behavior	-0.097	0.956
SE	Use Behavior	-0.056	0.951
ANX	Use Behavior	-0.155**	2.209
FC	Use Behavior	0.092	1.380

Use behavior measured with self reporting – questionnaire 3

Construct	Dependent Construct	Path	T-Value
BI	Use Behavior	0.009	0.156

The non-significant constructs (EE, ATUT, SE, Use Behavior) were removed.

Model tests without non-significant constructs – questionnaire 3

Construct	Dependent Construct	Path	T-Value
PE	BI	0.454***	4.852
SI	BI	-0.086*	1.630
ANX	BI	-0.180***	2.489
FC	BI	0.175**	1.910

r2=0.354 (medium)

Values of original UTAUT constructs – questionnaire 3

Construct	Dependent Construct	Path	T-Value
PE	BI	0.439***	4.878
EE	BI	0.188**	2.318
SI	BI	-0.037	0.846
FC	Use Behavior	0.099**	1.766
BI	Use Behavior	-0.066	1.022

The last model (Q3) had more significant constructs than previous models. An explanation could be, that with extended usage of the system, people built a rather valid opinion on the system. This is very relevant for other research in which the model was measured at one point in time only. To check for the impact of constructs, we tested the hypotheses derived from UTAUT theory.

Combined measurement model results

UTAUT PLS values – combined measurement model

Construct	Dependent Construct	Path	T-Value
PE	BI	0.327**	2.756
EE	BI	0.015	0.226
SI	BI	-0.050	0.958
ATUT	BI	0.130	1.216
SE	BI	0.042	0.896
ANX	BI	-0.161*	1.941
BI	Use Behavior	-0.025	0.493

Tests: r2=0.248 (medium) BI, r2=0.001 (not existing) Use Behavior. f2=0.06 (small, excluded PE). f2=0.00 (small, excluded EE), f2=0.00 (small, excluded SI), f2=0.00 (small, excluded ATUT), f2=0.00 (small, excluded SE), f2=0.03 (small, excluded ANX). The measurement model is weak.

Q2 is substantial above 0 for all constructs, except SE and Use behavior.

In the combined case, the results are very similar to the ones previously measured. PE and ANX seem to be strong predictors of BI. There was no statistically significant path from BI to use behavior either.

Use behavior measured with self reporting – combined measurement model

Construct	Dependent Construct	Path	T-Value
BI	Use Behavior	-0.030	0.510

The values did not change for the measurement with self-reporting system use.

Model tests without non-significant constructs – combined measurement model

Construct	Dependent Construct	Path	T-Value
PE	BI	0.425***	5.162
ANX	BI	-0.141**	2.073

r2=0.238 (medium to weak)

Values of original UTAUT constructs – combined measurement model

Construct	Dependent Construct	Path	T-Value
PE	BI	0.411***	4.489
EE	BI	0.083	1.031
SI	BI	0.019	0.410
BI	Use Behavior	-0.012	0.227

Again, in the original model PE is the strongest predictor of BI.

Case Study „Public Transport Company" - Pre-Test Questionnaire to select participants

PRE-TEST QUESTIONNAIRE „PUBLIC TRANSPORT COMPANY"

1.) Wie zufrieden sind Sie mit dem PTC-HandyTicket System insgesamt? Bitte kreuzen Sie einmal an.
- ☐ absolut zufrieden
- ☐ zufrieden
- ☐ eher zufrieden
- ☐ eher unzufrieden
- ☐ unzufrieden
- ☐ absolut unzufrieden

2.) Wie zufrieden sind Sie mit der aktuellen PTC-HandyTicket Software? Bitte kreuzen Sie einmal an.
- ☐ absolut zufrieden
- ☐ zufrieden
- ☐ eher zufrieden
- ☐ eher unzufrieden
- ☐ unzufrieden
- ☐ absolut unzufrieden

3.) Wie häufig nutzen Sie derzeit das PTC-HandyTicket System, um Fahrkarten zu kaufen? Bitte kreuzen Sie einmal an.
- ☐ 6 – 7 Tage pro Woche
- ☐ 4 – 5 Tage pro Woche
- ☐ 2 – 3 Tage pro Woche
- ☐ 1 Tag pro Woche
- ☐ 1 – 3 Tage pro **Monat**
- ☐ seltener
- ☐ nie / fast nie

4.) Würden Sie die Busse und Bahnen des öffentlichen Nahverkehrs bei vereinfachtem Ticketkauf noch häufiger nutzen? Bitte kreuzen Sie einmal an.
- ☐ Ja
- ☐ Nein

5.) Nutzen Sie die nachfolgenden mobilen Services. Machen Sie bitte in jeder Zeile ein Kreuz.

a.) mobiles Internet
- ☐ Sehr häufig
- ☐ Häufig
- ☐ Manchmal
- ☐ Selten
- ☐ Nie

Oder:
- ☐ 6 – 7 Tage pro Woche
- ☐ 4 – 5 Tage pro Woche
- ☐ 2 – 3 Tage pro Woche
- ☐ 1 Tag pro Woche
- ☐ 1 – 3 Tage pro **Monat**
- ☐ seltener
- ☐ nie / fast nie

b.) Stadtplan
- ☐ Sehr häufig
- ☐ Häufig
- ☐ Manchmal
- ☐ Selten
- ☐ Nie

Oder:
- ☐ 6 – 7 Tage pro Woche
- ☐ 4 – 5 Tage pro Woche
- ☐ 2 – 3 Tage pro Woche
- ☐ 1 Tag pro Woche
- ☐ 1 – 3 Tage pro **Monat**

	☐ seltener
	☐ nie / fast nie
c.) Klingeltöne	
	☐ Sehr häufig
	☐ Häufig
	☐ Manchmal
	☐ Selten
	☐ Nie
Oder:	
	☐ 6 – 7 Tage pro Woche
	☐ 4 – 5 Tage pro Woche
	☐ 2 – 3 Tage pro Woche
	☐ 1 Tag pro Woche
	☐ 1 – 3 Tage pro **Monat**
	☐ seltener
	☐ nie / fast nie
d.) Mobile Spiele	
	☐ Sehr häufig
	☐ Häufig
	☐ Manchmal
	☐ Selten
	☐ Nie
Oder:	
	☐ 6 – 7 Tage pro Woche
	☐ 4 – 5 Tage pro Woche
	☐ 2 – 3 Tage pro Woche
	☐ 1 Tag pro Woche
	☐ 1 – 3 Tage pro **Monat**
	☐ seltener
	☐ nie / fast nie

6.) Bitte geben Sie an, wie häufig Sie in der Regel die folgenden Verkehrsmittel nutzen. Machen Sie bitte in jeder Zeile ein Kreuz.

a.) Bus und Bahn des öffentlichen Nahverkehrs	
	☐ 6 – 7 Tage pro Woche
	☐ 4 – 5 Tage pro Woche
	☐ 2 – 3 Tage pro Woche
	☐ 1 Tag pro Woche
	☐ 1 – 3 Tage pro **Monat**
	☐ seltener
	☐ nie / fast nie
b.) Bahn im Fernverkehr	
	☐ 6 – 7 Tage pro Woche
	☐ 4 – 5 Tage pro Woche
	☐ 2 – 3 Tage pro Woche
	☐ 1 Tag pro Woche
	☐ 1 – 3 Tage pro **Monat**
	☐ seltener
	☐ nie / fast nie
c.) Auto	
	☐ 6 – 7 Tage pro Woche
	☐ 4 – 5 Tage pro Woche
	☐ 2 – 3 Tage pro Woche
	☐ 1 Tag pro Woche
	☐ 1 – 3 Tage pro **Monat**
	☐ seltener
	☐ nie / fast nie
d.) Flugzeug	
	☐ 6 – 7 Tage pro Woche
	☐ 4 – 5 Tage pro Woche

□ 2 – 3 Tage pro Woche
□ 1 Tag pro Woche
□ 1 – 3 Tage pro **Monat**
□ seltener
□ nie / fast nie

7.) Welches Handy nutzen Sie zurzeit für den Kauf Ihres PTC-HandyTicket?

Handyhersteller: _____
Handymodell: _____
Handynetz: _____

8.) Möchten Sie sich in Kürze ein neues Handy kaufen?

□ Ja ⇒ Filter: nachfragen, welches
□ Nein

a) Welches Handy möchten Sie sich kaufen?

9.) Ihr Alter:

10.) Ihr Geschlecht:

□ Männlich
□ Weiblich

Public Transport Company Questionnaire – Exemplary for Measurement point 3

QUESTIONNAIRE „PUBLIC TRANSPORT COMPANY" – Measurement point 3
TEXT: *Herzlichen Willkommen beim dritten Fragebogen zum Pilotprojekt* *„[...]"*
Als Teilnehmer an einer sehr innovativen und in Deutschland in der Art, einmaligen Testphase, hatten Sie mittlerweile drei Monate Gelegenheit, das Handy Ticketing mit NFC ausgiebig zu nutzen. Nun haben Sie noch einmal die Möglichkeit über Ihre Erfahrungen mit dem System zu berichten und Anregungen für die Zukunft zu geben. *Dies ist der letzte Fragebogen im Drei-Monatstest. Wir würden uns freuen, wenn Sie diesen ebenso gewissenhaft und ausführlich beantworten würden, wie die anderen beiden zuvor. Wir danken Ihnen an dieser Stelle sehr herzlich für Ihre hilfreichen Antworten und Kommentare, die wir nutzen möchten um das HandyTicket immer weiter zu verbessern und in Ihrem Sinne zu gestalten.* *Ihre Daten werden unter Beachtung der datenschutzrechtlichen Bestimmungen erhoben, verarbeitet und genutzt.* *Vielen Dank!* *Ihr [...] Team*
VORABFRAGE: Bitte geben Sie uns Ihre Mobilfunknummer an, mit der Sie Ihr neues Nokia 6131 NFC nutzen. (Format +491711234567). Ihre Mobilfunknummer:

1.) Wie zufrieden sind Sie mit dem System „PTC-HandyTicket für NFC-Handys" in Stadt insgesamt? Bitte markieren Sie Ihre Antwort.
        ☐ absolut zufrieden
        ☐ zufrieden
        ☐ eher zufrieden
        ☐ eher unzufrieden
        ☐ unzufrieden
        ☐ absolut unzufrieden

2.) Für den Erwerb der Fahrkarten mit Ihrem NFC-Handy halten Sie das Handy an den sogenannten „NFC Tag". Wie häufig nutzen Sie derzeit die NFC-Funktion mit dem NFC Tag um Fahrkarten zu kaufen?
        ☐ 6 – 7 Tage pro Woche
        ☐ 4 – 5 Tage pro Woche
        ☐ 2 – 3 Tage pro Woche
        ☐ 1 Tag pro Woche
        ☐ 1 – 3 Tage pro **Monat**
        ☐ seltener
        ☐ nie / fast nie

3.) Der Ticketkauf ist auch ohne NFC-Funktion möglich, also ohne Berühren des „NFC Tag". In diesem Fall müssen Sie das PTC-HandyTicket-Programm manuell öffnen und die Starthaltestelle am Handy eingeben. Wie häufig nutzen Sie derzeit diese Möglichkeit, um Fahrkarten zu kaufen?
        ☐ 6 – 7 Tage pro Woche
        ☐ 4 – 5 Tage pro Woche
        ☐ 2 – 3 Tage pro Woche
        ☐ 1 Tag pro Woche
        ☐ 1 – 3 Tage pro **Monat**
        ☐ seltener
        ☐ nie / fast nie

4.) Wofür steht die Abkürzung „NFC"?   ☐ National Football Conference

☐ Near Field Communication
☐ Near Frequency Communication
☐ Nirvana Fan Club
☐ New Field Communication
☐ Near Field Connections
☐ Nokia Field Communication
☐ Weiß nicht

5.) Wie gut schätzen Sie Ihre Kenntnis über die dem PTC-HandyTicket für NFC-Handys zugrunde liegende Technik der Near Field Communication (NFC) ein?

☐ Sehr gut
☐ Gut
☐ Mittel
☐ Schlecht
☐ Sehr schlecht

6.) Wie gut schätzen Sie Ihre Kenntnis über mögliche mobile Anwendungen mit der Near Field Communication (NFC) ein?

☐ Sehr gut
☐ Gut
☐ Mittel
☐ Schlecht
☐ Sehr schlecht

7.) Hatten Sie bereits vor diesem Test Kontakt mit NFC-Anwendungen?

☐ Ja, einmal
☐ Ja, mehrmals
☐ Ja, oft
☐ Nein, nie
☐ Bin mir nicht sicher
☐ Weiß nicht

8.) „Near Field Communication" (NFC) ist eine drahtlose Übertragungstechnik. NFC kombiniert die Eigenschaft der RFID Technologie und kontaktlosen SmartCards. NFC ermöglicht die Datenübertragung auf eine Distanz von 2-5 cm. Der Hauptvorteil von NFC ist die Einfachheit und Schnelligkeit, mit der Geräte eine sichere, drahtlose Kommunikationsverbindung aufbauen können.

Können Sie sich vorstellen, dass NFC bei den folgenden Anwendungen genutzt werden kann?

a.) Ersatz für Kreditkarten

☐ Ja
☐ Nein
☐ Vielleicht
☐ Weiß nicht

b.) Türöffner

☐ Ja
☐ Nein
☐ Vielleicht
☐ Weiß nicht

c.) Bluetooth Set-Up

☐ Ja
☐ Nein
☐ Vielleicht
☐ Weiß nicht

d.) WLAN Set-Up

☐ Ja
☐ Nein
☐ Vielleicht
☐ Weiß nicht

e.) Informationsabruf zu Produkten

☐ Ja
☐ Nein
☐ Vielleicht

☐ Weiß nicht

f.) Auto starten

☐ Ja
☐ Nein
☐ Vielleicht
☐ Weiß nicht

g.) Kostenpflichtige SMS Dienste

☐ Ja
☐ Nein
☐ Vielleicht
☐ Weiß nicht

h.) Kostenpflichtige MMS Dienste

☐ Ja
☐ Nein
☐ Vielleicht
☐ Weiß nicht

i.) Community, Verabredung und Unterhaltung

☐ Ja
☐ Nein
☐ Vielleicht
☐ Weiß nicht

j.) Mobile Spiele

☐ Ja
☐ Nein
☐ Vielleicht
☐ Weiß nicht

k.) Klingeltöne (Screensaver etc.)

☐ Ja
☐ Nein
☐ Vielleicht
☐ Weiß nicht

l.) Navigation in Städten via NFC Tags (Stadtpläne)

☐ Ja
☐ Nein
☐ Vielleicht
☐ Weiß nicht

m.) Sicherheit und Notfall

☐ Ja
☐ Nein
☐ Vielleicht
☐ Weiß nicht

n.) Bezahlfunktion (ÖPNV)

☐ Ja
☐ Nein
☐ Vielleicht
☐ Weiß nicht

o.) Zugang zu Portaldiensten (Beispiel: Yahoo GO!)

☐ Ja
☐ Nein
☐ Vielleicht
☐ Weiß nicht

p.) Mobiles Fernsehen über UMTS

☐ Ja
☐ Nein
☐ Vielleicht
☐ Weiß nicht

q.) Musikdienste

☐ Ja
☐ Nein
☐ Vielleicht
☐ Weiß nicht

r.) Kamerahandy

☐ Ja
☐ Nein
☐ Vielleicht
☐ Weiß nicht

s.) Kamerahandy mit Barcode Leser

☐ Ja
☐ Nein
☐ Vielleicht
☐ Weiß nicht

t.) Parken

☐ Ja
☐ Nein
☐ Vielleicht
☐ Weiß nicht

u.) Informationsdienste

☐ Ja
☐ Nein
☐ Vielleicht
☐ Weiß nicht

9.) Wie gut schätzen Sie Ihre Kenntnis über das PTC-HandyTicket mit NFC-Handys ein?

☐ Sehr gut
☐ Gut
☐ Mittel
☐ Schlecht
☐ Sehr schlecht

10.) Entwickeln und programmieren Sie selbst Anwendungen für mobile Endgeräte? (Java / Mobile Programming)

☐ Ja, das gehört zu meinem Beruf.
☐ Ja, privat habe ich damit ab und an zu tun.
☐ Ich kann programmieren, mache aber nichts für mobile Endgeräte.
☐ Nein, ich programmiere überhaupt nicht.

11.) Hätten Sie gegebenenfalls Interesse unsere NFC - Funktionalitäten (Anwendungen rund um den öffentlichen Personennahverkehr und darüber hinaus NFC)) mit uns weiter zu entwickeln? Dabei meinen wir nicht nur das Programmieren, sondern auch konzeptionelle Zusammenarbeit.

☐ Ja, ich habe Interesse. Bitte nehmen Sie mich in einen Ihren Email Verteiler auf.
　　Meine E-Mail-Adresse ist: _____
☐ Nein, ich habe kein Interesse.

12.) Nun kommen ein paar Fragen zum NFC Tag. Kam es <u>in den letzten 4 Wochen</u> vor, dass ein „NFC Tag" nicht funktionsfähig war?

☐ Ja ⟹ Filter -> 13
☐ Nein

13.) (FILTER) An welchen Stationen war der NFC Tag nicht funktionsfähig? Bitte nennen Sie uns die Station, die Anzahl, wie häufig der NFC Tag nicht funktionsfähig war und beschreiben Sie uns so konkret wie möglich was nicht funktioniert hat.

14.) Bitte markieren Sie in jeder Zeile die für Sie zutreffende Antwort [UTAUT QUESTION SET]:

Ich finde die NFC Tags nützlich für meinen Alltag.

☐ Stimme voll und ganz zu
☐ Stimme eher zu
☐ Teils/teils
☐ Stimme eher nicht zu

☐ Stimme überhaupt nicht zu
Ich finde die Kombination der NFC Tags mit dem PTC-HandyTicket für NFC-Handys nützlich für meinen Alltag
☐ Stimme voll und ganz zu
☐ Stimme eher zu
☐ Teils/teils
☐ Stimme eher nicht zu
☐ Stimme überhaupt nicht zu
Wenn ich das PTC-HandyTicket für NFC-Handys benutze, kann ich meine Fahrkarten leichter kaufe:
☐ Stimme voll und ganz zu
☐ Stimme eher zu
☐ Teils/teils
☐ Stimme eher nicht zu
☐ Stimme überhaupt nicht zu
Wenn ich das PTC-HandyTicket für NFC-Handys benutze, kann ich meine Fahrkarten schneller kaufen:
☐ Stimme voll und ganz zu
☐ Stimme eher zu
☐ Teils/teils
☐ Stimme eher nicht zu
☐ Stimme überhaupt nicht zu
Das System macht den ÖPNV für mich effizienter:
☐ Stimme voll und ganz zu
☐ Stimme eher zu
☐ Teils/teils
☐ Stimme eher nicht zu
☐ Stimme überhaupt nicht zu
Die Handhabung der Anmeldung zum PTC-HandyTicket für NFC-Handys störte mich nicht:
☐ Stimme voll und ganz zu
☐ Stimme eher zu
☐ Teils/teils
☐ Stimme eher nicht zu
☐ Stimme überhaupt nicht zu
Ich spare Zeit durch die Nutzung der NFC Tags:
☐ Stimme voll und ganz zu
☐ Stimme eher zu
☐ Teils/teils
☐ Stimme eher nicht zu
☐ Stimme überhaupt nicht zu
Ich spare Zeit durch die Nutzung des NFC Handys:
☐ Stimme voll und ganz zu
☐ Stimme eher zu
☐ Teils/teils
☐ Stimme eher nicht zu
☐ Stimme überhaupt nicht zu
Die Benutzung des Systems ist für mich jederzeit klar und verständlich:
☐ Stimme voll und ganz zu
☐ Stimme eher zu
☐ Teils/teils
☐ Stimme eher nicht zu
☐ Stimme überhaupt nicht zu
Ich muss das NFC Handy direkt an die NFC Tags halten. Diese auf Berührung basierende Benutzung des Systems ist für mich klar und verständlich:
☐ Stimme voll und ganz zu
☐ Stimme eher zu
☐ Teils/teils
☐ Stimme eher nicht zu

□ Stimme überhaupt nicht zu
Ich finde die Benutzung durch Berührung einfach:
□ Stimme voll und ganz zu
□ Stimme eher zu
□ Teils/teils
□ Stimme eher nicht zu
□ Stimme überhaupt nicht zu
Das Erlernen der Nutzung war einfach:
□ Stimme voll und ganz zu
□ Stimme eher zu
□ Teils/teils
□ Stimme eher nicht zu
□ Stimme überhaupt nicht zu
Ich nutze das System gerne:
□ Stimme voll und ganz zu
□ Stimme eher zu
□ Teils/teils
□ Stimme eher nicht zu
□ Stimme überhaupt nicht zu
Die Nutzung macht Spaß:
□ Stimme voll und ganz zu
□ Stimme eher zu
□ Teils/teils
□ Stimme eher nicht zu
□ Stimme überhaupt nicht zu
NFC Technologie mit einem Handy zu nutzen macht Spaß:
□ Stimme voll und ganz zu
□ Stimme eher zu
□ Teils/teils
□ Stimme eher nicht zu
□ Stimme überhaupt nicht zu
Das System macht das Fahren mit ÖPNV besser:
□ Stimme voll und ganz zu
□ Stimme eher zu
□ Teils/teils
□ Stimme eher nicht zu
□ Stimme überhaupt nicht zu
Ich hätte gerne weitere NFC-Anwendungen wie das PTC-HandyTicket:
□ Stimme voll und ganz zu
□ Stimme eher zu
□ Teils/teils
□ Stimme eher nicht zu
□ Stimme überhaupt nicht zu
Ich kaufe lieber HandyTickets als Papiertickets:
□ Stimme voll und ganz zu
□ Stimme eher zu
□ Teils/teils
□ Stimme eher nicht zu
□ Stimme überhaupt nicht zu
Menschen, die mir wichtig sind, denken positiv über Handy Ticketing:
□ Stimme voll und ganz zu
□ Stimme eher zu
□ Teils/teils
□ Stimme eher nicht zu
□ Stimme überhaupt nicht zu
Menschen, die mir wichtig sind, denken positiv über NFC:
□ Stimme voll und ganz zu
□ Stimme eher zu

☐ Teils/teils
☐ Stimme eher nicht zu
☐ Stimme überhaupt nicht zu

Ich fühle mich mit meinem Wissen über NFC in der Lage, das PTC-HandyTicket für NFC-Handys zu nutzen:

☐ Stimme voll und ganz zu
☐ Stimme eher zu
☐ Teils/teils
☐ Stimme eher nicht zu
☐ Stimme überhaupt nicht zu

Es gibt genug NFC Tags in Stadt:

☐ Stimme voll und ganz zu
☐ Stimme eher zu
☐ Teils/teils
☐ Stimme eher nicht zu
☐ Stimme überhaupt nicht zu

Es gibt genug NFC Tags an einzelnen Stationen:

☐ Stimme voll und ganz zu
☐ Stimme eher zu
☐ Teils/teils
☐ Stimme eher nicht zu
☐ Stimme überhaupt nicht zu

Ich hätte kein Problem, die Handymarke zu wechseln, um ein NFC-Handy zu haben:

☐ Stimme voll und ganz zu
☐ Stimme eher zu
☐ Teils/teils
☐ Stimme eher nicht zu
☐ Stimme überhaupt nicht zu

Ich würde mir einen direkten Ansprechpartner beim PTC wünschen:

☐ Stimme voll und ganz zu
☐ Stimme eher zu
☐ Teils/teils
☐ Stimme eher nicht zu
☐ Stimme überhaupt nicht zu

Ich möchte jemanden anrufen können, wenn es mit dem Ticketkauf nicht klappt:

☐ Stimme voll und ganz zu
☐ Stimme eher zu
☐ Teils/teils
☐ Stimme eher nicht zu
☐ Stimme überhaupt nicht zu

Ich mache mir Sorgen wegen der Benutzung des PTC-HandyTicket für NFC-Handys:

☐ Stimme voll und ganz zu
☐ Stimme eher zu
☐ Teils/teils
☐ Stimme eher nicht zu
☐ Stimme überhaupt nicht zu

Es macht mir Angst, dass der PTC genau wissen kann, an welchen Orten ich war:

☐ Stimme voll und ganz zu
☐ Stimme eher zu
☐ Teils/teils
☐ Stimme eher nicht zu
☐ Stimme überhaupt nicht zu

Ich zögere, das System zu benutzen, weil ich Angst habe, Fehler bei der Bedienung zu machen, die ich nicht korrigieren kann:

☐ Stimme voll und ganz zu
☐ Stimme eher zu
☐ Teils/teils
☐ Stimme eher nicht zu

□ Stimme überhaupt nicht zu
Das System wirkt einschüchternd auf mich:
□ Stimme voll und ganz zu □ Stimme eher zu □ Teils/teils □ Stimme eher nicht zu □ Stimme überhaupt nicht zu
Ich zögere, ein NFC System wie das PTC-HandyTicket für NFC-Handys zu nutzen, weil ich Angst um meine Privatsphäre habe:
□ Stimme voll und ganz zu □ Stimme eher zu □ Teils/teils □ Stimme eher nicht zu □ Stimme überhaupt nicht zu
Ich zögere ein NFC System wie das PTC-HandyTicket für NFC-Handys zu nutzen, weil ich Angst um den DATENSCHUTZ habe:
□ Stimme voll und ganz zu □ Stimme eher zu □ Teils/teils □ Stimme eher nicht zu □ Stimme überhaupt nicht zu
Mehr Angst als die NFC Technologie machen mir andere Aspekte des Ticketings:
□ Stimme voll und ganz zu □ Stimme eher zu □ Teils/teils □ Stimme eher nicht zu □ Stimme überhaupt nicht zu
Ich denke, es gibt keine gesundheitlichen Risiken durch Nutzung von NFC:
□ Stimme voll und ganz zu □ Stimme eher zu □ Teils/teils □ Stimme eher nicht zu □ Stimme überhaupt nicht zu
Ich würde das PTC-HandyTicket für NFC-Handys (wenn erhältlich) innerhalb der nächsten sechs Monate weiter nutzen:
□ Stimme voll und ganz zu □ Stimme eher zu □ Teils/teils □ Stimme eher nicht zu □ Stimme überhaupt nicht zu
Ich vermute, ich würde das System (wenn erhältlich) innerhalb der nächsten 12 Monate nutzen:
□ Stimme voll und ganz zu □ Stimme eher zu □ Teils/teils □ Stimme eher nicht zu □ Stimme überhaupt nicht zu
Ich plane, das System (wenn erhältlich) innerhalb der nächsten 12 Monate zu nutzen:
□ Stimme voll und ganz zu □ Stimme eher zu □ Teils/teils □ Stimme eher nicht zu □ Stimme überhaupt nicht zu
15.) Sind Sie bereit, neben Ihrem persönlichen Handy (Privat- oder Fimenhandy) ein zweites Handy zu nutzen, nur um die NFC-Technologie anwenden zu können, vorausgesetzt Ihr persönliches Handy ist kein NFC-Handy?
□ Ja □ Nein
16.) Würden Sie NFC-Handys Ihren Freunden und Bekannten weiter empfehlen?

☐ Ja
☐ Nein
☐ Vielleicht
17.) Unter welchen Voraussetzungen würden Sie innerhalb der nächsten 1-2 Jahre das Angebot kostenpflichtiger mobiler Services nutzen?
☐ günstigere Preise als heute
☐ höhere Qualität des Inhalts
☐ gebotener Mehrwert
☐ bessere Bedienbarkeit der Endgeräte
☐ bessere Darstellung des Inhalts (Displayqualität)
☐ höhere verfügbare Geschwindigkeit der Datenübertragung
☐ Ich würde keine kostenpflichtigen mobilen Services nutzen
18.) Unter welchen Voraussetzungen würden Sie innerhalb der nächsten 1-2 Jahre das Angebot kostenpflichtiger mobiler Services nutzen?
☐ günstigere Preise als heute
☐ höhere Qualität des Inhalts
☐ gebotener Mehrwert
☐ bessere Bedienbarkeit der Endgeräte
☐ bessere Darstellung des Inhalts (Displayqualität)
☐ höhere verfügbare Geschwindigkeit der Datenübertragung
☐ Ich würde keine kostenpflichtigen mobilen Services nutzen
19.) Könnten Sie sich vorstellen mit Ihrem Handy kontaktlos nicht nur Ihre Fahrkarten, sondern auch weitere Produkte und Services zu bezahlen?
☐ Ja, bei Beträgen bis unter 50 Cent
☐ Ja, bei Beträgen von 50 Cent bis unter 5 EUR
☐ Ja, bei Beträgen von 5 EUR bis unter 50 EUR
☐ Ja, bei Beträgen ab 50 EUR
☐ Nein, ich kann mir keinesfalls Bezahlen mit dem Handy vorstellen [*FILTER: NEIN -> 23,, Warum können Sie sich ...]*
20.) [*Only if answered YES in any of the above question*] Bitte geben Sie zu jedem der vorgegebenen Möglichkeiten an, ob Sie kontaktlos mit dem NFC-Handy (also nur durch Berühren) bezahlen würden:
☐ Allgemein
☐ Supermarkt
☐ Parken
☐ Gastronomie
☐ Museen
☐ Öffentliche Einrichtungen
☐ Freizeiteinrichtungen ...
☐ offene Antwort
a) Ja, sicher
b) Ja, vielleicht
c) Eher unwahrscheinlich
d) Nein, sicher nicht
21.) Wie wichtig sind Ihnen folgende Aspekte des mobilen Bezahlens:
☐ Das Vermeiden von Wartezeiten beim Bezahlen
☐ Weniger Bargeld mit sich zu tragen
☐ Keine weitere Karten (EC-/Kreditkarten) mehr mit sich zu tragen – das Handy ist ja sowieso dabei.
☐ Einfache Bedienung des Systems
☐ Die Anzahl der Akzeptanzstellen
☐ Internationale Nutzbarkeit
☐ Die Höhe der Transaktionskosten pro Bezahlvorgang
☐ Nur eine Abrechnung zu erhalten
a) Sehr wichtig
b) Wichtig
c) Teils/teils
d) Unwichtig
e) Sehr unwichtig
22.) Welcher Akteur würde Ihrer Meinung nach als Betreiber von mobilen NFC Bezahlverfahren in

Frage kommen?
☐ Banken ☐ Kreditkartenunternehmen (Visa, MasterCard, etc.) ☐ Spezialisierter Intermediär (PayPal, etc.) ☐ Telekommunikationsunternehmen (02, Vodafone, etc.) ☐ der PTC ☐ Sonstige, nämlich: [   ] ☐ Weiß nicht
23.) Beim PTC-HandyTicket ist die monatliche Abrechung über Bankeinzug oder Kreditkarte möglich. Welches Abrechnungsverfahren würden Sie für andere NFC-Bezahlverfahren nutzen?
☐ Direkte Abbuchung vom Bankkonto (Bankeinzug) ☐ Monatliche eigene Rechnung ☐ Kreditkarte ☐ Telefonrechnung ☐ Vorausbezahltes, Guthabenbasiertes Konto ☐ Sonstige ☐ Weiß nicht
24.) [*FILTER question from number 18*] Warum können Sie sich <u>nicht</u> vorstellen mit dem NFC-Handy kontaktlos zu bezahlen?
25.) Momentan müssen Sie den NFC Tag nur bei Fahrtantritt berühren und die Fahrkarte auswählen. Alternativ dazu gibt es Ticketing Systeme, bei denen Sie den NFC Tag vor und nach der Fahrt berühren, d.h. ohne weitere Aktionen. Wie beurteilen Sie dieses Verfahren?
☐ Finde ich besser als das derzeitige System ☐ Finde ich schlechter als das derzeitige System, ☐ Aus welchen Gründen finden Sie das System besser oder schlechter? Bitte begründen Sie Ihre Entscheidung. [   ]
26.) Das PTC - HandyTicket für NFC-Handys ist derzeitig in Stadt verfügbar. Würden Sie das PTC-HandyTicket System für NFC-Handys auch in anderen Städten nützen?
☐ Ja ⇒ Filter -> next question 26 ☐ Nein
27.) Bitte wählen Sie Ihre drei wichtigsten Städte aus, in denen Sie das PTC-HandyTicket für NFC-Handys nützen würden:
☐ Berlin ☐ Hamburg ☐ München ☐ Köln ☐ Stadt am Main ☐ Stuttgart ☐ Dortmund ☐ Essen ☐ Düsseldorf ☐ Bremen ☐ Weitere [   ]
28.) Wie häufig sind Sie in den Städten, die Sie eben angekreuzt haben, mit dem öffentlichen Personennahverkehr unterwegs?
☐ 6 – 7 Tage pro Woche ☐ 4 – 5 Tage pro Woche ☐ 2 – 3 Tage pro Woche ☐ 1 Tag pro Woche ☐ 1 – 3 Tage pro **Monat** ☐ seltener
29.) Wie häufig fahren Sie mit der Bahn in die Städte, die Sie eben angekreuzt haben?
☐ 6 – 7 Tage pro Woche ☐ 4 – 5 Tage pro Woche ☐ 2 – 3 Tage pro Woche

□ 1 Tag pro Woche
□ 1 – 3 Tage pro **Monat**
□ seltener

30.) Das HandyTicket mit NFC-Funktionalität erfüllt meine Erwartungen an ein Ticket-System.

□ Stimme voll und ganz zu
□ Stimme eher zu
□ Teils/teils
□ Stimme eher nicht zu
□ Stimme überhaupt nicht zu

31.) Welche Erwartungen werden nicht erfüllt?

32.) Sie haben nun das Nokia NFC Handy seit drei Monaten in Betrieb. Welche der folgenden Dienste möchten Sie zukünftig mit dem NFC-Handy durch Berühren eines NFC Tags nutzen? Weitergehende Informationen über den Standort:

□ Download von mobilen Spielen
□ Download von Klingeltönen (Screensaver, etc) an der Bushaltestelle
□ Sicherheit und Notfallfunktionen (Hilfe-NFC Tag)
□ Bezahlfunktionen für Tickets mittels NFC Tag (ÖPNV)
□ Produktinformationen im Handel mittels NFC Tags
□ Parken und das Bezahlen der Parkkarte via NFC Tag

33.) Mittels NFC-Technologie können Sie weitere Informationen schnell und unkompliziert abrufen. Wie schätzen Sie die folgenden Statements ein:

Mir fehlt häufig eine gewisse Information, die ich dringend benötige.

□ Stimme voll und ganz zu
□ Stimme eher zu
□ Teils/teils
□ Stimme eher nicht zu
□ Stimme überhaupt nicht zu

Ich würde das mobile Internet (Internetnutzung über Handy) häufiger nützen, wenn der Zugang dazu einfacher wäre.

□ Stimme voll und ganz zu
□ Stimme eher zu
□ Teils/teils
□ Stimme eher nicht zu
□ Stimme überhaupt nicht zu

Ich hätte gerne mehr Informationen zu meinem aktuellen Standort in meiner Stadt.

□ Stimme voll und ganz zu
□ Stimme eher zu
□ Teils/teils
□ Stimme eher nicht zu
□ Stimme überhaupt nicht zu

Ich hätte gerne mehr Informationen zu meinem aktuellen Standort in anderen Städten

□ Stimme voll und ganz zu
□ Stimme eher zu
□ Teils/teils
□ Stimme eher nicht zu
□ Stimme überhaupt nicht zu

Wartezeiten auf Bus oder U-Bahn sind unangenehm.

□ Stimme voll und ganz zu
□ Stimme eher zu
□ Teils/teils
□ Stimme eher nicht zu
□ Stimme überhaupt nicht zu

Die Wartezeiten auf Bus oder U-Bahn vertreibe ich mir mit meinem Handy (Telefonate, Spiele, etc.).

□ Stimme voll und ganz zu
□ Stimme eher zu
□ Teils/teils

☐ Stimme eher nicht zu
☐ Stimme überhaupt nicht zu
Während der Wartezeiten auf den Bus oder die U-Bahn würde ich gerne anderweitig unterhalten werden (Beispiel: Durch aktuelle Nachrichten).
☐ Stimme voll und ganz zu
☐ Stimme eher zu
☐ Teils/teils
☐ Stimme eher nicht zu
☐ Stimme überhaupt nicht zu
34.) Dieses ist der dritte und damit letzte Fragebogen zu unserem PTC-HandyTicket für NFC-Handys. Sie haben nun die Möglichkeit ein Abschlussfeedback zum Test allgemein, zu Ihren Eindrücken, Erlebnissen und zu der zukünftigen Nutzung zu geben? Wir freuen uns über Ihre interessanten Kommentare und Anregungen! Sie helfen uns damit das Produkt immer weiter zu verbessern!

TEXT:
Damit sind wir am Ende der dritten und damit letzten Befragung. Noch einmal vielen Dank für Ihre Bereitschaft, unsere Fragen zu beantworten. Als Dankeschön für Ihre zuverlässige Unterstützung dürfen Sie Ihr persönliches Nokia NFC Handy behalten. Damit können Sie auch bei anderen NFC Services von Anfang an dabei sein!
Wenn Sie weitere Informationen zu NFC möchten, oder sich über Veranstaltungen über NFC auf dem Laufenden halten möchten, dann senden Sie bitte eine Email an _____ (Email einrichten: [-> für Listenverteiler). Wir freuen uns über Ihr Interesse.
Falls Sie Ihren Freunden und Bekannten eine Freude machen wollen, das Nokia NFC Handy ist ab dem xxxx bei xxxxx in [...] erhältlich!   *Bitte klicken Sie nun auf den folgenden Button,*   *um die Befragung erfolgreich abzuschließen.*

GPSR Compliance
The European Union's (EU) General Product Safety Regulation (GPSR) is a set
of rules that requires consumer products to be safe and our obligations to
ensure this.

If you have any concerns about our products, you can contact us on

ProductSafety@springernature.com

In case Publisher is established outside the EU, the EU authorized
representative is:

Springer Nature Customer Service Center GmbH
Europaplatz 3
69115 Heidelberg, Germany